Henry S. (Henry Stedman) Nourse

The Military Annals of Lancaster, Massachusetts. 1740-1865.

Including Lists of Soldiers Serving in the Colonial and Revolutionary Wars

Henry S. (Henry Stedman) Nourse

The Military Annals of Lancaster, Massachusetts. 1740-1865.
Including Lists of Soldiers Serving in the Colonial and Revolutionary Wars

ISBN/EAN: 9783337134969

Printed in Europe, USA, Canada, Australia, Japan

Cover: Foto ©ninafisch / pixelio.de

More available books at **www.hansebooks.com**

THE

MILITARY ANNALS OF LANCASTER

MASSACHUSETTS.

1740–1865.

INCLUDING LISTS OF SOLDIERS SERVING IN THE COLONIAL AND REVOLUTIONARY
WARS FOR THE LANCASTRIAN TOWNS: BERLIN, BOLTON, HARVARD,
LEOMINSTER AND STERLING.

BY

HENRY S. NOURSE, A. M.

What heroes from the woodland sprung,
    When through the fresh awakened land
The thrilling cry of freedom rung,
And to the work of warfare strung
    The yeoman's iron hand.
                                —BRYANT.

LANCASTER:

1889.

PREFACE.

THE purpose of this work needs neither explanation nor excuse; its short-comings, perhaps no one will more severely accuse than the author, while none but he can well appreciate the difficulties that have beset his patriotic task. The names and exploits of the local heroes who, with lavish expenditure of labor and life, helped gain and perpetuate the political and religious liberty we inherit, are mostly unknown to our generation. We perfunctorily honor the memory of those who achieved national fame — those whose names by chance of opportunity or high place are emblazoned upon historic tablets. Equally entitled to our grateful remembrance are the humbler patriots who, setting the nation's safety and liberation from wrong above the dearest ties, went out from rustic homesteads patiently to do and suffer, even to mortal agony, in behalf of country, faith and freedom. Though but yeomen, uncult and obscure, they were imbued with a spirit of chivalry pure as that of any knight of romance. The stern virtues of Puritan ancestry again shone in them. If their deeds and sacrifices gained little lustre that time has not dimmed or destroyed, it is the fault of the local chroniclers. In this attempt to preserve for Lancaster an accurate compilation of its military history, the author asks credit only for faithful research and conscientious adherence to recorded facts.

In the words of William Camden : "If any there be which are desirous to be strangers in their own soil, and foreigners in their own city, they may so continue, and therein flatter themselves. For such like I have not written these lines, nor taken these pains."

LANCASTER, July 4, 1889.

NOTE.—Circumstances beyond control, and greatly regretted, have prevented the reproduction of the portraits of Generals John and Henry Whiting, Major Fabius Whiting and Captain Edward Richmond Washburn for presentation in this volume, as had been contemplated.

CONTENTS.

IV.

THE WAR FOR NATIONAL INDEPENDENCE.

VII.

THE CIVIL WAR, 1861-1865.

VIII..

APPENDIX.

IX.

INDEX.

MILITARY ANNALS

OF

LANCASTER, MASSACHUSETTS.

I.

THE WAR WITH SPAIN.

1739–1744.

IN The Early Records of Lancaster, printed by the author in 1884, the experiences of that town in warfare previous to 1725 have been fully detailed. Before that date Lancaster's adult male population were practically always soldiers, were constantly menaced by savage foes, and often fought in defence of their lives and homes. Two, at least, of her earliest pioneers, John Prescott and William Kerley, had probably served in the army of the mother land; certainly they brought with them into the wilderness the arms and armor characteristic of the Cromwellian soldier. Another of her leaders, Major Simon Willard, on his coming from England bore the title, captain, and, at the outbreak of the war called King Philip's, held the highest military rank then recognized in the colony, honoring the position by his bravery, energy and skill during the earliest horrors of that bloody episode in New England history. Lieutenants William and Henry Kerley and Thomas Wilder, and Ensigns John Divoll and John Moore trained the first military company of the town under the

2

immediate supervision of Major Willard. Scarce an inventory of the period but contains, listed among humble domestic appointments and the utensils of husbandry, various articles of a soldier's equipment. Jacob Farrar, the head of a family noted for its many martyrs in Indian warfare, possessed "a Culliver Gun." Reverend John Whiting, who, surprised by savages in the field, bravely refusing quarter fought until slain, had five "fire arms," appraised after his death at four pounds. In the property schedules of seven other Lancaster planters figure these items :

Three musketts, one sword, one pᵣ bandiliers and one pistoll and bullets, 3£ 16ˢ . . . .
4 gunns, 1 cutlash 3£. 3ˢ . . . .
Iron cloathes 2£.—military books . . . .
One muskett 12ˢ, one sword and Rest 12ˢ. . . . .
A snapsack and bag 3ˢ. A pike 2ˢ. 6ᵈ . . . . .
A muskett, a sword, one rest and a snapsacke 2£. . . .
One Gun, one sword 2£ 4ˢ; one hallbut 16ˢ, 2 musquetts one cutlash 1£ 18ˢ. . . . . .

Of a frontier town, standing in the advance guard of Puritan civilization, Lancaster's yeomen were too completely engrossed in the hard struggle for existence to spare volunteers for service on other battle grounds than those within a day's march of their own hearthstones. Nevertheless, some adventurous spirits joined the little armies from time to time organized for the invasion of Canada. In Sir William Phip's disgracefully unfortunate attempt upon Quebec in 1690, Benjamin Willard served as lieutenant, and of several townsmen who are supposed to have accompanied him were : Joseph Atherton, Jonathan Fairbank, John Pope, Samuel Wheeler and Timothy Wheelock. Of these, Wheeler, if not others, died in the service. The two Acadian expeditions of 1707 and 1710 had such enthusiastic support in Massachusetts that Lancaster was doubtless well represented therein ; but the only record thus far discovered to prove this, is an item in the inventory presented by the administrator of a deceased soldier, Ralph Houghton, filed in the Middlesex Probate Registry. Captains Jabez Fairbank, John White and Samuel Willard, during Lovewell's War, 1722–1726, leading their neighbors, won repute as able commanders of rangers, and made it hazardous for the savages to venture far south of the fountains of the Merrimac. For fifteen years the arts of peace had been undisturbed by war's alarms, and swords had grown rusty in their scabbards, when the recruiting officer in 1740 drummed for recruits in Lancaster.

Great Britain, committed to a blindly selfish commercial policy, held a monopoly of the trade in African slaves, and her merchants were enriched by the enormous gains of their smuggling and man-stealing ventures. She exercised the right of search upon the seas and denied it to Spain. She demanded the privileges of free trade from other powers, but persistently refused them to the North American colonies — a lesson of the mother land which they remembered and acted upon in after time. At length, having forced war upon Spain under pretended championship of free commerce, England called upon her colonies to aid in an expedition sent under command of Vice-Admiral Edward Vernon to assail the Spanish strongholds in the West Indies. Massachusetts was required to furnish a regiment, and the organization of one was nearly perfected, officers and men being enrolled and assembled at Boston. The bills for expenditures in levying some of its companies are extant, and the methods of the recruiting officers of that day are illustrated by the recurrence of such charges as these :

To Drummers and Liquor expended, ...
To Ribbons for cockades, 50 yards @ 2/ . . . .

For some reason only four captains' commissions were received from the king instead of the ten expected. These were bestowed upon John Prescott, who was to have been colonel of the regiment, Daniel Goffe, Thomas Phillips and George Stewart. The other companies were dis-

banded. Dr. William Douglass, in his Summary, states
that this disastrous enterprise cost the province seven thousand pounds sterling, and that "of the 500 men sent out
from Massachusetts Bay not exceeding 50 returned." The
majority fell victims to pestilential disease during the siege
of Carthagena, or at Jamaica, whither the enfeebled remnant of the defeated army was withdrawn. Joseph Willard,
Esq., in a note to page 50 of the History of Lancaster,
states that "there were eighteen or nineteen in this expedition who belonged to Lancaster; none of them lived to
return." He had good authority for claiming in behalf of
this little town so large an enlistment, although it seems
almost incredible that it should have furnished nearly one
twenty-fifth of the whole quota of the commonwealth.

The town's volunteers must be looked for in the company of which a Lancaster man, Jonathan Houghton, was
lieutenant; the other companies were recruited far from
here, and in their rolls, as found, no Lancaster family
names are discovered. Captain John Prescott of Concord
was a direct descendant of the founder of Lancaster, whose
name he bore. His enlistment roll, sadly mutilated, is
preserved in Massachusetts Archives, xci, 333. It was
written upon both sides of a single sheet, and the right-
hand columns of the first page, which included residences
and dates of muster, have been torn off and are missing.
Thereby thirty-six names borne upon the reverse page are
lost. The sixty-five names remaining follow :

A List of such Persons as are Enterd: as Vol. . . . .
In the West Indies Under the Command of . . . .

Persons Names	Of what Town born	Age	Calling	Time of Enlisting
Jonathan Houghton	Lancaster	37	Husbandman	July 14
Obadiah Foster	Billerica	18	Cordwainer	May 22
Jonª Heywood	Concord	22	Tanner	May 22
Gideon Powers	Lexington	33	Husbandman	July 14
Oliver Spaulding	Chelmsford	29	"	July 15
Thos Pool	Lynn	32	Physician	May 1st
Robert Waite	Weston	41	Husbandman	July 12
William Stevens	Dublin	30	"	July 23

Persons Names	Of what Town born	Age	Calling	Time of Enlisting
— Thos Johnson	Concord	24	Tanner	May 12
Asa Douglass	Plainfield	24	Cordwainer	May 20
Timothy Rigbee	Concord	30	Husbandman	May 28
John Train	Watertown	50	"	July 22
Joshua Parker	Groton	39	Gentelman	July 1
Jacob Wilder	Lancaster	23	Husbandman	July 14
Jona. Brown	Concord	41	Blacksmith	May 22
John Page	, South Carolina	24	Husbandman	July 25
Daniel Albert	Rainshall (?)	39	"	July 14
James Carey	Newport	24	Farmer	July 22
Peter Kendall	Woburn	29	Husbandman	July 14
John Fitzgerald	Cork	37	Nailer	May 15
Nehemiah Stevens	Almsbury	24	Cordwainer	June 2
Timothy Power	Littleton	24	Husbandman	July 14
Darias Wheeler	Marlborough	21	"	July 14
William Chubb	Woburn	25	Weaver	July 24
Demas Wells	Ireland	24	Labourer	July 11
Samuel King	Worcester	20	"	July 11
Thomas Queen	Ireland	21	"	July 12
James Billings	Concord	23	Nailer	May 15
Nathaniel Munroe	Lexington	20	Joyner	May 28
Benjamin Frey	Grafton	43	Labourer	July 12
Mathusala Oliver	Boston	17	"	May 15
John Parker junʳ	Sudbury	21	"	July 10
Ephraim Fletcher	Chelmsford	30	"	July 12
Ebenezʳ Lampson	Concord	24	Husbandman	May 15
Nathan Stow	Concord	18	Labourer	July 12
Benjamin Melvin	Charlestown	45	Blacksmith	July 23
Jona Jackson	Framingham	22	Husbandman	May 20
Daniel Barney	Concord	27	Millwright	May 12
Joshua Winship	Lexington	24	Labourer	May 15
John Norcross	Watertown	43	Cordwainer	May 20
John Nixon	Ireland	20	Husbandman	July 10
Mathew Galbreth	Ireland	18	"	July 13
John Parker	Billerica	42	"	May 14
✓ Richard Wheeler	Worcester	19	"	July 23
Isaac Knights	Sudbury	22	"	July 14
Christopher Stevens	Almsbury	20	"	July 20
John Stewart	Salem	25	Housewright	July 23
Stephen Kendall	Woburn	23	Labourer	May 25
Josiah Holt	Andover	19	Blacksmith	July 21
Ephraim Roper	Sudbury	23	Husbandman	May 25
Josiah Blanchard	Groton	40	Blacksmith	May 10
Ezekiel Kendall	Lexington	24	Husbandman	July 15

Persons Names	Of what Town born	Age	Calling	Time of Enlisting
Joshua Peirce	Woburn	22	Housewright	July 14
Jeremiah Smith	Needham	18	Blacksmith	July 27
Henry Durant	Billerica	39	"	May 23
Zachry Blood	Concord	33	Husbandman	May 21
Thos Barron	Concord	29	Tinman	May 23
William Day	Cape Ann	21	Husbandman	May 15
William Whitcomb	Lancaster	30	"	July 18
Henry Jones	Concord	23	Clothier	July 18
Richard Nevers	Woburn	20	Blacksmith	May 5
Jonathan Pike	Concord	23	Cordwainer	May 20
Benjamin Pollard	Billerica	23	Husbandman	July 15
Peter Grouts	Sudbury	25	"	May 25
Zach{n} Bunn	Concord	29	Peat-maker	May 20

Of the thirty-six missing names, four were of volunteers whose "present habitation" is recorded as Lancaster, and three were of Bolton. Identity in the dates of enlistment —July 14 and 15—and the bearing family names then common in the town, point to these fifteen as residents of Lancaster, although two or three of them may have been of Bolton:

Jonathan Houghton,	Timothy Power,	Isaac Knights,
Gideon Powers,	Darius Wheeler,	Ezekiel Kendall,
Oliver Spaulding,	Jacob Wilder,	Joshua Peirce,
Daniel Albert,	Benjamin Frey,	William Whitcomb,
Peter Kendall.	Ephraim Fletcher.	Benjamin Pollard.

Joseph Willard, Esq., quotes from a letter written by Jacob Wilder, at Jamaica, in December, 1740, wherein, after mentioning a number of his acquaintances who had died, he adds: "through the providence of God, I am in nomination for an Ensign, and I hope I may be fitted for it." By signatures to the oath of the officers, found in Massachusetts Archives, LXXII, 517, it appears that Jonathan Houghton held commission as a subaltern. Daniel Albert's name has a line drawn through it, which probably indicates that he did not go with the expedition. He had been a soldier in Lovewell's War, and was living in Lancaster after the close of the Spanish War. Two of the lost

Lancaster names are disclosed by a memorial dated 1742, found in Massachusetts Archives, XVIII, 64, wherein the petitioners are heirs of "David and Nathan Farrar, late of Lancaster, * * * both Died in his majestie's sarvis in the West Indies sometime Last year." Perhaps two others, John Hastings and Thaddeus Houghton, are given in this certificate subscribed to the roll :

SUFFOLK SS. BOSTON, ye 27th, 1740. It is hereby Certefied thatt John Hastings, Joseph Bulkley, James Jefferies, Thadeus Houghton mentioned in this List appeared before me and Severally Declared yt. they did Voluntaryly enlist in his maj'sty's Service under the Command of Capt. John Prescott. . . . . .

It seems not improbable that three or four of these men survived to return from the West Indies. The names Peter and Ezekiel Kendall, Joshua Peirce and William Whitcomb appear in muster-rolls again a few years later. But neither history nor tradition throws further light upon the deeds or sufferings of the Lancaster volunteers in this unfortunate expedition.

II.

KING GEORGE'S WAR.

1744–1749.

I. THE SIEGE OF LOUISBOURG.

WHEN the traditional rivals, France and England, became involved upon opposing sides in the War for the Austrian Succession, it was inevitable that sooner or later their provinces of New England and Canada should be drawn into the conflict; and the so called King George's War was but an episode in the great struggle over the balance of power between the European potentates. Nova Scotia, or Acadia as it was then named, including New Brunswick with boundaries ill defined, had been a British possession from its conquest in 1710, although its inhabitants were almost exclusively French Catholics; while the islands, including Cape Breton, were retained by France. The news of the formal declaration of war reached Breton three weeks before it arrived in Boston, and was taken advantage of by the French to surprise and capture Canseau, the inhabitants of which were carried prisoners to Louisbourg. The situation of affairs was ominous of ruin for Massachusetts. Her valuable cod fisheries must be abandoned, and her shipping lay at the mercy of French privateers. Acadia was nearly defenceless, and if forced to succumb even New England might not long be able to escape French domination. No boundary could be peacefully permanent that divided Jesuit from Puritan, and while the Catholic French could plan forays from the safe vantage ground of the impregnable fortresses of Louisbourg and

Quebec, so long the New England Protestants could expect to sow in fear, never certain of a harvest.

William Shirley, Governor of Massachusetts, was gifted with great political sagacity. His military ability, though not of a high order, commands respect, because contrasted with the obstinate adherence to traditional methods, the blundering and inefficiency of Braddock, Loudoun and Abercrombie. He clearly saw that only by the capture of Louisbourg could safety be insured New England, and, like Cato of old, he successfully impressed it upon the councils of the commonwealth that this Carthage must be destroyed. Some of the prisoners taken at Canseau, when exchanged, brought from Louisbourg reliable description of its fortifications and information that disclosed supposed vulnerable points. This fortress had been perfected in all the defences then known to military art, at a cost to France of thirty millions of livres. Over one hundred guns, mostly of heavy calibre, were mounted in the various batteries, and six months' provisions for the garrison were kept in store. An English officer familiar with the works wrote that an army assaulting them would have the same prospect of success "as the Devils might have in storming Heaven." Shirley, however, was in no way dismayed at the difficulties presented, and the people then trusted Shirley. The preparations for attack were made with all possible speed and secrecy. The greatest enthusiasm was aroused, accompanied with such religious fervor that the expedition resembled a crusade of the Middle Ages. In two months' time thirty-two hundred and fifty men of Massachusetts, with eight hundred and twenty from Connecticut and New Hampshire, were assembled.

Besides that of William Pepperrell, Esq., commander-in-chief of the land forces, there were five infantry regiments, led from Massachusetts by Colonels Samuel Waldo, Jeremiah Moulton, Robert Hale, Sylvester Richmond and Samuel Willard. The last officer was of Lancaster, and commanded the Worcester County regiment, known as the Fourth Massachusetts. The roster of its officers follows:

COMPANY.	CAPTAINS.	LIEUTENANTS.	ENSIGNS.
1	Colonel Samuel Willard.	Abijah Willard.	Jonathan Trumbull.
	Capt.-Lieut. Joshua Pierce.		
2	Lt.-Col. Thomas Chandler.	John Payson.	David King.
3	Major Seth Pomroy.	Ebenezer Alexander.	William Lyman.
4	John Warner.	Joseph Whitcomb.	William Hutchins.
5	David Melvin.	Eleazar Melvin.	Isaac Barron.
6	Palmer Goulding.	John Sterns.	Nathaniel Payson.
7	James Stevens.	Timothy Johnson.	
8	John Huston.	Reuben King.	Benjamin Sheldon.
9	Joseph Miller.	Samuel Chandler.	John Mann.
10	Jabez Olmstead.	James Frye.	John Bell.
		Jonathan Hubbard, *Adjutant.*	

Besides their larger commands, it was customary at this date for field officers to have companies; and general officers were also colonels of regiments. The three officers of the fourth company were of Lancaster, and both Whitcomb and Hutchins had served an apprenticeship in the art of war with Captain John White, in 1725. In this company and that of Colonel Willard were the volunteers of Lancaster and its neighborhood, probably full fifty in number; but much research has failed to discover any company rolls of this regiment, and our townsmen's names are mostly unknown. Colonel Willard's acceptance of his appointment, written with his characteristic orthography, is found among the Pepperrell Papers belonging to the Massachusetts Historical Society:

To the Honorable William Pepperell Esqur. In Boston
LANCASTER Feb^{ry}: ye: 25th: 1744

Honor^d: Sir. I Receiued orders from the Govener the 19th: day of Feb^{ry}: to take upon me the Command of a Rigement though very unequel to that Trust. I do it with a great deal more Plasure, hauing so good a general to Instruct me — Sir I hope you will Excuse me if I am not Ready So Soon as the others Colonals. I am Constonant Rideing both Night and day to accomplish my byseness and I intento wait upon your honnor Next week   Sir I haue a good Prospect of geting men   Sir I haue been in an Army Knowing the Diffeculty being in it — I think it my Deuty to

Put you in mind to See that the Committy byes a quantety of fat wethers for it is very Necessary for Solders when they are Sick and if the Committy Sends me word I could get a Score or more Honered Sir. Giue my Regards to Coll: Molten. So I Remain your Humble Servent–

SAMLL: WILLARD

The experience of an army which the colonel claims, had been gained in the scouts of Lovewell's War. When, in September, 1725, he commanded two companies of rangers, he dignified that force in his journal as "the army." The volunteers were required to clothe and arm themselves, and the pay of a private was but twenty-five shillings per month, *new tenor*—equal to about two ounces of silver,— although farm laborers at the time commanded nearly double that sum. As the expedition sailed from Boston March 24, 1745, it is evident from the date of Colonel Willard's appointment that he recruited his regiment, numbering about five hundred men, in thirty days. This testifies both to the popularity of the leader and the religious ardor that fired the troops. " In the name of God they set up their banners and away they sailed. *Pray for us and we will fight for you,* was the valiant and endearing language wherewith they left us," says Reverend Thomas Prince in his Thanksgiving Sermon, July 18, 1745. "Brown bread and the Gospel is good fare," was the proverb with which they cheered each other on in the trials of siege. One chaplain, if we may trust the story, armed himself with a hatchet for the express purpose of demolishing the images in the Catholic churches ; and George Whitefield is credited with furnishing the motto upon the flag, — *Nil Desperandum Christo Duce.* Arriving before Louisbourg on the thirteenth of April, "less than four thousand men, unused to war, undisciplined, and that had never seen a siege in their lives," landed on a dangerous coast in the face of the enemy, with Herculean labor dragged siege guns over rocky hills and through morasses, girt the fortifications about with batteries, and by sheer audacity compelled surrender on the seventeenth of June, 1745 — the

day made yet m re memorable in the calendar thirty years
later at Bunker Hill.   The English admiral, Peter Warren,
was present with his fleet to claim large share in the honors,
and grasp all the prizes of victory, but he did not fire a
gun during the siege, and the real glory of the wondrous
achievement belonged to the men of New England.

Massachusetts at this date had a population of about
two hundred thousand souls, and expended in this expedition more than two pounds sterling for her every man,
woman and child.   The prizes of war exceeded in value
a million pounds, but all the proceeds went to the navy and
the king's chest, while the provinces waited three years before their expenses even were repaid ; and then the re-
imbursement was granted as the gracious beneficence of
his majesty, not as a debt due.   William Pepperrell, Esquire,
who commanded the provincials, was knighted — the only
reward of distinguished service received by any New England officer.   The exalted estimate of the importance of
the victory at the time, is exhibited by the fact that as the
news of it reached in turn Boston, New York, Philadelphia
and even London, the people became wild with joyful excitement ; and as night came on, in each of these cities,
great bonfires and general illumination lighted crowds up-
roarious in unrestricted rejoicing.   A few days after the
surrender, Colonel Willard signed the following letter at
Gabarus Bay, the intrenched camp at that point having
been ordered to be destroyed, after removal of its stores to
the city of Louisbourg.   The report that a large body of
French and Indians was near at hand meditating an attack
upon it, accounts for the worthy colonel's very marked
uneasiness :

Honoured Sir:. According to your Honour's order I have Attended
my Duty at the Camp with Col⁰: Donnel Col⁰: Meshervay and Col⁰: Chandler, have with me eight comp⁵: of my own Regiment Except what are at
ye out housen and In ye City to attend ye Sick. Col⁰: Moulton has 160
men here belonging to his Regiment, Col⁰: Moore 140 belonging to his,
Col⁰ Hale about 18 men belonging to his, Col⁰ Burr 40 men belonging to

his ye others have Sent None to guard us Vizt: Brig^r Waldo, Col^n Storer Col^o Richmond and Col^n Gorham I would pray that your Honour would see us well Guarded. I am Ready and Willing always to obey your Honours Commands In every thing I am Capable of. I expected to have a sloop here to Day to take away all ye Stores but am Disappointed which makes all ye officers very uneasy.

I am your Honours Dutifull

Camp June 26th 1745.   Obedient and Very Humble Servant

SAM^{LL}: WILLARD.

P. S. Mr Cosbee has been here wth a french Gentleman to View ye Camp and is Returned (as I suppose) to ye City again and it gives us all matter of uneasiness had it been known Sooner some of ye officers would have taken them up and Confined them untill they had Known your Honours Pleasure.

I am your Honours Humble Servt.

Endorsed,—   SAM WILLARD

May it please your Honour Since ye Letter was Writt and Sealed up Several Vessels are Com to Recive y^r Stores (as I suppose)   S. W–

Superscribed,—

To Generall Pepperell, In the City of Cape Breton.

[Pepperrell Papers, 206.]

On July 31, Abijah Willard was promoted captain-lieutenant of the first company, and his brother Levi was made ensign. They were sons of the colonel, the former being twenty-one years of age, and Levi, eighteen. Endorsed upon a petition of certain officers of the regiment, asking that in the consolidation of the forces retained to garrison Louisbourg they and their men might be joined with Brigadier-General Samuel Waldo's regiment, is this letter:

His Excellency Wm Sherley Esqr:

This is to inform your Exelency That my Regiment is not Settl^d: so as to be in any Capassity of doing their duty as thay ought to do—and it is by Reason of ye Companys being Very much Broke: and in order for the Settlement of the Companys In my Regiment and for the Peace and Quietness of the Soldiers: I shall take it as a Grate Favour Done to me: if your Exelency would See Cause [To Commiteonate Those Gentleman Hereafter Nam^d: John Huston, James Fry, John Fry Nathl: Pettengell To be the officers over the men that belong^d to Leut: Coll^n Chandler's Company and Capt: James Stevens's Comp^a· Jona: Hubard Benijah Austin & Elisha Strong To be the officers over the men belonging To Maj^r Pomroy's

Comp^n: & Capt: Millers; Ephriam Hayward and John Bell & Dudley Bradstreet To be the officers over the men that are Left of Capt: Warner's Comp^n: & Capt: Omsteds. In So Doing you will Oblige your most obedient and Humble Servant   SAMLL: WILLARD

        LOUISBOURGE Oct^r: the 2 day 1745

                                              [Pepperrell Papers, 319.]

The rigors of the climate and the toil of the siege told severely upon even the hardy yeomen of New England, and the victims of disease far outnumbered the killed and wounded in the lines. Thomas Littlejohn fell in action, but how many others of Lancaster is unknown. Among those who died in hospital was Captain John Warner. Hundreds of the sick and enfeebled were at length permitted to return home, and the depleted companies were consolidated and garrisoned the fortified city until the following April. The Lancaster officers mostly escaped the winter's hardships and the terrible camp fevers which wasted the army that remained. The two documents that follow — numbers 331 and 335 of the Pepperrell Papers — close our record of Lancaster men in the Louisbourg campaign of 1745 :

To his Excellency William Shirley Esq,: Capt: Genl: &c.

May it please your Excellency Since my Company is Come under Capt: Hubbard I Would Pray your Excellency To Dismis me and Grant me the favour of going home with my father and allso John Warner son of Capt: John Warner who Died in this Place above a month ago he is a Lad of about Twelve years of age &c

        From your Excellency's most Humble Servt:

                                        ABIJAH WILLARD

Subscribed,—   LOUISBOURG 12th Octo 1745

Capt: Lieut Abijah Willard of Col^o: Samuel Willard's Regiment, having assigned over his Company by their Consent to Capt: Jonathan Hubbard in Brigadier Genl: Waldo's regim^t: and having petitioned for a discharge from the service is hereby accordingly dismissed, & permitted to return to New England & to take with him a youth of about twelve years old the son of Capt: John Warner late Dec^sd: W. SHIRLEY

                        LOUISBOURGE Octob^r: 17th 1745

Lt. Coll^o Pitts, Maj^r Hodges, Coll^o: Saml. Willard, Ensign Benj^a Blackston, Leut. Edwd Prat being unable to do duty by reason of a bad state of health and being desirous to be Dismist His Majesty's Service in this Garrison, it is hereby Granted and they Accordingly Dismist.

Pr   Warren W. Shirley
W. PEPPERRELL

The following year the country was in continual unrest, knowing that France had fitted out an armada, headed by forty war ships under the Duke d'Anville, to ravage the coast of New England. The militia to the number of over six thousand were stationed at Boston, and various forts upon the coast were rebuilt and garrisoned. A letter printed in American Archives, IV, I, 1168, states that "forty thousand men marched down to Boston and were mustered and numbered upon the Common, complete in arms from this Province only, in three weeks." Muster rolls of this period are not found, but a few items preserved testify to Lancaster's active participation in the public anxiety :

LANCASTER April ye 29, 1747

Maj. Larance, Sir, Please to pay Capt. Abijah Willard our wages and Billet which is Due to us upon your muster not paid for going downe to Boston upon a larm. In so doing you will oblege your humbel servants and his Receipt shall be your discharge.

		his
JOHN OSGOOD	JOHN WHITE	JOHN + HARIS
		mark
NATHANIEL WHITE	JAMES HOUGHTON	BENJAMIN HOUGHTON Jr.
		for Elijah.

October 10, 1746, the Council issued a warrant :

To Cp^t. Ephraim Sawyer and the Company, in His Majesties Service on the Frontiers, the sum of Two Hundred and nine Pounds two Shillings and nine pence (to each Person the sum set against his name) to discharge his Muster Roll beginning May 16. 1746 and ending June 30, 1746.

A letter from Secretary Josiah Willard to Admiral Warren — Massachusetts Archives, LIII, 195, — mentions Jacob Willard as a midshipman. For many weeks the people of Massachusetts, resolute but hardly hopeful of the result, were waiting in dread suspense the coming of their powerful foe. England made no effort to shield them from the

impending ruin, but Providence was upon their side. A
fierce tempest smote the French fleet and scattered it;
the sailors and soldiers were decimated by disease, and
D'Anville died on September 26. New England was
spared.

II.   INDIAN RAIDS.

We have no record that the soldiers of Lancaster were
again called into service until 1748, when, on July 5, a
band of fourscore savages made a revengeful raid under
the lead of a half-civilized Indian, Surdody by name, upon
the lonely garrison of John Fitch, a carpenter, living in
what is now Ashby. Zaccheus Blodgett and Jennings, two
soldiers there stationed, were slain, and Fitch, with his
wife Susannah, and children Catharine, John, Paul, Susannah and Jacob were carried away captive. Colonel Samuel
Willard ordered out various companies of militia from the
neighboring towns in pursuit; and the marauders would
probably have suffered dearly for their temerity, but for a
warning conveyed to the angry pursuers by a note which
Fitch fastened to a tree. The savages had resolved, if
attacked by the rangers, to kill their prisoners at once, and
he urged them to abandon further attempts at rescue.
Fitch tells his own story in a petition for aid, preserved in
Massachusetts Archives LXXIII, 609. He with his five
children returned in safety the following year by way of
New York and Providence, but his wife died in the latter
place on the way home, December 24, 1748. The following is one of Colonel Willard's orders "upon Hearing the
Exstroydnery News of Mr Fitches Family Being Takeing
from Lunenburge by the enemy."

To Capt. Ephraim Wilder Jun. in Lancaster.
    You are herby Directed forthwith to order as many off your Troop to
be Ready to march tomorrow morning as you can Posebel an I will Go

with you for ther is two souldirs Killed att fitches fort and the man and his wife and five Children are Caryed Into Captivity as is sususpected att Lunenburge. SAM^LL WILLARD *Coll*

LANCASTER July ye 7. 1748.

P. S. to go to Narengansitt No 2 and Paquoage and Neichewoage. you may Ride or go afoot as you Se good

[Massachusetts Archives, XCII, 144.]

Roll of Captain Ephraim Wilder.

Ephraim Wilder Capt	Israel Whitcomb	*William Richardson*
John Whitcomb *Lieut*	*Joseph Rugg*	Abiathar Houghton
Hezekiah Gates Cornet	*Sherebiah Ballard*	Joseph Polley
Hezekiah Whitcomb Q M	Eleazar Whitcomb	Jonas Whitcomb —
Joshua Moor Corporal.	*John Dupee*	*Phinehas Willard*
Jabez Fairbank *Co.*	*Aaron Dresser*	*Elijah Sawyer*
Samuel Burpee do.	Oliver Pollard	Poll Gates
Jonathan Wilder	William Sawyer	*Abijah Houghton*
Thomas Fairbank	*John Farrer*	Hezekiah Gibbs
James House	*Ebenezer Buss*	*Ephraim Osgood*
Thomas Sawyer	Samuel Moor	*John Prentice*
Phinehas Sawyer	*Shebiah Hunt*	*Stephen Johnson* —

The names in italics are of Lancaster men. The others —excepting Houghton and Polley, who were of Leominster—belonged to Bolton. The captain's brief journal accompanies his pay roll in Massachusetts Archives, XCII, 144:

A Journal of the march of Cap. Ephraim Wilder Juner and Company In July 1748.

July 7. In Mustering his men they belonging to Several towns.

July 8. In Marching to Narragansitt No. 2 and In Searching After the Indens that was the same day discovered there.

July 9. In Marching throw the woods to Paquage.

July 10. In Scouting And Marching to Necthewoage

July 11. In Scouting in the woods and Camped in the woods the same night.

July 12. In Scouting and In Returning to Lancaster—

EPHRAIM WILDER JUNER:

More than three months before, the governor had been notified by the anxious commander of the Lancaster regiment, that the frontiersmen were in peril from Indian raids:

3

To his Exelency William Sheerly Esq. Capt. general & Governer in Cheif in and over his majesties Province of the Massachusetts bay in New-england & to the Honrd his majesties Councel & house of Representa-tives in general Court assembled.

The memorial of Sam[ll]. Willard Humbly Sheweth, That wheare as many of the Towns in my Ridgement ly on the frountiers & are vary much expos[d] to the enemy, and the soldiers alradie Propos[d] for those Towns are not by any means (as I conceiue) sufficient for the protection of the peo-ple, since there is not many more soldiers then Garisons in sd Towns & theirfore cant carie on a scout which I think would be absolutely nassary & theirfore your memorialist Humbly moues that their may be Town's scouts appointed in each frountier Town who shall be Changed alternately as often as is thought best; whose Duty it shall be to maintain a constant scout on the Back of these Towns which seruice hath allways ben much for ye Safty of frountiers when faithfully Perform[d] & this mathod may also saue the Presing of a Considerable many more soldiers, & your memorial-ist as in Duty Bound Shall ever Pray.   SAM[LL]. WILLARD

April 8 1748

[Massachusetts Archives, LXXIII, 129.]

A few days after the raid he again wrote:

To the Hon[ble] Spencer Phipps Esq. Lieut. Gov[r] and to the Hon[ble] his maj-ties Council.

I think it my duty to lay before your Honours the Distrest Condition of the towns hereafter mention[d], lying between Merimack & Conecticut, by reason of the Indians. New Rutland, Nichwog, Naragansett No 2, Leominster, Lunenburgh, Groton West Precinct, who will not be able to do their Harvest & to get their hay without some Relief from your Hon-ours their being but sixty-two soldiers allowed & nineteen men for town Scouts to the towns aboue mention[d], which is by no means sufficient to guard them.   So I subscribe myself your humble Serv[t]

Endorsed.   SAM[LL]. WILLARD

Recd July 15, 1748

[Massachusetts Archives, LIII, 375.]

The Jesuits of Canada conducted warfare against the hated heretics, their Puritan neighbors, in a mode the most cowardly and barbarous known in modern history. By various arts they had won to their interest all the more savage tribes. The French peasants had been encouraged to take Indian wives. The priests found it easy to awaken the superstitious fears of the susceptible red men, and abused this power without scruple. The savage's cupidity

and love of finery were stimulated by judicious distribution
of gaudy presents, and the promise of bounties for services.
Bands of painted warriors were regularly equipped and
sent to the English frontier settlements to murder, burn and
plunder. These cunning. swift-footed marauders, skulking
about some lone cabin, would surprise its owner at the
plough or in the harvest field, tear off his scalp and drive
before them through the pathless forests to Canada his wife
and children, loaded with spoils from their own home. In
Montreal or Quebec the employers paid into the blood-
stained hands the promised bounty and ransom money.
To protect the adventurous pioneers of new settlements, it
again became necessary, as during Lovewell's war, to keep
parties of rangers almost constantly in motion; hence such
records as the following :

*A Muster Roll of a Number of Men that was sent Into the Woods under
Command of Jonathan Whitney Capt viz: By order of Coll. Samuel Willard. July 23 to 31.* [1748]

Jonathan Whitney, *capt* :	Hezekiah Willard	Phineas Pratt
Thomas Ball, *lieut* :	Stephen Haskal	Josiah Wetherby
Ephraim Gates, *sergr* :	John Davis	Elisha Gates
John Randall, *sergr* :	Amos Stone	Josiah Gates
Ebenezer Davis, *clark*	Benj^a. Sampson	Josiah Davis
Justinitian Holden, *corpl* :	Abnah Holt	Daniel Farr
Gabriell Preist, *corpl* :	Samuel Bruce	Joseph Wetherby
Thomas Wheler, Jun. *centu*:	John Sterns	William Skinner
William Farmer	Benj^a. Baley	David Jewett
John Warner	Benj^a. Marbel	Silas Wetherby
Ebenezer Worcester	Abijah Pratt	Daniel Bruce
William Harper	John Houghton	Jonas Wilder
Sam^ll. Harper	Daniel Whitney	Abraham Houghton

[Massachusetts Archives, XCII, 125.]

These men were of Bolton and Harvard; a company of
twenty was led from Lunenburg by Captain Jonathan Willard, and a smaller scout from Leominster was headed by
Captain Jonathan White.

LANCASTER July y⁰ 19. 1748.

LANCASTER July ye 19. 1748.

Captain White.

Having repeated accounts of the indians Shooting and being tracked aboue you, You are hereby Directed to send six able bodied men to Scout constantly aboue Lunenburg and Leominster untill further orders

Yours to serue   SAM^LL. WILLARD.

A Muster Roll of a Scout of men in his Majesties Service under the Command of Jonathan White Captain anno D 1748 [July 19 to August 12.]

Jonathan White, *capt.*	Oliver Carter	Nathaniel Carter
Joseph Beman	Gershom Houghton	Joshua Walker

[Massachusetts Archives, XCII, 130.]

A Muster Role of a Number of men that Scouted by order of Coll Willard under the Command of Sergt James Houghton. [Served six weeks from July 24, 1748.]

James Houghton, *sergt.*	Hezekiah Whitcomb	Nathan Burpee
John Wilder	John Hadley	Jonathan Powers
Asa Whitcomb	Joseph Kilborn	

Endorsed.   December the 31, 1748

These may Certifie that Having advise from Capt. Stevens of No 4, that a party of Indians ware Come Betwene the Revers I sent out the within named James Houghton & Company.

SAM^LL WILLARD

[Massachusetts Archives, XCII, 144.]

About this time "the Truck House above Northfield comonly called Fort Dumer," as its commandant writes of it in 1740, began to figure as a strategic position of some importance in connection with Charlestown No. 4, and Fort Massachusetts. Fort Dummer was in control of Colonel Josiah Willard of Lunenburg and his kindred, who owned the site and the lands about it. The pay rolls of the little garrison usually contain less than a dozen names, all told, and these nearly always of Willards or of families connected with them by marriage. Fairbank Moore and John Sargent of Lancaster were generally on duty here. Captain Phineas Stevens, who, like the Willards, was of Lancaster origin, was commander of Number Four, and sometimes two or three Lancaster soldiers are found in his muster-rolls. Among prisoners ransomed and brought to Boston from Canada in 1748, was John Henderson of Lancaster, "taken at Number Four." July 16, 1748. near Fort Dummer, a party of thirteen was waylaid by Indians, and three only escaped. Joseph Richardson, Nathan French, John Frost and William Bradford were slain; Henry Stevens, Benjamin Osgood, William Blanchard, Joel Johnson, Moses Perkins and Matthew Wyman were taken prisoners. The last named and two or three others were of Lancaster and adjoining towns. Wyman was soon ransomed, and the following petition is found:

The Petition of Matthew Wyman most humbly sheweth, That your Petitioner being in his Majesties service and employᵈ as a souldier under Capt. Josiah Willard by your Excellency's Order was taken by the Indian Enemy near Fort Dummer on ye 16 of June 1648, who took & finally Kept from me a Gun worth no less than 20£ old Tenʳ and a Hat worth 5£ of ye same Tenʳ and carried me to Canada. From which Captivity I obtained not my Liberty till about ye 5 of October following when I arrived in Boston with Capt. Britt of Newbury & above 40 other Prisoners of War. Which unhappy Bondage hath tended more than a little to ye Distress & Impoverishment of myself and Family. It is therefore ye earnest supplication of your Poor Petitioner that your Excellency and Honours will condescend to afford me some Relief such as in your Great Wisdom, Equity and Goodness you shall think proper, which will be a lasting obligation of Gratitude on your afflicted Petitioner who shall ever pray &c

January 10, 1748/9   MATTHEW WYMAN

[Massachusetts Archives, LXXIII, 321.]

Eight pounds in money and a gun were voted the petitioner. A few years later he is found again fighting for the King.

III.

THE FRENCH AND INDIAN WAR.

1754–1763.

I. THE CROWN POINT EXPEDITION OF 1755.

THE treaty of Aix-la-Chapelle, signed October 7, 1748, permitted for a time the semblance of peace between Jesuit and Puritan, but restored to the French all that had been wrested from them by the valor and sacrifices of the New England men. Again Louisbourg became a standing menace to the commerce of the English colonies in America. Lancaster's veteran colonel, who had honored himself and his birthplace by his conduct during the siege and capture of that famous fortress, now drops from our annals.

> We hear from Lancaster that on the 19th of this instant Novbr. Col. Samuel Willard was suddenly seized with an apoplectick fit, and died in three hours afterwards. He had attended the publick worship both forenoon and afternoon on the preceding day. He was decently interred on the Wednesday following. He has left a sorrowful widow and six children.
>
> [Boston Weekly News Letter, Nov. 30, 1752.]

Colonel Samuel was a grandson of Major Simon Willard, and the energy and executive ability of his distinguished ancestor shone again in him. Sixty-three years of age at his death, he was at the height of his prosperous and useful career. For twenty-five years he had been the ranking officer of the military district, and, with the exception of Chief-Justice Joseph Wilder, the most prominent citizen of the town. He had held the office of judge of the Court of Common Pleas for nearly ten years. Three of his sons following in paternal footsteps early showed marked taste for military life, and each attained the rank of colonel.

In 1753 it was determined to encourage the manufacture of linen in Massachusetts by substantial premiums, and to obtain a fund for this purpose a tax was imposed upon certain chattels deemed luxuries. The sum of ten shillings was annually levied upon each coach, five shillings upon a chariot, three shillings upon a chaise, and two shillings upon a calash or chair. The first year Lancaster paid tax upon three chairs; in 1754, upon one chaise; in 1755, upon two chairs and three chaises; in 1756, upon two chaises and two chairs. We can hardly err in assigning the chaises to Judge Joseph Wilder and the family of Colonel Samuel Willard. Bezaleel Sawyer was the proprietor of one of the chairs, but we are left to conjecture the ownership of the other. During the same years Harvard, Bolton and Leominster had but a single chair to the three towns. From the paucity of such conveniences for travel, we may judge of the austere simplicity of the times.

In attempting to carry out the provisions of the excise act of 1754, laying a tax upon certain table luxuries, by means of which the colonists were expected to contribute to the support of the government, unforeseen difficulties were met in this county, as told by the return of a committee, the two leading members of which were Lancaster citizens:

To his Excelency William Shirley Esq., Capt. General . . . . . .
October ye 18, 1754.

Whareas your Excelency & Honours appointed us the subscribers a Committe to farm out the excise of Tea, Coffe & Chine ware In the Countey of Worcester, This therefore Certifies that In pursuance of said order we Notified the whole Countey of our Desighn to meet at a publick Time and place when & where we attended, but when the acte Relating to that affair was Read, No person by Reson of some Clauses In said acte appered to bid for said excise, for which Reson, Notwithstanding our Time Trouble and Expences it Is Not farmed out

The Expences. To writing 23 Notifications & sending them to [so]
many Towns 0 .. 9 .. 0
To attendance on said affair, one Day & a
hafe a person 1 .. 7 .. 0
To Expences 0 .. 6 .. 0

Which we pray may be allowed

We are your Excellency & Honor. most Humble Servants,

JOSEPH WILDER
WILLIAM RICHARDSON } *Committe*
NATHAN TYLER

[Massachusetts Archives, CXIX, 685.]

The people who thus voluntarily denied themselves common luxuries, and jealously scrutinized every attempt to raise the smallest subsidy without their consent, were soon willingly impoverishing themselves and mortgaging their children's inheritance, for love of country and the religion of their fathers.

Preparations for a desperate and decisive struggle never ceased, and from time to time collisions upon the frontiers told of the unabated rage between the rival civilizations and creeds. In 1754 the mask of peace was dropped in the colonies, although the mother countries did not formally declare war until two years later. Colonel John Winslow was stationed upon the eastern frontier with a regiment, and with him, chiefly in the companies of Captains Phineas Osgood and Eleazar Melvin, serving from April to November, were these men of Lancaster, Bolton and Harvard:

Sergt. John Whitcomb.	Timothy Houghton.	Abraham Knowlton.
Sergt. Stephen Houghton.	Benjamin Hutchins.	William Larkin.
Nathan Barns.	Gordon Hutchins.	Josiah Priest.
Charles Holman.	Benjamin Kendall.	Jacob Willard.
Richard Holden.	Isaac Kendall.	Elijah Wood.
		Joseph Wood.

[Massachusetts Archives, XCIII, 136–8.]

Captain Gershom Flagg was engaged in the construction of Fort Halifax on the Kennebec, from July to November of this year, and with him were Henry Haskell, Uriah

Tucker, and perhaps other carpenters of Lancaster. The town was also represented upon the western frontier during the same season.

LANCASTER Sept. the 11th, 1754.

Collo Israel Williams Sr. I haue Received a Copey of your Letter from Collo. John Chandler wh ch Gaue me a Count that you had order from his Excellency the Capt. General's Warrant to Rayse such forces out of the seueral Regiments with n the Counties of Hamshire and Worcester for the Defence of his majestys subjects in the Western parts of the Prov-ince and also I haue received from Collo John Chandler the Proportson of men which is fourteen and accordingly I haue corsed that number to be impressed and ordered them to yourself for further order. So I Reman your Hum. Servent   OLIVER WILDER

and haue put Mr John May Ensign ouer the Detachment of fourteen Raysed In our County Expecting Collo Chandler will put an offiser ouer him.

Ensign John May	W^m. Pollard	Mathias Larkin
Elijah Holton, *sgt*.	James Houghton	Elias Haskell
Ephm. Sawyer	David Atherton	Solomon Stone
Danl. Bruce	Jona Kendall	Mathew Knight
Nahum Houghton	Jos : Beeman	Joseph Dexter in

Ephm. Sawyer's place to be muster^d from ye day of Sawyer's Enlistment.

[Col. Israel Williams' Papers, 79.]

The French, alert and aggressive, not only claimed by right of discovery the Mississippi and its tributaries to their sources in the Alleghanies, but had gone far to make their claim good by encircling the English colonies with a cor-don of block-houses and forts from the St. Lawrence to the Ohio. Against this French line of occupation in 1755 four great expeditions were planned, and four Colonial and British armies were sent out, aiming at widely separated points : Fort Duquesne at the head of the Ohio River, Fort Niagara on Lake Ontario, Crown Point on Lake Cham-plain, and the Acadian Forts at the head of the Bay of Fundy. The first expedition met with ignominious disas-ter, the second and third missed their aim, and the fourth won inglorious victory. With the last two, only, is Lan-caster history intimately connected.

Enlistment Roll found among papers of Colonel Oliver Wilder.

We the Subscribers Do acknowledge to Haue Volentareley Inlisted our Selues as Priuate Solders to Serue his majestey King George the Seccond In a Regiment of foot Now a Raising In the Prouince of the Massachusets Bay In New England oute of the Seueral Regiments of horse and oute of the Regiment in partickular whareof Olivar Wilder Esq'. Is Collonal to Reinforce the armey under the Command of Major General Johnson Destined for Crown Point and under such Collonal as his Honour the Left. Gouener Phips shall se good to apoint as witness our hands this fifteenth Day of September in the year of ouer Lord 1755.

LUKE JARVIS accepted in ye Rome of Stephen Tuttle

BENJAMIN WILDER [*lieutenant*]	OLIVER POLLARD
PHINEHAS CARTER [*ensign*]	FAIRBANK MOOR
JONATHAN POWERS	SETH OAK
PAUL SAWYER	BENJA BRIDGE
NATHAN^L. HOUGHTON	MOSES WHITNEY
NATHANIEL WHITE	SIMON BLANCHER, *impressed*
NATHANIEL HUDSON	PHINEHAS WILLARD
JONATHAN HOUGHTON	CALEB SAWYER
ISRAEL GREENLEAF	ZADOCK DAVIS, *trompt*
JOHN MOOR, Jr.	WILLIAM HOUGHTON
OLIVER WARNER	GORDON HUTCHINS
SAMUELL CUMMINGS, Juner.	JEREMIAH LAUGHTON, *corp.*
SIMON WILLARD	DANIEL HOUGHTON
JOSEPH WHEELOCK	NATHANIEL COBLEIGH
JONAS WHITCOMB, *trompt*	OLIVER TENNEY
EPHRAIM ✕ HOUGHTON (his mark)	ROBERT WHITCOMB
	BENJAMIN HALE, *corp.*

These soldiers from Lancaster and neighboring towns served in the regiment of Colonel Josiah Brown, and in the companies of Captain Jeduthan Baldwin of Brookfield, and Lieutenant-Colonel John Cummings, whose musterrolls are in Massachusetts Archives, XCIII, 206 and 215, and XCIV, 8, 27 and 71.

Samuel Willard, eldest son of the late colonel, was authorized to raise a regiment of eight hundred men for this expedition, and John Whitcomb of Bolton was commissioned its lieutenant-colonel, Timothy Houghton of Bolton, adjutant, and Phineas Phelps of Lancaster, surgeon's-mate. Colonel Willard was mustered in command of the regiment from August 9 to October 26, at which date John Whitcomb was commissioned colonel. Samuel Willard had been taken sick shortly after joining the army, and died at Lake George. He was not quite thirty-seven years of age. For a time he had lived at Petersham, having an estate there, was justice of the peace, and highly esteemed for his uprightness and ability. He had returned to his boyhood's home, however, before the war broke out, and was chosen town clerk of Lancaster. The election of his successor to the clerkship for 1755, is recorded as "in room of Samuel Willard absent in his majesty's service." He left no children. Colonel John Whitcomb's company of fifty men had in it the following soldiers from Lancastrian towns, the remainder being mostly from Stow and Marlborough:

OF LANCASTER:

Hezekiah Whitcomb, *lieutenant, (died)*. Aaron Dresser, Thomas Dole, John Whitcomb, *(died)*. Abner Osgood.

OF BOLTON:

Gabriel Priest, *sergeant*. Abram Holman, James Townsend, Nathaniel Longley, *clerk*. Francis McFadden, Eleazar Whitcomb, John Whitcomb, Jun, *drummer*. Josiah Priest.

OF HARVARD:

Uriah Holt, *corporal*. Joseph Houghton, John Sawyer, Isaac Gates, Elkanah Keyes.

OF LEOMINSTER:

Job Spofford, *corporal*. Jonas Spofford, Benjamin Street, *(died)*. Elias Carter.

[Massachusetts Archives, XCIV, 52.]

In the company of Captain Samuel Hunt of Lunenburg, there were:

OF BOLTON:

Silvanus Sawyer, *drummer*, Francis Fullam.

OF LEOMINSTER:

John White, *sergeant*, William Boutell, *corporal*, Luke Richardson, Benjamin Whitcomb.

[Massachusetts Archives, XCIV, 63.]

In the company of Captain Stephen Hosmer of Concord, were:

OF LANCASTER:

William Richardson, Jr. *lieutenant*, Samuel Warner.

In the company of Captain William Peirce of Stow, were:

OF HARVARD:

Judah Clark, *lieutenant*, Isaac Stone, *corporal*, Phineas Pratt,
Benjamin Hutchins, *sergeant*, Samuel Corey.

[Massachusetts Archives, XCIV, 76.]

Josiah Whitney and Samuel Meed of Harvard were in other companies of the same regiment.

Most of the soldiers of this neighborhood, however, were in three companies of a regiment commanded by Colonel Timothy Ruggles, which suffered severely in the battle of Lake George, September 8. 1755, when the gallant Dieskau was defeated by the undisciplined valor of New England rustics under the energetic leadership of General Phineas Lyman, despite the woful mismanagement of the commander-in-chief. The muster-roll of Captain Joseph Whitcomb's company is in Massachusetts Archives, XCIV, 86. The time of service was from March, 1755, to the close of the year:

Joseph Whitcomb, *capt.* Lancaster	Ebenezer Snow,	Lancaster
Benjᵃ. Whitcomb, *lieut.* Leominster	Robert Forskit	"
Benjᵃ, Hastings, *ensign*, Bolton	John Wheeler	"
Hezekiah Walker, *clerk*, Lancaster	Joseph Robbins	"
Dennis Locklin, *sergt.* Bolton	Jonᵃ. Houghton	"
John Barnard " "	Cyrus Gates	"
Samuel Patch " Stow	Marmaduke Jos. Hamilton, "
Jonas Johnson, *corp.* Leom'ster, (*died*)	Abram Knolton	"
Benjᵃ. Marble " Bolton	Josiah Pratt. Senʳ.	"
James Cresfield " Lancaster	Abraham Bruce	"
Joseph Robbins, Jr. " (*died*)	Joseph Evelith, Stow	
Joshua Sawyer "	Ebenezer Patch, " (*died*)	
Josiah Pratt, Jr. " (*died*)	Henry Keyes, Shrewsbury	
Robert Longley "	Robert Fletcher, *clerk*, Lancaster	
John Richardson "	Joseph Polley, Leominster	
Nathaniel Holman "	Ebenezer Knight "	
Abijah Cole "	James Clark "	
Joseph Shewally, Leominster, (*died*)	William Porter, Shirley	
Ethan Phillips, Lancaster	Peter Kendall, Lancaster, (*died*)	
Zecariah Eager, Shrewsbury	John Davidson, Stow	
William Willard, Lancaster	Micah Gates "	
Phineas Randell " (*died*)	Silas Bouker, Shrewsbury	

Peter Houghton, Leominster   Joseph Bigelow, Framingham
John Scott, Lunenburg   Comfort Brabrook, Shrewsbury (*died*)
Jona. Priest Whitcomb, *drummer*, Lancaster

The muster-roll of Captain Asa Whitcomb is in Massachusetts Archives, xcv, 88 :

Asa Whitcomb, *capt*. Lancaster   Ithamar Bennett, Lancaster, (*died*)
Ezra Houghton, *lieut*.   "   Fortunatus Taylor, Shrewsbury
Elijah Houghton. *ensign*,   "   Thomas Fairbanks, Lancaster
Joshua Hide, *sergt*. Petersham   Silas Bennett, Petersham
Reuben Keyes " Shrewsbury (*died*)   Joseph Woolly, Rutland
Eph'm Bennett " Holden, (*died*)   Oliver Dresser, Lancaster
Philemon Houghton, *clerk*, Lancaster Caleb Wright, Harvard
Jacob Hinds, *corp*. Shrewsbury   Nathan Garey, Lancaster
Isaac Kendall " Lancaster, (*died*)   John Harvey. Shrewsbury
Ebenezer Engalsbe, *corp*. Shrewsbury David Allen. Petersham
Sam'l Fairbanks,*corp*.Lancaster,(*died*) Joshua Bailey, Lancaster
Wm. Fairbanks, *drum'r*, "   (*died*) Tilley Littlejohn   "
John Farrar   "   (*died*) Eliphalet Cutting, Shrewsbury
John Brooks   "   Oliver Osgood, Lancaster, (*died*)
Benjamin Flood, Westborough   Charles Holman, Bolton, (*died*)
Daniel Stone, Shrewsbury   Jonathan Goodale, Marlborough
Jedediah Belknap "   (*died*)   Nahum Houghton, *drummer*, Lan-
Francis Temple   "   caster.

The muster-roll of Captain Benjamin Ballard is in Massachusetts Archives, xciv, 123, and contains forty-nine names, eleven being of Lancaster, three of Leominster, and one of Harvard ; the lieutenants and many of the privates being from Townsend and vicinity.

OF LANCASTER :

Benjamin Ballard, *captain*,   William Barron,   Elisha White,
Sherebiah Hunt, *sergeant*,   Josiah Fairbanks,   Elijah Woods,
Timothy Whiting. *clerk*,   William Kendall,   Joseph Woods,
Samuel Ballard,   John Manning,   John Rugg (*killed*)

OF LEOMINSTER :

Abiathar Houghton, *sergeant*,   Jon*. White, Jr.   Aaron Brown.
William Babcock of Harvard.

These three companies were in the bloody "morning fight," and those recorded as "died" were, with the exception of Farrar, killed or mortally wounded on that day. Petitions presented by certain of the survivors will serve to

picture some of the trials endured by these patriots after
the dangers of the battle-field were safely passed, while
they suggest comparisons and contrasts with our modern
experiences of war :

Jonathan Powers * * * * * Inlisted himself a privet under the
Command of Capt. Jeduthan Ballding In Collonal Brown's Regiment to go
in the Expedition against Crown point the Last year, and so it was * * *
I was Taken sick at Lake George and so Continued for thre wekes and
after Recovering some small strength I was Imbarked In a wagon and got
Down to Albany with much Deficultey and thare Taried thre Days and
then I being Verry Disirous of Giting hom attemted a tryel and Traveled
as my strength would bare untill I Got to Kingston and sent Home for
Horse and man to Come to my assistance, I being unable to proced any
further I had got so weke.

To what it cost me for said man & two Horses thre Days &
    Expences   £1 – 0 – 0
and after I got Home I was Confined to my house with fevour
    & flucks for thre wekes and was obliged to aply to Dr
    Harvey whose Bill Is herwith exhibited and Is   1 – 7 – 6
and for Nursing and other Nesecareys During said thre wekes   10 – 8

                                 2 – 18 – 2

Your Pettioner Humbly Prays your Honour & Honours to Repay him
the apove said sum. * * * *   JONATHAN POWERS

                         [Massachusets Archives, LXXV, 691.]

To His Honour Spencer Phips Esq . . . . . July ye 1 1756.

    The Pettion of Aaron Dresser Humbley Shewing that he Inlisted
himself a privet solder In Collonel Whitcomb's Companey In Collonel
Willard's Regiment the last year In the Expedition against Crown point
and so it was may it plese your Honouer and Honours that I was Taken
sick at the Camp and was unable to Travil and Brought Down to Albaney
In a wagon and Remaind sick at Albaney thre wekes & thre Days and
then was unable to travil on foot and was forst to Hire a man and Horse to
Carrey me homward.

To what it Cost me at Canterhook while sick there for Nurising
    and Nesecarys I was obliged to get   1£– 5ˢ–11ᵈ
To what it Cost me for man and Horse and expenses Home to
    Lancaster which ye man was 15 Days a performing I being
    so weke   3 – 18 – 6

Your Pettioner Humbley prays your Honouer and Honouers to Repay
him the above said sum of five pounds four shillings and five pence which
Cost and Charge he has actuley ben at as In Dutey bound shall Ever Pray.

                             AARON DRESSER

    [Massachusetts Archives, LXXV, 686.]

To the honble his Majesties Counsell & house of Representatives in Generel Court Assembied. April ye first 1757.

The Pettition of William Willard humbleley shewing That he was an Inlisted soildier under the Command of Capt. Joseph Whetcomb in the Reigement wherof Timothy Rugles Esq: was Conll: in the Crown Point Expedition in the year one Thousand Seaven hunderd and fivety-five, and so it was, may Please your Honours, That your poor Pettitioner was taken Sick att Lake George & I was obliged for to hire a horse, and make the Best of way home with the Leave of my Superor officers leave and was Obliged for to Lay by four days on my Jorney home I being so very sick and week, & the fourteenth Day with great Difficultey I arrived att my home att Lancaster, & there was Confined to my Room & bed for five weeks with the feaver and Camp Destemper and my bodey and Leggs being Swelld for fonr or five months afterwards which Cost me in money besides all other Nessesery Charges, as to Candles & boarding nurses &c. which sum of one pound twelve Shillings, your poor pettistioner would humbleley pray your honours to Repay him. As in Duttey bound Shall ever pray. WILLIAM WILLARD.

WORCESTER Ss, LANCASTER April ye 11. 1757. The before Named William Willard apered and made oth the Truth of the foregoing Pettonn before me WM RICHARDSON *Justice Pacis.*

Subscribed,—

The Comttee allow one pound twelve shillings In full. SAMLL WITT

pr order

Similar petitions to those above given were presented by Ethan Phillips, Daniel Houghton, William Kendall, James Johnson and others of the same companies. Two from Lancaster widows are as follows:

To His Honour Spencer Phips Esq: * * * *

The Pettition of Mary Farrar administratrix to Hur Late Husband John Farrar Late of Lancaster Decesed Humbley Shewing that Hur Said Husband Inlisted under the Comand of Capt. Asa Whitcomb In Collo Rugeles Regiment In the Crown Point Expedition In ye year 1755 and that he was well During the sumers Campain untill a few Days before his Dismision at the Camp but was then Taken out of order and with Grate Dificultey got home and was Verey poorley for some wekes after he got home but Notwithstanding the grate Dificulteys he met with the year before, your Poor Pettition' Husbands zele was so grate for ye good of his Cuntrey that when thare was a motion to goe a seccond time In ye servis of his King & Cuntrey he freley Entred Into said servis the Last year and Continued In it till he was Dismissed and was Taken Sick In his [return] at Shefield and thare Died : and so it was may it plese your Honour and Honours that my said Husband's Entering Into the servis ye Last year he

had not an opurtunity to get his Billiting money for his Returning Back ye
year before & I often herd my said Husband saye he bore all his own expences In his Return from ye said Expedition In ye yeare 1755, as also ye
afe Davit of two others herwith Exhibited, and that your pettioner was at
the Cost & Charge of sending man & horse twice whi'st my said Husband
Lay sick at Shefield which cost me thirty-six shillings for expences besides
the two men & their horses who was one of them gone a fortnight & the
other a weke which I aprehend to be well worth thirtey shillings. Your
poor Distresed pettitioner therefore Humbley Prayes your Honour &
Hon^rs to take Hur case Into your wise and Just Consideration & Give hur
a Power to Draw ye Billiting for hur husbands' Return from ye Expedition
In ye year 1755 & to allow the thirtey shillings for ye two men & two Horses
that went to hur said Husbands asistance or Grant Hur Relief In shuch
other way as your Honour & Honours In your Grate wisdom shall Direct.
as In Duty Bound shall Every pray   MARY FARRAR

    WORSESTER : Ss : LANCASTER March ye 6th 1757

    Mary Farrar appered and made oth to ye truth of ye facts set forth
In ye forgoing pettition before me—

                    WILLIAM RICHARDSON *Justice Peace.*

    Endorsed—Your Honour & Honours within mentioned pettitioner
further Humbley prayes you will alow Hur ye accounts also Here with Ex-
hibeted payed Dr Harvey for Doctering hur Husband which Is ten shillings & five pence as in further Dutey shall Ever pray.

                                          MARY FARRAR.

    [Massachusetts Archives, LXXVI, 366.]

*To His Honour the Leut. Governour and Comander in Chief for the time
    being.   To the Honourable His Majesties Council and House of
    Representatives in General Court Ascembled Jany. 6th 1757.*

    The Petition of Hannah Woods Humbly Prays that shee had two sons
Listed under Capt. Ballard in Coll : Rugglesses Regement in the first Expedition Against Crown Point, Vizt : Joseph and Elijah. Elijah Attended
His Duty in the Province Service till the 26th Day of Oetober 1755 at
which time he had a furlow being unfit for Service and Remained Ill twenty
weeks unable to Do aney Business all of which time I Nussed & Billited s^d
Elijah : that Joseph Continued in the Service till he was Dismissed from
the Expedition and Returned Home so Ill that He was not Capable of
Doing aney thing for ten weeks after his Return at which time I Billited
and Loked after Him. therefore the said Hannah Humbley Prays that she
may be allowed for Nussing Billiting and for what shee paid for Doctring
Hir two Sons an Account of which accompaneys this Petition and as in
Duty bound shall Ever Pray * * * *   HANNAH WOODS

                              [Massachusetts Archives, XCV, 188.]

  Though barren of far reaching victory, and foiled of

its real purpose, the first Crown Point Expedition gave needful experience and confidence in themselves and their own officers to the soldiers of New England ; while Braddock's defeat could not but suggest to them comparisons that made them thereafter more impatient than ever before of the arrogant claims of superiority constantly obtruded upon them by the British regulars.

II.   LANCASTER IN ACADIA AND THE ACADIANS IN LANCASTER.

It is one hundred and thirty years

" . . . . Since the burning of Grand-Pre,
When on the falling tide the freighted vessels departed,
Bearing a nation, with all its household gods, into exile ;
Exile without an end, and without an example in story."

Of the numerous Lancaster readers of Evangeline few now suspect how nearly the sad tale of ravaged Acadia touched our town history.   Upon the crown officials then in authority over the Province of Nova Scotia, historian and poet have indelibly branded the stigma of a merciless edict of expulsion, which devastated one of the fairest regions of America, and tore seven thousand simple peasants from a scene of rural felicity rarely surpassed, to scatter them in the misery of abject poverty among strangers speaking a strange tongue and hating their religion. Discussion of the question of military necessity would be out of place here.   The agents who faithfully executed the decree were chiefly Massachusetts men reluctantly obedient to "his Majesty's orders," given them specifically in writing by Charles Lawrence, lieutenant-governor of Nova Scotia.

On the twentieth of May, 1755, Lieutenant-Colonel John Winslow embarked at Boston with a force of about two thousand men, organized in two battalions.   They

4

were enlisted for the term of one year, unless sooner discharged, for the special service of dislodging the French
from their newly fortified positions along the north side of
the Bay of Fundy and upon the isthmus connecting New
Brunswick and Nova Scotia. Among the vessels of the
fleet was a sloop called the Victory, and to this was
assigned a company belonging to the second battalion,
Lieutenant-Colonel Scott's, which was largely composed
of, and officered by, Lancaster men. A descriptive roster
of this company, compiled from the Captain's Orderly Book
and the Journal of Colonel John Winslow, follows :

	Age	Occupation	Residence	Birthplace
Abijah Willard, *captain*	[31]		Lancaster	Lancaster
Joshua Willard, *lieutenant*			"	
Moses Haskell "			"	
Caleb Willard, *ensign*			Lunenburg	
Thomas Beman, *sergeant*	25	husbandman	Lancaster	
James Houghton "	25	"	"	
Edmund Brigham "	30	"	Marlboro'	
Nathan Stone "	21	"	Petersham	Framingham
Jacob Willard, *corporal*	21	"	Lancaster	
Aaron Taylor "	25	"	Lunenburg	Littleton
Thomas Willard "	23	"	Lancaster	
Nathaniel Foster "	25	"	Chelmsford	
Joel Phelps *drummer*	21	"	Lancaster	
Joseph Farnsworth "	20	"	"	
Luke Aldridge	20	laborer	Deerfield	
Aaron Allen	30	"	Petersham	
Benjamin Atherton	20	"	Harvard	
David Atherton	21	"	Lancaster	
Phineas Atherton	16	"	"	
Timothy Baker	24	tailor	Petersham	Littleton
Joseph Bayley	30	laborer	Lancaster	
Jonathan Brown	17	"	"	Stow
Roger Bruce	21	"	Marlboro'	
Michael Bryant	21	"	Shrewsbury	
John Bunn or Bur	20	"	Petersham	
William Burt or Burk	28	"	Groton	
Joseph Chandler	21	"	Petersham	
William Chesnutt	22	"	Shrewsbury	Boston
Josiah Chamberlain	25	"	Groton	

	Age	Occupation	Residence	Birthplace
Henry Coffin	17	joyner	Lunenburg	
Joseph Collin	24	tanner	Worcester	
Jonathan Creasy	25	laborer	Harvard	Groton
Samuel Davis	20	"	Lunenburg	
Isaac Day	17	cooper	Harvard	Malden
Peter Day	24	laborer	Springfield	London
Phineas Divol	20	"	Lancaster	
Abel Farnsworth	22	husbandman	"	
John Farnsworth	30	laborer	Harvard	Lancaster
Jeremiah Field	18	"	Lancaster	Boston
John Fitch	21	"	Lunenburg	
David Fling	30	tailor	Marlboro'	Ireland
Joseph Foster	22	cordwainer	Lunenburg	
Samuel Foster	25	laborer	Chelmsford	
Samuel Gates	26	"	Marlboro'	
Levi Goodenough	19	"	"	
Luxford Gooding	24	"	Westboro'	
Peter Gore	21	"	Petersham	Watertown
Ephraim Goss	22	"	Lancaster	
Nehemiah Gould	21	"	Groton	
Daniel Harper	21	"	Harvard	
Elias Haskell	19	cooper	"	
Thomas Henderson	40	laborer	Lancaster	Ireland
Nehemiah How	21	"	Groton	
Samuel How	19	"	Marlboro'	
Andrew Hutchins	25	husbandman	Chelmsford	
Eliakim Hutchins	22	laborer	"	
Enos Hutson	20	"	Petersham	Westboro'
William Hutson	22	cordwainer	Lancaster	
John Johnson	22	laborer	"	
Samuel Kilham	20	"	Marlboro'	
Matthias Larkin	30	"	Lancaster	
James Leach	21	"	Lunenburg	
David McClelhan	18	joyner	Worcester	
Samuel Martin	18	cooper	Groton	Lunenburg
Artemas Maynard	20	laborer	Shrewsbury	
Joseph Metcalf	21	cooper	Harvard	
Daniel Moody	25	laborer	Marlboro'	
Uriah Morse	24	"	Worcester	
Samuel Neagus	22	"	Petersham	Westboro'
Jabez Norcross	20	"	Lunenburg	
Joseph Patterson	25	"	Groton	
Ebenezer Phillips	30	"	Grafton	

	Age	Occupation	Residence	Birthplace
Joseph Pratt	30	laborer	Lancaster	
Joseph Priest	45	"	"	
Nathan Rugg	20	"	Marlboro'	Lancaster
John Russell	35	weaver	Shirley	Ireland
David Saunders	19	laborer	Lancaster	Groton
John Simon	23	"	Lunenburg	
Andrew Spear	21	"	"	Ireland
Robert Spear	45	"	"	
Jacob Stiles	19	housewright	Lancaster	Lunenburg
David Stone	18	laborer	Petersham	Framingham
Hezekiah Stowell	21	"	Worcester	Watertown
Isaac Sullendine	21	"	Lancaster	
Zechariah Tarbel	22	"	Lunenburg	Groton
John Taylor	25	"	"	Littleton
John Turner	22	"	Petersham	Lunenburg
Joseph Turner	20	"	"	Lunenburg
Lemuel Turner	18	"	Lancaster	Groton
Nathaniel Turner	18	"	"	Groton
William Turner	18	"	"	Lancaster
John Warner	20	husbandman	"	
William Warner	20	"	Leominster	Lancaster
Eliphalet Warren	20	laborer	Westboro'	
Barnard Wilde		"	"	
Aaron Wilder	20	"	Lancaster	
James Willard	18	"	"	
Silas Willard	19	"	Harvard	
David Wilson	18	"	Petersham	
John Wilson	20	"	Lancaster	
Jonathan Witherby	20	"	Lunenburg	
Levi Woods	20	"	Lancaster	
Matthew Wyman	40	"	"	Woburn
Uriah Wyman	21	apothecary	"	Woburn
Robert Zewers	30	laborer	Worcester	Concord

David Atherton died the second day of May, on board the sloop, in Boston Harbor; Sergeant James Houghton died October 21, at Fort Cumberland; William Hudson was killed in the assault made by the enraged Acadians upon Major Frye's detachment, when burning the "mass house" at Peticodiac. Besides the natives of Lancastrian towns above named, these appear in other companies:

	Age	Occupation	Residence	Birthplace	Company
John Buttrick	39	yeoman	Leominster	Stow	Capt. Jones's
Jesse Howe		"	"		Col. Shirley's
Nath¹. Johnson	25	"	"	Lancaster	Capt. Jones's
Jonas Moore	32	"	Bolton		"
John Rugg	31	"	South Hadley	Lancaster	Capt. Stevens's
William Warner	18	"	Leominster	"	"
David Wilde	21	blacksmith	Nutfield	"	Capt. Gilbert's

The Orderly Book of Captain Abijah Willard, in possession of Dr. Robert Willard of Boston, contains a journal kept from April 9, 1755, on which day he marched from Lancaster with his company, until January 6, 1756, when it abruptly closes. From this brief record of daily events we ascertain that the Lancaster company actively participated in the capture of Fort Beau Sèjour, and Willard records that in repelling an attack of the French and Indians upon the camps:

We Killed the Chief Indian a Sagamore from the Island of Saint Johns which are known by the name Mickmack, he Liued aboute 5 hours after he was Shott and behaued as bold as any man Could Do till he Died but wanted Rum and Sider which we gaue him till he Died, he was shott throug the Bodey just below his Ribs, he was supposed to be 6 feet and two inches and very Large bon'd but very poor.

The captain, with his friends Captain Phineas Stevens and Chaplain Phillips, took an early opportunity to visit two or three of the Acadian villages, and his picture of Evangeline at home adds no graces to the poetic ideal of modern artists; he writes:

I saw a Grate many french women and Garls, their Faces Loock well bnt their feet Loock verey strange with wooden shoes they all wore.

The battalion was drawn up to hear prayers at six o'clock every morning, and Chaplain Phillips regularly upon Sunday, "held forth both forenoon and afternoon." Chapter and verse of his texts are faithfully recorded. One day the men were deprived of their usual ration of strong drink, and Winslow's battalion "was in an uproar and cried *No Rum* till Late in the Evening." Some of

these too thirsty soldiers condoned their offence the next day
by a two hours' ride upon the wooden horse. There appear throughout the journal frequent intimations of a hearty
dislike between the Massachusetts soldiers and the regulars. Governor Shirley, in a letter, mentions hearing "that
so good an harmony as could be wished did not subsist
between the officers of the New England Regiments and
those of his Majesty's Regular Troops." Captain Willard
evidently thought that by far the largest share of hard and
disagreeable fatigue and picket duty was allotted to the
Massachusetts men; and once breaks out petulantly with
the complaint that his company were "made cattle on for
to Draw barils." Lieutenant-Colonel Robert Monckton,
the King's officer at the head of the expedition, appears in
Willard's pages in very unfavorable light, as a cold-blooded
martinet, caring little for the comfort of his soldiers. With
plenty of cattle roaming wild on the meadows about them,
the soldiers were forbidden fresh meat. Several were
arrested for going out to gather some green peas, a great
abundance of which were growing on the marsh, and the
journal adds:

> Their was a grate uprore in the Camp concerning the peese, for it was
> thought that Coll. Munckton had much Rather the Cattle should Eate the
> peese, than the soulders that Came from New England or his one troops,
> which by Credible Information of oure officers. I thought it very hard.

Our captain seems, however, to have won the good
graces of Monckton, for on August 5 he received the command of a party of two hundred and fifty men, and was
sent with sealed orders to the head of Minas Bay. A party
of regulars under a captain-lieutenant was to join the expedition at some point in advance, and Captain Willard,
knowing that by custom this regular officer, though of
inferior rank to himself, would then assume the command
over him, refused to accept the position and submit to such
indignity. He therefore received written instructions to
support his authority, which seeing, the British officer "was

sumthing Blank to think a New England Capt. should Take Command of a Capt. Lt. of the Regulars, and Emediatly he said he was much Fatigue with his Traveling so much and Desired to have the Liberty of Coming on to Cobequid ;" Willard declined to relieve him.

The impudent claim of the Englishmen that the royal commission entitled them to precedence above every Provincial of the same grade, whatever his term of service in that rank, was so constant a source of bitterness and strife, that Pitt was compelled, in the interest of the public service, to promise redress of the wrong before the organization of Abercrombie's army could be effected in 1758. Captain Willard's march along the shore of Minas Bay came near ending in a tragedy, which would have carried mourning into many a home in Lancaster. He had been traversing the beach, the banks of which were precipitous and nearly one hundred feet in height, when the increased roaring of the tide attracted attention. and a Frenchman warned them that their lives depended upon swift retreat. The journal continues :

I ordered the party to Return back as fast as they Could; the men being frighted Traveled as fast as possible. We was obliege to Travell 2 miles before we could escape the tide and before we Got to the upland where we could Gett up the Banks was obliege to waid in the Rear up to their midles and Just escape being washed away and when come to this case sum of the men very much fatigued and att this plase by the best observation the tides rise 80 foot.

When the expedition reached Tatmagouche, Captain Willard, according to instructions, opened his secret orders, and he records them as—"suprising to me for my orders was to burn all the houses that I found on the Road to the Bay of Verts." The captain made suitable disposition of forces, and began to carry out his disagreeable duty. All the inhabitants of the district were summoned to assemble, and when collected and surrounded by the soldiers he went among them :

* * * and told them that they must Go with me to fort Cumberland and Burn all their Buildings which made them Look very sober and Dejected, one of the french askt me for what Reason for he said he Never had Taken up arms against the English sence they had the fight at menas, and sence swore by the bible that he Never would, before Maj^r Philips of anopilis: and he was Ready to swear now and all the Rest mad the same Reply; after this I told them they was Rebbelios, the frenchman askt me In what, I answered him In harbouring the Indians from Saint John's Island to go to the English Settlements in New England and Noviscotia and find them provitions and ammonition which they answered me and said they was oblige to or the Indians would kill them. I told them if they had been true they might of ben protected by the English and I told them they might Cary their familys with them if they thought best; and upon that they ast me for to have the Liberty to go with their familys to the Island of Saint Johns but soon answered them itt Did not Lie in my power to Do itt, and they askt me Liberty for 2 hours to Consult wether they thought Best to Cary their familys. I Granted them the Liberty and after they had Consulted with each other they sent for me and they made this Reply that they had chose to Leave their familys, which I Readyly Granted for I Did not want the Trouble of the women and children. * * * this afternoon I ordered the whole to be Drawed up in a Bodey and bid the french men march of and sott fire to their Buildings and Left the women and children to Tack Care of themselues with grate Lamentation which I must Confess itt seemed to be snmthing shoking.

And thus the pillage and destruction, the wailing of women widowed and children made fatherless went on from hamlet to hamlet, and when the torch had desolated the district assigned to him, Captain Willard marched back to Fort Cumberland and reported to Colonel Monckton. That magnate seemed much pleased with his conduct, and invited him to supper in his tent. That this service was not only inglorious and ungrateful to the brave, but attended with much hardship, is attested by the following documents from Massachusetts Archives, LV, 62 and 63. They are in the handwriting of Secretary Josiah Willard:

Sir: I have received your Letter giving me an acct. of the Hardships your poor Soldiers are exposed to. I sincerely Compassionate their unhappy case & I pray God to find out some Way for their Relief. The Governor is not expected here till the month of Decembr. When he arrives I shall endeavour to mention the affair to him. In the mean time,

I have written a Letter to Major General Winslow which I have left open, Leaving it with you to deliver it or not as you shall judge best, first sealing it before you deliver it. The Council being informed that I had a Letter from you upon the subject of these Hardships of the Soldiers desired me to communicate it to them, which I did. What they will do upon it I know not.

October 31, 1755.　　　　　　　　*To Abijah Willard.*

BOSTON, Oct. 31, 1755

Sir: I have lately rec^d a Letter from my Kinsman Cpt. Abijah Willard expressing his tender concern for his soldiers who are exposed to ly in Tents in this cold season now coming on and their cloath now worn out. I would fain use any Interest I could make that may contribute to the Relief of these and other the Provincial soldiers in Nova Scotia in the like circumstances, but I am a perfect stranger both to Governor Lawrence & Coll. Monkton. But the acquaintance I have of you & my knowledge of your compassionate spirit, especially towards the soldiers under your command in like circumstances, urges me to write to you on this occasion (not from any Distrust I have of your care in these matters, but possibly as your Distance from the Place where this Company is quartered may keep you in some Ignorance of the Difficulties these poor men labour under) to desire you would interpose your best offices for their Relief. It seems that these men can be of little service in act of Duty required of them while they are so destitute of the necessary Comforts & Refreshments of Life. You will excuse this Freedom. With my earnest desires of the gracious Presence of God with you & particularly to prosper your enterprises for the Good of your nation & Country I am, Sir, Your very humble servt,　　　　　　　　　　JOSIAH WILLARD.

The Lancaster soldiers, ill clad, often inefficiently provisioned, and suffering much from the rigors of the climate, spent the dreary Canadian winter in barracks at Fort Cumberland. In April, 1756, they were allowed to return to their homes. As we have seen, this was not Captain Willard's first experience of Nova Scotia, nor was it to be his last. Little more than twenty years passed from the time when he assisted in forcing the broken-hearted Acadian farmers into exile, and again he sailed for Nova Scotia, himself a fugitive, proscribed as a Tory, his ample estate confiscated and his name a reproach among his life-long neighbors. As thousands of French Neutrals, from Georgia to Massachusetts Bay, sighed away their lives with

grieving for their lost Acadia, so we know Abijah Willard,
so long as he lived, looked westward with yearning heart
toward that elm-shaded home so familiar to all Lancastrians.   On the coast of the Bay of Fundy, about ten miles
west of St. John, is a locality yet called *Lancaster*.   Colonel Abijah Willard gave it the name.   It was his retreat
in exile, and there he died in 1789.

Of the thousand Acadians apportioned to the Province
of Massachusetts, the committee appointed by General
Court for the duty of distributing them among the several
towns, sent three families, including twenty persons, to
Lancaster.   These were: Benoni Melanson, his wife Mary,
and children Mary, Joseph, Simeon, John, Bezaleel, Carrè,
and another daughter not named; Geoffrey Benway, Abigail his wife, and children John, Peter, Joseph, and Mary;
Theal Forre, his wife Abigail, and children Mary, Abigail
and Margaret.   The Forre family were soon transferred to
Harvard.   These exiles arrived in February, 1756, and the
accounts of the town's selectmen for their support were regularly rendered until February, 1761.   They were destitute,
sickly, and apparently utterly unable to support themselves,
and were billeted now here, now there, among the farmers,
at a fixed price of two shillings and eightpence each per
week for their board.   Sometimes a house was hired for
them, and, in addition to rent paid, we find in the selectmen's charges such items as these:

	£	s	d	qr
To cash pd for an Interpreter and paper,		3	4	
To what Nessecareys we found them,	1	o	8	o
To 472 weight of Befe cost,	3	3	2	1
To Corn that they have had & yoused, with Sauss,		10	8	
To one Bushel of Salt & Salting the Befe,		5	6	
to one washing tub, 2 earthen pots & pail,		4	o	
to wood for the winter season for the year 1757,	1	6	8	

Direct evidence to the helpless condition of the two families of French Neutrals in Lancaster is given in a letter
from the selectmen, dated January 24, 1757, found in Massachusetts Archives, XXIII, 330:

and here Foloweth an account of the curcumstances, age and sexes of those people. thare Is to famles Consisting of fifteen In Number, the whole to witt. Benoni Melanso with his wife of about fourty four or five years of age, and they have seven children thre Boyes and four Girlls, the Eldest Girl about 17 years old, the boye Next about 15 years old, Sickly. Can Do Nothing. ye Next Boy 12 years old. ye Next boy 10 years old, and ye four Girlls all under them Down to two years old, and the woman almost a Criple. . . . . . . The Name of the others is Jefray & his wife. he almost an Idiot and aboute 46 years old. . . . . . they have four children 3 Boyes & one Girll. ye Eldest Boye 10 yeares old & ye Rest Down to two years old.   Wᴹ RICHARDSON ⎱ *Selectmen*
                                 JOHN CARTER   ⎰ *of*
                            JOSHUA FAIRBANK ⎰ *Lancaster*

Shortly after the date of the above, these unhappy people suddenly disappeared from their habitation. Reckless with homesickness, they had stolen away and made a bold push for the sea, in the vain hope that on it they might float back to the Basin of Minas. This was in the depth of winter, February, 1757. They reached the coast at Weymouth, where they soon encountered the questioning of local authority, and to excuse their intrusion Melanson made complaint against his Lancaster guardians. The history of the case is in Massachusetts Archives, XXIII, 356 :

> The Committee to whom was referred the Petition of Benoni Melanzon in behalf of himself and sundrie other French People, Having met and heard the Petition and one of the Selectmen of Lancaster, relating to the several matters therein Complained of and also have heard the Representative of Weymouth where the French People mentioned in sᵈ. Petition at present reside : Beg leave to report as follows. Viz : That it doth not appear that yᵉ Petitioner had any Grounds to complain of the selectmen of Lancaster or either of them relating the matter complained of, and therefore Beg leave further Report that the Committee are of oppinion that the said French People be ordered forthwith to Return to Lancaster from whence they in a disorderly manner withdrew themselves. all which is Humbly submited.   pr order of the Comitte
>   SILVANUS BOURN.

In Council, February 24, 1757.

Read and ordered that this Report be so far accepted as relates to the Petitioners Complaint of his Treatment at Lancaster being without Grounds, but inasmuch as the Petitioner offers to undertake for the support of himself and the other French removed from Lancaster except in the article of Firing and House Room, and is likewise willing that two of his sons be placed out in Families and inasmuch as the Petitioner is by employment a Fisherman, which cannot be exercised at Lancaster, therefore, Ordered that he have liberty to reside in the Town of Weymouth untill this Court shall otherwise order, and the Selectmen of said Town are impowered to place two of his sons in English families for a reasonable term and to provide House Room for the Rest, & the liberty of cutting as much Firewood as is necessary in as convenient a Lot as can be procured. The account of the Charge of House Rent and Firewood to be allowed out of the Province Treasury.

Sent down for concurrence.

Feb. 25, 1757. THOS. CLARKE, *Depty. Secy.*

In the House of Representatives.

Read and unanimously non concurred, and ordered that Report of the Com[tee] be accepted & y[t] the said French Neutrals so called be directed to return forthwith to ye Town of Lancaster accordingly.

Sent up for Concurrence.

T. HUBBARD, *Spkr.*

In Council, Feb. 25, 1757.

Read & Concurred. A. OLIVER, *Secy.*

Consented to. S. PHIPS.

They were soon again in the quarters whence they fled. In June, 1760, the Melanson family were divided between Lunenburg, Leominster, and Hardwick, while the Benways remained. Among the petitioners for leave to go to "Old France," a little later, appear "Benoni Melanson and Marie, with family of seven," and from that date the waifs from Acadia appear no more in the annals of Lancaster.

III. THE SECOND CROWN POINT EXPEDITION AND FORT WILLIAM HENRY.

1756–1757.

Hardly had Captain Abijah Willard tasted the comforts of home after returning from Acadia, before the following letter came to him from his late commander:

ALBANY, May 27, 1756.

His Excellency General Shirley haveing Directed me to acquaint you that as he is Determined for the Good of His Majesty's Service to raise an

Independant Company on the Terms by him proposed and herewith Inclosed and being Sensable of your Abilletys for such a Command has proposed you for their Captain and Doubt not of your acceptance and has also appointed Jotham Gay (whom you Know) as Lieut and the other officers you will appoint prefarance allways to be Given those that wer with us at Nova Scotia and as many of those men to be employ'd as Can be Obtained being somewhat used to This Kind of Duty. What Inlistment you want you will apply to Mr Draper, money you find to Mr Apthorp. But should it so happen that your Curcumstances will not Admitt of your proceding on the Expedition his Excellency has reposed the Trust In you Either to Grant the favour to you Intended To Capt. Bailey or Jones as It best Suits and you Judge for the Good of the Service hope to see you Soon as your very humble serv⁺

JOHN WINSLOW.

To Capt. Abijah Willard.

[Winslow Papers of Massachusetts Historical Society, 63.]

No reply from Willard is found, but his domestic affairs doubtless demanded his presence, for he did not enter the service under his old commander. War was at last formally declared between France and Great Britain. Shirley's plan of the campaign for 1756 was the same as that of the preceding year, and its results were as meagre. The provincial forces assembling at Albany awaited the arrival of the royally commissioned general, Shirley having been superseded. Abercrombie came in June, and awaited his superior, Earl Loudoun. Loudoun arrived late in July, and energetically continued the loitering policy. The Massachusetts men were in the field early in the spring. John Whitcomb, Esq., of Bolton, was one of those appointed March 9, 1756, by the council, "a Committee to reside at Albany or parts adjacent * * * to take care of the transportation of the provisions and other stores for the use of the forces of the Province." Hezekiah Gates of Lancaster served as their assistant, and William Richardson of Lancaster as purchasing agent. Certain letters of theirs contain matters of interest relating to the quartermaster's department of the army:

LANCASTER March ye 31, 1756.

To the Honrble. John Osburn Esqr. & the Rest of Honrble Committee of Warr.

Gentlemen, this Is to Inform you that I am Just Returned from the westward from purchising Cattle & to Let you Now that I have secured aboute seventey two or thre & I had the fortune to be first In the affair for as I came Back out of hadley I met Collo Murey a going In.   I have with a great Deel of Trouble got Good Cattle but thay at the first asked me twentey pence pr pound those having Given eighteen pence for ye Govener's servis & paid thre pounds pr weke for caping till thay went, but fineley I purchised for eighteen pence & some for sixteen & thay must goe the 13th or 14th of April which time I shall set out, thay Not being able to Cape them Longer.   I shall be at Boston the 5th Day of April to wait upon your Honrs for aboute 250 pounds more.   I being obliged to promis ye owners of ye Cattle to pay the Rest when I tak away ye Cattle.   No more present. Begg Leve to subscribe my self your Honours friend & most Humble sert.   WM RICHARDSON.

    P. S.   Cattle are Very carse & I believe Coll Murey wont be able to get above 100 for the Province if he Dos yt that are good.

                              [Massachusetts Archives, LV, 162]

To the Honrble John Osburn Esqr & the Rest of ye Honrble Committee of Warr.

Gentlemen.   This is to Inform you that my son withe the Rest of the people Returned from Albany ye 28th of April with a Recepte for 68 Cattle one of the fatest tired at Shefield but Mr. Ashley one of the Commissioners said he would take Care and Get him up after he had Rested, but it is Verey Surprising to me that men equal to such a trust as is Reposed In them should send me a Recept for 68 Cattle part for Befe & part for working, it Is true there was as I told your Honours aboute 12 or 14 that I told you was Not so fat as the Rest, but not one but what was Handsom befe. but we was unfortunate as to set oute them 3 first Days which Tok their stumock of from eating & my son telles me they eate Verey Little all ye way to Albaney, which Caused them to Look Verey thin which misfortune I conld not help, but the Rest of the Cattle was the Best that Could be got In the Countrey & was fatt Cattle & some of the Best Sort. however I Take it that Mr Livermore & Mr Foye that was the Commissioners that ware at Albaney either would not make a Resonable alowance for the Cattle being Drove so farr or modestly speking they had not Judgment so to Do, but however thay may Right I am sure In this that I have Done all the Justice that I am capable of.   My people telles me that thay were Detained two Days at Albaney thay promising to send a Gard to the hafe moon, but fineley sent none & sent for ouer people to bring the Cattle over the River which thay Did the Cost of which with ye two Days Expences amounted to upwards of thirteen pounds the Gentlemen I understand was so busey aboute their tea Dishes and other Delights of Life, thay could not attend & This Gentleman from your frend & Humble ser^t.

W$_M$ RICHARDSON

LANCASTER, April y^e 30th, 1756.

[Massachusetts Archives, LV, 202.]

STILLWATER, May 25, 1756

We Arived hear yesterday about the middle of the Afternoon and find timber Redy hewed to build the Greatest part of the fourt and store house and bords for all and find a Good place to build on whare the River that Runs from the Saw-mill Coms to the Great River; the things which you sent me a List of are Come, thare is no Great pot nor pail nor Large brass kettle nor tents which the other Committee men have, which things we cannot well do without, for we have nothing to fetch water in nor to wash in, nor any Gun tent which we much need, 3 or 4 bags of bullits we want. I hope we shall Go to build your Station in about 3 days, we have about 300 men with us and we shall want about 200 more for part must be Imployed in bringing the stores hear. Your most obedient Servant

HEZEKIAH GATES

N. B. pray sir send the tin Kettles for Cap Ballard's Company if they are come. I hope sir you will find it out for I was obliged to wright upon my Knee.

Superscribed: Colln John Chote at Albany.

[Massachusetts Archives, LV, 272.]

UPPER FALLS, June 14, 1756

We are Generaly well hear. I have Received about 1000 bls of stores and sent to fourt Edward above 800 bls of stores. the cheaf Commander of fourt Edward is a man of Government. I do not think he Incorigeth our people to Go in the battoes from this fourt we man but 10 battoes and 6 or 7 from the fourt the commanding offisser thare sends word to us our people had best Lodge thare thay have once don it and ware obliged some to Gard the Rest to Ly under the battoes and if they are obliged to Lodge thare I cannot Git aney to Go in the battoes and if so the stores will be much stopped hear, but Cap Nelsons is this day Gone up to the fourt to see what he can do. I had the affair in so Good a way before this happened the stores went as fast as thay came, above 130 bls, in one day and was Increasing— pray sur send me money to pay the battoe men as soon as may be, for I shall pay them all the money I have of my own now to Incorrage them for they say the promisses made to them Last year was not fulfiled and It will be so this. bullits we have none the bl of powder we have is cannon powder, pray send Bullits and pistol powder. Sur I desire you will send me some cider, sugar, and chocolat. We have none to speak of. Cap Whipple is Gone to fourt Edward to Receve the Stores with Sum of his men, pray send Cap Houghton's men as soon as may be for we have 30 in battoes, 40 In the Gaurds to fort Edward out of about

115 men, the duty is hard : to onlode the stores and store them and deliver them to the battoes, 4 or 5 ol' Leut Hunts men do It. but they are worn out, thayer fingers blead and sore with handling Barrels, and desire to Go in the battoes. pray sir if you Intend to forward the business hear, send Cap. Houghton's men and money to pay the battoe men with. I am your most obedient Servant   HEZEKIAH GATES.

Superscribed: Coll John Whitcomb. At the Half Moon.
[Massachusetts Archives, LV. 326.]

Hunt's and Houghton's men, referred to in this letter, were of Lancaster, Bolton and adjoining towns. From the headquarters of General Winslow, at Half Moon, a road ran beside the Hudson to Stillwater. Thence stores were conveyed by water to Saratoga, where they were again loaded upon wagons and carried to Upper Falls to be transported by batteaux to Fort Edward, an irregular fortification built of hewn timber, on the east bank of the Hudson, about fifty miles above Albany. Fort William Henry was supplied from Fort Edward over a wagon-road of fourteen miles' length. The next month Gates is farther north upon the river :

FORT MILLER July 22, 1756

After my humble duty to your Honour, I would Inform your Honour that I have taken the names of 36 men by their Consent to serve in the Battoes but several of them are gone already from me. Capt. George Harmer has ordered his men to Lave the Battaux Service. Capt. Andrew Fuller's men are gone from me, the officers Discourageing them by Calling them Cowards and Otherways. Peter Graves Charles Boyles with others are gone from me. Sr. I wait your Orders and Directions in these affairs for If the Battaux are Stopt for want of men to go in them the Expedition will be hindred for here is a Quantity of Warr like Stores already and Other Stores daily Coming here. No Doubt In your great Wisdom you will direct In the Best manner In these affairs. Your most humble and Obedient Servant.   HEZEKIAH GATES.

To General Winslow.
[Winslow Papers, II, 92.]

The Lancaster soldiers of 1756 were mostly in the regiment of Colonel Jonathan Bagley, and the company of Captain Benjamin Ballard, the roll of which, containing fifty names, is in Massachusetts Archives, XCV, 17 and 18 :

Benjamin Ballard, *captain*, Henry Bridgeman, Joseph Priest,
Sherebiah Hunt, *lieutenant*, Josiah Divol, Samuel Ross,
Henry Haskell, *sergeant*, Andrew Goodfry(*died*), David Thurston,
James Crosfield, *corporal*, Benjamin Houghton, Gardner Wilder
John Manning " Joseph Houghton, Elijah Woods,
Samuel Ballard, *clerk*, Abner Haskell, Samuel Woods,
Elijah Beeman, Jeremiah Dickenson, (*died*).

Captain Timothy Houghton, also in Colonel Bagley's command, led a company largely recruited by his lieutenants from Waltham and Newton. The following were of Bolton :

Captain Timothy Houghton, Zachariah Glazier, Josiah Priest,
John Whitcomb, *sergeant*, Marmaduke Jos. Hamilton,
Jonas Wilder " Robert Longley, Richard Townsend,
Abraham Bruce, Francis McFadden, Levi Whitcomb,
James Carruth, Samuel Nichols, Silas Whitcomb.

[Massachusetts Archives, XCIV, 382.]

Hezekiah Gates of Lancaster was mustered with this company, but detached as assistant quartermaster by the war committee of the commonwealth, as heretofore stated.

In Captain Thomas Hartwell's (Littleton) company of the same regiment were these men of Harvard :

Benjamin Bridge, *lieutenant*, Abijah Coles, Uriah Holt.
Justinian Holden, *clerk*, Isaac Day, Benjamin Hutchins,
Gershom Hale,

[Massachusetts Archives, XCV, 50–51.]

In the company of Captain James Reed of Lunenburg, attached to Colonel Timothy Ruggles's regiment, were the following of Leominster :

David Johnson, *lieutenant*, Peter Houghton, William Warner,
Jonathan Houghton, Philip Sweetser, Phineas Wheelock,
Jonathan White.

William Barron of Lancaster, enlisted in this company, was appointed adjutant of the regiment in September.

[Massachusetts Archives, XCIV, 354; XCV, 131–2.]

To the Hon Spencer Phips Esq Leut Governr and Commander in Chief in and over his Majesties Province of the Massachusetts Bay in New England.

In Obedience to his Excellencey's Command to me Directed on the

5

15th of April Inst. to Coll my Companys together on the 22d Instant & agreable thereto I did & ther enlisted & Impressed as follows:

Inlisted, Josiah Divoll
Henry Bridgman
Saml. Ross
Willm. Warner
Manahsah Littel
Benja. Hutchins
Benja. Willson, Jun.
John Munroe
Zachh. Parker, Jun.
Jona. Holdin
Zachh. Farnsworth

Impressd, Abel Davis & *he hired*
William Barron
Joseph Hartwell
Thos Smith, Jun.
John Littel *he hired*
John Brown

I subscribe myself your
Most obedient Hble. Servant
OLIVER WILDER

LANCASTER, April 23d, 1756.
[Massachusetts Archives, XCII, 157.]

William Larkin and Gilbert Canady served in Colonel Richard Gridley's regiment of artillery at Fort William Henry; Josiah Holt, Joseph Ballard, Darius Hudson, Nathaniel Hudson and William Richardson, Jr., were also in the service. In the Boston Weekly News Letter for Thursday, April 22, 1756, Benjamin Ballard of Lancaster published an advertisement, offering twelve dollars reward for the return of a lost "Buckskin Purse, containing the following Pieces of Gold, viz: 13 Pieces of 18£ each, 12 Pieces of 13£ 10ˢ, and one Piece of 36£, Old Tenor." A subsequent petition of Captain Ballard's is given below:

*To His Honour Spencer Phips * * * * May 5, 1756.*

The Humble Memorial of Benjamin Ballard of Lancaster in Worcester County Sheweth that in March last having obtained a Captaincy in the Troops raised to go against Crown Point he took out of the Treasury of the Province about one hundred & forty pounds Lawful money, but as it was mostly in gold, he coud not pay the men who Inlisted without changing the same into silver and on ye ninth of April last going towards No. 2 he unfortunately lost out of his pocket fifty seven pounds & 12ˢ part of the sum first mentioned as he was going to get it changed & he has never found it or any part of it again and unless he is relieved by your Honr & Honrs, tho about forty of his Company are gone forward & the rest are all ready, he cannot proceed in the Expedition as he proposed — therefore he humbly prays that the Treasurer may be ordred (upon your memost giving good security) to advance to him that sum out of the Treasury: and to stop so much hereafter out of what shall be due to your memorialist & his

Company, or that he may be otherwise Relieved by your wisdom & goodness, & as in duty bound shall pray—   BENJ^N. BALLARD.

[Massachusetts Archives, LXXV, 543.]

While Loudoun and Abercrombie debated and dallied,
vigilant Montcalm dared, and the close of the year 1756
saw the churches of Montreal and Quebec decorated with
British colors captured at Oswego. The two much vaunted
expeditions against Crown Point, in the preparations for
which New England had enthusiastically taxed all her resources, had never moved from the base of supplies. With
the year 1757 a new plan of operations was resolved upon,
Louisbourg being made the single point of attack. But
Loudoun proved more earnest in asserting the royal prerogative in the colonial councils than in "seeking the bubble
reputation in the cannon's mouth," and his masterly inactivity again gave Montcalm his opportunity. Nothing was
won in the East, and Fort William Henry was lost in the
West. Scant record is found of our townsmen during the
year's campaigning. Colonel Joseph Frye marched from
Fort Edward, August 2, with his regiment of Massachusetts men and two hundred British troops, to succor Fort
William Henry, then besieged by Montcalm with an overwhelming force of French and Indians. On the surrender
of that fort, August 9, a massacre ensued, from which Colonel Frye and most of his men escaped with the loss of
everything but life. How many and what soldiers of Lancaster shared the horrors of that day will never be known,
but Captain Hartwell of Lunenburg, Captain Arbuthnot
of Marlborough and Captain Bailey served in the regiment, each leading from his neighborhood a company of
one hundred men.

To his Excelency Thomas Pownal . . . . . humbly sheweth Phineas
Atherton of Lancaster in the County of Worcester that your Petitioner
was a soldier in Captain Hartwell's Company in Col^o. Fry's Regiment in
the public service A. D. 1757 and that whilst he was in that service he was
taken sick of the small Pox at Albaney by means of which he was put to
the expence of six pounds twelve shillings York currency for nursing and

other necessarys, & your Petitioner therefore prays he may be reimbursed that sum or that such other relief may be granted to him as to your Honours shall seem good and your Petitioner as in duty bound shall ever pray.

PHINEAS ATHERTON.

[Massachusetts Archives, LXXVIII, 81.]

A similar petition of Caleb Willard is in Massachusetts Archives, LXXVII, 596. In the regiment of Colonel Israel Williams, during 1757, served the following:

Benjamin Harris,	*aet.* 24	Abel Wilder, *aet.* 21	Samuel Rugg,	*aet.* 59
Silvanus Harris	" 18	Moses Chandler " 25	Tho⁵. White	" 17
Elijah Prouty	" 17	John Wilder " 44	George Wheeler "	17

At the general alarm consequent upon the expectation that Montcalm, flushed with his victory at Fort William Henry, would make a bold push for Albany, the fourth part of the militia of Massachusetts were hurried towards that point with all possible speed. Captains Israel Taylor and Samuel Haskell of Harvard, Thomas Wilder of Leomster, John Carter and Nathaniel Sawyer of Lancaster, marched with from fifty to sixty men each as far as Springfield, whence, Montcalm having retreated to Canada with the rich spoils of easily bought success, they were recalled. The rosters of their companies follow. A few of the soldiers doubtless were not inhabitants of the town with whose company they served, but it is found impossible accurately to designate them:

A Muster Roll of a Foot Company Commanded by Nathaniel Sawyer of Lancaster, Detached out of Collo Oliver Wilder's Regimt. that Marchd on the late Alarm for the Relief of Fort William Henry, as far as Springfield.

Capt. Nathᵘ. Sawyer	Moses Sawyer	Russel Knight
Lieut. John White	Josiah Divoll	Joshua Johnson
Ensign Reuben Rugg	Joshua Fletcher	John Stewart
Sergt. Joseph White	Lemuel Houghton	Willᵐ. Dunsmore
" Amos Rugg	Peter Larkin	Ezekiel Kendall
" Wᵐ. Richardson, Jr.	Josiah Fairbank	David Willard
" Gershom Flagg	Moses Baily	Jonᵃ. Buss
Corp. Ephᵐ. Willard	Cyrus Fairbank	Samˡ. Houghton
" Josiah Sawyer	Samᵘ. Ballard	Solomon Houghton

Corp. Jacob Smith
" Tho⁹. Kendall
Private Jona. Kendall
Josiah Locke
Willᵐ. Kendall
Aaron Tufts
Elijah Osgood
Moses Wilder

Nahum Houghton
Jacob Bennet
Elijah Beman
Matthew Wyman
Benjᵃ. Houghton
Jeremiah Haskell
Joseph Woods
Willᵐ. Willard
Jonᵃ. Whitney

John McBride
Nathˡˡ. Hastings, Jr.
Joshua Baily
Jona. Osgood, Junʳ.
Samˡˡ. Snow
Samˡˡ. Prentice
Daniel Rugg
Edward Robbins

[Massachusetts Archives, XCV, 497.]

A Muster Roll of a Mounted Company Commanded by John Carter of Lancaster, Detached out of Collᵒ Oliver Wilders Rigement that Marchᵈ in the late alarm for the Fort William Henry as far as Springfield.

Capt. John Carter
Lieut. Hezekiah Gates
Cornet Jonᵃ. Wilder
Quar. Mr. Nathˡ, Longley
Chaplin Moses Hemingway
Corpˡˡ. Manasah Divoll
" Abiathar Houghton
" Gabriel Priest
" Abijah Wyman
Trumpeter Simon Butler
" Abijah Houghton
Jonas Whitcomb
Phineas Sawyer
Ephraim Fairbank
Daniel Priest
Thomas Beckford

James Carter
Hezekiah Gibbs
Elijah Woods
Eleazar Whitcomb
Josiah Carter
Sherebiah Hunt
Oliver Pollard
Hooker Osgood, Jr.
Joseph Heidrick
Ephᵐ. Wilder, Jun.
Paul Sawyer
Samˡˡ. Thurston
John Moor, Jun.
Levi Woods
Stephen Greenleaf
Daniel Robbins
Ezekiel Snow

Nathan Burpee
Jacob Stiles
Joseph Houghton
Hezekiah Whetcomb
James Townsend
Thos. May
Nathˡˡ. Houghton
Edward Houghton
James May
David Osgood, Jr.
Benjᵃ. Hastings
Asa Whitcomb
James Ross
Joel Houghton
Elijah Houghton
Jonᵃ. Robbins

[Massachusetts Archives, XCVI, 181.]

A Muster Roll of a Foot Company Commanded by Thomas Wilder of Leominster. . . . .

Capt. Thomas Wilder
Lieut. Samuel Nurse '
Ensign Josiah Bayley
Sergt. Nathaniel Page
" Caleb Sawyer
" Oliver Hale
" Nathan Bennett
Corporal William Wilder
" Nathaniel Hastings

James Ballard
Gardner Wilder
Philip Vorbach
Silas Bayley
Jacob Houghton
Obadiah Gill
Samuel Moore
Henry Sartel
Jonas Fife

Joseph Davis
Reuben Wyman
Jacob Gould
Aaron Taylor
Jonathan Page, Jr.
Ephraim Osburn
Timothy Fox
Seth Dodge
John Leach

Corporal Phineas Wheelock	Abijah Pratt	Zebulon Dodge
" John Pollard	James Snow	Jonathan Wood
Benjamin Whitcomb	Matthew Knight	Silas Dutton
Jonathan White	Samuel Bruce	Jonathan Holt
James Simonds	Wil iam Pollard	Asa Sartell
Rufus Houghton	James McBride	William Kimball
Amos Kendall	Jabez Bears	Reuben Smith
Kendall Boutell	Elij ih Wilson	John Symonds
Joseph Polley	Jonathan Holman	Amos Hazeltine
Nathaniel Colburn	John Pyper	William Steward
Luke Richardson	John Grout	Samuel Hodgkin
Asa Johnson	Jonathan Messard	David Peirce
Oliver Wyman	Jonathan Page	

[Massachusetts Archives, XCVI, 4 and 535.]

Captain Wilder's lieutenant and many of his men were residents of Bolton, but as the residences are not recorded in the roll, it is not always possible to locate the soldier.

A Muster Roll of a Foot Company Commanded by Israel Taylor of Harvard . . . . .

Capt. Israel Taylor	Joseph Houghton	William Withington
Lieut. Daniel Whitney	Jonathan Sampson	Amos Ray
Ensign Phineas Fairbank	John Houghton	Thomas Osburn
Sergt. Oliver Stone	Amos Fairbank	Elisha Gates, Jr.
" Silas Wetherby	Hezekiah Whitney	Phineas Taylor
" David Jewett	Abel Davis	Jeremiah Whitney
" Joseph Wetherby	Nathaniel Gates	Samuel Farr
Corporal Zebulon Peirce	Samuel Mead	John Davidson
" Isaac Stone	Samuel Mead, Jr.	Daniel Rand
" Abel Farnsworth	Richard Whitney	Jabez Brown
" William Sanderson	Josiah Whitney	John Whitaker
Joseph Eveleth	Nathan Warner	Jonathan Conant
Elias Stone	William Farmer	Daniel Allen
Abijah Cole	Micah Stone	Jonas Brown
Gordon Hutchins	Abraham Willard	William Jewett
William Burt	John Atherton	Asa Willard
Benjamin Barnard	Deliverance Davis	

[Massachusetts Archives, XCV, 489.]

A Muster Roll of a Company of Troopers commanded by Samuel Haskell of Harvard . . . .

Capt. Samuel Haskell	Isaac Gates	Charles Willard
Lieut. Samuel Tuttle	Samuel Finney	Josiah Priest, Jr.

Cornet Samuel Fellows
Quartermaster Jonª. Reed
Corp. Benjamin Hale
" Jeremiah Laughton
" Jonathan Wheeler
Barnabas Davis, Jr.
Jonas Peirce
Stephen Tuttle
Aaron Rand
Simon Blanchard

Moses Whitney
Nathaniel Holman
Oliver Tenney
Phineas Willard, Jr.
John Meriam
Ezekiel Haskell
John Cobleigh
Aaron Davis
Thomas Wright, Jr.
Judah Clark

John Sawyer
Caleb Sawyer
William Houghton
Daniel Houghton
Robert Whitcomb
Nathaniel Houghton
Peter Fox
Peter Willard
Thomas Houghton
James Crosfield

[Massachusetts Archives, XCV, 533.]

III. THE CONQUEST OF CANADA.

1758–1763.

The return of William Pitt to power, practically as dictator, took place in June, 1757. The sagacity and vigor of his war policy were quickly felt wherever England had an enemy. He repaid to the colonies the expenditures incurred by them in the contest with the French, and promised them protection from the official rapacity and arrogance under which they had long suffered, thus inspiring them with new confidence. The ever unready Loudoun disappeared from American shores, and Major-General Jeffrey Amherst succeeded to the chief command. He too was cautious to excess, but thoroughly reliable, and associated with him was the impetuous Brigadier, James Wolfe. The military imbecile, Abercrombie, was unfortunately retained, but, to atone for this chief's lethargy, the king's cousin, "the Bayard of the British army," Lord George Augustus Howe, was joined with him in command, and the inspiration of his chivalric energy soon pervaded the conduct of the campaign. The days of sloth and inactivity appeared to be at an end. England furnished over twenty thousand of her best troops, and the colonies strained their every resource, resolved to close the long contest by a vigorous onslaught along the whole line of debatable territory. At the north, Louisbourg fell under the daring and skilfully directed as-

saults of the British naval and land forces.   At the south,
Washington, under General John Forbes, planted the British colors over the fortress of Duquesne.

The central column, under Abercrombie, to which had
been allotted the capture of Ticonderoga, met with the
wonted ill fortune of its commander, owing to his disgrace-
ful mismanagement.   With this column were the Massachusetts men, seven thousand in number.   The expedition,
consisting of twenty-four regiments, and numbering over
fifteen thousand men, started out July 5, in batteaux, down
Lake George, and, landing at a point near its outlet, the
next day began the march towards the French fort in two
divisions, upon both sides of the stream.   An advanced
detachment of the enemy was encountered in the dense
woods, and a brisk engagement ensued, lasting less than
an hour, which resulted in the rout and capture of the
French ; but the victory was bought at a fearful price, with
the loss of the dearly beloved Lord Howe, who was killed
while pressing forward in the van of the right division.
The diary of the Reverend John Cleaveland informs us
that Colonel Jonathan Bagley's Massachusetts regiment
made the charge upon the right, and Dr. Caleb Rea, surgeon of that regiment, records that "Colonel Bagley behaved extremely well in battle."

Abercrombie seems to have lost, after Lord Howe's fall,
whatever judgment he possessed, and timidly fell back to
ponder over the situation.   Advancing again on the morning of July 8, he drew up his forces, four-fold those of
Montcalm, before the outworks of the fortress, which was
protected by water and impassable swamps on all sides but
one.   Hitherto always dilatory, he now became foolhardy.
Following the advice of a rash staff-officer, without awaiting his artillery and in contempt of the urgent remonstrance
of experienced provincial leaders — among whom was
Stark — he at once ordered an assault by columns upon
intrenchments bristling with formidable abatis.   Four hours

of desperate and useless fighting followed. About two thousand brave men were sacrificed, and the next day the dazed "Mrs. Nabby Crombie" was leading an ignominious retreat from a force vastly inferior to his own, to resume his normal occupation — planning fortifications. Again the colonies saw themselves hampered rather than helped by the royal officers. Again their enthusiasm and sacrifice had been brought to naught by official dawdling and stupidity. Remembering Louisbourg, the veteran provincial leaders might well regret that they had not been left unaided by the king's troops in their contest with Canada.

In the regiment of Colonel Bagley, John Whitcomb was lieutenant-colonel and his brother led a company of ninety-eight, thirty-six of whom were credited to Lancaster, twenty-six to Bolton, and thirteen to Shrewsbury. Several of these last resided in a precinct then, in part, Lancaster territory, and the roll will therefore be given in full. The service was from March to December, 1758:

Muster Roll of a Company of Capt. Asa Whitcomb in a Regiment raised by the Province of the Massachusetts Bay for the Reduction of Canada, whereof Jonathan Bagley, Esq., is Colonel.

Asa Whitcomb, Esq., *capt.*, Lancaster
Benja. Hastings, *lieut.*, Bolton
Francis Temple, " Shrewsbury
Zachariah Longley, *ensign*, Groton
Stephen Greenleaf, *sergt.*, Bolton
Jacob Smith, *sergt.*, Lancaster, (*died*)
Abner Cranson, " Marlborough
Abner Osgood, " Lancaster
Artemas Maynard, *corp.*, Shrewsbury
Micah Harthan, " Lancaster
John Wheeler, " Bolton
Timothy Hale, " Littleton
Josiah Priest, *drummer*, Bolton
Benjamin Atherton, Lancaster
Micah Briant, Shrewsbury
Thomas Bennett, Shirley
John Brooks, Lancaster
Benj. Bruce, Bolton
Ephraim Browne, Bolton
David Goodman, Shrewsbury
Jonathan Goodnow, "
Job Harris, Holden
John Houghton, Bolton
Nathan Harrington, Shirley
Jotham Houghton, Bolton
Ezekiel Hutson, Shrewsbury
Joseph Hale, Bolton
Nathaniel Hastings, Lancaster
Darius Hutson, Shrewsbury
Daniel Johnson, Lancaster
John Ingoldsby, Shrewsbury
Joshua Johnson, Lancaster
Phillip Jeno, " (*died*)
Joseph Keyes, Bolton
Eli Keyes, Jr., Shrewsbury
Mathias Larkin, Bolton
Wm. Larkin, Lancaster
Edmund Larkin, "

Asaph Butler, Lancaster
Shubael Baily, Jr., Lancaster
Willm. Brabrook, Lancaster, (*missing*)
Isaac Brooks, Bolton
Abraham Bruce, "
Jabez Bears, "
John Baily, Lancaster
Jabez Bigelow, No. 2
Joseph Bigsby, Lancaster
Willm. Barrack, Shrewsbury
Eben Bigelow, Lancaster, (*died*)
Saml. Bigsby, Shrewsbury
John Browne, Marlborough
Benoni Biglow, Bolton
Abraham Barnes, Marlborough
Jedediah Cooper, Lancaster
James Carruth, Bolton
Oliver Dresser, Lancaster
Oliver Dinsmore, "
Nathan Eager, "
Joseph Eveleth, Stow
Robert Fletcher, Lancaster
Phineas Goodale, "
John Gourden, Stow
Daniel Goss, Shrewsbury
Jonathan Geary, Lancaster, (*died*)
Ephraim Goss, "
Joseph Goodale, Marlborough
David Goodale, Bolton
James Goodnow, Shrewsbury

W^m. Longley, Shirley
Joseph Longley, "
Francis McFadden, Bolton
John McBride, Lancaster
Abner Marble, Stow
Amos Meriam, Bolton
Joseph Pratt, "
Amos Ray, Marlborough
Richard Roberts, Bolton
W^m. Simons, Jun., Shirley
Moses Sawyer, Lancaster
Nathan Smith, Shirley
William Sawyer, Bolton
Ezekiel Snow, Lancaster
Jacob Smith, Shrewsbury
James Squireen, Lancaster
Aholiab Sawyer, Bolton
John Sampson, Lancaster
Jonathan Taille, Groton
Benj^a. Townsend, Bolton
Aaron Tufts, Lancaster
David Thurston, "
Jonathan Townsend, Lancaster
Asa Taylor, No. 2
John Whitney, Shirley
Phineas Wilder, Lancaster
Josiah Woods, Bolton
Silas Warner, Lancaster
Levi Whetcomb, Bolton
Elijah Woods, Lancaster
Jedediah Woods, "

[Massachusetts Archives, XCVI, 102, 478–81.]

In the company of Captain Salmon Whitney of the same regiment were these Lancaster soldiers:

William Farmer,   John Larkin, (*died*)   Joseph Woods.

Of Harvard were these:

Lieut. Judah Clark,   Jonas Davis,   Asahel Nickerson,
Sergt Abraham Willard,   Josiah Davis,   Jonathan Parkhurst,
Sergt. Jonathan Whitney, Samuel Fellows,   John Rugg,
Corp. Samuel Mead,   Stephen Gates,   David Sampson,
John Burt,   James Haskell,   David Sanderson,
David Brown,   Solomon Haskell,   Amos Stone,

John Cole,	Aretus Houghton,	Samuel Wetherby,
John Daby,	Joseph Houghton,	Hezekiah Whitney,
		Asa Willard.

[Massachusetts Archives, XCVI, 473.]

In the regiment of Colonel Timothy Ruggles, Captain Joseph Whitcomb of Lancaster and Captain James Reed of Lunenburg led companies. Billeting rolls only of these commands have been found, and in them no residences are given. Colonel Ruggles assembled his command at Northampton, started thence June 3, and marched for five days — through what was then a wooded wilderness, absolutely without white inhabitants — to Albany. During the battle of Ticonderoga the regiment was detailed as rear guard at the saw-mills, where it threw up earthworks. Thenceforward it was engaged in rebuilding and improving the military roads between Saratoga and Albany, until it was marched home in November. Serving under Captain Whitcomb were the following men known to belong to Lancaster :

Joseph Beaman,	Amos Knight,	Richard Proutee,
William Brown,	Jonathan Phillips,	George Wheeler,
John Headley,	James Pratt,	Asa Whitcomb,
Levi Kendall,	Benjamin Priest,	Joseph Whitcomb, Jr.
Simon Kendall, (*died*)	Joshua Proutee,	Henry Wyman.

There were from Leominster :

| John Beaman, | Joshua Pierce, | Oliver Wyman, |
| | Peter Houghton. | |

Of Harvard were :

Jonathan Conant,	William Jewett,	Jonathan Whitney,
John Davidson,	John Taylor,	Thomas White.
	Israel Hale.	

In Captain Reed's command were Lancaster men :

| Phineas Bailey, | Simeon Johnson, | Josiah Locke. |
| Benjamin Hinds, | William Kendall, | Tilley Wilder. |

Of Leominster were :

| Timothy Boutell, | John Grout, | John Simonds, |
| Elias Carter, | Nathaniel Page, | Abel Wheelock. |

Of Harvard were :

John Conn,	Phineas Farnsworth,	Isaac Stone,
Jonathan Creasy,	Ephraim Robbins,	Jonathan White,
Joseph Davis,	Samuel Sanderson.	

Of Bolton were :

Hezekiah Gibbs,	Joseph Hazletine,	Joseph Snow,
	Jacob Gould.	

[Massachusetts Archives, XCVI, 137–8.]

In various other rolls proof is found that the following men from Lancaster served during 1758 :

Joseph Bailey,	John McCarty,	Joseph Stewart,
Samuel Ballard,	Ebenezer Pike,	Jotham Wilder
Elijah Beaman,	Moses Redman,	Nathaniel Willard,
Isaac Eveleth,	Joseph Squirean,	Aaron Willard.

The last named led a light-infantry company in the regiment of Colonel Oliver Partridge, and was severely wounded in the battle at Ticonderoga. He had been a lieutenant with Captain Caleb Willard of Lunenburg, and while in service was placed in command of a company of light infantry, Nathaniel Willard serving with him as subaltern. The following undated petition is in Massachusetts Archives, LXXVIII, 224 :

Province of the Massachusetts Bay. To his Excellency Thomas Pownal Esq. To the honourable his Majesty's Councill, the honourable the House of Representatives : humbly sheweth Aaron Willard of Lancaster that your Petitioner was a Captain in the Provincial Service in the Regiment of Light Infantry at the late Battle of Ticondaroga, that in that Engagement your Petitioner was shot through the Trunk of his Body about the bottom of his Breast, with which wound he lay a long time in a hopeless condition and so weak that he could not be moved to any Hospital for above a month and from thence your Petitioner got home by slow degrees about the end of September in a languishing Condition unable to do any work and continueing to this day under the care of a Physician ; by means of all which your Petitioner has been put to great and extraordinary expences of living in a manner sutable to his wounds and Consumptive habit, abroad and at home, besides the loss of time and great Damage to his future strength of body. Your Petitioner therefore humbly prays your Excellency and Honours to consider his case and grant that the sum of Twenty-one pounds which he has expended for surgery medicines and many necessary things since your Petitioner received his wound may be allowed him, or grant such other relief as in your Wisdom you shall see meet, and your Petitioner as in Duty bound shall ever pray. AARON WILLARD

Numerous memorials in the state archives instruct us in the spirit and manners of the time, and the sacrifices of the patriotic soldier. Extracts from some of these follow :

LANCASTER Sept. 18, 1758. These may sertify that my son Samuel Ballard was Taken Captive near Ticondaroga about the 25th June Last being with Leut. Stephens ; he was a Ranger in Capt. John Stark's Company. BENJN. BALLARD.

To the Honble Andrew Oliver Esq. Secy. in Boston.
[Massachusetts Archives, LXXVII, 722.]

To His Excellency Thomas Pownall Esq. . . . Dec. 29, 1758.

The Pettition of Phinias Wilder of Lancaster Humbley shewing that he Inlisted himself Into his majesties forces In the Expedition against Cannada in 1758 under the Command of Capt. Asa Whitcomb in Collo Bagley's Regiment and was taken sick aboute the first of September last with the Camp Distemper with a Grate Dele of Deficultey that I underwent by being brought some of the way in a Cart & some of the way by water to Green Bush whare I layd aboute a fortnight as they tell me I not being in a posture to Recolect the time myself and then I was Brought part of the way from Green Bush on a horse & part of the way In a horse Litter an arived at home but Just in Life & Remained above six wekes after I got home the Bigest part of In Dout of Life & the Cost and Charge I was at In order to Get home & after I got home amounts to six pounds two shillings & five pence as pr. account. . . . . PHINEHAS WILDER
[Massachusetts Archives, LXXVIII, 56.]

In the same volume as the last are similar petitions from John Bailey and Asaph Butler.

. . . . The Pettition of Thomas Garey of Lancaster . . . . Humbly Shewing to your Excellency & Honours that his son Jonathan Gary was Inlisted soulger under the Comand of Capt. Asa Whitcomb . . . and as my said Jonathan was a serving his King & Countrey in ye Expedition against Cannada he was taken sick at Lake George & was Brought in a Cart or wagon as far as the outermost barn in hafe moon & thare sent me a Letter earnestly Intreting me to Come or send some bodey to his Relief upon which Information I sent a man & Horse with Nesecareys for his Relief as soon as possiable I could fix him away but my poor son was Dead before my man & horse arived at the hafe moon. . . . .

THOMAS GEARY

[Massachusetts Archives, LXXVIII, 244.]

. . . . . The pettition of Peter Larkin of Lancaster . . . . . . his Brother John Larkin was an Inlisted soulger . . . . . in the Expedition against Cannada in yᵉ year 1758, under the Comand of Capt. Whitne in yᵉ Regiment of Collᵒ Bagley. . . . . my said Brother John was taken sick at Lake George but with some help by the Carts & wagons he got Down as far as Shefield & could get no farther & sent for me to Come to his assistance, accordingly I went to him to Shefield & set out & got him as far as Westfield with much a Do & thare taryed with him two or three Days, but he being unabele to Travil aney farther I was obliged to Leve him and he continued aboute ten or eleven Days & Expired & Died. . . .

PETER LARKIN

[Massachusetts Archives, LXXVIII, 247.]

Chaplain John Cleaveland, before mentioned, was the intimate friend of Lieutenant-Colonel John Whitcomb, and joint tenant with him of a rude hut in the encampment. Cleaveland's diary and that of Surgeon Rea afford pictures of the life of the soldiers in the intrenchments upon Lake George, detailing the supercilious deportment of the British officers, and the jealous dislike of them felt by the New England men ; the daily prayers and psalm singing, and the Sunday exhortations among the provincials, contrasted with the drunkenness, ribaldry and profanity of camp ; the perpetual delving upon the fortifications ; the court martials and infliction of punishments characteristic of rigid military discipline.   As the autumn days sped, the ill cooked and tainted provisions, and the universal filthiness of the camps engendered fevers and dysentery to an alarming extent, and the fort became one vast hospital.   It would doubtless be a harsh judgment, but one can hardly help suspecting, reading the diary of the pious surgeon in connection with the stories of his patients — the sick soldiers already quoted — that he interested himself less in his own business than in that of the chaplain ; earnest rather to edify spiritually, than to apply his energy and skill to the improvement of sanitary conditions.   In the disaster of Ticonderoga he sees the wrath of Providence towards "the horrid cursing and swearing there is in yᵉ camp, more especially among yᵉ Regulars.   I can't but Charge our defeat on this sin." He was tender of heart, however, for he writes :

Altho there is almost every day more or less whiped or Piqueted or some other ways punished I've never yet had ye curiosity to see 'm, the shrieks and crys being Satisfactory to me without ye Sight of ye Strokes,

One bright ray of sunshine relieved the gloom of the situation in the West. Lieutenant-Colonel John Bradstreet, obtaining the reluctant consent of his superiors, led three thousand provincial troops two hundred miles through the wilderness to the shore of Ontario, crossed the lake in boats, captured the important fort and naval station of Frontenac, and destroyed the French fleet. Soon after, General Amherst, with several regiments from Louisbourg, reached New York and joined Abercrombie early in October; but their jointd eliberations evolved no plan of action until the frosts were upon them, and then all that could be done was to dismiss the armed yeomanry to their farms, and distribute the regulars in their winter quarters.

The campaign for 1759, as planned by Pitt, contemplated a direct attack upon Quebec by a select army of English troops commanded by Wolfe, to be seconded by a vigorous advance towards Montreal by way of Lake Champlain. By the end of June Wolfe was planting his batteries opposite the Gibraltar of America; but Amherst lingered three weeks later, adding to the superfluous earthworks of Fort William Henry, before he ventured upon the single day's journey down Lake George to the scene of Abercrombie's disgrace the preceding year. The colonial troops had been long assembled, awaiting orders. The following list shows the Lancaster men enrolled in March and April:

Return of the Men enlisted or impressed for his Majesties Service within the Province of the Massachusetts Bay in the Regiment whereof Oliver Wilder Esq. is Colonel, to be put under the immediate Command of His Excellency Jeffrey Amherst Esq. General & Commander in Chief of His Majesties Forces in America for the Invasion of Canada.

John Willard,	Aged 19	
Jona. Hutchins	" 20	Served, 1757, at Lake George.
Robert Phelps	" 18	

Jonᵃ. Phillips	Aged 30	Served 1755
Wᵐ. Perham	" 34	*Impressed.*
Joseph Turner	" 16	"
Thoˢ. Barney	" 39	"
Abner Osgood	" 20	" 1758, at Lake George. (*Hired.*)
Jonᵃ. Townsend	" 20	" " " "
Mathias Larkin	" 32	" " " "
John Headley	" 36	" " " "
Phinehas Baily	" 18	" " " "
Jotham Wilder	" 40	
Joshua Proutee	" 21	" 1758, at Lake George.
Daniel Allbert, Jr.	" 28	
Peter Larkin	" 27	
Frederick Allbert	" 20	
John Bailey	" 40	" 1758, at Lake George.
Jonᵃ. Goodnow	" 21	
Stephen Kendall	—	
Samˡˡ. Kendall	" 17	
Levi Kendall	" 23	" 1758, at Lake George.
Henry Wyman	" 17	" " " "
Joseph Bixpy	" 18	" " " "
Jedediah Cooper	" 19	" " " "
Ephraim Goss	" 26	" " " "
John McCarty	" 25	" " " "
Joseph Squirean	" 19	" " " "
•Ebenʳ. Pike	" 32	" " " "
Joseph Bailey	" 28	" " " "
Samˡˡ. Goodenow	" 30	
Daniel Cook	" 17	
Reuben Walker	" 19	
John McBride	" 23	" 1758, at Lake George.
Joseph Stewart	" 27	" " " " (*Hired.*)
John Dunsmoor	" 11	(*Impressed.*)
George Bush, Jr.	" 37	"
John Crosly	" 36	(*Hired.*)
James Pratt	" 20	Served, 1758, at Lake George.
Phinehas Wilder	" 28	" " " "
Isaac Eveleth	" 24	" " " "
Moses Redman	" 37	" " " "
Micah Briant	" 24	" " " " (*Hired.*)
Nathaniel Wright	" 40	
Joseph Turner	" 16	(*Impressed.*)

HARVARD MEN:

Micah Stone,	Aged 24				
Jonathan Peirce	" 23	Served, 1756, at Lake George,			
Jacob Emerson	" 22	"	1758,	··	"
Jacob Harris	" 18				
William Sanderson	" 39				
John Houghton, 3d,	" 24				
Amos Stone	" 29				
Nathaniel Bray	" 22				
Josiah Davis	" 30				
Abraham Whitney	" 51				
David Brown	" 21	Served, 1758, at Lake George.			
Joseph Proctor	" 19	"	"	"	" "
Asahel Nickerson	" 17	"	"	"	"
John Conn	" 19	"	"	"	"
Jonathan White	" 17	"	"	"	"
John Cole	" 18	"	"	"	"
Isaac Holden	" 17	"	"	"	"
John Daby, Jr.	" 18	"	"	"	"
Ephraim Robbins	" 41	"	"	"	"
Samuel Whippy	" ?	"	"	"	"
Samuel Corey	" 42	"	"	"	"
John Burt	" ?	"	"	"	"

BOLTON MEN:

Josiah Priest,	Aged 23	Served, 1758, at Lake George.	
Benjamin Marble	" 32	"	1755
Jonathan Holman	" 23	"	1758
Ephraim Ward	" 25		
Josiah Pratt	" 59	"	1755
Joseph Pratt	" 32	"	1758
John Wilder	" 17	"	"
Benoni Bigelow	" 18	"	"
John Wheeler	" 25	"	"
Aholiab Sawyer, Jr.	" 17	"	"
Jonas Pollard	" 25		
John Pollard	" 29		
John Townsend	" 17		
Jonas Whitcomb	" 24	"	1755
Dennis Lockling	" 39	"	"
Josiah Moore	" 32	"	"

6

LEOMINSTER MEN:

Asa Butterick,	Aged 40	Served, 1758, at Lake George.
Joshua Peirce	" 18	" " " "
Abel Wheelock	" 20	" " " "
Benjamin Whitcomb	" 21	" 1756
Joseph Harper	" 17	
Ebenezer Harris	" 36	
James Symonds	" 17	
Rufus Houghton	" 35	
Elias Carter	" 21	
Richard Stewart		
Paul Hale		

[Massachusetts Archives, XCVIII, 373.]

One hundred and forty-two men in all were furnished from the Lancaster regiment, those not here given being chiefly from Lunenburg.

Colonel Wilder's account of services rendered as mustering officer is a curiosity in its way, and is appended unabridged:

Province of the Massachusets Bay Is Dr:

To one Warrant I Received from his Excellency Governor Pownell Requiring me to Raise one Hundred and fourtey two men and to apportion them as Equaley as I could to and amongst the Respective Companys in my Regiment in March the 26, 1759.

To filling a Leven warrants and sending a Leven expresses to a Leven Captains.	£ 1– 5–0
To Mustering said 142 men Raised out of my Regiment which s^d servis I attended two Days by Reson of the Captains not making their Respective Returns ye first Day in seson	0–12–0
To what Expences I was Nesesaryley at while attending s^d servis	0– 6–0
To one Days servis more in mustering the other Leveys Raised out of my Regiment that went under Coll^o Abijah Willard	0– 6–0
To my Expences in said servis	0– 3–0
To one Journey to Boston to Receive the Bountey money for the soulgers which toke me thre Days	1– 0–0
To my Expences in said Journey	0– 8–0
To two Days I went to Boston to make Return to the Adjutant General of the men I Raised according to the Governor's order & to Retourn 23 Retournes	0–12–0
To my Expences said Journey	0– 6–0

To two Days time I was obliged to spend in going over to Worster at the Request of the Expedition Captains who could

not make up their Billeting Roles without the Listing papers
which by an unhapey mistake was Never sent to me and I
having obtained the favour of Coll⁰ Chandler of some Blanck
Listing papers was first to be at the trouble of Listing the men
all a new again   0–12–0
To my Expences on said affair   0– 6–0
                                                                  ──────
                                                                  £5–16–0

OLIVER WILDER, *Colo*

LANCASTER, December yᵉ 27, 1759.

[Massachusetts Archives, LXXXIX, 432.]

The above named volunteers were divided between the
companies of Captains Aaron Willard of Lancaster and
James Reed of Lunenburg. The former led one hundred
men, the latter ninety, and both were probably attached to
the regiment of Colonel Timothy Ruggles, which included
two battalions. Captain Willard's Lancaster men were:

Lieut. Jacob Stiles,	Thomas Barney,	Jonathan Phillips,
Sergt. Jonathan Hutchins,	John McCarthy,	Joshua Proutee,
" Peter Willard,	Silvanus Johnson,	Moses Redman,
Benjamin Atherton,	Abner Osgood,	James Squirean,
John Bailey,	William Perham,	Joseph Turner,
	Robert Phelps.	

Of Bolton were:

Sergt. Josiah Moore,	Benjamin Marble,	Edward Roach,
Benoni Bigelow,	Jonas Pollard,	Aholiab Sawyer,
Jonathan Holman,	Joseph Pratt,	Ephraim Ward,
John Law,	Josiah Pratt,	John Wilder,
Dennis Locklyne,	Josiah Priest.	

Of Harvard were:

Sergt. John Burt,	Jacob Emerson,	Josiah Proctor,
Corpl. Samuel Corey,	Jacob Harris,	Ephraim Harris,
" John Daby,	Isaac Holden,	William Sanderson,
Nathaniel Bray,	John Houghton,	Micah Stone,
David Brown,	Asahel Nickerson,	Samuel Whipy,
John Cole,	Jonathan Pierce,	Jonathan White,
John Conn.		

Of Leominster: Richard Stewart.

[Massachusetts Archives, XCVII, 398.]

Captain James Reed's Lancaster men were:

Lieut. Til'ey Wilder,	Isaac Eveleth,	John McBride,
Sergt. Joseph Bailey,	Jonathan Goodenough,	Joshua Peirce,
Daniel Albert,	Samuel Goodenough,	Ebenezer Pike,
Frederick Albert,	John Headley,	James Pratt,
Phineas Bailey,	Levi Kendall,	Joseph Stewart,
Joseph Bixby,	Samuel Kendall,	Jonathan Townsend,
Micah Bryant,	Stephen Kendall [*died*],	Reuben Walker [*died*],
George Bush [*died*],	Peter Larkin,	Jotham Wilder,
Daniel Cook,	Mathias Larkin,	Phineas Wilder,
John Dunsmore,	William Lee,	Henry Wyman.

Of Leominster were:

Asa Buttrick,	Joseph Harper,	Benjamin Whitcomb.
Jonathan Grout,	Ebenezer Harris,	

[Massachusetts Archives, XCVII, 310.]

Samuel Kendall and John Headly presented petitions to the General Court for help, which are preserved in Massachusetts Archives, LXXIX, 147 and 322.

The regiment of Colonel Abijah Willard contained eighteen companies, coming from all parts of the commonwealth. The complement of each company was fifty, rank and file.

A Roll of the Field & Staff Officers in His Majestie's Service of a Regiment whereof Abijah Willard Esq. is Colonel. [April 17 to December 30, 1759.]

Abijah Willard, Esq., *Colonel*, Lancaster.
Stephen Miller, Esq., *Lieutenant-Colonel*, Milton.
Richard Godfrey, *Major*, Taunton.
Caleb Willard, *Major*, Lunenburg.
Cyrus Fairbanks, *Adjutant*, Lancaster.
Manassah Divol, *Quartermaster*, Lancaster.
William Crawford, *Chaplain*, Worcester.
John Taylor, *Chief Surgeon*, Harvard.
John Tappan, *Surgeon's Mate*, Newbury.
John Preston, *do.* Harvard.
Jonathan Bowman, *Commissary*, Dorchester.

[Massachusetts Archives, XCVII, 372.]

Captain Benjamin Hastings led a company in Willard's regiment. These men of Lancaster were in his command:

Lieut. Thomas Beaman,	Joshua Baily,	Jonathan Kendall,
2d Lieut. Manasseh Divoll,	Benjamin Chase,	Josiah Prentice,
Sergt. John Warner,	Nathan Eager,	Joseph Priest,
" Paul Richardson,	Ephraim Goss,	Nathan Pusha,
" Levi Woods,	Thomas Henderson,	Jeremiah Stewart,
Corpl. Ebenezer Knight,	Nahum Houghton,	Jonathan Wheelock,
Drummer Levi Divoll,	Joshua Johnson,	Jason Wyman.

These were of Bolton:

Capt. Benjamin Hastings,	Cyrus Houghton,	James Townsend,
Corpl. John Richardson,	Francis McFadden,	David Whitcomb,
Ephraim Butler,	Andrew McElwain,	Ezra Wilder.

These were of Harvard:

Jonathan Gates,	Ambrose Hale,	David Taylor.
Elias Haskell,	Gordon Hutchins,	

Of Leominster, was Ebenezer Rice.

[Massachusetts Archives, XCVII, 389.]

Thomas Beaman succeeded to the command of the company in September. John Warner was promoted to be ensign in the company of Captain Elijah Smith, and Peter Willard to be ensign in Captain William Bayley's company.

Under Captain Thomas Cobb of the same regiment were Joshua Mosman, Samuel Mosman and Asa Rugg of Lancaster. Samuel Woods, according to the Lancaster church records, was "Killed by ye Enemy" this year.

The orderly book of Colonel Willard unfortunately closes July 17, four days before the movement upon Ticonderoga began. His first regimental orders are dated June 26, at camp near Fort Edward:

It is my Order that the Commanding officer of Each Company See that their orderly Sergeants turn out their Companies to Prayers every morning by Six o Clock and by Seven in the Evening; and every Captain with his officers to lead their Companies on the Perade themselves and also to see that every man appears on the Perade for Guard that they are Clean and Soldierlike; and also that the officers appear in Camp like Gentlemen officers, for I observe that they are very Negligent in their Dress . . . . . . and that the officers of my Regiment Put off their Highland

Caps, for it is Disagreeable to the Commanding officer [*Montgomery, colonel of the Royal Highlanders*] now at Fort Edward.

Lemuel Wood of Boxford, who served in Captain Francis Peabody's company of Willard's regiment during the campaigns of 1759 and 1760, kept a diary which has been published in the Essex Institute Collections, xix. He records that "it Came out in orders . . . . . that no Officer in ye Regiment should wear a Scotch bonnet." Generally the officers only in provincial regiments were uniformed. They usually appeared in blue coats faced with red, but dress for the most part was left to individual taste and convenience. From orderly book and diary we learn that in camp at Lake George, throughout June and July, the troops were kept constantly drilling, and practice in firing was daily exacted. Frequent courts-martial were summoned and fearful sentences were imposed upon those found guilty of grave military crimes. "One thousand lashes with a cat of nine tails" was one punishment for desertion, although executions for this offence took place, the whole army being drawn up to witness the dismal ceremony. Wood relates that "two sargants . . . . for not going to hear Prayers . . . . were sentenced to yͤ ranks" by Colonel Willard; but were subsequently pardoned. Captain Benjamin Hastings of Bolton was during September "Dismessed ye Servis with Desgrace" for mutinous behavior. Abraham Austin, "Capt of the waggons," being convicted of stealing some tools, was condemned . . . .

to Receive thirty six lashes with a Cat of nine tails at the head of Each of the four Regular Battallions and the seven Provinciall Regimtˢ. in Camp, Beginning with Forb's and Ending with Scuyler's, and be then turned out of Camp and Deemed unworthy of ever Serving in the Army again.

Ten teamsters who connived at the same theft were ordered to be . . . .

marched Round the Camp, and see the Punishment above on Austin, and they all to be marched Back to Saratoga, from thence to Bring the tools that ware stolen Back together.

Colonel Willard, by the evidence of his regimental orders, appears an energetic, soldierly officer, exacting firmly every military duty, but diligently caring for the well-being of his men. He turned the captains out to drill their companies in platoon exercise at five o'clock in the morning, and had all the officers exercised in the same manner by the senior captains twice daily. He orders:

That every Tent shall have one side Turned up every Fair Day from Eight in the morning untill ten . . . . . it being much for the health of the men. Likewise that every sick man have his hands, feet and leggs washed in warm water, and carefully dryed every other Day.

Amherst's immobility already argued ill for any aid from his column to Wolfe. At the advance, finally begun July 21, Ticonderoga and Crown Point fell with only the pretence of contest, as they probably would have done had the movement been made a month earlier. Niagara had already been surrendered to Sir William Johnson. Instead of pushing northward on Lake Champlain at once, Amherst now set about rebuilding the captured forts, constructing roadways to them from various points, and planning a navy. Regardless of the positive orders of Pitt, while Wolfe was daring impossibilities, Amherst resolved to take no risks. The glory of Wolfe was the greater, and all New England, in the general thanksgiving for his victory at Quebec, mourned him as their benefactor. It was not until the middle of October that the newly built fleet cleared Lake Champlain of the French. Soon the wintry frosts had sealed the northern waters, and Colonel Willard, with his townsmen, were again by their own firesides, relating to interested listeners their varied experiences upon the frontier, and preparing for the final campaign of 1760.

The enlistments recorded for Lancaster in the spring months of the next year, as found in Massachusetts Archives, xcviii, are:

John Years,	aged 29 (a Frenchman).	Moses Redman, aged 37 (Irish).
Joseph Farrar,	" 17	John McCarty, " 29
Nathan Farrar,	" 18	James Squirean, " 22

Oliver Power, *aged* 18	Michael McLong, *aged* 24
John Prentice, " 19	Richard Wiles, " 49
Josiah Prentice, " 18	Benj. Houghton, " 20
Stephen Foster, " 30	Ephraim Goss, " 26
Nathan Turner, " 23	

These were, however, not a fifth part of the town's soldiers actually in service. Colonel Abijah Willard again led his regiment to the front, having the same staff, except that John Miller of Milton acted as chaplain, and Samuel Ward, of Worcester, later to become an honored citizen of Lancaster, served as adjutant. One company was chiefly of Lancaster and adjacent towns, and served from April to December. Levi Willard is recorded as "sutler" of the regiment. The Lancaster soldiers of Captain Beaman's company were:

Captain Thomas Beaman,	Daniel Cook,	John Richardson,
Lieut. Sherebiah Hunt,	James Crosfield,	Paul Richardson,
Sergt. Daniel Warner,	Isaac Eveleth,	Isaac Sollendine,
Corporal Nathan Gary,	Thomas Fairbanks,	Richard Stewart,
Drummer Ephraim Fairbanks,	Phineas Goodell,	David Wilder,
Benjamin Atherton,	Thomas Henderson,	Ezra Wilder,
Charles Beamis,	John Lock,	Nahum Wilder,
Joseph Bigsbey,	Joshua Peirce,	James Willard,
Jedediah Blaney,	Ethan Phillips,	Levi Woods,
William Brown,	Amos Powers,	Henry Wyman.
John Burroughs,	Benjamin Priest,	

Of Leominster were:

Sergt. Benjamin Whitcomb,	Asa Buttrick,	Jonathan Kendall,
Corporal John Beaman,	Francis Corey,	John White,
Simeon Butler,	Joseph Daby,	Josiah White.

Of Bolton were:

Sergt. Benoni Bigelow,	Andrew McElwain,	Ezekiel Snow,
Jonadab Moore,	Francis McFadden,	Benjamin Townsend.
	Richard Roberts,	

Of Harvard were:

| Sergt. Caleb Wright, | Solomon Haskell, | Benjamin Whittemore. |
| David Dickenson, | Peter Snow [*died*], | |

Rufus Putnam, who became a brigadier-general and the

chief engineer of the patriot army in the revolution, was ensign of Captain Beaman's company.

Daniel Stone of Lancaster served in the company of Captain Timothy Hamant, and in Captain Richard Sykes' company there were of Lancaster:

Lieut. Frederick Howe,	Nathaniel Gates,	Jacob Williams.
Abel Farnsworth,	Robert Spear,	

James Burt of Harvard and Henry Dunn of Bolton served under the same captain.

[Massachusetts Archives, XCVIII, 280; 312.]

Colonel Ruggles, as brigadier, commanded the five Massachusetts regiments. In his own regiment were two battalions, and in these probably served the following men; the company rolls give no clue to their regimental organization. Of Lancaster:

Captain Aaron Willard, Sergt. Josiah Prentice [*died*], Silvanus Johnson. Lieut. Jacob Stiles,

In Captain Willard's company there were from Harvard:

Timothy Bowers,	Stephen Gates,	Asahel Nickerson.
Silas Corey,	Maximilian Jewett,	

Of Leominster:

Edward Kendall,	Samuel Rogers,	Jeremiah Stearns.
David Robbins.		

[Massachusetts Archives, XCVIII, 223, 389.]

Under Captain James Reid of Lunenburg were of Lancaster:

Ephraim Carter, Jr.,	Jedediah Cooper,	Daniel Johnson,
Jonas Carter,	David Dufore,	Henry Wyman.
	Thomas Henderson,	

Of Leominster:

Joseph Harper,	Edward Joyner.	Richard Stewart.

[Massachusetts Archives, XCVIII, 339.]

With Captain Jonathan Butterfield were of Lancaster:

Benjamin Houghton,	Edward Robbins,	Joseph Robbins.

Of Bolton: Ephraim Goss.

Of Harvard :

Silas Farnsworth,	Jabez Keep,	Coleman Sanderson,
Uriah Holt,	Jonathan Reed,	John Sanderson.

Of Leominster were :

Barzillai Moore, Abijah Sawyer.

[Massachusetts Archives, XCVIII, 307–9.]

With Captain William Barron of Concord were eight Lancaster men :

Stephen Foster,	Moses Redman,	Jos. Turner,
John McCarthy,	James Squirean,	John Years.
John Prentice,	Nat. Turner,	

[Massachusetts Archives, XCVIII, 254–5.]

Colonel John Whitcomb's regiment, of eighteen companies, served in the campaign of 1760, and in it were a few men of Lancaster. In the Southboro' company of Captain Nathaniel Brigham were :

Lieut. Ephraim Sawyer,	Obediah Gross,
Levi Divol,	Joseph Stewart [*drowned Aug.* 14].

[Massachusetts Archives, XCVIII, 287.]

With Captain William Williams of Marlborough were :

Lieut. Henry Haskell,	Amos Atherton,	Joseph Woods,
Corporal Joshua Johnson,	Daniel Johnson,	Jasher Wyman.

[Massachusetts Archives, XCVIII, 291.]

With Captain Jonathan Rolfe were of Bolton :

Ensign Joseph Hendrick,	Robert Holdea,	Thomas Mears,
Sergt. John Barnard,	Matthias Larkin,	James Townsend.
Obediah Gill,	Robert Longley,	

[Massachusetts Archives, XCVIII, 247–8.]

In other companies were of Lancaster :

Ensign Josiah Locke,	John Hinds,	Robert Phelps,
John Bailey,	Nathaniel Jones,	Caleb Sawyer,
Gershom Flagg,	Levi Kendall,	Josiah White.
Josiah Flagg,		

[Colonel Whitcomb's Orderly Book, and Massachusetts Archives, XCVIII, 231, 248, 287, 291, 323.]

During winter and spring and summer General Amherst studied over and elaborated the plan of a combined movement by all his forces upon Montreal ; the very method by

which an able general would have swept the French power
from Canada the preceding autumn. It was the tenth of
August before the main army at Oswego, and Colonel
William Haviland's force at Crown Point, began the advance. From Colonel Whitcomb's orderly book we learn
that his own and the regiments of Colonels Willard and
Ruggles, under Haviland, proceeded leisurely down Lake
Champlain in batteaux. On the sixteenth the expedition
landed on the east side of the River St. Johns, near the
Isle aux Noix, and Colonel Whitcomb was ordered to
throw up works under the direction of the engineers for the
protection of the fleet of batteaux, while the rest of the
army moved to the siege of the island which had long been
fortified. On the morning of the twenty-eighth it was discovered that the enemy had evacuated their works and fled
in the night through the swamps. Quickly pursuing, Colonel Haviland issued the following order on arrival at
Therese :

As the army is now going into the inhabitable part of the Country,
therefore it is ordered that none of the inhabitants are plundered or ill used
on any pretence. Whosoever is detected disobeying these orders will be
hanged. Milk, Butter or Provisions, or anything else must be regularly
paid for; this to induce the inhabitants to stay in their villages, as good
usage will prevent their men from joining the French army.

It was much to expect of the men of New Hampshire
and Massachusetts, almost every one of whom had rankling recollections of loss by some bloody raid of demons
who spared neither age nor sex, that they should enter as
conquerors the territory of those who had for years insti-
gated their merciless spoilers, without exhibiting great ex-
ultation, and at least an inclination towards retaliation. It
speaks well for these Protestant soldiers quartered in the
hamlets of their priest-ridden and treacherous enemies,
that on September 7th they should hear read upon parade
these words :

It gives Coll. Haviland pleasure to find the troops under his command
have so strictly complied with his orders of the 31 of August, with respect

of not plundering the inhabitants and paying for such things as they get from them. It is obvious to every one the good effects it has had on many. Hundreds have delivered themselves up here and at Chambly. . . . . .

On the eighth General Amherst announced in general orders :

. . . . The Marquis Vaudreuil has capitulated. The troops of France in Canada have laid down their arms and are not to serve during the war. The whole country submits to the Dominion of Great Britain.

On the tenth, the Massachusetts men were marching back to Crown Point, and there for the next two months they were busily employed in extending and completing fortifications and barracks. The orders recorded relate chiefly to guard, fatigue duty, sick call, and rations—the humdrum routine of ordinary camp life. There was, however, one variation which to the soldier of today would be a novelty, thus set forth in special orders :

Spruce Beer will be served out from Brewing, from 6 to 8 O clock Daily which is to be paid for as usual.

The price of this aromatic but not too exhilarating beverage was one half-penny per quart, and its use throughout the army was greatly favored for its supposed tonic value. It could not alleviate homesickness, however, and the patriotic yeomanry, now that the purpose of their enlistment was accomplished, could see no need for their further detention in the western wilderness. A grumbling discontent became epidemic, and a few left for home without leave. In November the veteran Colonels Willard and Whitcomb marched their regiments through the woods across Vermont to Charlestown Number Four, and thence to Lancaster, where they arrived about December 1. The jubilation at their return we must imagine, for no gossip of the period has preserved any notes of the joyous event for us. More than a month before, however, the ministers from their pulpits had voiced the universal joy of victory, and these are some of the utterances heard in Lancaster :

Could we have thought, some years since, that we should at this Time, have celebrated a Thanksgiving for the entire Reduction of *Canada*, the compleat Conquest of the Country of our ancient, inveterate and restless enemies? the Source of most of our Wars and Troubles with the Natives, and the perpetual Impediment to our Settlements and the Inlargement of our Territories? the Occasion of so much Bloodshed, Murder, Massacre, Grief for butchered captivated Relatives, Impoverishment of Families, Desolation of Towns, Fears, Alarms, and endless Expence and Damage? . . . . The war with us has lasted six years; Three of them Years of Prosperity and Plenty; and three of them Years of Rebuke, Misfortune and Drought. . . . . . Our late decisive Victories and valuable Acquisitions have not been purchased with a Song, though they occasion Joy and Singing. They have been obtained at the Expence of much Blood and Treasure. Many a precious Life has been sacrificed to these glorious Atchievements. Brave Generals and noble Lords, accomplished Officers, and great numbers of fine soldiers, have laid down their Lives. Many of the British Troops and Provincial Volunteers have fallen in Battle, and died in the Bed of Honour. Many who could not be otherwise conquered have been overcome by Disease and expired in fatal Hospitals. What year can be mentioned that has not sifted out some of the Flower of our Towns, and thinned our religious Assemblies? *Here* a father has Sacrificed a son; *there* another his First-born: one mourns the Loss of a Father, another a Brother, and the veiled *Widows* cloathed in Sackcloth, have come forth in a yearly succession.

[Rev^d. John Mellen's Sermon, October 9, 1760.]

In the appendix to his sermon, Mr. Mellen records the names of nineteen men belonging to his parish who lost their lives during the war. These will be found scattered through previous pages in their proper commands, but the list, which it would seem was intended to be arranged in the order of the soldiers' deaths, will be given with the addition of dates:

Samuel Fairbanks, killed Sept. 8, 1755.			William Brabrook, missing	1758.	
William Fairbanks,	"	"	Ebenezer Bigelow, died	"	
Isaac Kendall,	"	"	Sergt. Jacob Smith, "	"	
Ithamar Bennett,	"	"	Jonathan Geary, died Sept.	"	
Lt. Hezekiah Whitcomb, died,		1755	Philip Geno, died	"	
John Whitcomb,	"	"	Reuben Walker, "	1760	
Jacob Glazier,	"	"	Stephen Kendall, "	"	
Simon Kendall,	"	1758.	George Bush, Jr., "	"	
John Farrar,	"	1756.	Joseph Steward,		
Jeremiah Dickenson,	"	"	drowned Aug. 14, "		

Unfortunately, no similar contemporary statement of the loss in the First parish exists. The following list, doubt-

less a very imperfect one, contains all deaths found anywhere recorded :

Oliver Osgood,	killed September 8, 1755.
John Rugg,	" "
Joseph Robbins, Jr., "	"
Josiah Pratt, Jr., "	"
Phineas Randall, "	"
Peter Kendall, "	"
David Atherton, died May 2,	"
Col. Samuel Willard, died October,	"
Sergt. James Houghton, died Oct. 21,	"
William Hudson, killed in Acadia,	"
Andrew Goodfry, died 1756.	
John Larkin, " 1758.	
Samuel Woods, killed 1759.	
Sergt. Josiah Prentice, died 1760.	

The two years that followed before the treaty of Paris
confirmed to England the fruits of the conquest of Canada,
were years of peace to the colonies, but the forts at Halifax
and Crown Point were garrisoned by New England men.
Those of Lancaster serving on the western frontier in 1761
and 1762, under Colonel Richard Salstonstall, were :

Joseph Bixby,
Josiah Brown,
Nathaniel Gates, *drummer*,
Stephen Gates,
George Hadley,
John Hadley,
John Hadley, Jr.,
Jeremiah Haskell,

Abner Hibera,
Dole Johnson,
Joshua Johnson,
Simeon Johnson,
Aaron Kilburn,
Isaac Kilburn,
Matthias Larkin,
Jonathan Lawrence,

Timothy Powers,
Benjamin Priest,
Richard Prouty, Jr.,
Benjamin Spaulding,
David Stimpson,
John Sulandine,
Oliver Wilder, Jr.,
Jacob Winn,
Henry Wyman.

Of Bolton were :

Thomas Barney,
Ephraim Butler,

Joseph Pratt,
Ezekiel Snow,

Josiah Wood.

Of Harvard were :

James Burt,
Silas Corey,
Thomas Daby,
Abel Farnsworth,

Samuel Fellows,
Jacob Harris,
Uriah Holt,
James Reed,

Ephraim Stone,
Paul Willard,
Abijah Worster,
Samuel Worster,
Thomas Wright.

Of Leominster :

Jedediah Cooper,	Edward Joyner,	Abijah Smith,
Joshua Johnson,	John Rowe,	Asa Smith,
		Elijah Wheelock.

At Halifax, with Captains James Reed and Edmund Lawrence, were of Lancaster :

Josiah Brown,	Thomas Henderson,	Jonas Pollard,
Jonas Carter,	Joseph Jewett,	William Swan,
David Dufore,	Daniel Johnson,	Elijah Woods,
Levi Divoll,	Ephraim Moore,	Abijah Wyman,
Isaac Eveleth,	Abner Osgood,	Jasher Wyman.

Of Harvard were :

Abijah Cole,	Stephen Gates, Jr.,	Paul Willard.
Stephen Gates,	John Harper,	

[Massachusetts Archives, XCIX.]

The second regiment of militia in Worcester county, known as the Lancaster Regiment, at this period was organized as follows :

Joseph Wilder, Esq., Col⁰. and Capt. of the first company in the Town of Lancaster.
Peter Atherton, Esq., Lt. Col⁰ and Capt. of the first company in the Town of Harvard.
John Carter, Major & Capt. of second company in the Town of Lancaster.

Lancaster 1st. Co.
James Wilder, *capt.-lieut.*
John White, *2d lieut.*
Joseph White, *ensign.*

Lancaster 2d. Co.
Elisha Sawyer, *1st lieut.*
Elijah Houghton, *2d lieut.*
Tilley Moore, *ensign.*

Lancaster 3d. Co.
Caleb Wilder, *capt.*
Nathll Sawyer, *lieut.*
Josiah Ballard, *ensign.*

Lancaster Troop.
Hezekiah Gates, *capt.*
Nathl. Willson, *lieut.*
Jona. Wilder, *cornet.*
James Carter, *quartermaster.*

Lunenburg 1st Co.
Benjamin Goodridge, *capt.*
George Kemball, *1st lieut.*
David Goodridge, *2d lieut.*
Joseph Hartwell, *ensign.*

Lunenburg 2d. Co.
Jonathan Wood, *capt.*
Josiah Bailey, *lieut.*
John Buss, *ensign.*

Harvard 1st. *Co.*	*Harvard* 2d. *Co.*
Joseph Fairbank, Jr., *capt. lieut.*	Phineas Fairbank. *capt.*
Benjamin Stow, *lieut.*	Jerem. Laughton, *lieut.*
Peter Atherton, Jr., *ensign.*	Jason Russell, *ensign.*

Bolton Co.	*Leominster Co.*
Samuel Baker, *capt.*	Benjamin Whitcomb, *capt.*
Oliver Barrett, *lieut.*	Jonan. Carter, *lieut.*
William Wilder. *ensign.*	Oliver Hale, *ensign.*

Westminster Co.	
Nicholas Dike, *capt.*	Moses Wilder,
Benja. Butterfield, *lieut.*	*Adjutant,*
John Woodward, *ensign.*	

[Massachusetts Archives, XCVIII.]

In 1766, John Carter had become colonel of the regiment; Caleb Wilder was lieutenant-colonel, and James Wilder and Levi Willard, majors. A Fitchburg company had been added. and in 1767, a second Bolton, a second Leominster and a fourth Lancaster company appear. In 1771, Caleb Wilder was colonel; Levi Willard, lieutenant-colonel; James Richardson and Gardner Wilder, majors. The regiment at that time consisted of sixteen infantry companies and two troops, as follow: Lancaster, four companies; Lunenburg. two; Harvard, two; Bolton, two: Leominster, two: Westminster, two; Fitchburg, one; Ashburnham, one. The first troop was from Lancaster, Harvard and Bolton; the second from Lunenburg, Leominster and Fitchburg.

The Lancaster companies were officered thus in 1771:

1st. *Company.*	3d. *Company.*
Nathaniel White, *capt.*	Samuel Ward, *capt.*
William Phelps, *lieut.*	Ephraim Carter, *lieut.*
Hooker Osgood, *ensign.*	Moses Smith, 2d. lieut.
	Phineas Houghton. *ensign.*
2d. *Company.*	
Ephraim Wilder, *capt.*	4th. *Company.*
Samuel Prentice, 1st. *lieut.*	Daniel Robbins, *capt.*
Thomas Gary, Jr., 2d *lieut.*	Enoch Gerrish, *lieut.*
Jona. Osgood, *ensign.*	Asa Wilder, *ensign.*

Troop.

James Carter, *capt.*
Jeremiah Burpee, *lieut.*
Elijah Sawyer, 2^d. *lieut.*
Thomas Gates, *cornet.*
Elijah Houghton, *quartermaster.*

Three years later, obedient to the demands of the county convention, these officers all resigned their commissions, and, in the new elections, men perhaps younger or more in accord with the fevered political sentiment of the day took their places. It is certain not one of the above entered the continental service, and but three of them appear in the rolls of the Lexington Alarm.

7

IV.

THE WAR FOR INDEPENDENCE.

I. FROM TOWN-MEETING TO CONTINENTAL CONGRESS.

"The voice of Otis and of Adams in Faneuil Hall, found its full and true echo in the little councils of the interior towns: and, if within the Continental Congress patriotism shone more conspicuously, it did not there exist more truly, nor burn more fervently; it did not render the day more anxious, nor the night more sleepless; it sent up no more ardent prayer to God for succor; and it put forth in no greater degree the fulness of its effort, and the energy of its whole soul and spirit, in the common cause, than it did in the small assemblies of the towns."

[Daniel Webster, in the Massachusetts Convention of 1820.]

The pastor of the second parish in Lancaster, John Mellen, printed a sermon, "preached . . . . October 9, 1760, on the General Thanksgiving for the Reduction of Montreal and Total Conquest of Canada," in which he rapturously predicts the glorious future awaiting the English colonies forever relieved from the machinations of papists and the terrors of French invasion. He estimates the population of these colonies at that time to be one million, and foresees that, by the ordinary rate of increase, "one century and a half will people the British Empire in America with upwards of Sixty Million Souls." This vision of one wiser than most of his generation is now more than realized. But even his clear prophetic sight probably caught no glimpse of the great political changes that hinged upon the expulsion of the Bourbons from Canada; nor could he have dreamed that the long struggle then just closed was but the first act of a revolution which was to bind thirteen weak and jealous colonies, widely separated

not more by distance than by historic and religious sympathies, into a stable, independent republic, soon to become
the mightiest in the history of governments.

New England, in lavishly expending blood and treasure,
ostensibly for the aggrandizement of George II, was edu-
cating herself in warlike arts and self reliance to throw off,
when the times grew ripe, all allegiance to kings; and the
more southern provinces, especially Virginia, were fitting
themselves to follow.   Massachusetts had always led in the
contest.   One man out of her every four able for service
was kept in the ranks of the provincial regiments, equipped,
fed and paid from the colonial treasury.   When in 1760
the Crown re-imbursed the colonies in the sum of two hundred thousand pounds, allotting each a share proportionate
to its contributions for the common cause, three-tenths fell
to Massachusetts.   Lancaster had not been behind her sister towns in sacrifice.

The distracted country was stained along its inland borders, from the river Ohio to Nova Scotia, with the blood of
helpless women and children, as well as brave men, sav-
agely slain.   Peace had come at last; plenteous harvests
had been gathered from the rich soil, and safely housed.
With reason the hearts of all throughout the land went up
in thanksgiving.   But below the surface of joyous calm
slept the elements of a greater explosion of popular will
than any yet seen upon this continent, waiting only the excuse of some petty tax, some nagging encroachments upon
chartered privilege, to begin a new chapter in the history
of mankind.   Until the occasion should arrive, the inspired
leader was waiting ready.   He had passed through the
stern preparatory lessons for his heaven-appointed task in
the wilds of Pennsylvania and Virginia.   In every town
were men clad in homespun and busy in shop, at trade, or
on the farm, who had led regiments or commanded companies under Winslow, Loudoun, Abercrombie, and Amherst.   Few of these but had rankling memories of super-

cilious insolence received from the gorgeously accoutred officers of the royal troops,—whose contemptuous assumption of superiority was rarely based upon campaign experience or personal worth, but begot of insular pride, fostered by martinet discipline, and supported by parliamentary regulations which ranked the king's above the provincial commission, regardless of precedence in date.

Among other causes of disaffection in Massachusetts was the hereditary rage of Puritanism against prelacy, which, though soon hidden from sight in the smoke of actual conflict, was none the less pervasive and powerful. But in this the yeomanry had become more radical than the clergy. A schism in the little Bolton church grew, during 1774, into a controversy so bitter that it seriously shook the pulpits in all the neighboring parishes. This, widely known as the Goss and Walley war, finally turned upon the question of the churches' independence of clerical councils. The ministers were united under the leadership of Reverend Zabdiel Adams, who won the sobriquet, "Bishop of Lunenburg;" while it is noteworthy that the most prominent among their opponents were the men soon to become the military and legislative leaders of the community in political rebellion—the Whitcombs, Fairbank and Dr. Dunsmoor.

Little more than four months had passed since the thanksgiving day, on which, from hundreds of pulpits, there had issued a flood of loyal declamation adulatory of "his gracious majesty King George II," when James Otis, advocating the peoples' privilege, inveighed with fiery eloquence in open court against the arbitrary and restrictive commercial policy adopted by the ministry of George III. And speedily, like an echo of the bold utterances of Otis, there came from aristocratic Virginia the voice of the plebeian lawyer, Patrick Henry, proclaiming that even the divine right of an anointed king is naught if not used solely for the good and by the consent of the governed.

The Stamp Act struck like a stunning blow, and loyalty seemed to many no longer compatible with patriotism. Hastened by the heat of just wrath, remonstrance scorned was fast ripening into revolt. Yet revolt against so powerful an oppressor, however well justified, seemed to the sober-minded hopeless; and hopeless it was without unanimity, long and secret preparation, and external aid. The repeal of the stamp act availed to quiet the other colonies, but not Massachusetts. Here the public heart was fired with patriotic frenzy, and would not be restrained. Any suggestion of a temporizing policy met with contempt. Liberty poles were raised in every village. At every new attempt to enforce royal prerogative the spirit of resistance became more outspoken and determined, and the materials of revolution, everywhere abundant, began to flame. Puritanism personified in Samuel Adams, recognized the exigency and shrewdly organized rebellion by inspiring the Committees of Correspondence with courage and enthusiasm. The newspaper suddenly rose to great political power in the land. The Massachusetts town-meeting became at length the arena where were rehearsed the dramatic scenes soon to be enacted by the various provincial congresses. In the town-meeting, the village orator found and improved his opportunity; the local demagogue and radical stirred the passions of the people; but the old men, the captains and colonels scarred in conquest of Canada, delayed rash action by their conservative counsel, weighty with the teachings of experience. Among the most honorable pages in the records of Lancaster, is that upon which are engrossed the liberty-breathing resolutions passed in town-meeting the first month of 1773; resolutions boldly protesting against the attempted encroachments of the Crown upon the constitutional freedom of the Province, and demanding "radical redress of grievances;" resolutions anticipating in nobly simple phrase, by three and one-half years, the grandest sentiments of the Declaration of Independence.

A warrant for a Town meeting ye first wednesday of Jan. 1773.

WORCESTER, ss. To the freeholders and other Inhabitants of the town of Lancaster legally qualified to vote in town affaiers, Greeting:

In his majestie's name you are hereby requierd to meet at the meeting-house in the second precinct in Lancaster on the first wednesday in January Next at Ten of the Clock in the forenoon then and there to act on the Following articles viz:

1ly. To chuse a moderator for the goverment of sd. meeting.

2lly. To take into consideration the Dangerous condition of our Publick affaiers in Perticular the Independancy of our Superiour Judges and take such measures as shall then be thought proper.

3dly. To chuse a Committee to Draw up our greveances and Infringements upon our Liberties and to Lay them before the Town when the Town shall so order.

4ly. To consider and act upon the Request from Boston Committee.

5ly. To give to our Representative such Instructions as the Town shall think proper Relative to our Priveledges.

6ly. To Chuse a Committee to return an answer to Boston Committee and to correspond with aney other Committee Relateing to our priveledge and to Inform the Town of their Transactions from time to time.

7ly. To act and do any thing that the Town shall see proper to withstand the Preasent Progress of our Enemies in Indevering to take away our Priveledges.

Dated at Lancaster Decembr 22d 1772, and in the Thirteenth Year of his majestie's Reign.

By order of the selectmen.

Entred by DANIEL ROBBINS, *Town Clerk.*

At the meeting thus summoned, Deacon Oliver Moore was chosen moderator, and a committee of seven, elected under article third, consisting of Doctor William Dunsmoor, John Prescott, Aaron Sawyer, Josiah Kendall, Joseph White, Nathaniel Wyman and Ebenezer Allen, were instructed to report on Tuesday, the nineteenth of January, to which date the meeting was adjourned. It is worthy of note that the first three named upon this committee could claim inheritance of the blood of John Prescott, the founder of Lancaster, and they proved themselves inheritors of his brave, independent spirit. On the appointed day, the town, at the meeting-house in the first precinct, voted to hear the report of the committee, to report the town's doings to the Boston committee, and to instruct their representative at General Court. Both resolves and instructions were published in the Boston Gazette for May 17, 1773:

At a legal Meeting of the Freeholders and other Inhabitants of the Town of Lancaster, by Adjournment.

The Committee appointed by the Town to take into Consideration the State of publick Affairs beg leave to report the following Resolves and Instructions:

1. *Resolved,* That this and every other Town in this Province have an undoubted Right to meet together and consult upon all Matters interesting to them when and so often as they shall judge fit; and it is more especially their Duty so to do when any Infringment is made upon their Civil or Religious Liberties.

2. *Resolved,* That the raising a Revenue in the Colonies without their Consent, either by themselves or their Representatives, is an Infringment of that Right which every Freeman has to dispose of his own Property.

3. *Resolved,* That the granting a Salary to his Excellency the Governor of this Province out of the Revenue unconstitutionally raised from us is an Innovation of a very alarming Tendancy.

4. *Resolved,* That it is of the highest Importance to the security of Liberty, Life and Property that the publick Administration of Justice should be pure and impartial, and that the Judge should be free from every Bias, either in Favour of the Crown or the Subject.

5. *Resolved,* That the absolute Dependancy of the Judges of the Superior Court of this Province upon the Crown for their support, would if it should ever take Place have the strongest Tendancy to bias the Minds of the Judges, and would weaken our Confidence in them.

6. *Resolved,* That the Extension of the Power of the Court of Vice-Admiralty to its present enormous Degree is a great Grievance and deprives the Subject in many Instances of that noble Privelege of Englishmen, Trials by Juries.

7. *Resolved,* That the Proceedings of this Town be transmitted to the Town of Boston.

DR. WILLIAM DUNSMOOR,
JOHN PRESCOTT,
JOSIAH KENDALL,
EBENEZER ALLEN, } *Committee for Grievances.*
NATHANIEL WYMAN,
JOSEPH WHITE,
AARON SAWYER,

Attest: DANIEL ROBBINS, *Town Clerk.*

To Captain Asa Whitcomb.

SIR: As you are chosen to represent this Town in the General Assembly of this Province, we take this Opportunity of informing you of our Sentiments relative to the unhappy State of our publick Affairs: You will perceive by the Resolves which are herewith sent to you, the Light in which we view the encroachments made upon our Constitutional Freedom; particularly you will observe our serious Opinion of a Dependancy of the Judges of the Superior Court on the Crown for their Support. That they are already so dependant, or that it is in Contemplation to render them so, we have great Reason to fear. Also an Act passed in the late Session of the British Parliament entitled An Act for the better preserving his Majesty's Dock-Yards &c., does in a most essential Manner infringe the Rights and Liberties of the Colonies, as it puts it in the Power of any wicked Tool of Administration, either from Malice or Policy, to take any Inhabitant from the Colonies and carry him to Great Britain, there to be tried; which, by the Expence and long Detention from his Occupation, would be the Destruction of almost any Man among us, altho' his Innocence might finally appear in the Clearest Manner; and further the late Commissions for taking Persons in our Sister Colony, Rhode-Island, and sending them to Great Britain, there to be tried upon Suspicion of being concerned in burning his Majesty's Schooner Gaspee, is an Invasion of the Rights of the Colonies, and ought to excite the Attention of the whole Continent. We expect that you will use your utmost Efforts this Session of our General Assembly to obtain a Radical Redress of our Grievances, and we wish you Success in your Endeavours, and which we cannot but flatter ourselves from the late happy Change in the American Departments, you will meet with. We confide in your Ability and Firmness in all Matters which may come before the General Court, assuring you of the Support of this Town in all your legal Proceedings, and earnestly praying that the great Governor of the World may direct and bless you in all your Ways.

Attest: DANIEL ROBBINS, *Town Clerk.*

Other town-meetings, following in quick succession, were called alternately at the meeting-houses of the two parishes, which were over five miles apart. Captain Hezekiah Gates generally acted as moderator. The warrant for a town-meeting on Monday, September 5th, 1774, contained these articles:

. . . . 2dly. To see if the Town will do any thing towards the Relief of the suffering Poor of the Town of Boston occationed by a Late Act of Parliment for Blockeing up the Port of said Town or to Act or Transact any thing Relateing thereto.

3dly. To see if the town will come into any agreement for non-Importation & non-Exportation of Goods to or from Great Britain or to act or Transact any thing Relateing thereto.

4th. To chuse a Committee or Committees to act or do any thing or things that the Town shall think Propper to be done or acted by any agreement with any other Town or Towns in order to get Releaf in the best and most easy way from our Present Difficultys Inflicted on us by the Late Acts of Parliment and to act and do any matter or thing that the Town shall see needfull to be done & Report to the Town from time to time what they have done & to Receive the Town's orders to act & do what the Town shall think Propper to be done & acted. . . . . .

7th. To see what way the Town will come into to pay their Part of the Present charges of ye Proposed Congress.

8th. To Grant money to Purchase a Town stock of Ammunition and to order how much shall be Purchased & where it shall be kept & under whose care & direction it shall be.

9th. To Pass such votes as the Town shall think Propper to be done to get Releaf from these Oppressive Acts of Parliment which hath been Inflicted on us Lately and to act any thing that said Town shall think needfull Relateing to the Congress and to accept and Rattify what they shall do if the town thinks fit.

10th. To Pass any Votes that may be thought needful in order to get Releaf in our Present Distressed Circumstances by our just Rights and Previledges as we think being taken from us.

11th. To see if the Town will vote to abide by our charter Rights & Previledges.

By order of the selectmen of Lancaster.

JOSEPH MOOR, *Constable.*

LANCASTER, July 30th, A. D. 1774.

At the meeting so warned :

. . . . 2dly. Voted to Choose a Committee to Consist of seven Persons to be a Committee of Correspondence for ye County. Chose Doctr. William Dunsmoor, Deacon David Wilder, Aaron Sawyer, Capt. Asa Whitcomb, Capt. Hezekh. Gates, John Prescott, Ephraim Sawyer, as a Committee of Correspondence.

Voted, that the above Committee make Report to the Town of their doeings from time to time as expressed in the warrant.

Voted, that any number even less than a majority of the above Committee shall be sufficient to Represent the Town as a Committee of Correspondence.

Voted, that the Town will Indemnify the Constable for not returning a List of the Freeholders for Jurors under the Late Act of Parliment.

Voted to Raise Fifty pounds for to buy Ammunition with to be a Town Stock. . .

Attest : SAM. WARD, *Town Clerk.*

The meeting adjourned to the second precinct, on Monday the nineteenth of September, and at this adjourned meeting :

. . . . 2ᵈ. Voted, That there be One Hundred men Raised as Volunteers to be Ready at a minutes Warning to Turn out upon any Emergency, and that they be Formed into Two Companys & Choose their own officers.

3ᵈ. Voted, that the said volunteers shall be Reasonably paid by the Town for any services they may do us in defending our Libertys & Previledges.

4ᵗʰ. Voted, that Doctʳ. Wᵐ. Dunsmoor be Impowerᵈ. to Enlist 50 men in the old Parish to serve as Volunteers.

5ᵗʰ. Voted that Capt. Asa Whitcomb be Impowerᵈ. to Enlist 50 men in the Second Parish to serve as Volunteers.

6ᵗʰ. Voted to Buy one field peice for the use of the Town.

7ᵗʰ. Voted that the Gentlemen Committee of Correspondence for this Town be a Committee to Purchase the said Field Gun. . . . .

At a meeting held by adjournment, Wednesday, September 28 :

. . . . 2ᵈ. Voted to choose one man for the Proposed Provencial Convention to be held at Concord on the second Tuesday of October next.

3ᵈ. Voted, & chose Doctʳ Wᵐ Dunsmore for the Proposed Provencial Convention to be held at Concord on yᵉ 2ᵈ Tuesday of October next.

4ᵗʰ. Voted, that notwithstanding the Town Passed a vote at their Last meeting to buy one field piece, yet if the committee appointed for that Purpose thinks fit they may buy Two 2 Pounders in place thereof. . . .

Lancaster was represented in this first Provincial Convention by Captain Asa Whitcomb and Doctor William Dunsmoor; Leominster, by Thomas Legate, Esq., and Israel Nichols; Bolton, by Captain Samuel Baker and Ephraim Fairbanks; Harvard, by Reverend Joseph Wheeler. It was the last named who, October 25, presented in the convention a letter suggesting that while they were attempting to save themselves from slavery, they should "also take into consideration the state and circumstances of the Negro Slaves in this Province."

LANCASTER, December 12, 1774. At a meeting of the Freeholders & other Inhabitants of the town of Lancaster by adjournment, the Meeting being Opened, Passed the Following Votes, viz:

Voted, to choose a Committee of 3 Persons to Draw up an Association League & Covenant for Nonconsumption of Goods, &c., for the Inhabitants to sign.

Voted, & Chose Doc^r. W^n. Dunsmoor, Capt. Hez^h Gates & Capt. Asa Whitcomb a Committee for the above purpose. . . . . .

LANCASTER, October 18th, 1774. *At a meeting of the Freeholders* . . . *by adjournment.* . . . . .

Voted, to chuse a Committee to Reckon with the Constables and Collectors of Taxes and see what moneys they have in their hands and to Direct them not to pay out any Public moneys out of their hands without the Town's order, and make Report to the Town of their Proceedings as soon as may be, and that Messr^s. Doct^r. Josiah Wilder, Aaron Sawyer & Ephraim Sawyer be a Committee for the above Purpose.

The Committee appointed to Purchase Field Peices, Reported to the Town that they had Purchased Two 4 Pounders for Eight pounds, therefore voted to accept of what they had done in that Respect.

Voted, to buy 5 hundred w^t. of Ball suitable for ye Field Peices.

Voted, to buy 3 hundred w^t. of Grape Shott.

Voted, that Messr^s. Aaron Sawyer & Ephraim Sawyer be empower^d to Receive the money due from the Town of Brookline to Pay for the field Peices, Ball & Grape Shott.

Voted, that one Field Peice shall be Kept in the old Parish & the other in the new Parish, and the Grape Shott & Ball to be kept in the same manner.

LANCASTER, October 31, 1774. . . . .

Voted to choose a Committee to Receve the Province & County moneys from the several constables and to give the said constables Propper discharges for the same so that they may be Indemnified from any demands that may be made on them hereafter by the Province Treasurer or County Treasurer.

Voted and chose Messrs. Aaron Sawyer, Ephraim Sawyer & Doct^r. Josiah Wilder a committee for the above purpose, and they are hereby directed to Pay the said moneys as fast as they may Receve them to Henry Gardner Esqr. of Stow, Receiver General.

Voted that the above Committee be Empower'd also to Receve the moneys Likewise of the several Constables which is Granted by the General Court & now to be assessed, & Pay the same to Henry Gardner Esqr.

Voted to choose a Committee to Post up all such Persons as continue to buy sell or consume any East India Teas, in some Public Place in Town, and that Doct^r. Josiah Wilder, Ephraim Sawyer & Aaron Sawyer be a Committee for the above Purpose.

Voted to build Two Carriages suitable for the Field Peices, & that Deacon Oliver Moor & Aaron Sawyer build one Carriage, and that Elisha White & Joel Phelps build the other Carriage. . . . . .

LANCASTER, January 2^d. 1775. . . . . . .

Voted to Choose a Committee to receive Subscriptions & Donations for the Suffering Poor of the Town of Boston occationed by the Late Boston Port Bill.

Voted & Chose Doc^r. Dunsmore, Deacon David Wilder, Ephraim Carter, Deacon Asa Whitcomb, Capt. Daniel Robbins & Ephraim Sawyer as a Committee for the above Purpose.

Voted to Carry in the Donations to some one of the Committee in a Fortnight from this day.

Voted to adopt & abide by the spirit and sence of the Association of the Late Continental Congress held at Philadelphia.

Voted to Chose a Committee to see that the said Association be kept & observed by the Inhabitants of said Town.

Voted, That the above Committee have no pay but do the Business *gratis*.

Voted & Chose John Prescott, Capt. Gates, Deacon David Wilder, Ephraim Carter, Doc^r. Wilder, Doct^r. Dunsmore, Samuel Thurston, Ebenez^r. Allen, Ephraim Sawyer, Capt. Asa Whitcomb, Capt. Robbins, Josiah Kendall Jr., Jon^a. Fairbanks, David Osgood and Jonathan Wilder as a Committee for the above Purpose.

Voted & Chose David Osgood as a Committee man to Reckon with the Constables & Receive the moneys in the stead of Aaron Sawyer deceas^d.

Voted and Chose Levi Moor & Israel Moor as a Committee to Compleat the Carriage for the Field Peice.

Voted & Chose Capt. Asa Whitcomb & Doc^r. W^m. Dunsmore to Represent the Town of Lancaster in the said Provincial Congress to be held at Cambridge on the 1st day of Feb^{r}y. next. . . . . .

SAM. WARD, *Town Clerk*.

Monday, March sixth, 1775.

Voted that the selectmen be a Committee to Receve the Donations of the several gent'men of the Town to furnish the Poor of sd. town with good arms for the use of said Town.

Voted the selectmen are Impowered to provide suitable Persons to use the grate goons. . . . . .

DANIEL ROBBINS, *Town Clerk*.

. . . Third Monday of May, 1775. . . . .

Voted to Choose two men for the Provential Congress.

Voted and Chose Dea. David Wilder & Doc^t. W^m. Dunsmoor.

Voted to add two more men for Correspondancy for the County—Chose Dea. Thos. Fairbank & Mr. Jonathan Wilder.

Voted to Choose one man more & Chose Doc^r Josiah Wilder. . . .

Voted to reconsider this meeting and Dismissed Deacon David Wilder and Chose De^c. Thomas Fairbank as a member of Congress. . . . .

. . . . . Monday, the seventeenth Day of July, 1775. . . . . .

Voted and Chose Capt. Hezekiah Gates and Mr Ebenezer Allen to Represent the Town this Presant year.

It is curious to contrast with these early utterances in Lancaster of the rebellion against King George's ministry the following title of a pamphlet published, in the year 1772, by the first of these representatives elect, then captain of the mounted company of the town, who had served under Shirley and Abercrombie:

KING GEORGES RIGHT

TO THE

' *Crown of GREAT BRITAIN*

Displayed:

Being a Collection from History, from the first Known Times to the present year 1769 Extracted for the Benefit of those in the Province of Massachusetts Bay who have not Leisure to Study History.
Shewing it to be the Duty of all Officers and others to defend the Heirs of SOPHIA being Protestants upon the British Throne, and the undoubted Right that King GEORGE the third hath to the Crown of Great Britain.

Extracted by

HEZEKIAH GATES

of Lancaster in NEW ENGLAND.

The loyal Captain Gates, two years later, is found in the first Committee of Safety fiercely opposing the royal prerogative, and his only son headed the Lancaster troopers who galloped down the Bay Road to Lexington, April nineteenth, 1775, when the alarm courier brought news that the British were come out of Boston.

A panel of fifteen grand jurors attending the summons of the superior court at Worcester, in April, 1774, before consenting to take the oath, presented a written protest which all had signed, refusing to serve should Chief Justice Peter Oliver take his seat in that tribunal. He alone of the judges had refused to yield to the authority of the Provincial Assembly, and retained his salary from the royal treasury. This act of the jurymen, in contempt of a court wielding almost unlimited power to fine or imprison any one disturbing or obstructing its mandates, well illustrates the temper of the times. Deacon David Wilder of Lancaster was the foreman of this patriotic jury.

On Tuesday, August 9, 1774, a convention of the committees of correspondence and delegates of several towns of Worcester county met at the house of Mrs. Mary Sternes, in Worcester. Lancaster was therein represented by Doctor William Dunsmoor, Deacon David Wilder, Mr. Aaron Sawyer, Captain Samuel Ward, Captain Asa Whitcomb, Captain Hezekiah Gates, Mr. John Prescott and Mr. Ephraim Sawyer; Harvard, by Reverend Joseph Wheeler; Bolton, by Captain Samuel Baker and Lieutenant Jonathan Holman; Leominster had no delegate then present. Captain Samuel Ward and Lieutenant Jonathan Holman were members of the committee of ten who presented the patriotic resolves which were passed by the convention. At the adjourned meeting of August 30, convened at the court house, Captain Samuel Ward was elected one of a committee of nine to present resolutions for the consideration of the assembly. On September 6, the people of the county gathered upon Worcester green to the number of six thousand, armed and under their military leaders, ready to repel, by force if must be, the British troops which Gage was expected, and had proposed, to send to the protection of the court and its royalist officials. This demonstration of popular feeling had been foreshadowed in the discussions at the previous meeting of the delegates, and it seems probable that the governor, knowing well the certainty of a collision, feared to carry out his avowed intention. The delegates, meeting at the house of their chairman, adjourned to join the mass convention on the green. A committee of three, Captain Asa Whitcomb of Lancaster being one, was chosen to wait upon the justices and obtain their signatures to the declaration already agreed to by the judges. The forty-three protesting royalists of Worcester and the justices who had signed the loyal address to Governor Thomas Gage, were marched between the parallel lines of the armed assemblage, their principals reading the recantation which they had signed. Of these justices, Joseph Wilder, Abel Willard and Ezra Houghton were of Lancaster. Captain Samuel Ward was the same day chosen chairman of a committee of nine, whose duty it was made to arrange, with the help of the judges, means to prevent any stay in the course of justice. This duty was happily effected by the acceptance of their report, offered the following day, retaining the services of such officials of the court as had not become too obnoxious to the people.

The convention of September 20, 1774, was principally engaged in organization of the militia. Seven Worcester county regiments were established, the third or Lancaster regiment to include the companies of Lancaster, Bolton, Harvard, Leominster, Lunenburg, Fitchburg, Ashburnham and Westminster. All commissions then in force were to be resigned, and new elections of line officers to take place at once. The company officers chosen were to elect the field officers. Many subsequent meetings of the delegates were held, but their records are brief during 1775. Doctor William Dunsmoor of Lancaster appears prominently as a leader in affairs, his pronounced radical views suiting better the hot temper of the times than did the more prudent counsels of his astute neighbor, Captain Samuel Ward. The recorded action of the delegates does not especially concern our local history.

The nature of the provocations that were fast severing the colonies from the mother-land are not alone visible in the grave protests against ministerial encroachment upon charter rights, made by town-meeting and popular convention. Outcries of indignation from classes and individuals are scattered through the diaries and printed journals of the day. On September 8, 1774, the blacksmiths of Worcester county met at the county seat, and adjourned to November 8, when they made declaration of their principles, in a series of resolutions which were published in the papers of the period. They pledged themselves to do no labor which could directly or indirectly be held to aid or countenance any person whom they esteemed "enemies to their country commonly known by the name tories," or those "that shall not strictly conform to the affiliation or covenant agreed upon and signed by the Continental Congress lately convened at Philadelphia." Of the forty-three sons of Vulcan whose names are appended to the document were: Samuel Sawyer, Jr., Mark Heard, Ebenezer Belknap and Seth Heywood of Lancaster; Job Spofford and Jonathan White of Leominster; Thaddeus and John Pollard, and Samuel Jones of Harvard and Bolton.

In the Boston Evening Post for Monday, August 15, 1774, may be found the following notice, signed by a prominent innholder of Lancaster:

The subscriber finding that he could get no Satisfaction in a legal Way, takes the Freedom to acquaint the Publick with the Treatment that he met with at the Boston Neck Guard, by the Officer of the Guard, Lieut. Willm Cochran of the 23^d Regiment, and he does it the rather on account of the many Insults, Abuses and Wrongs that he understands have been daily offered to others. On the 12th of this Instant, driving his Waggon out of Town, which was not loaded with any Contraband Goods, he was, Contrary to Law, stopped and detained by the above officer near two Hours with his Waggon, putting him under Guard, using him with rough and Officer like Language, & not suffering him to go out to give anything to his Cattle, some of the Soldiers at the same time taking a cag of Rum out of his Cart, which he was obliged to consent to their doing, after they had propos'd it, to prevent greater Abuse and Wrong &c. And when set at Liberty by the Officer of the Guard, demanding satisfaction for this cruel Treatment, all the satisfaction that I could get was, that if I did not go about my Business he would put me under Guard again.

Attest, JONAS WYMAN, *of Lancaster*.

BOSTON, 13 August, 1774.

II. THE LEXINGTON ALARM.

As the men of Lancaster in the various wars of the preceding hundred years were found wherever the service of king and country called them, from Carthagena to Quebec, so in the great contest for civil liberty Lancaster patriotism has its history in every arm of the service, and at every post of duty. When, on the morning of the nineteenth of April, 1775, the hurrying horseman sped through the town shouting news of the sudden irruption from Boston of Gage's hated red-coats, almost before the clatter of galloping hoofs had faded away as a fresh horse bore the alarm courier westward, the roar of the town's four-pounder fieldpieces signaled the not unexpected tidings, and speedily there swarmed from farm and shop down the Bay Road, under six company leaders, two hundred and fifty-seven resolute men, eager to meet and drive the invaders back. They marched to Cambridge, and General William Heath, in his Memoirs, tells us that "General Whitcomb was in this day's battle." It is therefore possible that his regiment of minute men, or some portion of it, arrived in season to take active part in the fray, although no casualties in it were reported. The companies remained at Cambridge about two weeks, but many of the men were allowed to return to their homes some days sooner. About one in three enlisted for the remaining months of 1775, in the provincial service.

The colonels of the two Lancastrian regiments, the brothers John and Asa Whitcomb, natives of Lancaster, and direct descendants of the original proprietor, John Whitcomb, had seen varied field service during the French and Indian wars. As has been detailed in previous pages, both served in the scouts of 1748. John held the rank of colonel in the first Crown Point expedition, and served during 1756, 1758 and 1760. Asa was captain of a company in 1755 and 1758; and in 1768 he was one of the much extolled "ninety-two" representatives who refused —

notwithstanding a mandate from the crown and the persistent dictation of the royal governor—to rescind the action of the previous legislative session, by authority of which a circular letter touching the sovereign's encroachments upon colonial rights had been sent to the other provincial assemblies in America. Both Whitcombs had large farms, were deacons in their precincts, and greatly respected for their ability and probity. They had been left orphans at a tender age, and upon their attaining manhood the court had assigned to John the ancestral estate in the easterly part of Bolton, and to Asa lands upon Wickapeket Brook, in the west precinct of Lancaster, now Sterling. Upon these they resided in 1775.

The "minute men" at this date differed little from other troops; for the whole adult male population were armed and in training for strife. The "alarm list" embraced all able-bodied men between the ages of sixty-five and sixteen, save the few exempted because of profession or official position. The "training bands," as the militia companies were called, included all males between fifty and sixteen years of age, with the same exempts. The "minute men" composed about one-third of the militia, being those selected for their skill in the use of arms, exercised and equipped for active service at short notice. These distinctions disappeared early in the war. A regiment at first was nominally ten companies of one hundred men, but the complement varied in different states and from time to time. In the eight months' service of 1775, the company complement in Massachusetts was fifty-nine privates, two musicians, four corporals, four sergeants, one ensign, a lieutenant and captain; and the regiment was composed of ten companies. The continental regiment was finally established to include eight companies of ninety men each. Every soldier at first was expected to be fully armed and accoutred at his own expense, unless too poor to provide his own equipments, when the town was enjoined to supply him. He was required to carry (besides his gun, bayonet, blanket and knapsack) a cutting sword or hatchet, a jack-knife, six flints, forty bullets, one hundred buck-shot, a powder-horn and powder, some tow for wadding, and a wooden canteen holding a quart. Both powder and lead were scarce, and early in the war the housewife's pewter platters, and even leaden sash, were not seldom melted down in the home manufacture of musket-balls.

The dress of the soldier was his ordinary homespun garb. Even the officers rarely had a distinguishing uniform or arms by which they could be known, until Washington required them to wear cockades in their hats. Field officers wore red cockades, captains yellow, and subalterns green; sergeants had a red stripe, and corporals a green one, upon the right shoulder. It must be added, moreover, that the fashions of the day permitted much variety of shape and color in masculine attire. This is best seen from the personal description of deserters published in the weekly papers during the siege of Boston. Reading them, one is inclined to exclaim, parodying the melancholy Jacques, "Motley's the only wear." James Bridge of Bolton is described by his captain as having "a large head of hair almost black and very long which is commonly cued with a black ribband," and as wearing "an old blue surtout, cloth-colored coat and jacket, a pair of Cotton breeches and two shirts, tow and linen." John Chowen of the same company, "a molatto but calls himself Indian," had on "a dark colored coat and a pair of breeches something lighter." Other combinations thus advertised are as follows :

A blue coat, red waistcoat, blue breeches.—A blue coat, black vest, and metal buttons on hat.—A green coat, and old red great-coat.—A sad red coat, pale blue vest and dark brown thickset breeches.—A green coat and thick leather breeches.—A blue coat with metal buttons, leather breeches, blue yarn stockings and plated buckles.—Buckskin breeches, brown surtout coat, and white yarn stockings.—A blue coat faced with red and bound with yellow.—A lightish colored cloth great-coat and short sailor's jacket, leather breeches and white yarn stockings.

From the note-book of Captain David Nourse, used

while in service during 1777, is this memorandum of the allowance of rations to the soldier of that date :

One Pound of beef or ¾ of Pound of Pork or one Pound of Salt fish Pr : Day.

Three Pints of Peas or Beans Pr : Week or Vegetables at one Dollar Pr : Bushel for Peas or Beans.

One Pint of Milk Pr : Day or at the Rate of 1/72 of a Dollar.

One half Pint of Rice or one Pint of Indian Meal Pr : Week.

One Quart of Spruce Beer or Cyder Pr : Man Pr : Day or nine Gallons of Molasses Pr : Company of 100 Men Pr : Week.

Three Pounds of Candles to 100 men Pr : Week for Guards.

Twenty-four Pounds of Salt or eight Pounds of hard Soap for 100 Men Pr : Week.

This differs but slightly from the allowance in the Massachusetts army of 1775. The money commutation for vegetables not supplied is often spoken of in the settlement of soldiers' accounts as sauce money. The troops at first were paid by the week : a captain receiving thirty shillings ; a first-lieutenant, twenty shillings ; an ensign or second-lieutenant, seventeen shillings six pence ; sergeants, twelve shillings ; corporals, eleven shillings ; and privates, ten shillings. Each soldier was paid a penny per mile for actual travel, going and returning.

The Lexington-Alarm rolls for Lancaster and the towns formed from its original territory give the following lists of names. The columns of dates, wages, etc., as well as the sworn certificates of commanding officers appended to the rolls, and most of the headings, are omitted as of minor interest. In the spelling of names, that of the muster rolls is strictly copied :

A list of Men & the time they spent & distance they traveled in their March to Cambridge on the 19th day of April 1775, to defend the Country against General Gage & his troops, under the command of Capt. Thomas Gates of Lancaster.

Capt. Tho. Gates,	John Hawks,	Shadrach Hapgood,
Lt. Jonⁿ. Priest Whitcom,	James Goodwin,	Jona. Puffer,
Lt. Ricᵈ. Townsend,	Joel Osgood,	Eben. Allen,
Sgᵗ. Wᵐ. Hutson,	Phin. Fletcher,	Asa Rugg,
Sgᵗ. Peter Thurston,	Reuben Gary,	Jos. Blood,

Sg^t. Thos. Brooks,	Dav^d. Willard, Jr.,	Israel Willard,
Corp. W^m. Whitcom,	John May, Jr.,	Gardner Moors,
Corp. Moses Burpee,	Eph. Willard, Jr.,	Simeon Hemenway,
Corp. Jonas Wyman,	Thos. McBride,	Jere. Willard,
Priv. Lem. Sawyer,	Benj. Bruce,	Gab. Priest,
	Uriah Ward,	Joel Phinney. 32

[Massachusetts Archives, Revolutionary Rolls, XII, 95.]

This mounted company was known as the "Lancaster Troop," and a few years earlier had been commanded by Captain Hezekiah, the father of Thomas Gates. Father and son lived at the junction of the two main roads leading from Lancaster to Sterling, and there kept an inn known far and wide as the Gates Tavern. This ancient hostelry was torn down about forty years ago. The Lancaster Troop kept up its organization and attended annual musters until 1825. Lieutenant Townsend and seven of the troopers were of Bolton. The last ten upon the roll enlisted in the continental service for eight months. Joseph Willard, Esq., writing in 1826, says: "Of this company, James Goodwin, the oldest man in Lancaster, Moses Burpee, Samuel Sawyer, John Hawkes, Phineas Fletcher and Joseph Blood are living." We have much to regret in the fact that the limit set by Mr. Willard to his Sketches of the Town of Lancaster, did not permit him to record for us the reminiscences of these and other soldiers of the Revolution, and also of the surviving veterans of the French and Indian Wars, who were in his day fighting over the battles of their youth at many a fireside. Only few and faint traditions now survive to hint to us of the thrilling stories of personal daring and suffering, which, sixty years ago, could have been taken down from the lips of many an aged continental soldier.

. . . . *The Command of Capt. John Prescott of Lancaster.*

Captn. John Prescott,	Priv. Abner Haskell,	John Ballard,
Lieut. John White, Jr.,	Will Jewett,	Joseph Phelps,
Serj. Elisha Allen,	Adam Fleeman,	Josiah Phelps,
Serj. James Fuller,	Jacob Zewer,	Robert Phelps,
Serj. Salmon Godfrey,	Jona. Phillips,	Peter Ayers,

Serj. Joseph Beeman,	Ichabod Garey,	David Robins,
Corp. Seth Sergeant,	Asa Sterns,	Jona. Atherton,
Corp. Jonª. Wilder,	Abiel Abbot,	Eben. Flagg,
Corp. Wᵐ. Shaw,	Luke Carter,	Moses Brewer,
Corp. Nath. White,	John Maning,	Oliver Houghton,
	Jona. White,	John Baker. 32

[Mass. Archives, Revolutionary Rolls, XIII, 68.]

This Roll contains the travel and service of Capt. Joseph White and the Militia men under his command in Colᵒ Asa Whitcomb's regiment who in consequence of the Alarm on the nineteenth day of April last marched from Lancaster in the County of Worcester to Cambridge for the defence of this Colony against the Ministerial troops.

Captⁿ. Jos. White,	Corp. Moses Wilder,	Jonª. Whitney,
1 Lt. Cyrus Fairbanks,	Priv. Jno. White,	Asel Phelps,
2 Lt. Moses Sawyer,	Nat. White,	Jos. Fairbanks,
Serj. Sam. Thurston,	Wᵐ. Richardson,	Josiah Bennet,
Serj. Josh. Fletcher,	Phineas Wilder,	Wᵐ. Phelps,
Serj. John Clarke,	Jos. Lewis,	Joseph Beman. 19
Corp. Peter Larkin,		

[Mass. Archives, Revolutionary Rolls, XIII, 189.]

Provincial Ridgement of foot of militia men Commanded by Coll. Asa Whitcomb, part of the Larram Company whereof Cap. Jonth. Wilder Commanded, who marched to Cambridge in consequence of an alarm order of the Coll. and returned again not listed in the American Service. [April 19 to 22.]

Jonᵗʰ. Wilder, *sert.*,	Jonth. Fairbanks,	Nathˡ. Jones.
	Caleb Whitney,	

Then by request of General John Whetcomb we marcht to Cambridge again. [April 29 to May 4.]

Jonath. Wilder, *sert.*,	Jonath. Fairbanks,	Caleb Whitney.

We bore our own expenses both for ourselves and our horses all the time we were from home.

[Mass. Archives, Revolutionary Rolls, XIII, 173.]

Provincial Regiment of foot of Militia Men Commanded by Colᵒ. Asa Whitcomb, Part of the Second and Thirtieth Companies whereof Capt. Daniel Robbins Commands, who marched to Cambridge in consequence of an alarm by order of the Colᵒ and returnd again not Listed in the American Service.

Daniel Robbins, *captⁿ*.	Josiah Wilder, Jun.,	Ephraim Bowker,
Asa Wilder, 1ˢᵗ *lieut*.	Abraham How,	Elijah Wilder,
Fortunatus Eager, 2ᵈ *lieut*.	Joseph How,	David Whittecor,
Edward Newton, *ensign*.	John Robbins,	Samuel Jewett,

Josiah Kendall, 1st *lieut.*
Jonathan Baley, *ensign.*
Samuel Baley, *sergt.*
Nathaniel Wright, Jr., "
John Dresser, "
Thomas Mears, "
Samuel Thompson, *corp.*
Thomas Ross, "
Samuel Herring, "
Simeon Lyon, "
Benjamin Whitemore,
Seth Fairbank,
Ephraim Wright,
Thomas Wright,

Seth Brooks,
Gamaliel Beaman,
Benjamin Beaman,
Josias Baley,
Jonathan Thompson,
John Kilburn,
William Palmer,
Calvin Moor,
James Houghton,
George Hibris,
Joshua Sawyer,
Joseph Dunsmore,
Jonathan Prescott,
Thomas Sawyer, *quartermaster, as a private.*

Samuel Holman,
Asa Smith,
Hugh Moore,
Timothy Wilder,
Joshua Whitney,
Elijah Dole,
David Gray,
Daniel Farrar,
Noah Kendall,
Seth Ross,
Jonas Beaman,
Oliver Fairbank,
Reuben Moore, 53

[Mass. Archives, Revolutionary Rolls, XIII, 77.]

Provintial Regiment of foot of Minute Men Commanded by Col. John Whitcomb, second Company of sd. Regiment whereof Samuel Sawyer was Captain, ... not Inlisted in the American Service.

Samuel Sawyer, *capt.*
Manassa Sawyer, *leut.*
Joel Houghton, *ensign.*
Ebenezer Ross, *corporal.*
Lemuel Fairbanks, "
Jabez Brooks,
Jonathan Wilder, Junr.
Samuel Churchel,

Timothy Hawood,
Ephraim Powers,
Jacob Robins,
Aron Kilburn,
John Spafford,
Thomas Sawyer, Jun.
Silas Rice,

John Persons,
Oliver Powers,
Ezra Sawyer,
Asa Smith,
Ephraim Wiman,
Obediah Grose,
Abel Bigelow.

[Mass. Archives, Revolutionary Rolls, XIII, 84.]

. . . . ingaged in the provintial service.

Ephraim Richardson, *leut.*
Seth Hawood, *sergeant.*
Ephraim Bointon, "
Ebenezer Pike, "
Luther Graves, "
Jiles Wills, *corporal.*
Timothy Brown, "
John Wheler, *drummer.*
William Kindall, *fifer.*
Ebenezer Belknap, *private.*
Thomas Blockit,
Israel Coock,

Thomas Kleland,
Elijah Dresser,
John Densmore,
Aaron Gary,
Ephraim Goss,
Joshua Kindall,
Israil Manning,
Jonathan Phillips,
Elisha Prouty,
Jacob Piper,
Josiah Person,

Isaac Tower,
Ephraim Winship,
Jacob Wilder,
Roger Bartlet,
Nathaniel Brown,
Mathias Larkin,
Samuel Rice,
Solemon Holeman
Menassa Powers,
John Sawyer,
Jude Sawyer. 56

[Mass. Archives, Revolutionary Rolls, XIII, 115.]

Captain Sawyer and most of his company were from the second precinct.

This Roll contains the names and service of Capt[n] Benjamin Houghton &
the minute men under his command in Colo. John Whetcomb's Regi-
ment. . . . . .

Capt[n]. Benj. Houghton,
2[d] Lieut. Sam[l]. Josslyn,
Serj. Nath. Sawyer,
Serj. Sam. Wilder,
Corp. Aaron Johnson,
Corp. Will[m]. Wilder,
Drum. W[m]. Wheelock,
Drum. Eph. Kindall,
Priv. Paul Sawyer,
  Thomas Bennet,
  Abijah Hawks,
  Henry Willard Farmer,

Jona. Kendall,
John Willard,
Jona. Knowlton,
Steph. Wilder,
Titus Wilder,
John Dana,
Elijah Ball,
Daniel Knight,
John Thurston,
Edm. Larkin,
Joseph Josslyn,
David Horseley,

Reuben Lipenwell,
John Bennet,
Jonas Prescott,
Nathan Esterbrook,
Elisha Houghton,
Stanton Carter,
Joseph Jones,
Josh. Fairbanks,
Abijah Houghton,
Mathew James,
John Chowen.

The following persons did enlist into the Continental Army.

First Lt. And[w]. Haskell,
Sarg. Jon[a]. Sawyer,
Sarg. John Kendrick,
Corp. John Farwell,
Corp. Jere. Haskell,
Fifer John Wheelock,
Priv. Mark Heard,
  Jacob Wilder,
  Eber Sawyer,

Abel Wyman,
Benj. Ballard,
Jos. Beaman,
Dan. Wyman,
John Baker,
Josiah Bowers,
Joseph Phelps,
Josiah Phelps,
Abel Allen,

Sam. Adams,
Thos. Goodwin,
Elisha Rugg,
Jona. Ross,
Jacob Phelps,
Isaac Eveleth,
Abijah Phillips,
Benja. Houghton,
                    61

[Mass. Archives, Revolutionary Rolls, XII, 14.0]

Three companies marched from Leominster at the Lexington Alarm; ninety-nine men in all. As the names will
show, very many of these soldiers were lineal descendants
of the Lancaster pioneers:

Captain Joshua Wood's Company of Militia. . . . . .

Capt. Joshua Wood,
Lieut. Nathaniel Carter,
Lieut. Edward Phelps,
Sergt. Joseph Beaman,
Sergt. Samuel Stickney,
Sergt. Phillip Sweetser,
Sergt. Thomas Wilder,
Corp. Daniel Nichols,
Corp. Elijah Fairbank,
Corp. Ephraim Carter,
Corp. Benjamin Perkins,
Drummer John Wood,

Priv. Elisha White,
John Jewett,
Jonas Gates,
William Boutell, Jr.
Luke Richardson,
Abiathar Houghton,
Samuel Hale, Jr.
Joseph Wilder, Jr.
John Bennet,
Josiah White,
James Boutell,

Ebenezer Osgood,
Benjamin Hale,
Caleb Cummins,
David Fleeman,
Isaac Whitman,
John Bowers,
Abraham Houghton,
Jese Slack,
Charles Eames,
John Hale,
David Hale.   34

[Mass. Archives, Revolutionary Rolls, XIII, 161.]

*Captain David Wilder's Company of Minute Men, Colonel John Whit-
comb's Regiment. . . . . .*

Capt. David Wilder,	Phinius Carter,	William Nichols,
Lieut. Joseph Bellows,	Israel Wiman,	Ebenezer Stewart,
2d Lieut. Thomas Harkness,	Richard Fowler,	Ephraim Buss,
Sergt. Elijah Gaffil,	Jonathan Marting,	David Clarke,
" John Locke,	David Kendal,	Josiah Colburn,
" Rufus Houghton,	Josiah Whetcomb,	Asa Kendal,
" Abijah Butler,	James Joslin,	Richard Stewart,
Noah Dodge,	David Willson,	Ruben Gates. 24

[Mass. Archives, Revolutionary Rolls, XII. 175.]

*Captain John Joslin's Company of Minute Men, Colonel John Whitcomb's
Regiment. . . . . .*

Capt. John Joslin,	Corp. Nathan Colbourn,	Nathan Johnson,
Lieut. Thomas Gary,	" Aaron Kendall,	Francis Parker,
2d Lieut. Phinehas Carter,	Private Thomas Page,	Benjamin Smith,
Clark Oliver Houghton,	" Tolham Bennett,	Enoch Chase,
Sargent Joseph Joslin,	Nathaniel Evens,	David Boutell,
" Robert Legate,	Abraham Goodnow,	Moses Osgood.
" John Colbourn,		

Enlisted in Army.

Ensign Timothy Boutell,	Zebedee Symonds,	Joseph Smith,
Sergt. William Warner,	Jonathan Colbourn,	Nathaniel Chapman,
Corp. Josiah Carter, Jr.	Amos Brown,	Benjamin Stearns,
Corp. Samuel Buss,	Joshua Pierce,	Benjamin Gary,
Drummer Luke Aldridge,	Stephen Chase,	Luke Johnson,
Fifer Abijah Haskell,	John Stone,	Joshua White,
Private Jonathan Kendall,	Joshua Proute,	James Wood. 41
Levi Warner,		

[Mass. Archives, Revolutionary Rolls, XII, 159.]

Four companies are credited to Harvard in the Lexington Alarm rolls, containing one hundred and sixty-four
men :

*Captain Jonathan Davis's Company of Minute Men in Colonel John
Whitcomb's Regiment. . . . . .*

Capt. Jona. Davis,	Fifer Jacob Davis,	Ebenr. Davis,
Lieut. Elisha Fullam,	Priv. Jacob Fullam,	Charles Warner,
2d Lieut. Jona. Pollard,	Reuben Garfield,	John Wood,
Ensign James Haskell,	Thaddeus Pollard,	David Whitney,
Sergt. Jabez Keep,	Thomas Pratt,	John Farnsworth,
" John Mead,	Solomon Haskell,	Ezekiel Cox (*deserted*)

Sergt. Isaac Holden,
" Abraham Munroe,
Corp. Benjⁿ. Laurance,
" Josiah Whitney,
" Prince Turner,
" Josiah Gates,
Drummer Cyrus Fairbanks,
" Jona. Davis,
Fifer Abijah Worster,

Joshua Bowers,
Benj. Robbins,
Jacob Whitney,
Jacob Priest,
Josiah Davis,
Manasseh Stow,
John Knight,
Francis Farr,
George Gleason.

Abijah Warner,
Nath^{ll}. Farnsworth,
Philemon Priest,
Oliver Mead,
Daniel Furbush,
Thomas White,
Isaiah Whitney,
(deserted).
43

[Mass. Archives, Revolutionary Rolls, XII, 36, 41, 48.]

Captain Isaac Gates's Company of Militia in Colonel Asa Whitcomb's Regiment. . . . . .

Capt. Isaac Gates,
Lieut. Josiah Haskell,
Lieut. Amos Fairbank,
Ensign John Daby,
Sergt. Sim. Willard,
" Saml. Hill,
" John Houghton,
" John Daby,
Corp. Gibson Willard,
" Israel Whitney,
Drummer Lem^l. Willard.
Priv. John Sawyer,

Benj^a. Barnard,
Lem^l. Farnsworth,
Asa Farnsworth,
Barzillai Willard,
Malbery Kingman,
Joseph Knight,
Saml. Farnsworth,
Joseph Wood,
Phineas Fairbank,
Nicholas Patterson,
John Atherton,
Lem^l. Haskell,

Elijah Willard,
Edwd. Cheney,
Joseph Atherton,
Zaccheus Stevens,
Josiah Willard,
Jere^h. Bridge.
Eph^m. Barnard,
Jon^a. Sawyer,
Levi Fairbank,
Asa Haven,
Benj^a Stow,
Jon^a. Symonds.

Enlisted in American Army.

Eben^r. Warner,
Saml. Worster,
Saml. Finney,
W^m. Bennett.

Thos. Chamberlin,
Joel Finney,
W^m. Haskell,
Benj^a. Willard,

W^m. Safford,
W^m. Harris,
Aaron Priest,
Saml. Furbush.   48

[Mass. Archives, Revolutionary Rolls, XII, 99.]

Captain Joseph Fairbank's Company in Colonel Asa Whitcomb's Regiment. . . . . .

Capt. Jos. Fairbanks,
Lt. W^m. Burt,
Lt. Phineas Willard,
Ensign Jos. Willard,
Sgt. Jona. Reed,
" Jona. Clark,
" Benja. Cutler,
" Rich^d. Whitney,
Corp. John Priest,

Israel Taylor, Esq.
Jos. Wheeler, Esq.
Lem^l. Willard,
Jer^h. Laughton,
W^m. Sanderson,
Jos. Atherton,
Jos. Houghton,
Abr. Willard,
Jona. Adams.

Oliver Whitney,
Phineas Fairbanks,
Jer^h. Priest,
Elijah Houghton,
Joseph Blanchard,
Eben^r. Burges,
Stephen Randall,
Manasseh Sawyer,
Isaac Haile.

Corp. Isaiah Whitney,   Ward Safford,   James Perry,
   " Saml. Meed,   Oliver Whetcomb,   Oliver Wetherbe,
   " Timo. Willard,   Aaron Davis,   35

[Mass. Archives, Revolutionary Rolls, XII, 74.]

Captain James Burt's Company. . . . . .

Capt. James Burt,   George Coon,   David Sterns,
Lt. Phinehas Farnsworth,   Coleman Sanderson,   Lemuel Stone,
Lt. Jacob Robins,   Aaron Whitney,   Jona. Crouch, Jr.
Ensign Caleb Sawyer,   Silas Whitney,   Willis Secomb,
Sergt. Hezek. Whitney,   Saml. Brown,   Aaron Warner,
   " Ephraim Davis,   Dan. Houghton,   John Sartell Farwell,
   " Joel Stone,   Moses Hale,   Joseph Wetherbe,
   " Charles Taylor,   Timo. Phelps,   Richard Whitney,
Corp. James Whitcom,   Timo. Crouch,   Joseph Park,
   " Silas Rand,   Abijah Reed,   Joseph Blanchard,
   " Simon Cooper,   W^m. Park,   Jabez Keep, Jr.
   " Abel Whitcom,   David Farwell,   Jerem. Willard,
Jotham Barnard,   Abel Farnsworth,   James Willis.   40
Simon Whitney

[Mass. Archives, Revolutionary Rolls, XI, 196.]

Three companies from Bolton (including Berlin district) marched to Cambridge at the Lexington Alarm ;— one hundred and twenty-seven men :

Captain Benjamin Hastings's Company, Col. John Whitcomb's Regiment.

Capt. Benj^a. Hastings,   Abel Moore,   Jonathan Whitcomb,
Lieut. Jonathan Houghton,   William Biglow,   Abraham Whitney,
2 Lieut. Jonathan Merriam,   William Sawyer,   Josiah Sawyer, 3^d.
Sergt. Benjamin Gold,   Israel Sawyer,   Jeremiah Wilson,
   " John Wilson,   Nathaniel Holman,   Nathan Ball,
   " Timothy Mosman,   John Ross,   Cyrus Gates,
   " David Moore,   Hezekiah Gibbs,   Joseph Amsden,
Corp. James Townsend,   Levi Meriam,   Benjamin Marble,
   " Andrew McWain,   Nathaniel Hastings,   Lemuel Bruce,
   " Silas Welch,   Samuel Stanhop,   Samuel White,
   " James Briges,   Abraham Holman,   William White,
Josiah Cooledge,   Calvin Holman,   Nathl. Oakes,
Ephraim Fairbank,   Joel Fosket,   Elijah Foster,
John Houghton,   Simon Houghton,   Josiah Moore,
John Hasting,   Sanderson Houghton,   Joshua Townsend,
Abner Moore,   Jeremiah Priest,   William Sawyer,
Joseph Pratt,   Josiah Sawyer, Jr.   John Welch,

Jonathan Robins,　Joseph Sawyer,　Amos Fuller,
William Ross,　Thomas Atherton,　Jacob Houghton.　58
Jonas Welch,

[Mass. Archives, Revolutionary Rolls, XII. 135.]

Captain Artemas How's Militia Company. . . . . .

Capt. Artemas How,　Samuel Baker,　Eben. Worcester,
Lieut. David Nurss,　John Coolidge,　Nathan Jones,
2 Lieut. Joseph How,　Joseph Woods,　John Bruce,
Sergt. W^m. Pollard,　Solomon Jones,　Asa Fay,
　"　W^m. Jones,　Benj^a. Bailey,　Silas Bailey, Jr.
　"　Jotham Maynard,　Eben. Bailey,　Benj. Muzzy,
　"　David Rice,　George Sawyer,　Asa Johnson,
Corp. Josh. Johnson,　Jonas Johnson,　Silas Bailey, Sen.
　　Timo. Bailey,　Samuel Jones,　Jacob Moor,
　　Elisha Hodson,　Nath. Longley,　John Barnard,
Drum^r. Jabez Fairbank,　Thos. Pollard,　Robert Fife,
Fif. Samuel Jones, Jr.　Amos Osgood,　Steph. Bailey.　36

[Mass. Archives, Revolutionary Rolls, XIII, 194.]

Company of Captain Robert Longley, Colonel Asa Whitcomb's Regiment.

Capt. Rob. Longley,　Beriah Oak,　Saml. Bruce,
Lieut. Paul Whitcomb,　David Stiles,　Asa Nurss,
Lieut. Thos. Osborn,　Jabez Walkett,　Benj. Nurss,
Sergt. John Townsend,　Thaddeus Pollard,　Israel Foster,
　"　Oliver Barrett,　Sam. Blood,　James Flood,
　"　Phin. Moore,　Epm. Whitney,　W^m. Cooledge,
　"　Abel Piper,　David Stratten,　[Cyrus] Gates,
　"　Oliver Jewett,　Jonas Whitcom,　Josiah Edwards,
Drummer Jon^a. Priest.　John Peirce,　Richard Hazeltine,
Gabriel Priest,　Jon^a. Whitcom, Jr.　Jacob French,
Jon^n Nurss,　Sanderson Houghton,　Eph^m. Chamberlain.
Isaiah Bruce,　　　　　34

[Mass. Archives, Revolutionary Rolls, XII, 182.]

Field and Staff of the regiment of minute men.

Colonel John Whitcomb, of Bolton.
Lieutenant-Colonel Thomas Legate, of Leominster.
First-Major William Dunsmoor, of Lancaster.
Second-Major Ephraim Sawyer, of Lancaster.
Adjutant Jeremiah Gager, of Westminster.
Quartermaster David Osgood, of Lancaster.

Field and Staff of the militia regiment.

Colonel Asa Whitcomb, of Lancaster.
Lieutenant-Colonel Josiah Whitney, of Harvard.
First-Major Josiah Carter, of Leominster.
Second-Major John Rand, of Westminster.
Adjutant Eliakim Atherton, of Bolton.
Quartermaster Jeremiah Laughton, of Harvard.

[Mass. Archives, Revolutionary Rolls, XXVI, 318, 336.]

III. BUNKER HILL AND SIEGE OF BOSTON.

The day before the battle of Lexington, the Committee of Safety and Supplies, having met at Newton, designated Lancaster as one of nine towns wherein depots of military material were to be established.   It was ordered that besides infantry ammunition, one company of matrosses, two iron three-pounder cannon with thirty-three rounds each of grape, canister and round shot, two medicine chests and one hundred and fifty tents should be kept in this town. The exigency, however, quickly concentrated all the scanty military stores of the Province in and about Cambridge. To be near the camps, the Provincial Congress re-assembled at Watertown, and on April 25 resolved to raise an army of thirteen thousand men from the state militia, trusting to the other colonies to augment this to thirty thousand.   Enlistments began at once, and Lancaster's quota was soon in camp, the volunteers mostly joining two companies recruited for Colonel Asa Whitcomb's regiment.   Colonel John Whitcomb had received the promotion due to his experience.

During the later months of 1774 five general officers had been chosen by the Provincial Congress : Honorable Jedediah Preble, a brigadier of the French and Indian War, now nearly three score and ten years of age ; Honorable Artemas Ward, who had been a lieutenant-colonel under Abercrombie, but had won his chief repute in civil pursuits ; Colonel Seth Pomeroy, who had served as major in Colonel Samuel Willard's regiment at Louisbourg, now seventy years old ; Colonel William Heath, skilled as yet only in the theory of war, but commander of the Ancient and Honorable Artillery ; Colonel John Thomas, Shirley's staff surgeon, and commander of a regiment in 1759 at Crown Point. General Preble declined service on account of growing infirmities. Artemas Ward was made Commander-in-Chief, and General Thomas lieutenant-general, by the Second Congress. "Honorable John Whitcomb, Esq.," of Bolton, was, on February 15, 1775, added to the list of generals, and at the first council of war, convened at Cambridge the day after the Concord Fight, he was one of the three general officers present. On the sixth of May he and Colonel Benjamin Lincoln were appointed mustermasters. General Whitcomb declined this service, "on account of various avocations," and his younger brother, Colonel Asa Whitcomb, was three days later chosen to fill the vacancy. June 13th, John Whitcomb was elected "first major-general of the Massachusetts army," and the following day Joseph Warren was chosen the "second major-general." A committee was appointed to wait upon both officers and desire their immediate acceptance. General Whitcomb hesitated, it is said on account of his health, and a committee was ordered "to draw a complaisant letter to Gen. Whitcomb, to desire a more explicit answer," which letter follows :

WATERTOWN, June 16, 1775.

Sir : Your letter wherein you express yourself willing to continue in the Service of this Colony, until the army is regulated and properly encamped and then rely on a discharge, was read with much concern by this Congress, who earnestly hope you will continue in office till the conclusion of the campaign, and must beg your further and more explicit answer.

On the next day was fought the battle of Bunker Hill, and its chief martyr, the second major-general of Massachusetts, is a famous name in history ; while Major-General John Whitcomb, second in command of the state forces at

Cambridge that day (although he had not received his commission), being held in reserve at Lechmere Point — probably by order of the commander-in-chief, who expected the British to attack Cambridge — had no opportunity to win laurels. In Massachusetts Archives, cxlvi, 246, is found his reply to the "complaisant letter :"

To the Honble Congress :

Whereas you Desire of me to Giue a more Explicit Answer as to my opintment, as the Surcumstances of the army is so Deficult and the Enemy so ner I excep the Scruis to Do my Duty as far as I shall Be Able. I am your mst obedeint Ser.

JOHN WHETCOMB, *Colo.*

CAMBRIDGE, June yᵉ 22ᵈ, 1777.

He was at once commissioned major-general of Massachusetts forces, to date from June 21, and the commission was handed to him by the President of Congress June 26. The following letter indicates that his lack of literary attainments did not prevent a generous appreciation of his military services and ability :

In the HOUSE OF REPRESENTATIVES, July 22, 1775.

Sir : This house approving of your services in the station you were appointed to in the army by the Congress of this Colony, embrace this opportunity to express their sense of them, and at the same time to desire your Continuance with the army, if you shall judge you can do it without Impropriety, till the final determination of the Continental Congress shall be known with regard to the appointment of General officers. We assure you that the Justice of this House will be engaged to make you an adequate conpensation for your services. We have such intelligence as affords us confidence to suppose, that a few days will determine whether any such provision shall be made for you as is consistent with your honor to accept and shall give you encouragement to remain in the service.

By order of the House.

[Massachusetts Archives, LVII, 264.]

Similar letters were sent to Generals John Thomas and James Frye. Much heart-burning had resulted from the selections made by the Provincial Congress for the highest military officers, and the appointments of the Continental Congress increased dissatisfaction among the battle-scarred veterans of former wars. No record shows that John

Whitcomb resented the slight put upon him — any more than did the sturdy patriot, Pomeroy — although he was the senior in years, military experience and rank in service, to every one of the congressional appointees. June 5, 1776, he was commissioned brigadier-general in the continental army, and General Washington announced to Major-General Artemas Ward, upon resignation of the latter, that he proposed to order General Whitcomb, so soon as he should accept his commission, to assume command of the forces in Massachusetts. [See American Archives, iv, vi, 929.] John Whitcomb, however, returned the commission, "desiring to be excused on account of age and a diffidence of not being able to answer the expectation of Congress." He served for four years an honored member of the council, to which he was elected July 25. He had been chosen to the same position in 1773, but then declined the office, prefering to remain in the House of Representatives. The historian, Frothingham, describes him as "one of the sterling, disinterested officers of the early revolution," one who "appears to have enjoyed to a great degree the respect and confidence of his contemporaries." He died November 17, 1785, in the seventy-third year of his age. The epitaph upon the unpretentious stone that marks his grave in Bolton's oldest burial ground ignores his military honors, giving only his civic title.

The Lancaster regiment was among the first filled. By provincial regulations the complement required ten companies of fifty-nine rank and file. On the twenty-fifth of May, Colonel Asa Whitcomb reported eleven companies encamped at Cambridge, containing five hundred and sixty volunteers. The field and staff officers were as follows: Colonel Asa Whitcomb of Lancaster, Lieutenant-Colonel Josiah Whitney of Harvard, Major Ephraim Sawyer of Lancaster, Adjutant Jeremiah Gager of Westminster, Quartermaster Jeremiah Laughton of Harvard, Surgeon William Dunsmoor of Lancaster, Surgeon's Mate Moses

Barnard of Harvard.   Eliakim Atherton of Bolton was appointed a deputy commissary of the Province.

Here followeth an account of the Subbaltons in the several Companies Belonging to Colo. Asa Whetcomb's Regament Recommended to the Committee of Safty for their approbation. By the sevral Capt. who has Rec⁴ their Comitions.

Capt's. Names.	*Leut's. Names.*	*Ens's. Names.*
John Fuller,	Ebenezer Bridge,	Jared Smith,
Ephraim Richardson,	Seth Haywood,	Ephraim Boyenton,
James Burt,	Ebenezer Woods,	Jabez Keep,
David Wilder,	Jonathan Gates,	Timothy Boutal,
Andrew Haskell,	John Kendrick,	Jonathan Sawyer,
Robert Longley,	Silvanus Smith,	Ephraim Smith,
Agrippa Wells,	Jacob Poole,	Ezekiel Foster,
Jonathan Davis,	Elisha Fullom,	John Meed,
Abner Cranson,	John Wyman,	Benjamin West,
Edmond Bemis.	John Hore.	David Foster.

Camp at Cambridge, June yᵉ 3ᵈ, 1775.

ASA WHITCOMB, *Colᵒ.*

Adjutant Jeremiah Gager.

'[Massachusetts Archives, CXLVI, 156.]

Of the eleventh company Colonel Whitcomb says :

I have a full Regᵗ. exclusive of Benj Hastings who has 53 in his Company, and he has done Duty with me and declines joining any other Regᵗ. and I desire that the officers of that Company may be commissioned & join my Reg'mt.   ASA WHITCOMB.

Benj Hastings, *capt.* Jonathan Houghton, *lieut.* Jonathan Meriam, 2ᵈ. *lieut.*

CAMP NO. 2, CAMBRIDGE, June 30, 1775.

This may certify, that we, the subscribers, being chosen Officers of a Minute Company, in *Bolton,* have taken orders to raise a Company in the present Army: and having fifty-three able-bodied, effective men, fit for service, in our Company, and having done duty in Colonel Whetcomb's Regiment from our first taking out orders, we desire that we may be commissioned under the above said Colonel, which was the expectation of the Company.   BENJAMIN HASTINGS, *Captain.*

JONATHAN HOUGHTON, *Lieutenant.*

JONATHAN MERIAM, *Second Lieutenant.*

To the honourable the Provincial Congress.

[American Archives, IV, II, 828.]

Haskell's and Richardson's companies were mostly of

Lancaster; Burt's and Davis's of Harvard; Longley's of
Bolton and Shirley; Hastings's of Bolton; Wilder's of
Leominster and Ashburnham; Fuller's of Lunenburg;
Bemis's of Westminster; Cranson's of Marlborough; and
Wells's of Greenfield, etc. The regiment lost five killed,
eight wounded, and two missing in the battle of Bunker
Hill, according to the official returns. The historian, Bancroft, says "from the regiment of Whitcomb of Lancaster
there appeared at least fifty privates, but with no higher
officers than captains." The loss as well as other facts
seem to prove that more than twice fifty were at the front.
Richard Frothingham states that it was represented in
action by "a few companies," and, upon what authority is
not discovered, adds that probably Captain Burts' and
Wilders' companies were of these. He also relates that
"one account by a soldier states that Captain Benjamin
Hastings . . . . . led one company of thirty-four, and took
post at the rail fence." Sergeant Robert Phelps of Haskell's Lancaster company was mortally wounded and died
a prisoner in Boston; and David Robbins of the same company was killed. In Massachusetts Archives, CLXXXI, 73,
is a petition of Elisha Houghton, a Lancaster man in Captain Hastings's company, alleging that he was in the battle
and helped Jacob Davis, who was wounded, off the field.
This wounded man was of Harvard, belonged to Captain
Burt's company, and was discharged October 6th, on account of his injury. Among resolves passed by the House
of Representatives, February 6, 1776, for the payment of
accounts for losses at Bunker Hill, were the following:

To the heirs, or Master of David Robbins, who was killed, 2 .. 12 .. 0
To Robert Phelps, wounded, 2 .. 0 .. 0
To Israel Willard, 2 .. 0 .. 0
To Joseph Wilder, 1 .. 0 .. 0

These names are all found in the company roll of Captain Andrew Haskell.

By casualties in their ranks therefore we have proof

that Haskell's, Burt's and Hastings's companies were in the battle upon Bunker Hill. Judging from those recorded as died and discharged after that day, it seems probable that Longley's, Davis's and Bemis's commands were also in action. There is a tradition among old families that one or more companies of the Lancaster regiment were crossing the Neck towards the battle-ground when the retreat began, and that others had marched to re-enforce Prescott earlier.

The names of soldiers who enlisted in the eight-months' service of 1775 are found in the so-called "Coat Rolls." April 23d the Provincial Congress, in establishing the pay of the troops, passed a resolve that, in addition to the monthly stipend, "a Coat for a uniform be given to each of the Non-commissioned officers and Privates, as soon as the state of the Province will admit of it." July 5, thirteen thousand coats were ordered for the army, each town being required to furnish a share of these proportionate to its last provincial tax. Lancaster's proportion was determined to be one hundred and sixteen ; Bolton's, fifty-five ; Harvard's, fifty-six ; Leominster's, forty-three. A certificate was ordered sewn to the inside of each coat, giving the name of the town that furnished it, that of the maker, and the name of the weaver of the cloth, if home-made material was used. American cloth was to have preference. Soldiers providing their own coats were entitled to receive twenty shillings in money.

The Lancaster regiment, upon the organization of the army for the siege of Boston, was placed in a brigade with the Rhode Island troops, under General Nathaniel Greene, forming part of the Second—General Charles Lee's—division. According to Paul Lunt's Diary, it joined the brigade Friday, July 28, and was posted on Prospect Hill. It was the largest of the twenty-six Massachusetts regiments before Boston. Tents were few, and each squad usually planned and constructed some sort of hut with such materials as were most easy to obtain. Turf, stone, boards, brick, logs and sail-cloth were wrought into rude forms of shelter, which, in their disorderly quaintness, may have been picturesque, but lacked military convenience and cleanliness. As an officer of the command has told us, the whole army, consisted of less than fifteen thousand militia, "without a shade of uniformity in its organization, pay, dress, arms or exercise, destitute of subordination and discipline, and fluctuating from day to day as the caprice of the men inclined them to absent themselves or to rejoin their colors." General Greene, however, is credited with having the neatest encampment and the best disciplined brigade in the patriot lines. With less than twenty rounds of powder per man, this motley aggregation of brave yeomen held Boston in close siege for ten months, and finally compelled the dilatory Sir William Howe to take refuge in the British fleet.

Captain Andrew Haskell's Company of Lancaster. . . .

Capt. Andrew Haskell,
Lt. John Kindrick,
Lt. Jonathan Sawyer,
Ser. John Hewitt,
" Abijah Phillips,
" Robert Phelps,
" Jeremiah Haskell,
" Joshua Fairbank,
Cor. Josiah Bowers,
" Benjamin Houghton,
" Ebenezer Allen, Jr.
" Jacob Wilder,
Drum. Nathaniel White,
Fifer John Wheelock,
Surgeon's ⎰ Jonas Prescott,
Waiters ⎱ Abel Allen,
Abijah Houghton,
Abel Wyman,
Benjamin James,
Daniel Clark,
Daniel Wyman,

Eber Sawyer,
Elisha Rugg,
Ebenezer Abbott,
George Richardson,
Gershom Flagg,
Israel Willard,
Joseph Phelps,
Jacob Phelps,
Josiah Phelps,
Jonathan Ross,
Joseph Wilder,
Jacob Pike,
Isaac Kilbourn,
Isaac Eveleth,
Isaac Bailey,
John Fletcher,
Jonathan White,
Jotham Wilder,
John Warner, Jr.
Mark Heard,

Matthew James,
Nathan Easterbrooks,
Peter Airs,
Peter Manning,
Samuel Barret,
Stanton Carter,
Thomas Goodwin,
William Phelps,
William Deputron,
David Robbins,
Samuel Adams,
John Baker,
William Cally,
John Myres, *seaman*,
David Hosley,
Joseph Beaman,
William Shaw,
Benjamin Ballard,
John Ballard,
Winslow Phelps.

[Mass. Archives, Coat Rolls, LVI, 147.]

Against Sergeant Robert Phelps's name is recorded:

"Wounded and in captivity, June 17;" against David Robbins's, "Killed on Bunker Hill June 17;" against Samuel Adams, John Baker, William Cally and John Myres is written: "Enlisted into the Train, May;" against David Hosley, Joseph Beaman and William Shaw is: "in the works;" against the last three names is written: "in command." John Ballard and Abel Wyman died in the service, the former of small-pox. Sergeant Jeremiah Haskell was an older brother of the captain.

Captain Ephraim Richardson's Company of Lancaster.

Capt. Ephraim Richardson,	Aaron Gary,	Elisha Prentice,
Lt. Seth Heywood,	Asa Rugg,	John English, Salem.
Lt. Eph^m. Boynton,	Benjⁿ. Smith,	John Bunn,
Sergt. Ebenezer Pike,	Calvin Fairbank,	James Sawyer,
" Luther Graves,	David Pike,	Manasah Powers,
" Sam^{ll} Rice,	Eph^m. Goss,	Reuben Moor,
" Falls Wills,	Elijah Dole,	Seth Ross,
Corp. Eph^m. Sawyer,	Elihu Goss, Bolton.	Tho. Blodgett,
" Nath^{ll}. Brown,	Jude Sawyer,	Tho. Cleeland,
" Mathias Larkin,	Isaac Tower,	Tho. Proser,
" Elijah Dreser,	Jacob Wilder,	Benjⁿ Hines,
Fifer Will. Kendall,	Israel Cook,	Tho. Smith,
Drummer John Wheeler,	Josiah Pearson,	Jonathan Phillips,
Amos Dole, Shirley.	Joshua Whitney,	Jacob Piper,
Aaron Glazer, Shrewsbury.	Jonas Beaman,	Luther Rice,
Stephen Harris, Charlemont.	Jacob Kilburn,	Asa Farrar,
Asa Robbinson, Lexington,	John Dunsmore,	Eph^m. Pike,
Benjⁿ. Glazer, Arvinshier.	Israel Maning,	James Wall,
Benjⁿ. Treadway, Princeton.	Jabez Brooks,	Joseph Savage,
Eph^m. Winchupp, Lexington.	Joshua Kendall,	Josiah Brunson.

Captain Richardson died in the service. Nathaniel Brown, Elijah Dole, Jabez Brooks, Stephen Harris and Thomas Smith "went to Quebec, September 11, 1775." Joseph Savage and Josiah Brunson enlisted "in the train." Thomas Proser and James Wall are reported deserters, in May. The transfers to the train were by authority of the Provincial Congress which, May 16, 1775, ordered that any officer of artillery might enlist men from any other arm of the service, taking, however, no more than four from any company. Special inducements were also given to those volunteering for the expedition under Colonel Benedict Arnold, which, by the route of the Kennebec and Chaudiere rivers, traversed the wilderness and joined General Montgomery in the disastrous attack upon Quebec. Those who thus enlisted from Lancaster served in the company of Captain Samuel Ward. Brooks and Brown were wounded, but are again found in their country's service, and Elijah Dole, although taken prisoner, returned in safety, as the following letter proves:

To the Committee for Clothing the Continental Troops:

Gentlemen: The Bearer Elijah Dole belonging to my Company in Colo. Asa Whitcomb's Regiment, engag^d in the American Service immediately after the 19th of April 1775, march^d from Cambridge on September 13th following to Quebec; has never drawn a Coat according to the resolve of the Provincial Congress; wou^d be glad to have the amount of it in money; has apply^d to me to inform your Honours in his behalf.

SETH HEYWOOD, *Lieut.*

LANCASTER, Decr. 2, 1776.

[Mass. Archives, Coat Rolls, LVII, 15.]

Captain James Burt's Company, of Harvard, etc.

Captain James Burt, Harvard.	Jonathan Atherton, Lancaster.
Lieut. Ebenezer Wood, Fitchburg.	Moses Brewer, "
" Jabez Keep, Harvard.	Simeon Hemmenway, Bolton.
Adjutant Isaac Holden, Harvard.	John Bowers, Leominster.
Sergt. Maj. Thos. Hovey, Lunenburg.	Abiathar Houghton, "
Sergt. Thomas Hill, Fitchburg.	Jesse Slack, "
" Samuel Finney, Harvard.	William Slack, "
Corp. William Haskell, "	Jonathan Cummings, Fitchburg.
" Benjamin Willard, "	David Goodel, "
" William Safford, "	Thomas Harris, "
" Reuben Dodge, "	John Hastings, "
Joseph Blanchard, "	Edom Lonnon, "
Solomon Burges, "	Joseph Simons, "
Daniel Burt, "	John Woods, "
Thomas Chamberlain, "	Joseph Woods, "
Jonathan Clark, "	Uriah Holt, Ashburnham.
Joseph Fay, "	Abraham Hager, Shrewsbury.
John Sartle Farwell, "	John Bennett, Westborough.
Joel Finney, "	Nathaniel Tufts, Cambridge.

William Harris,	Harvard.	Abijah Eveonden, Stoughton.	
Joseph Park,	"	Jonathan Stone, Mason.	
James Turner,	"	Thomas Harris, Jr., Boston.	
Joseph Wetherbee,	"	John Adam Rupp,	"
Jeremiah Willard,	"	Henry Rimer, Boston, *dischd Oct*. 6.	
James Willis,	"	Edw. Holowell, Lynn, *deserted May*.	
Andrew Park,	" *died July* 6.		

Quartermaster Jeremiah Laughton, Harvard, *died August* 11.
Sergeant Israel Willard, Lancaster, *died September* 13.
Jacob Davis, Harvard, *discharged October* 6.
Ebenezer Flagg, Lancaster, *enlisted in ye Train*.

[Mass. Archives, Muster Rolls. LVI, 143.]

Captain Jonathan Davis's Company, of Harvard, etc.

Captain Jonathan Davis, Harvard.		Thomas Pratt,	Harvard.
Lieut. Elisha Fullam,	"	Thaddeus Pollard,	"
" John Mead,	"	Benjamin Robens,	"
Sergt. Abraham Munro,	"	James Robens,	"
" Josiah Gates,	"	Gideon Sanderson,	"
" Mikel Ceary, Boston.		Isaac Sanderson,	"
" William Kendall. Townsend.		Manasseh Stow,	"
" Francis Farr, Harvard.		Ebenezer Warner,	"
Corp. Charles Warner, "		Jacob Whitney,	"
" Thomas Etheridge, Boston.		Samuel Worster,	"
" Joshua Bowers, Harvard.		Nathan Osgood, Lancaster.	
" Samuel Forbush,	"	Ephraim Whitcomb,	"
Jonathan Adams,	"	Samuel White, Leominster.	
Ebenezer Davis,	"	Jedediah Felt, N. Rutland.	
Josiah Davis,	"	Joseph Putney, Ashby.	
Jacob Fullam,	"	Joseph Holden, Barrington.	
Reuben Garfield,	"	Thomas Cogney, Sandwich.	
George Gleason,	"	Francis Dizer, Charlestown.	
Solomon Haskell,	"	James Rand,	"
John McCoy,	"	Antony Shezzerel,	"
Aaron Priest,	"	Gilbert Coleworthy, Boston.	
Jacob Priest,	"	Benjamin Dolbee,	"
Job Priest,	"	Ebenezer Gofe,	"
Fifer Abijah Worster,	" *deserted*.	George Treat,	"

Corporal Benjamin Lawrence, Harvard, *died August* 26.
Drummer Cyrus Fairbanks, " *discharged Sept*. 11.

[Mass. Archives, Coat Rolls, LVI, 150.]

Captain Benjamin Hastings's Company, of Bolton, etc.

Capt. Benjamin Hastings,	Josiah Coolidge,	Abner Moore,
Lieut. Jonathan Houghton,	Ephraim Fairbanks,	David Moore,

Lieut. Jonathan Meriam,   John Hastings,   Joseph Pratt,
Sergt. Benjamin Gould,   Joseph Hoar,   William Ross,
  "   Timothy Mosman,   John Houghton,   Benjamin Sawyer,
Corp. William Bigelow,   Joseph Houghton,   Jonas Welch.
  "   William Sawyer,   Abel Moore,   William Whitcomb.
  "   Israel Sawyer,   Sergt. Silas Welch, *died Sept.* 8.
James Bridges,   Amos Southgate, *died Sept.* 21.
Isaac Buck,   Seth Muzzy, Worcester, *died*.
John Chowen,   Elisha Houghton, Lancaster. . . . . . .

[Mass, Archives, Coat Rolls, LVI, 145.]

Hastings's company numbered fifty-six men. Those not here given were from various localities, eleven being from Putney.

Captain Robert Longley's Company, of Bolton, Shirley, etc.

Capt. Robert Longley,   John Coolidge,   John Longley, Jr.
Sergt. Oliver Jewett,   Josiah Edwards, *died.* Gabriel Priest,
Corp. Gardner Moore,   Jacob French,   Joseph Woods,
  "   Joseph Blood,   Richard Hazelton,   Simon Farmer, Harvard.
Thomas Burnam,   Samuel Jones,   Dan¹. Fleeman, Lancaster.
. . . .

[Mass. Archives, Coat Rolls, LVI, 144.]

There are sixty-three names upon this roll, most of those not here given being of Shirley.

Captain David Wilder's Company, of Leominster, Ashburnham, etc.

Capt. David Wilder.   Amos Brown,   Asa Kendall,
Lt. Josiah Gates, Ashburnham.   Stephen Chace,   James Boutell,
Lt. Timothy Boutell,   Nathaniel Chapman, Josiah Colburn,
Sergt. William Warner,   Ebenezer Osgood,   David Fleeman,
  "   Josiah Carter,   David Clark,   Isaac Whitmore,
Corp. Levi Warner,   Joseph Smith,   Joshua White,
  "   Samuel Buss,   Benjamin Stearns,   Luke Johnson,
  "   James Butler,   John Stone,   James Wood,
Drummer Thomas Rogers,   Elisha Carter,   David Hale,
Fifer Abijah Haskell,   Benjamin Hale,   Abel Bigelow,
Charles Evans, *died Sept.* 27. Joshua Prouty,   Luke Wilson,
Jonathan Kendall,   Zebedee Symonds,   Asa Priest,
Jonathan Colburn,   Reuben Gates,   John Battle,
Josiah White,   John Hale,   Levi Blood. . . . .

[Mass. Archives, Coat Rolls, LVI, 148.]

There are sixty-eight names upon this roll, the Ashburnham names being here omitted.

Several soldiers of the Lancaster towns served during the siege of Boston under other regimental commanders. Of Colonel Ephraim Doolittle's command there were from Lancaster : Surgeon Enoch Dole ; Joseph Beaman, in the company of Captain David Wilder of Winchendon ; Joseph Bailey, in Captain John Jones's Princeton company ; Jonathan Knowlton, in Captain Jacob Miller's Holliston company ; John Wheelock, drummer in Captain Adam Wheeler's Hubbardston company. In Captain Josiah Stearns's Lunenburg company were these men of Leominster ;

Sergt. Nathan Colburn,	Ebenezer Houghton,	Francis Parker.
Nathaniel Evans,		

[Mass. Archives, Coat Rolls, LVI, 153-7.]

In the regiment of Colonel Jonathan Ward and the company of Captain Samuel Woods of Northborough, were these Bolton soldiers :

David How,	Moses Hudson,	Solomon Jones,
John Hudson,	Jonas Johnson,	George Sawyer.

These Leominster men were in the same regiment under Captain Job Cushing of Shrewsbury :

Joshua Pierce,	William Prentice.

In the regiment of Colonel William Prescott, Moses Osgood served under Captain Samuel Gilbert of Littleton ; Phineas Whitney of Harvard, with Captain Joseph Moore of Groton ; Abel Wetherbee, Caleb Wetherbee and Joseph Swatridge of Harvard, with Captain Samuel Patch of Stow ; drummer Jonathan Wheelock and fifer Lemuel Gates of Lancaster in Captain Abijah Wyman's Ashby company ; Israel Davenport of Lancaster served in Captain Joseph Butler's company of Colonel John Nixon's regiment.

In Colonel Richard Gridley's regiment of artillery, serving under Captain John Popkin, were :

Corporal Joseph Jones,	John Baker,	Simeon Hemmenway,
Ebenezer Flagg,	Joseph Blanchard,	Joseph Savage.
Samuel Adams,	William Calley,	

Captain Henry Haskell, who led a Shirley company of eighty men at the Lexington Alarm, in Colonel William Prescott's regiment, was at Bunker Hill commanding a company of seventy militia, and for meritorious service was promoted to the lieutenant-colonelcy of Colonel Nicholas Dike's, afterwards the Fifteenth Massachusetts regiment of the Continental army. He removed to Lancaster at the close of the war.

It was generally believed that the Acadians favored the American cause, and it was deemed expedient to ascertain the exact military condition of the province of Nova Scotia and the disposition of its people, with the view of organizing an expedition thither. The delicate task of making the investigation was entrusted in November, 1775, to special commissioners, Aaron Willard of Lancaster and Moses Child. Washington's instructions to them are to be found in The Writings of George Washington, III, 169. Upon reaching the province the commissioners, learning that under recent proclamations of the Governor they were liable to arrest and summary treatment as spies, lost courage for further adventure and returned, reporting in February, upon hearsay evidence, that the Acadians "would engage in the common cause of America, could they be protected," and that the defences of the province were insignificant. [See American Archives, iv, iv, 1150.] A report grounded upon such insufficient reconnoissance could of course afford no basis for military action.

December 1, 1775, the army was seriously weakened by the departure of the Connecticut troops, who insisted upon going home the day their term of enlistment expired. In order that the fortifications of Cambridge and Roxbury might be properly manned, General Washington besought re-enforcements of Massachusetts and New Hampshire, to the number of five thousand men, whose service should end January 15th. The quota of Lancaster under this call was forty-six. The following accounts for eighteen of

those who represented the town, but the others have not
been found :

LANCASTER, March yᵉ 11, 1776.

This may certify that wee whose Names are under written Have Recevᵈ, yᵉ whole of oᴜr wages while wee was under Capt. White from the 8ᵗʰ
of December 1775, to the 17ᵗʰ of January 1776, of Lieut. Samuel Sawyer
we say Recevᵈ.

EPHRAIM WILDER,	NATHAN GEARY,	JONAS BALEY,
TIMOTHY WILDER,	SETH FAIRBANK,	EBENEZER BURPEE,
THOMAS MAY, Jr.,	ASA ROPER,	JOHN STUART,
OLIVER BOWKER,	PETER PRESCOTT,	WILLIAM PALMER,
LEVI WILDER,	HIRAM PRESCOTT,	JOSEPH SEAVER,
OLIVER MOORE,	SAMUEL THOMPSON,	MARY BROOKS.

[Mass. Archives, Muster Rolls, LII, 17 a.]

Again, in January, General Washington called upon
Massachusetts, New Hampshire and Connecticut for temporary re-enforcements of militia to emphasize an offensive
movement upon Boston. Ten regiments were asked for.
Of the six furnished by Massachusetts, one was commanded
by Colonel Josiah Whitney of Harvard. William Warner
of Leominster served in this as adjutant. The quota of
Lancaster was forty-six, of Harvard twenty-five, of Bolton
twenty-three, of Leominster thirteen. No rolls of the
companies are found, but the officers' names are preserved :

*Officers of a company of militia who re-enforced the American Army Feb-
ruary 13, 1776: joined Col. Whitney's Regt.*

Nathaniel White, *capt.* [Lancaster.]
JamesBurt, 1ˢᵗ *lt.* [Harvard.]
Joseph How, 2ᵈ *lt.* [Bolton.]
Ezra Sawyer, *ensign, deceased.* [Lancaster.]
Jonathan Whitcomb, in room of Ezra Sawyer deceased.

[Mass. Archives, Muster Rolls, XXVIII, 61.]

The service ended April 1.

In the re-organization of the army besieging Boston, to
bring the provincial regiments to the standard continental
establishment, consolidation became necessary, entailing
the discharge of many officers. Among the field officers
dropped by the commander-in-chief after consultation with
the division and brigade commanders, was Colonel Asa

Whitcomb of Lancaster. The reason alleged for this re-
tirement was his advanced age. He was at this date in his
fifty-sixth year, and other considerations may perhaps have
had more weight in the advisory council. Colonel Whitcomb's great local popularity seems to have been in large
degree due to noble qualities of heart. He was evidently
a lovable as well as able man, a practical christian, an un-
compromising patriot, a brave and tried soldier. While he
may have been an unexceptional leader of men in days
like those of Lexington and Bunker Hill, it needed but a
brief campaign to show that he was too amiable to become
a military disciplinarian. This weakness is plainly pointed
at in more than one of Washington's orders, is shown
by the record of the regiment, and is incidentally mentioned in a letter from General Greene to Washington,
dated March 11, 1776. The story of Colonel Whitcomb's
re-instatement was told in the New London Gazette, and
copied into the New England Chronicle for Thursday,
January 11, 1776, and other papers of the period.

ANECDOTE.

DEACON WHITCOMB of Lancaster (who was a member of the Assembly
of Massachusetts Bay till the present war commenced, had served in former wars, and been in different engagements), served as Colonel in the
Continental Army; but on account of his age was left out upon the new
regulation. His men highly resented it, and declared they would not list
again after their time was out. The Colonel told them he did not doubt
there were sufficient reasons for the regulation, and he was satisfied with
it; he blamed them for their conduct, and said he would enlist as a private.
A Colonel Brewer heard of it, and offered to resign in favour of Colonel
Whitcomb. The whole coming to General Washington's ears, he allowed
of Colonel Brewer's resignation in Colonel Whitcomb's favour, appointed
the former Barrack-Master till he could further promote him, and ac-
quainted the army with the whole affair in general orders. Let antiquity
produce a more striking instance of true greatness of mind.

Confirmation and correction of this story is found in a
petition preserved in Massachusetts Archives, CLXXXI, 77 :

*To the Hon. Council & House of Representatives in Genl. Court assembled
at Watertown, June 4, 1776:*

The memorial of Jonathan Brewer of Waltham, in the County of Middlesex Colony aforesaid, Esq. Humbly sheweth, That no sooner were Hostilities commenced by the British Troops against the Liberties of America than he Voluntarily enter^d the Field for the Defence thereof & obtained of the Hon^d Congress then convened in this Colony a Colonel's Commission & raised a Regiment, & he flatters himself that he so behaved himself in that Department as to Merit the approbation of his country & in Perticular so distinguished himself in the Memorable Battle of Bunker Hill wherein he had the Honour of a command & was still continued in command by his excellency General Washington, after the Troops were taken into Continental service, and *in complyance with the Request of the Genl*, he gave up his Regiment to the command of Colo. Whitcomb, and at the General's like Request officiated as Barrack Master General until some other suitable Birth should offer, in which case he had the General's Promise for further Promotion, and as Vacancys now exist, your memorialist being heartily inclined to serve his Country further and lend his assistance in this Glorious Struggle for our Invaluable Privelidges, Prays the Hon^d Court would Recommend him the Memorialist to the Honb^le Continental Congress for further Promotion. I have the Promise from Genl. Washington which will be accompan^ed with his Letters to the like Purpose, and as in Duty bound shall ever pray.

J. BREWER, *Col.*

Washington's order was as follows :

Head-Quarters, CAMBRIDGE, November 16, 1775.

Motives of economy rendering it indispensably necessary that many of the Regiments should be reduced, and the whole put upon a different establishment, several deserving officers, not from any demerit, but pure necessity, have been excluded in the new arrangement of the Army; among these was Colonel Whitcomb; but the noble sentiments disclosed by that gentleman upon this occasion, the zeal he has shown in exhorting the men not to abandon the interest of their Country at this important crisis, and his determination to continue in the service even as a private soldier, rather than by a bad example, when the enemy are gathering strength, to put the public affairs to hazard—when an example of this kind is set it not only entitles a gentleman to particular thanks, but to particular rewards; in the bestowing of which, Colonel Jonathan Brewer is entitled to no small share of credit, in readily giving up to Colonel Whitcomb the Regiment which he was appointed to command. Col. Whitcomb, therefore is henceforward to be considered as Colonel of that regiment which was intended for Colonel Brewer; and Colonel Brewer will be appointed Barrack-Master until something better worth his acceptance can be provided.

[American Archives, IV, III, 1614.]

In the old army organization, of thirty-eight infantry

regiments Colonel Whitcomb's had been the Twenty-third;
under the new establishment it became the Sixth Foot,
there being twenty-seven infantry regiments in all, of eight
companies each. Although the favor of the commander-
in-chief had retained their old colonel in the service, his
men nearly all returned to their homes at the expiration of
the eight months for which they had enlisted. In the
weekly return of January 8, 1776, the regiment numbered
but three hundred and forty-seven all told, and but a single
one of the old company officers, Captain Abner Cranson,
continued in the command.

The Lancaster regiment of militia, now called the Second Worcester County Regiment, was re-organized in
March, Josiah Whitney of Harvard being chosen colonel,
Ephraim Sawyer of Lancaster, lieutenant-colonel, Silas
Bailey of Bolton, first-major, and Ebenezer Jones, second-
major. The line officers were commissioned as follows,
the third and eighth companies being of Harvard, the
fourth and seventh of Bolton, and the other six of Lancaster :

1
John White, Jr., *capt.*
Daniel Rugg, Jr., *lieut.*
Salmon Godfrey,   "

2
John May, *capt.*
Timothy Heyward, *lieut.*
Solomon Stewart,   "

3
Samuel Hill, *capt.*
Amos Fairbank, *lieut.*
John Daby,   "

4
Jonathan Houghton, *capt.*
Richard Townsend, *lieut.*
Thomas Osburn,   "

5
Daniel Goss, *capt.*
Samuel Wilder, Jr., *lieut.*
Levi Wilder,   "

6
Fortunatus Eager, *capt.*
Edward Newton, *lieut.*
Jabez Fairbank,   "

7
David Nourse, *capt.*
Joseph Howe, *lieut.*
William Pollard, *lieut.*

8
Hezekiah Whitney, *capt.*
Ephraim Davis, *lieut.*
Jabez Keep,   "

9	10
Wm. Greenleaf, *capt.*	Manasseh Sawyer, *capt.*
Samuel Joslin, *lieut.*	Elisha Sawyer, Jr., *lieut.*
Nathaniel Sawyer, *lieut.*	Ephraim Sawyer, Jr., *lieut.*

The names of many of these officers are found later in
various short service rolls, the militia being frequently
called upon to protect the New England states from threatened invasion. In June, 1776, Ephraim Sawyer, Jr.,
received a commission as lieutenant in the Fifteenth Massachusetts, Colonel Timothy Bigelow's regiment in the
Continental army. Samuel Sawyer was made captain of
the second militia company, to fill a vacancy caused by the
removal of John May from town.

Colonel Asa Whitcomb's regiment, which had for several months been in the intrenchments upon Prospect Hill,
was transferred to the brigade of General Thomas near the
close of January, and, on February 22, 1776, was ordered
to Roxbury, where it occupied the mansion known as Governor Shirley's residence. Before dawn on March 5, the
anniversary of the Boston Massacre, it was marched to relieve the five thousand men who had in one night, "with
an expedition equal to that of the genii belonging to Alad-
din's wonderful lamp"—as a British officer of distinction
wrote home—thrown up at Dorchester Heights two re-
doubts commanding the city of Boston. These were
wholly built of timber and fascines, the earth being at the
time frozen to a great depth. James Thacher, the surgeon's mate of the regiment, has recorded how, upon the
discovery of these frowning works at daylight, the forts
and fleet of the enemy opened upon them with all their
available artillery :

Cannon shot are continually rolling and rebounding over the hill; and
it is astonishing to observe how little our soldiers are terrified by them. . .
The royal troops are perceived to be in motion, as if embarking to pass
the harbor and land on Dorchester shore, to attack our works. The hills
and elevations in this vicinity are covered with spectators to witness deeds
of horror in the expected conflict. His Excellency General Washington
is present, animating and encouraging the soldiers, and they in return

manifest their joy, and express a warm desire for the approach of the enemy; each man knows his place, and is resolute to execute his duty.

General Howe was prevented from the contemplated assault by a fierce easterly storm that lashed the waters of the harbor into waves too formidable for heavily laden boats to encounter, and the mettle of the militia was not tested. The day passed, the works were enlarged and strengthened, and the tired regiments were relieved by others. The end of the long siege was evidently near at hand. Lancaster was to lose one more of her sons, however, before the victory. In the Memoirs of Major-General Heath, under date March 9, 1776, is written :

This night a strong detachment went down to open a work on Nook Hill in Dorchester still nearer to Boston. Some of the men imprudently kindled a fire behind the hill previous to the hour for breaking of ground. The enemy discovered the light of the fire; and there was, during the evening and night, a continual roar of cannon and mortars from the castle and guns on Boston Neck, south end of that town ; as well as from the Americans at Roxbury, Cobble Hill and Leechmore's Point at Cambridge. The second shot from the British at the old fortifications south end of the town of Boston killed 4 Americans who were standing around the fire before mentioned at Nook Hill; one of whom was Dr. Dow of Connecticut.

For *Dr. Dow* should here be read *Doctor Enoch Dole* of Lancaster, surgeon of Colonel Ephraim Doolittle's regiment, as an epitaph in the old cemetery at Littleton tells :

Here lies yᵉ Body of Dr Enoch Dole of Lancaster A. E. 33 Years 5 mo & 3 days, he unfortunately fell with 3 others yᵉ 9ᵗʰ of March 1776 by a cannon Ball from our cruel and unnatural Foes yᵉ British Troops while on his Duty on Dorchester Point.

> No warning giv'n ! Unceremonious fate !
> A sudden rush from Life's meredian joys.
> A wrench from all we are ! from all we love
> What a change
> From yesterday !* Thy daring hope so near,
> Long labour'd prize ! O how ambition flushed
> Thy glowing cheek ambition truly great,
> Of virtuous praise.
> And oh ! ye last, last, what (can word express
> Thought read) ye last, last silence of a friend.

* Meaning his entrance into Boston which so soon took Place & on which his Heart was much sett.

Colonel Whitcomb's regiment was one of three detailed to garrison Boston, and on March 20 it entered the town, greeted with a joyful welcome by the impoverished citizens, as it marched through the squalid streets desolated by a ten months' siege. Comfortable quarters in unoccupied houses were assigned the soldiers, and as small-pox was prevalent the surgeons were kept busy inoculating for that disease. Occasional events of interest relieved the commonplace of garrison duties. Thirteen vessels of the British fleet, including the ship Renown of fifty guns, remained off Nantasket, blockading the harbor. June 13 an expedition under Colonel Whitcomb, and including a part of his regiment, embarking from Long Wharf, proceeded by night to Long Island, and throwing up earth-works planted a battery, which opened upon the surprised Commodore Banks in the morning and compelled him to make hasty departure.

July 18, the Declaration of American Independence was formally proclaimed from the State House balcony, the commands of Colonels Whitcomb's and Paul Dudley Sargent's parading on King street in thirteen divisions, with a section of artillery which fired a salute of thirteen guns. The regiment had gone through the dangers from small-pox with the loss of one man only, a negro. August 7, with the inspiration of drum and fife and flying colors to prevent sorrow at enforced departure from showing too prominently, it marched for Ticonderoga. Arriving there about the first of September, it spent the winter in comfortable log huts, strengthening the works, and awaiting an enemy that showed no disposition to assault that formidable position. Colonel Whitcomb certainly added nothing here to his reputation as an officer. Before entering upon an account of the event that closed his military history, a brief sketch of the habits and peculiarities of the New England soldier may be necessary. The distinction between the military organizations North and South was not more marked at the

10

outset of our late civil war than it was in the days of 1776. In that earlier time, also, the Northern soldiers were to the Southern officer fanatics, clod-hoppers and mud-sills; and the better uniformed and more rigidly disciplined Southerners were to the Northern patriots "buck-skins" and "macaronies." The heirs of Puritanism scoffed at the bumptious coxcombry of their Southern allies, and were stung with retaliatory sneers at their own bumpkin ways and stinginess. The two classes often evinced for each other a dislike only less intense than that they naturally felt for the "lobsters," as the British regulars were nicknamed. It was the old, old quarrel—Stoic versus Epicurean, swaggering Cavalier jostling against psalm-singing Roundhead. The New England regiment was a voluntary association of equals enlisted in patriotic duty for a few months, usually less than a year. The officers, from colonel down, were practically elected by the votes of their neighbors—by men as well educated and of as good family as themselves. To gain a captaincy popularity with the mass of the people was essential, and aristocratic lineage or mien counted naught. A brave, intelligent race, and passionately patriotic, the soldiers excelled as pioneers or skirmishers, or in defensive warfare, and wherever independent action and judgment could most avail. Their discipline was, however, of the loosest description. The Southern officers usually stood upon an entirely different plane—recognizing no equality with their men, accustomed to deference and rigidly exacting it. These officers, gentlemen by accident of birth and generally by education, naturally viewed with prejudice the social equality displayed among their northern allies, and the epithet, *Yankee*, fell from their scornful lips with provoking tone and frequency. A Maryland subaltern wrote in his diary:

. . . . . On entering the camp near Boston I was struck with the familiarity which prevailed among the soldiers and officers of all ranks; from the colonel to the private I observed but little distinction; and I could not refrain from remarking to the young gentlemen with whom I made acquaintance, that the military discipline of the troops was not so conspicuous as the civil subordination of the community in which I had lived.

Colonel Whitcomb is described by the surgeon of the regiment as "a serious, good man, but is more conversant with the economy of domestic life than the etiquette practised in camp." Each officer was entitled to the services of a private soldier as his waiter, and a regimental commander had two. Colonel Whitcomb selected his own sons for this service, and one of them wishing to turn an honest penny by plying his trade of shoemaking, the good country deacon saw no impropriety in allowing the cobbler's bench to be set up in the room he occupied as regimental headquarters. This republican simplicity at once excited the fiercest contempt of the officers of other organizations in the encampment, and one night the lieutenant-colonel of Wayne's regiment, when half crazy with drink, made an assault upon the offensive bench, which having succumbed to his valiant sword, he knocked the colonel down, and ended by calling out some of his own battalion and raising a bloody riot. Sundry papers in Massachusetts Archives, CLXXXII, 205–209, give details of the shameful occurrence, selections from which follow :

Deposition of Ensign Ralph H. Bowles.

In the evening of the 25th of Decr Last I Past on the Parade of Collo Whitcomb's Regt, to my Lodgings & observed that the above Regt. was still & Quiet & Returned to my hutt to Repose myself for sleep. But after Being in Bed a few Moments I heard a Person Repeatedly say "Don't kill me," & then I heard a Person which I Thought was Coll. Whitcomb say " what is the Rout?" & then I started up in Order to Dress myself & the next answer was, " Dam you do you take his Part." & the above Coll. said " Don't strike me," & then I heard a Blow, & I Repard to the Door of the hutt & saw Collo. Whitcomb on the Ground & Lt Collo. Craig kicking him & striking him with his sword Drawn & then I Looking toward Major Whiting's hutt saw two Men with Drawn Swords in their hands which was offrs. & a Number of soldiers with them of the second Pennsylvania Battalion & some of them with Guns, & their Language was "Dam the Yankeys," & Began to demolish the hutt that I lodged in. But by speaking to them they Quitted & advanced to the hutt of Capt. Danforth & then I Repared to the Markee of Doctor Townsend. But hearing Lt

Collo Craig say to the second Pennsylvania Battalion, "Dam you turn out," & in a very short Time a Number of Armed Men with Bayonetts fixt came from the said Battalion headed by said Collo. & then entering the hutts of offrs. & soldiers Plundering & Firing into the same & Daming & stricking both offrs. & soldiers that was Peacably in their hutts. & after Marching several times acrost the Parade they Returned to their Habitations.   RALPH H. BOWLES, *Ensign.*

Deposition of Captain Lemuel Trescot.

I Lemuel Trescott Late of Collo Whitcomb's Regiment testify and declare that on the evening of the 25th day of Dec 1776, being at Ticonderoga I was in my tent & heard a noise as of somebody fighting with swords, upon which I turned out of my tent & saw Lt. Col. Craige calling upon his men to turn out. I also heard him order sd. men so turned out to fire upon Coll Whitcomb's encampment which they accordingly did & committed great disorder there, in a riotous and hostile manner passed thro sd encampment abusing all they met with. The deponent further said that he saw sd Craige personally abuse sd Whitcomb, calling him "damned old scoundrel," that he took him by the ear pulled him & with his drawn sword or cutlass, as the deponent supposed, cut the sd Whitcomb's ear, & otherwise so abused him as to leave him in a most bloody condition, and all this outrage committed by said Craige appeared to me to be without any provocation from any person whatsoever.

                                    LEMUEL TRESCOT.

At the close of a similar deposition, from Major Daniel Whiting of Dedham, is this statement:

. . . . . Col Whitcomb immediately entered a complaint against the said Thomas Craige to the Commandant & the said Thomas was arested, but as Colo Whitcomb was obliged to return home, & the Tryal of the said Thomas was not likely to take place soon, the said Colo Whitcomb withdrew his complaint so far as concerned himself & received satisfaction for himself of the said Thomas.

James Thacher gives a whimsical account of how this satisfaction was managed:

Colonel C. sent some soldiers into the woods to shoot a fat bear, with which he made an entertainment, and invited Colonel W. and his officers to partake of it; this effected a reconciliation; and Colonel W. was induced to overlook the high-handed assault upon his own person and on the lives of his soldiers.

How many and what Lancaster men followed the fortunes of the regiment to the end of its service, the rolls that are extant are insufficient to show; but they were doubtless very few. The consolidation, and expiration of brief terms of enlistment, totally changed the regimental roster, so that not one of the original Lancaster officers is found at Ticonderoga. Colonel Whitcomb's services ended April 1, 1777, and he returned to his farm, then the largest in the second precinct of the town. He experienced some trouble, because of imperfect records, in settling his accounts as Paymaster-General of the Massachusetts forces, an office which he held for some time during the siege of Boston. No suspicion, however, of his entire integrity, his unselfish patriotism, or his bravery, ever dimmed his reputation. Before the close of the war he removed to Princeton, served that town in the legislature, and there he died March 16, 1804, at the ripe age of eighty-four years.

IV. THE CAMPAIGN OF 1776—TOWN ANNALS 1776-8.

After the departure of the American army serious apprehensions arose lest the British should return to re-occupy Boston. The militia were therefore summoned to the defence of the coast and harbor; while the continental regiments which had been left in occupation of the city constructed defensive fortifications about it. To garrison Hull and other important points in the approaches to the harbor, two battalions were raised in April, 1776, the complement of each being fixed at eight companies of ninety men. They were commanded by Colonels Josiah Whitney and Thomas Marshall. A memorial of the Harvard colonel, found in Mass. Archives, CLXXXI, 293, dated "Camp at Hull, Oct. 29, 1776," complains that his men are not paid "continental pay" as are other troops about them, but the smaller stipend allowed by the provincial laws. He states that the battalion took the field early in the spring, and that their duty has been hazardous and fatiguing. In this regiment Captain William Warner of Winchendon commanded a company, in which were:

LANCASTER SOLDIERS.

Lieut. Jonathan Sawyer,	Jeremiah Haskell,	Peter Manning,
Sergt. Abijah Phillips,	Samuel Jewett,	John Nichols,
Drum^r. John Wheeler,	Samuel Johnson,	Moses Osgood,
John Chowen,	Thomas Kendall,	Edward Thomas,
Nathan Esterbrooks,	John Manning,	Robert Younger.

LEOMINSTER SOLDIERS.

Sergt. Benjamin Stearns,	Nathaniel Evans,	Joseph Robbins,
Corp. Jonathan Kendall,	Edward Fuller,	Silas Smith,
" David Clark,	Israel Hale,	Phillip Sweetser,
John Bowers,	Robert Houghton,	William Warner.
Silas Carter,	David Johnson,	

BOLTON SOLDIERS.

Levi Gates,	Ezra Whitcomb,	Silas Whitcomb.
	Simeon Gates,	

HARVARD SOLDIERS.

Joseph Fry,	William Stevens.

In Captain Aaron Guild's company of the same regiment were:

LANCASTER SOLDIERS.

Benjamin Ballard,	Amos Rugg,	Daniel Wyman.
John Bowers,	Jonathan Wheelock,	

BOLTON SOLDIERS.

Richard Hazeltine,	Benjamin Sawyer,	Robert Townsend.
Willard Moore,	Joseph Sawyer,	

[Mass. Archives, Muster Rolls, XXIII, 200; XXIV, 17–83; XXV, 53.]

In Colonel Thomas Marshall's battalion, at Hull, was a company of seventy-nine men, commanded by Captain Andrew Haskell of Lancaster, in which were the following:

LANCASTER MEN.

Capt. Andrew Haskell,	William Ball,	Carter Knight,
Lieut. John Hewitt,	Thomas Bennett,	Daniel Knight,
Sergt. Jonas Johnson,	John Coolidge,	Judah Piper,
" David Hosley,	Francis Davis,	William Richardson,
Corp. Elisha Rugg,	Gershom Flagg,	Levi Warner,
" John Willard,	John Fletcher,	John Warner,
Drum^r. Benjamin James,	William Flood,	Enoch Whitcomb,
John Baker,	Thomas Houghton,	Jotham Wilder,
David Baldwin,		James Willard.

LEOMINSTER MEN.

James Boutell,	Abiathar Houghton,	Benjamin Stewart,
John Buss,	Michael Nichols,	John Stone,
—— Graves,	Levi Phelps,	James Wilder.

HARVARD MEN.

| Simon Farmer, | Jonathan Simons, | Consider Turner. |

BOLTON MEN.

Corporal Joseph Wood, John Barnard.

[Mass. Archives, Muster Rolls, XXV. 71.]

John Whitcomb and Samuel Baily of Lancaster were "at the castle."

A resolve of the General Court, June 25, 1776, responsive to a request of the Continental Congress for five thousand militia to co-operate with the armies at New York and in the department of Canada, made it incumbent upon Lancaster to furnish seventy-two men. To Harvard were allotted thirty-six, to Bolton thirty-three, to Leominster twenty-four. A bounty of three pounds was promised each volunteer, and eighteen shillings were allowed each soldier for the use of arms and accoutrements, if furnishing them himself. The term of service ended December 1, 1776. Four battalions were destined for Canada, and three, including all companies from Worcester county, were to serve at New York in the brigade of General John Fellows. Captain Samuel Sawyer of Lancaster with eighty, Captain Jabez Keep of Harvard with eighty-two, and Captain Jonathan Houghton of Bolton with seventy-five men marched July 22, to join their regiment, which was commanded by Colonel Jonathan Smith. The lieutenant-colonel, Robert Longley, and the surgeon, Daniel Greenleaf, were citizens of Bolton. These companies, entering service for four months, contained a few soldiers of experience, but consisted chiefly of a hasty levy of farmers fresh from the furrowed fields, knowing nothing of camp discipline and little of the value of system and co-operation. They might have defended intrenchments with success, but could not withstand the onset in open field of the splendidly equipped and disciplined Hessian corps. They participated in the unfortunate affair of Kips Bay, September 15. Captain Sawyer's order book has been preserved in the state archives. The roll of his company, nearly all of Lancaster, follows:

Capt. Samuel Sawyer,	Joseph Houghton,	Elijah Wilder,
Lieut. Salmon Godfrey,	Ephraim Cheney,	John Joslyn,
2d Lieut. Nathl. Sawyer,	Simeon Burt,	Nathan Parmiter,
Ensign Ebenezer Belknap,	Joseph Beaman,	Josiah Winn,
Sergt. Benjn. Parkings,	Samuel Holman,	Jacob Piper,
" Elisha Allen,	Levi Wilder,	William Fairbank,
" Joseph Fairbanks,	Calvin Moor,	Abel Bigelo,
" Artemas Maynard,	Hezekiah Whetcomb,	Daniel Page,
Corp. John Bennitt,	David Houghton,	Jonas Rice,
" Amos Knight,	Jonathan Ross,	Roger Bartlitt,
" Samuel Chirchel,	Joseph Wilder,	Luther Rice,
" Elijah Bawl,	Jacob Phelps,	Thomas Blodget,
Drummer Seth Ross,	Samuel Bowers,	Stanton Brown,
Fifer Calvin Kilburn,	Joshua Rugg,	Joseph Bennitt,
Peter Airs,	John Bowers,	Nathaniel Beaman,
Jonathan Wilder,	Thomas Mears,	Joseph Wood,
Samuel Carter,	Edmund Larkin,	Jonathan Emerson,
John Brooks,	Asa Priest,	Aaron Glazier,
Reuben Lipingwell,	Joseph Hoar,	Abner Moors,
Timothy Stearns,	Thomas Hale,	Ephraim Rugg,
David Whitcomb,	Jasher Wyman,	Nathaniel White,
Jacob Swear,	Samuel Flood,	Jonas Wyman,
Benjamin Priest,	Shubal Bayley,	Ephraim Powers,
James Clerk,	Elisha Whitney,	Joseph Persons,
Jonas Brooks,	Benjamin Smith,	Abel Wright,
John Thurston,	Nathaniel Jones,	Jacob Robbins.
Samuel Johnson,		

Jacob Piper, David Houghton, Stanton Brown and Ephraim Rugg were reported "missing September 15, on the retreat from New York." As their names do not again appear during the war, it is probable that they were killed or captured at Kip's Bay. Benjamin Smith died October 15; Josiah Winn and Hezekiah Whitcomb on November 8; and John Bennett at a date unrecorded. Corporal Knight and Joseph Beaman were discharged November 12.

These men may have been wounded in some of the engagements in which the brigade is known to have taken part. Among the regimental orders, one dated September 6 is characteristic of the times :

> Jonas Brooks, soldier in Capt. Sawyer's Company, convicted by Regimental Court Martial, whereof Capt. Dewey was President, of theft, Sentenced Him to Receive fifteen Lashes on the Naked Back and to Return stolen goods to the owner. The Col. approves the above sentence, and orders it to be put into Execution at the Head of the Regiment at Halfe after 5. O.clock in the afternoon, then to be Discharged and Return to his Duty.

Corporal punishment was of quite frequent occurrence, but, except for the very gravest offences, no more than thirty-nine lashes were ever inflicted. The regimental drum-major was charged with the duty of carrying out the sentence, and by his collusion the punishment was sometimes only severe in the disgrace attached to it. Surgeon James Thacher relates that the victims about to come under the cat customarily placed a lead bullet between their teeth, which was supposed to help them in concealing lack of fortitude in suffering.

The roll of Captain Jabez Keep has not been found. That of Captain Jonathan Houghton is in the orderly book of Nathaniel Longley, Mass. Archives, Worcester Rolls, LVI, and LV, 20, 22, 25. The majority of the company were from Westborough and Northborough. The Bolton names are these :

Capt. Jonathan Houghton,	Jonas Bruce,	Levi Meriam,
Sergt. Samuel Baker,	Benjamin Gould,	Stephen Pratt,
" William Sawyer,	John Greenleaf,	Eliakim Rice,
Corp. Nathaniel Longley,	John Hastings,	William Ross,
Silas Bailey,	John Houghton,	Joseph Rugg,
William Bigelow,	Edward Johnson,	George Sawyer,
Samuel Blood,	Jonas Johnson,	Jesse Walcot,
Adam Bartlet,	Solomon Jones,	Deliverance Wheeler,
Benjamin Bruce, Jr.	Joseph Keyes,	William Whitcomb,
Benjamin Bruce,	John Longley,	Ephraim Whitney.
Daniel Bruce,	David Maynard,	

The General Court, July 10, 1776, ordered two regiments to be raised to strengthen the northern army under General Philip Schuyler at Ticonderoga, by drafting every twenty-fifth man of the train band and alarm lists. When the Council sought colonels for these regiments, Aaron Willard and Samuel Brewer were selected. Captain Aaron Willard, Jr., scarred with the terrible wound received at the battle of Ticonderoga in 1758, lived in Lancaster, a near neighbor to his noted cousins, Abijah, Levi and Abel. Unlike them, however, he was an ardent patriot. He accepted the colonelcy proffered him, but by accident "put his knee out of joint," and his command was led to its destination by other field officers. (See Council Records, xix, 141, 156, 167, 207.)

The Lancaster men were not, however, in that command. August 18, Captain Manasseh Sawyer marched with ninety-two men, drafted under the order of July 10, from Lancaster and neighboring towns. The company served for eight months, being for most of the time stationed at Dorchester Heights, and attached to the regiment of Colonel Nicholas Dike, of which Henry Haskell was lieutenant-colonel. Enrolled in this company were :

OF LANCASTER.

Captain Manasseh Sawyer,	Nathaniel Burpee,	David Pike,
Corporal John Loring,	Stanton Carter,	Nathaniel Roper,
" Elias Farnsworth,	Reuben Geary,	Thomas Sawtell,
Drummer Timothy Wilder,	Darius Harvey,	Abner Sawyer,
Fifer Oliver Bowker,	James Houghton. Jr.	Thomas Sawyer,
" Elisha White,	Nathaniel Houghton,	John Snow,
David Bennett, Jr.	Thomas Houghton,	Joseph Wheelock,
William Boardman,	Joshua House,	Ephraim Wilder,
David Amory Boynton,	Benjamin May,	Joshua Willard,
Ebenezer Burpee,	Levi May,	John Winn.
Elijah Burpee,	Samuel Mosman,	

OF LEOMINSTER.

Ensign Josiah Carter,	Thomas Joslin,	Joseph Sweetser,
Sergeant Jeremiah Underwood,	Jacob Spafford,	Philemon Sweetser,
David Boutell,		John Whitcomb.

OF BOLTON.

Sergeant Gardner Moore,	David Hemmenway,	John Powers,
" Abel Piper,	Nathaniel Holman,	Peter Stanhope,
Corporal Henry Powers,	Jonas Houghton,	Abel Whitcomb,
Joseph Amsden,	Jesse Jewett,	Richard Whitcomb,
John Barnard,	John Moore,	Abel Wilder,
William Coolidge,	Abel Priest,	Paul Wilson.
James Fife,		

OF HARVARD.

Sergeant Daniel Laughton,	Philemon Priest,	Abel Wetherbee,
Corporal Reuben Conant,	Jonathan Puffer,	Amos Wetherbee,
Joseph Atherton,	Benjamin Stow,	Josiah Whitney,
John Hill,	Manasseh Stow,	Salmon Whitney.
John Laughton,		

In Captain John Hartwell's company of the same regiment were :

OF LANCASTER.

Sergeant Sam. Dickenson,	Benjamin Farmer,	John Priest,
Nathan Easterbrook,	Simon Farmer,	Benjamin Priest,
William Flood,	John Nicholls,	John Warner,
Daniel Fleeman,	Eleazar Priest,	Daniel Willard.

OF HARVARD.

Samuel Farnsworth,   Joseph Farnsworth.

Joshua Johnson was in Captain Joseph Stetson's company, and Benjamin Warner, of Harvard, in Captain Bang's company of this regiment. Ebenezer Prescott of Lancaster died October 15, 1776, at Dorchester, in the service.

[Mass. Archives, Muster Rolls, III, 148, 174, 176, and XXVI, 77, 419-422.]

A few Lancaster men are found credited as serving in the Canada expedition of 1776: Jacob Bennett and John Johnson in Captain Lamb's company: William Flood and John Moore in Captain Morgan's ; Sergeant Luther Fairbanks in Captain Topham's ; Elijah Dole in Captain Ward's.

In the regiment of militia commanded by Colonel James Converse of Brookfield, of which Ephraim Sawyer of

Lancaster was lieutenant-colonel, the following officers were serving at Dobb's Ferry and Tarrytown:

Capt. Daniel Goss, *of Lancaster.* Capt. Samuel Hill, *of Harvard.*
Lieut. Jabez Fairbank, *do.* Lieut. Simon Cooper, *do.*
Lieut. Joseph How, *of Bolton.* Lieut. Luke Richardson, *Leominster.*

[Mass. Archives, Muster Rolls, LII, 46.]

No roll of their companies is found.

Captain David Nurse, with a company of sixty-four men, nine of whom were from Princeton, the rest from Bolton and Harvard, served, "in the Jerseys," from December 12, 1776, to March 26, 1777. The following is a copy of his roll:

Capt. David Nurse,
Lieut. Ephraim Davis,
Lieut. Thomas Mason,
Sergt. Simeon Willard,
  " David Moore,
  " Isaac Norcross,
  " John Townsend,
Corp. Philemon Priest,
  " Isaac Moore,
  " Charles Warner,
  " Levi Fairbank,
Drumr. Jacob Norcross,
Fifer Barnabas Sawyer.
Carpenters, James Burt,
  William Burt,
  John Wilson,
  Phineas Warner,
  Joseph Houghton,
  William Ross,
  Oliver Willard,
Teamsters, John Trask,
  Jeremiah Bridge,
  Joseph Blanchard,

Teamsters,
  Samuel Davis,
  William Parkis,
  Joseph Fry,
  Jabez Keep,
Privates,
  Solomon Haskell,
  Stephen Whitney,
  Josiah Hovey,
  Jotham Johnson,
  Dwelly Turner,
  Daniel Gibbs,
  Wm. Stevens, *died.*
  Simon Whitney,
  Joshua Mosman,
  Jona. Whitcomb,
  Jotham Whitcomb,
  Jabez Fairbanks,
  John Hill,
  Joseph Woods,
  George Sawyer,
  Joseph Keys,

Oliver Mosman,
John Cooledge,
Joseph Sawyer,
Carter Knights,
Josiah Maynard,
Joseph Gibbs,
William Chace,
Abel Harrington,
Jonathan Farnsworth,
Benjamin Bridges,
Jonathan Symonds,
Abel Baker,
Abel Priest,
Samuel Atherton,
Manasseh Farnsworth,
Jonathan Hutchins,
John Whitney,
Robert Townsend,
John Burnam,
Thomas Burges,
Luther Parmenter,
Joseph Ward.

[Papers of Capt. David Nurse.]

The inconveniences and serious dangers incident to the system of short enlistments popular in New England — and at first favored generally through dread of a standing army — had long been a source of disquiet to Washington.

Congress, reluctantly convinced of the decay of that martial spirit which had characterized the outbreak of revolution, at length saw that the depleted ranks of the patriot army must be permanently filled and rigid discipline enforced, or success was hopeless. In the autumn of 1776 every exertion was put forth to replace the state militia whose terms of service expired during the year, with regular troops enlisted for three years or during the war. To encourage volunteering, twenty dollars bounty, one suit of clothes per year, and one hundred acres of land were promised each soldier enlisting for the war. The monthly pay of the troops, in addition to subsistence, was established as follows :

Colonel,	$75.00	Captain,	$40.00	Sergeant,	$8.00
Lieut.-Colonel,	60.00	Adjutant,	40.00	Corporal,	7.33
Major,	50.00	Lieutenant,	27.00	Drummer and Fifer,	7.33
Surgeon,	33 33	Ensign,	20.00	Privates,	6.67

The army was re-organized into eighty-eight battalions of infantry, of six hundred and eighty men each ; and the proportion demanded of Massachusetts was fifteen regiments, or more than one-sixth of the whole number to be raised. December 27, 1776, sixteen additional infantry battalions were authorized, three of which were assigned to Massachusetts. To hasten enlistments, which were at first discouragingly slow, the province also offered a bounty of twenty dollars, and promised to make good any deficiency caused by depreciation of the paper currency in which wages were paid. The quota of each town was fixed, one man in every seven being required for service. As time went on, the selectmen or a specially chosen committee were authorized to bid for recruits, and offered special bounties even for the shorter terms of service ; and individuals who were drafted often hired substitutes for the whole or part of a "turn of duty." Many receipts for such bounty and substitution are extant, a few specimens of which are here given :

LANCASTER, Feb: yᵉ: 1ˢᵗ: 1777.
Received of Levi More twelve Pounds for going into the three year service.   LUTHER FAIRBANKS.

LANCASTER, April 26, 1777.
This may Certify that I have Recᵈ of Mr. Peter Thurston the sum of Ten Dollars for Doing two months' Service to Rhode Island for him.
                          Witnes my hand   JOSIAH PHELPS.
Attest LUKE WILDER.

LANCASTER, January 31, 1777.
Then Recᵈ of Thomas Gates the sum of six pound thirteen Shillings and four pence for Doing a turn in the Continental Servis, Eighteen months from the Date hearof as Witnes my hand.
                                              DANEL WYMAN.

LANCASTER, June 21 Day, 1776.
These may Sertyfay whome it may Consarn that Dannel Wyman this day have Inlisted under me In the Arme, In behalf of Cap Thomas Gatts and Exsepted by the Subscriber to do a turn for the above Cap Gatts.
    In aknogement whairof   TIMO MOSMAN, *Leftenant.*
test. JOHN MOORE   JOSIAH WHITNEY *Col.*

LANCASTER, June 21, 1776.
I Received of Capt. Thomas gatts three pounds in full for doing a turn for him till the first day of December next as witnes my Hand
    test. JOHN MOORE.   DANEL WYMAN

BOLTON, August the 1 : 1776.   then Recᵈ of Lieut. James Goddard Eight pound for half a turn of Soldring a-going to Canaday. I say Recᵈ By me   EZEKEIL FOSGAT.

Occasionally a learned medical authority was invoked to aid some citizen in escaping from military duty :

this may Sartify the Gentelmen whom it may Concarn that Mr John Nurse has a wickness in his Eye and is Lame and by Reson of them things in my Judgement is not fitt to Do Duity as a Solger in the malishea
    STOW Augᵗ 21ʳʰ 1776   CHARLES WHITMAN *Phasihion*

But John paid a substitute, in spite of the "Phasihion," and got this receipt :

This may certify that I Solomon Jones Received two pounds twelve shillings and six Pence of John Nurse for doing a quarter of a turn in the Continental Service to be done at New York.
                                              SOLOMON JONES.

BOLTON, July ye 2nd. 1776

Then Rec^d. of my Honoured Father Sam^{ll} Baker Twelve pounds Including the Bounty of three pounds From this Govrment For my Intring into the Service of s^d Cont Govrment in an Expedition to New York in ye Room and Stead of Abel Baker a minor and Son of my said Father.

Rec^d p me   SAM^{LL}. BAKER JR.

Occasionally the bondman's services were sold by his master in behalf of the nation's freedom :

WALTHAM, May 23^d 1777

Then Received of Joseph How and Eliakim Atherton the sum of Thirty Pounds l. m. for my Servent negro man Named York Rugles who Has inlisted and passed muster Before Coll. James Barrat of Concord for the tarm of three years in Cap Ashley's Company of Coll. Badison's [Patterson's] Rigement in the Continental armey. I further Promis and Say that my Negro York I sett to the afors^d How and Atherton to do a turn for Bolton in the Continental armey as witnis my hand. [Signature missing.]

To insure the correct apportionment of quotas throughout the commonwealth, a census of the male citizens of military age was ordered, returns of which were made to the Secretary of State and the commander of the military district to which the town belonged.

LANCASTER, Sept. 8, 1777, State of Massachusetts Bay.

According to a Resolve of this state of Dec. 9, 1776, Directed to the Selectmen to take the Number of their Male Inhabitants from sixteen years old and upwards, and Deliver the same into the Secretary's office on or before the Last Day of January 1777, in Compliance with orders Rec^d. from the general assembly Dated July 3, 1777, Directed to the Selectmen to make a Return of all the male Inhabitants from sixteen years old and upwards, the amount of the whole of the male inhabitants in the town of Lancaster at Dec. 9 1776, was six Hundred and fifty-nine ; the selectmen would inform the hon'able court that we Never Rec^d any orders from the assembly Before that Baring Date July 3. 1777, therefore we Beg to be excused from any Neglect in Regard to orders from said assembly.

EPH^M. WILDER,
W^M. GREENLEAF,
SOLOMON JEWETT,
NATH. BEAMAN,

} *Selectmen of Lancaster.*

[Sworn to before "W^m. Dunsmoor, Justice Peace."

[Massachusetts Archives, CLXI, 148, 154.]

There is added in the return to Colonel Josiah Whitney, "and thirteen negroes".

The revolutionary action of Lancaster town-meetings, all too briefly recorded by the town clerk, has been copied in former pages to the close of the year 1775. At the annual March meeting in 1776, among the officers regularly elected were the "Committee of Correspondence and Safety," consisting of these nine men :

Cyrus Fairbank,	Jabez Fairbank,	David Wilder,
Josiah Kendall, Jr.	Ephraim Sawyer,	Jonathan Wilder,
Ebenezer Allen,	William Dunsmoor, Esq.	Joshua Fletcher.

Warrant for Town Meeting on the Last Monday of Sepr. 1776. . . .

WORCESTER COUNTY, in the Colony of the Massachusetts Bay. To the Freeholders and other Inhabitants of the Town of Lancaster—Greeting.

In the Name of the people and authority of the American States: You are hereby Notify^d and warn^d to meet at the Meeting-house in the first parish in Lancaster on the Last of this Instant September at 9 O.Clock in the forenoon then and there to Act on the following Articles.

1^stly   To Chuse a moderator for the Goverment of said Meeting.

2dly.   To see if the Town will Raise money to hire men to go into the Service against our Enemies, whenever we have orders from the Congress and Genl. Court to turn out Men for that End.

3.   To see if the Town will Vote to have the Money asses^d and made into a Rate as our other Sums are Rais^d to Defray Town Charges provided there sh^d. Be a Sum Rais^d for that purpose above mentioned.

4.   To See if the Town will Chuse a Committee to provide men from time to time with said Money if sent for. Or act any thing Relative thereto as the Town shall think proper.

5.   To see if the town will allow and Except of the Receipts & Certificates of those that have paid out money to Get Men to go into the Service against our Enemies & Let Each man draw his Respective sum or sums out of the Town Treasure when said money is Colected.

6.   To See if the Town will Come into any measure Concerning those that have Done a Turn in this War, Longer or shorter without being hir^d : without any Bounty in Money for Encouragement from the province, this being Request of Phineas Beaman and others.

7.   To See if the Town will Chuse a person agreeable to a Late Act of the Genl. Court provid^g a Speedy and Cheep Course for Receiv^g of Debts.

8^thly.   To See if the Town will Make Choice of a County Treasurer.

9.   To See if the Town will Make Choice of a County Register.

DANIEL ROBBINS, *T. Clerk.*

Dated at LANCASTER, Sepr 12th. 1776.

At the meeting thus warned the propositions of Beaman

and his abettors were dismissed without comment recorded. To satisfactorily equalize payments for patriotic duty performed, proved undoubtedly a difficult problem — as it has to many wise bodies since. Doctor William Dunsmoor was chosen "to Take Cognisance of Debts." The next town-meeting was specially summoned on Monday, the seventh of October.

. . . . 2. To Consider and determine wether you will give yᵣ Consent that the present house of Representatives of this State of the Massachusetts Bay in New England together with the Counsel aforesaid if they Consent in one Body with the house & by Equal Voice, should consult, agree on & enact such a Constitution & form of Government for this State as the said house of Representatives & Counsel as aforesaid on the fullest and most mature deliberation shall judge will most conduce to the safety & peace & hapiness of this State in all after Sucessions & Generations & if you would direct the same to be made publick for the Inspection & perusal of the Inhabitants before ratification thereof by the Assembly.

At this meeting it was

Voted that the Town Impower the present house of Representatives to Draw up a Form of Goverment and Transmit Back for the Town's Ratification.

The same day Doctor William Dunsmoor was elected representative. The next four pages of the town's records are occupied by a copy of the Declaration of Independence, which Congress had ordered should be read by the clergymen in each parish "as soon as Divine Service is Ended in the Afternoon of the first Lord's Day after they shall have Received it," and then be recorded by the town's clerk in the Town Book, "there to Remain as a perpetual Memorial thereof." The leading article in the warrant for a town-meeting, held the sixth day of January, 1777, was as follows :

2ᵈˡʸ. To see if the Town will come into some methods for ye Providing men to reinforce the American army as they shall be Cal'd for from time to time by Authority in order for ye Defence of our Enestemable Liberties, either by a Just Assessment according as other Taxes are made, or some other way which shall be most Advantageous to the Publick in general and for this Town in Particular, and in general to act and Transact

11

all matters and things which shall appear for ye Peace and Prosperity of this Town—it being yᵉ Request of Mr Jonathan Wilder and others. . . .

When the town met, it was

Voted, to Consider what Each man has Done in the war sence ye 19ᵗʰ April 1775 and make a Proper Allowance to each man for what he has Done to this time.

Voted to Chuse a Committee to Estemate what Each man has Done towards ye war sence ye 19ᵗʰ of April 1775 to this time and also what they will give a month for the Futer to Each man. . . . . . Chose Capt. Wᵐ. Greenleaf, Capt. Wᵐ. Putnam, Samuel Thustin, Capt Jonathan Wilder, & Caleb Whitney to make ye above Estemation. . . . . .

January ye 20ᵗʰ 1777 then meet according to Adjournment. . . . . .

1ˡʸ. Voted, that the Commision officers be excluded from having any bounty from ye town.

2ˡʸ. Voted, to accept the Estemation of yᵉ Committee.

3ˡʸ. Voted to Chuse a Committee to Receive the Certificates of those that have Done Service.

4ˡʸ. Voted that the Commision officers be a Committee to Receive the Diffrante Certificates & Recptˢ of yᵉ men in servis. . . . . .

At adjourned meeting First Tuesday in Febr.

Voted that those Persons that Belongeth to either of yᵉ Companyˢ in Lancaster that have omitted bringing in their Certificates & Recpts at this time shall be Intitled to Lay their several Certificates & Recpts before the Respective officers.

Voted not to Raise a sum of money to encorage yᵉ solders to go into ye servis according to the Estimation Drawn up by the Committee Chose for that Purpos. . . . . .

At an adjourned meeting held on Tuesday the 11 day of March 1777.

Voted and Chose Col. Asa Whitcomb, Capt Thomas Gates, Joshua Fletcher, Elisha Allen, Jabez Fairbank, as a Committee of Correspondence and Safety in Lancaster.

The warrant for the town-meeting of November 24, 1777, had special reference to two matters of recent legislative action, and the freeholders were :

. . . . . 2ⁿᵈˡʸ. To take into Consideration the Late act made for Puting Large Sums of the Bills of Credit Emitted by this State on Intrest on or before the first Day of January Next, and to act or Transact anything Relating said act as they shall think Proper. . . . . .

4ᵗʰˡʸ. to See if the town will act on a Resolve of this State of Sepʳ 29 1777 of Supplying the families of Such Persons, Non Commisioned officers and Soldiers in the Continental Service for three years or During the war. . . . .

The meeting having expressed its hostility to the act concerning the Bills of Credit, chose Colonel Asa Whitcomb, John Prescott, Frederick Albert, Jonathan Fairbank and Thomas Fairbank a committee to draw up a statement of the matter, and then —

7thly. Voted to accept the Committees Report, which is as followeth: this Town Taking into Consideration the Late act made for Putting Large Sums of the bills of Credit Emitted by this State on intrest on or before the first Day of December Next, and for Sinking in the hands of the Possesors all Sums Less than ten Pounds Excepting those bills Less than one Dollar. Therefore this town are Clearly of oppinion that said act in Connection with a Tax we understand is soon to Come out is a grevence we Look upon greater than to Sink Said Money by a Tax or Taxes, as the People are Able to Bare; and Further we Look upon it Very Extrodanary that Said Court Should Lay a Fine on the Tendering sd money when at the same time the face of sd bill saith it shall be of Such Value, and Recd in all Payments. Therefore Resolvd to Petition sd Court for Redress of said Agrevence.

ASA WHITCOMB, *Chairman of sd Committee.*

February 5, 1778. . . . . . .
Voted to accept the articles of Confederation and Perpetual Union between the United States of America.

March 2, 1778. . . . . . .
Voted and Chose Capt. Jonathan Wilder, Jonathan Fairbank, Elisha White, Capt. Benjamin Houghton, Ephm Roper, a Committee of Inspection and Safety.

V. SHORT SERVICE ENLISTMENTS, 1777–82.

It will be more convenient, before giving a roster of Lancaster soldiers enrolled in the continental army for three years or during the war, to complete the records of short-service enlistments.

RHODE ISLAND SERVICE.

In December, 1776, General Sir Henry Clinton and Admiral Sir Peter Parker, having been foiled by General Lee in their attack upon Charleston, occupied Rhode Island with about six thousand troops. This was a convenient point whence to attempt marauding excursions when opportunity favored, or to make a diversion in aid of Burgoyne's southward movement from Lake Champlain. Congress, recognizing the threatening danger, ordered the raising of a corps of militia in the three southern New England states to hold this hostile force in check or destroy it, and General Joseph Spencer was placed in command. The movements of this officer were so deliberate that he became familiarly known to his own troops as "Granny Spencer." It was October, 1777, before he was ready for a descent upon the island. On an appointed night the army was drawn up at Tiverton, but a sudden storm made the passage of boats hazardous; the expedition was delayed, and the campaign finally ended ingloriously without action.

Besides Colonel Thomas Craft's artillery and half the militia of Massachusetts, drafted to serve during October under General Hancock, three thousand troops, specially enrolled by the state for this service, were present. Among the last, serving in Colonel Abijah Stearns's regiment, under Captain Joseph Sergeant of Princeton, were the following:

OF LANCASTER.

Sergeant Jacob Wilder,
William Beman,
John Brooks, Jr.
Daniel Burditt,

Thomas Grant,
Samuel Johnson,
Joseph Jones,
Phineas Phelps,
Josiah Phelps,

John Snow,
Nathaniel Taylor,
Ephraim Wiles,
Elijah Wilder.

OF BOLTON.

Corporal Samuel Baker,
Benjamin Bruce,

Thomas Burnham,
John Longley,

Josiah Sawyer,
John Whitcomb.

OF HARVARD.

Qr.-M. Sergt. Jacob Whitney,
James Burt,
Joseph Fry,

Jacob Robbins,
Jonathan Simonds,

Reuben Whitney,
Solomon Whitney.

OF LEOMINSTER.

Second-Lieut. Thomas Wilder,
Shubael Bailey,
Phineas Carter.

Asa Johnson,
Simeon Perry,

Benjamin Stevens,
Josiah White.

[Mass. Archives, Muster Rolls, 111, 162-3.]

In the regiment of Colonel Danforth Keyes, Captain Francis Wilson's company, were these Lancaster men, serving from August to December, 1777 :

Samuel Brown,	Jonas Houghton,	Reuben Ross,
Ebenezer Burphy,	David Pike,	Asa Rugg,
Elijah Burphy,	Elisha Prouty,	Nathan Taft,
Jonas Gary,	Peter Putnam,	Francis Temple,
John Dunsmoor,	Jonas Rice,	John Winn.

[Mass. Archives, Muster Rolls, XXIV. 156.]

Again, in 1778, an attempt was made to recover Newport, by the combined efforts of the newly arrived French fleet, commanded by the Count d' Estaing, and an army of ten thousand men under General John Sullivan, with General Nathaniel Greene and the Marquis de Lafayette as division commanders. A plan of combined attack was agreed upon, and on August 9 the advance began. The American forces occupied Quaker and Butt's Hills, and the French troops, four thousand in number, were preparing to disembark, when suddenly the English fleet was reported in sight, and the Count d' Estaing, with favoring wind, went out to meet it. Everything seemed to promise triumph ; but a tempest of unexampled severity set in, and, on the night of the tenth, drove both fleets to sea, damaging them seriously and causing much suffering in the camps. When, on the twentieth of August, d' Estaing again entered Newport harbor, he deemed it necessary to proceed at once to Boston for repairs, and abandoned the enterprise so favorably begun. In view of the fact that re-enforcements might at any hour arrive from New York to the assistance of the enemy, retreat was now unavoidable. On the twenty-eighth, at night, General Sullivan abandoned his siege works and marched to the northern end of the island. The British veterans were the following morning led to an assault upon the American lines, but were repelled by the combined force of militia and continentals, after several hours of hard fighting. In this action, known as the Battle of Quaker's Hill, the Massachusetts

detachments won much praise. The next day the retreat
was skilfully completed without molestation, and thus
ended an expedition that for a time gave fair promise of
putting a glorious end to the war.

The second Worcester regiment of militia, commanded
by Coloniel Josiah Whitney of Harvard, was one of those
detailed for the Rhode Island campaign, and was engaged
for one month and fifteen days from August 1, 1778. Captain Manasseh Sawyer's company of this regiment numbered sixty-four rank and file, belonging to Lancaster,
Harvard and Bolton. Its roster, found in Massachusetts
Archives, xxii, 207, follows, Lancaster names being in
italics :

Capt. Manasseh Sawyer,	*James Fuller*,	*William Putnam*,
Lieut. Richard Townsend,	Elisha Fullam,	Nehemiah Ramsdell,
Lieut. John Daby,	*David Geary*,	*Tilley Richardson*,
Sergt. David Sampson,	James Goddard,	Ebenezer Ross,
" *Ebenezer Pike*,	*James Goodwin*,	*Aaron Rugg*,
" *Jonathan Wilder*,	David Greenleaf,	Thaddeus Shattuck,
" *William Phelps*,	*Oliver Hale*,	*Joshua Stiles*,
Corp. Nathaniel Roper,	*Abner Haskell*,	Manasseh Stow,
" *Joshua Rugg*,	Stephen Hastings,	Jesse Walcot,
" *David Whitcomb*,	Silas Holman,	Ebenezer Warner,
" *Amos Sergeant*,	John Hoppin,	*Oliver Wheelock*,
Daniel Albert,	*Nathaniel Houghton*,	*Enoch Whitcomb*,
Oliver Atherton,	*Josiah Kendall*,	*Phineas Whitcomb*,
John Brigham,	Edward Martin,	Israel Whitney,
Ebenezer Burpee,	John Mead,	Richard Whitney,
Stephen Coolidge,	Willard Moore,	Abel Wilder,
William Coolidge,	*Joseph Nichols*,	*Asaph Wilder*,
Micah Davis,	*Jacob Norcross*,	*David Wilder*,
James Divol,	William Pollard,	*Elijah Wilder*,
Jonathan Fairbank,	Jacob Priest,	*Joshua Willard*,
Francis Farr,	*John Priest*,	*Joseph Wright*,
Phineas Fletcher,		

In the regiment of Colonel Nathaniel Wade, serving in
Rhode Island during the year 1778, in the companies of
Captains Ebenezer Belknap, Nathan Fisher, Elisha Jack-
son, etc., were :

LANCASTER MEN.

Sergt. William Fairbanks,	Josiah Cutting,	Jacob Sawyer,
" John Wheelock,	Jacob Glasier,	Jonathan Whitcomb,
Corp. Thomas Kendall,	Ephraim Houghton,	Samuel Whitcomb,
Drummer Timothy Kendall,	Jonas Houghton, Jr.	David Winch,
Peter Ayres,	Joshua Phelps,	John Winn,
Lazarns Brabrook,	Reuben Ross,	John Wyman.
Jonas Brooks,		

BOLTON MEN.

Sergt. William Whitcomb,	Jacob Houghton,	Abel Priest,
Nathan Ball,	Jonas Houghton,	Jonas Welch.
Nathaniel Holman,		

HARVARD MEN.

Corp. Phineas Warner,	William Sanderson, Jr.	Abel Wetherbee,
Oliver Edwards,	Prince Turner,	Jonas Whitney, Jr.
John Hale,	Calvin Warner,	

LEOMINSTER MEN.

Corp. Nathan Colburn,	David Hale,	Luke Johnson,
Thomas Follinsbee,	Joel Hale,	Jacob Symonds,
Calvin Hale,	Robert Houghton,	Zebedee Symonds.

[Mass. Archives, Muster Rolls, LV, M. 56, 59; XLII, 10, etc.]

At a town-meeting in Lancaster, September 9, 1779, it was

Voted to hier the men to go to Rhod Island, sent for by order of Council 28. August.

. . . . . *Capt. David Moore's company, Col. John Jacobs' regiment, serving in Rhode Island from October 1, 1779, two months.*

LANCASTER MEN.

Sergt. Sherebiah Hunt,	Oliver Glazier,	Reuben Lipenwell,
Fifer John Wheelock,	Daniel Knight,	Joseph Sever,
Stanton Carter,	Edmund Larkin,	James Snow,
Solomon Fleeman,	Ephraim Larkin,	Jotham Wilder.

BOLTON MEN.

Capt. David Moore,	John Moore,	Jonathan Whitcomb.
Joseph Houghton,	Richard Townsend,	

HARVARD MEN.

Sergt. John Hill,	James Furbush.	Nathaniel Hazeltine,
Thaddeus Brown,	Nathan Garfield,	David Stone,
		Jonas Whitney.

[Mass. Archives, Muster Rolls, III, 9.]

July 25, 1780, intelligence came that Sir Henry Clinton meditated an attack upon the French encampment at Newport, and the short service recruits raised for the re-enforcement of the Continental army were ordered to Rhode Island. These Lancaster officers led them :

Capt. Fortunatus Eager, Lieut. Timothy Hayward, Lieut. Samuel Wilder.
[Mass. Archives, Muster Rolls, I, 11.]

In Captain Joseph Elliott's company, Colonel William Furnas's regiment, at Butt's Hill, December 1, 1781, were the following :

OF LANCASTER.

Lieut. Joseph White,	Ephraim Hale,	John Whitcomb.
Corp. Abel Thayer,	James Haten, Jr.	

OF BOLTON.

James Haten,	David Wetherby,	Elihu Whitcomb.

OF HARVARD.

Samuel Haskell,	Nehemiah Ramsdell,	Samuel Russell.

OF LEOMINSTER.

Benjamin Brown,	Ephraim Lincoln,	Benjamin Tarbox.

[Mass. Archives, Muster Rolls. II, 13.]

Roll of Capt. David Moore's Company of Militia in Lt.-Col. Enoch Hallet's Regt. 3 mos., according to an Act of the General Court of the 22d June last. Rhode Island, July 21, 1781.

David Moore, *capt.*	Edmund Larkin,	Silvester Roper,
John Houghton, *lieut.*	Calvin Wilder,	Jonas Bailey,
Timothy Bailey, *lieut.*	Ignatius Fuller,	Josiah Fairbank,
Harry Rice,	Rufus Moore,	Levi Robins,
Ephraim Fairbank.	Benjamin Haskell,	Solomon Holman,
Jonathan Bush,	Daniel Wilder,	Nathaniel Taylor,
Daniel Carter,	John Willson,	Artemas Willard,
Moses Hudson,	Benjamin Hastings,	James Brown,
Peter Fletcher,	Walter Pollard,	Thomas Blodget,
Jonas Houghton,	Daniel Harris,	Benjamin Wheelock,
Abel Houghton,	Benjamin Gould,	William Park,
Stephen Ross,	Benjamin Sawyer,	Abnah Whitcomb,
Joseph Parson,	John Cooledge,	Abel Wetherbee,
Reuben Wilder,	William McBride	Benjamin Warner,
Nathan Wilder,	Eleazar Parker,	Oliver Hail,
Benjamin Robins,	Timothy Shattuck,	Peter Stickney,

Elisha Rugg,
William Burges,
Jacob Wilder,
Aaron Rugg,
Jonas Welch,
John Wheelock, *drummer*.
Benjamin Richardson, *fifer*.
John Barnard,
Lemuel Barrett.
John Wheelock,
Ephraim Larkin,

Jotham Whitcomb,
Joseph Beaman,
Haran Eger,
Oliver Tenney,
Solomon Sawtel,
Abijah White,
Levi Preast,
Nathan Burpee,
John Roper,
Oliver Dresser.
Samuel Kilburn,

Thomas Peabody,
Isaac Burbank,
John Dudley,
Ephraim Corey,
Elijah Preast,
Joseph Houghton,
David Farwell,
George Gleason,
Israel Hail,
Moses Dickenson,
James Richardson.

[Mass. Archives, Muster Rolls, XXI, 61.]

Residences are not given in the roll. The officers were all of Bolton, but the privates seem nearly equally divided between Lancaster, Bolton and Harvard, with a few from adjoining towns.

BENNINGTON ALARM.

In the month of July, 1777, the abandonment of Ticonderoga and the subsequent disasters to the patriot cause at Skenesborough and Hubbardton, naturally spread consternation through New England; for the victorious march by Burgoyne southward threatened a division of the country into two sections, and the probable subjugation of each in turn by the united armies of the king. An unmerited distrust of General Schuyler throughout the Eastern states, and the importance of garnering the hay and grain crops, had dangerously retarded the re-enforcements of the Northern army. The Massachusetts Council of War, at last rudely awakened to the hour's necessity, showed abundant zeal, and despatched the militia in hot haste to the rescue. Thousands reached the field in time to aid the impetuous valor of Morgan and Arnold in reaping for General Gates the glorious victory at Saratoga, which his predecessor's wisely laid plans had made secure. The call to arms reached the Lancaster captains in the following form:

In consequence of orders from Col. Whitney you are Immediately to Draught one-sixth part of the Train band and alarm List in your Company to march to Bennington to oppose the Northern Army; hereof fail not, and make Due Return — given under my hand this 27th Day of July 1777.

SILAS BAILY, *Major.*

N. B. they are to be equipt according to Law with six Days provision.

August 2, heavy re-enforcements were again demanded for the increase of the Massachusetts forces under General Benjamin Lincoln, then harassing the rear of Burgoyne's army. The Bolton major therefore issued this second order :

To Capt[n]. David Nurse, Greting.

In Consequence of orders receved this moment from Col. Whitney I order you to corse one half of the traning band together with the allarm list to march to Benington immediately with eight dayes provison and arms and ammunition as the law directs agreabel to s[d] orders.

SILAS BAILEY, *maj.*

For several weeks the mechanic was missed from his bench, the husbandman from the fields, and the care of cattle and crops devolved upon the women and children waiting in prayerful suspense. The Lancaster men answering to the summons are found in the muster-rolls of Captains John White and Solomon Stuart :

Captain John White's company which marched to Bennington on alarm July, 1777, and served one month eight days under Col. Job Cushing.

John White, *captain.*	Levi Larkin,	John Fletcher,
John Kenrick, *lieutenant.*	Enoch Roper,	Nathaniel Houghton,
Andrew Haskell, *substitute.*	John Spofford,	Ephraim White,
Luke Wilder, *sergeant.*	Phinehas Wilder,	Jacob Sawyer,
Ruben Garey, "	John Robbins,	Elijah Rugg,
David Hosley, "	Noah Kendall,	Amos Sawyer,
William Fairbank, *sergeant.*	Jacob Wilder,	Josiah Phelps,
Jonas Powers, *corporal.*	Abijah Houghton,	Joseph Jones,
Ebenezer Brooks, "	Nathaniel Taylor,	Solomon Fleeman,
Solomon Holman, "	William Goss,	David Bennett,
Joshua Rugg, "	Joseph Pearson,	Thomas Wright,
John Wheelock, *drummer.*	Jonathan Knight,	Ephraim Pike,
Calvin Kilburn, *fifer,*	Samuel Jewitt,	Peter Manning,
Abel Allen,	Daniel Page,	Joseph Beaman.
Amos Allen,	Joshua Phelps,	Elisha Woods,
Jotham Wilder,	James Divol,	Onesimus ——,
Moses Dickenson,	Benjamin Bosworth,	David Whitecar.
David Andrews, *Shrewsbury.*		

[Mass. Archives, Muster Rolls, III, 250.]

. . . . . Solomon Stuart's Co. in Coll. Josiah Whitney's Reg^t: marched on alarm at Bennington on August ye 21, 1777.

Solomon Stuart, *capt.*
Edward Newton, *1st lt.*
Elisha Sawyer, *2d lt.*
Samuel Bayley, *1st sert.*
Samuel Thompson, *2d sert.*
Ephraim Willard, *3d sert.*
Cornelius Sawyer, *4th sert.*
Ephraim Goss, *1st corp.*
Oliver Fairbank, *2d corp.*
Ephraim Bowker, *3d corp.*
Aaron Sawyer, *4 corp.*
William Kendall, *fifer.*
David Osgood,
William Putnam,
Micah Harthan,
Ebenezer Buss, Jr.
Jonathan Pierce,
Ephraim Wright,
Abel Richardson,

Caleb Whitney,
Ephraim Powers,
Elijah Dresser,
Samuel Snow,
Moses Burpee,
Timothy Brown,
Jonathan Nelson, Jr.
Joshua Willard,
Elihu Wilder,
William Putnam, Jr.
Manasseh Roper,
John Roper,
Levi May,
Nathan Burpee, Jr.
Samuel Brown,
Eathan Kendall,
Ephraim Wilder, Jr.
Jonathan Thompson,
Ebenezer Ross,

Josiah Kendall,
Samuel Mason,
Thomas Sawyer,
John Willard,
William Palmer,
David Wilder,
Jonathan Prescot,
Oliver Moor,
Peter Prescot,
Joshua Brooks,
Samuel Rice,
Elijah Wilder,
John Chandler,
Israel Cook,
William Eaton,
Calvin Moor,
John Brooks,
Tilley Richardson.

[Mass. Archives, Muster Rolls, XXIII, 64.]

August 21-25.

Captain Hezekiah Whitney's Company of Bolton; Bennington alarm, July 30, 1777.

Capt. Hezekiah Whitney,
Lt. Richard Townsend,
Lt. Thomas Mason,
Sergt. Jacob Moore,
" James Burt,
" William Haskell,
Corp. Uriah Moore,
" Gabriel Priest,
Fifer Isaac Crouch,

Richard Townsend,
Silas Whitcomb,
David Whitney,
Simon Houghton,
Richard Whitney,
Jonathan Clerk,
Thaddeus Pollard,
Jonathan Symonds,
James Fife,

William Willard,
Oliver Atherton,
Jonathan Stearns,
John Hill,
Josiah Whitney,
Enoch White,
Edward Martin,
Nathaniel Longley,
Samuel Davis.

[Mass. Archives, Muster Rolls, XXIV, 25 and 36.]

Lieut. Samuel Stickney's Company in Colonel Abijah Stearns's Regiment of Militia, marched to Saratoga on the 9 of Oct. 1777, by order of General Court, to assistance of General Gates. [of Leominster.]

Left. Samuel Stickney,
Left. Thomas Wilder.
Sargent John Colburn,
Sargent Levi Warner,
Corp. Abijah Butler,

John Bowers,
Ebenezer Butler,
Abijah Carter,
Josiah Carter,
Jonathan Colburn,

Ebenezer Houghton,
David May,
Francis Parker,
Jacob Spaford,
Josiah Swan,

Corp. Josiah Whitcomb,	Jonas Gates,	Elisha White,
David Boutell,	Silas Hail,	David Wilder,
William Boutell,	Abiathar Houghton,	James Wood.

[Mass. Archives, Muster Rolls, XXIII, 49.]

RE-ENFORCEMENTS OF CONTINENTAL ARMY.

. . . . Capt. John Drury's Co., Col. Ezra Wood, Ticonderoga, May to December, 1778.

John Drury, *captain*.	Stanton Carter,	Jacob Miller,
John Kindrick, *lieut.*	Benjamin Farley,	John More,
James Burt, *lieut.*	William Grout,	Joseph Nowell,
James Burt, *sergt.*	Jonathan Gale,	Marshall Newton,
Noah Eager, "	Solomon How,	Samuel Phelps,
Spencer Maynard, "	Ephraim Holland,	Ephraim Parkiss,
Enoch Roper, "	Jonathan Houghton,	Lewis Smith,
Abraham Townsend, *corp.*	Joseph Houghton,	Lemuel Shed,
Benjamin Sawyer, "	Joseph Houghton, Jr.	John Stacy,
John Fay, "	Samuel Jewett,	Thomas Severy,
Jonathan Knowlton, "	Joseph Jewett,	Jonathan Stearns,
Abijah Herrington, *fifer.*	Ebenezer Lyon,	Benjamin Sadler,
Nathaniel Andrews,	Benjamin Larkin,	Robert Townsend,
Amos Allen,	Edmund Larkin,	Jotham Wilder,
Abel Amsden,	John Larkin,	John Wilson.
Joseph Beeman,	Ebenezer Mann,	

[Mass. Archives, Muster Rolls, XLVI, 89, 101, 115, 129, 141.]

No residences are given in the original, but most of the list are of Bolton and Lancaster.

Capt. Ephraim Stearns's Co., Col. Ezra Woods' Regt. . . . 1778.

David Hemmingway, *sergt.*	Benjamin Dolbear,	Josiah White,
James Wilder, "	Phineas Fullam,	John Whitemore,
Joseph Newton, "	Jacob Hutchins,	Solomon Wilson,
Nathaniel Bosworth, *corp.*	Samuel Houghton,	George Wood,
Daniel Harris, "	Thomas Lawton,	Jonathan Wood,
Thomas Dodge, "	Joseph Priest,	Silas Wyman.
John Boutell,	John Thurston,	

[Mass. Archives, Muster Rolls, XLI, 188.]

A List of the Men Procured from the County of Worcester . . . . for the term of nine Months from the time of their arrival at Fish Kills. . . .

	Age.	Stature.	Complexion.
John Todd,	27	5 ft. 6 in.	`
Elisha Wood,	19	5 " 6 "	Dark.
William Flood,	19	5 " 6 "	"
Jacob Wilder,	20	5 " 10 "	"

	Age.	Stature.	Complexion.
John Brooks,	20	5 ft. 8 in.	Dark.
Benjamin Smith,	26	5 " 8 "	"
Jonas Baley,	26	6 "	"
Moses Bruer,	23	5 " 10 "	"
Charles Henry,	40	5 "	Negro.
Joshua Kendall,	30	5 " 6 "	Dark.
Joseph Patterson,	25	5 " 10 "	"
Jonathan Baley,	44	6 " 1 "	"
Benjamin Sterns,	29	5 " 6 "	Light.
Ephraim Fuller,	16	5 " 6 "	"
Benjamin Bosworth,	25	5 " 5 "	Dark.
Able Allen,	22	5 " 8 "	"
Andrew Haskell,	30	5 " 10 "	"

The list contains seventy-nine names, the above being Lancaster's quota of seventeen. Harvard's quota was nine; Bolton's, eight, and Leominster's, six. Captain Andrew Haskell led the men to Fishkill, arriving there June 17, 1778.

[Massachusetts Archives, Muster Rolls, XXVIII, 133; IV, 283; XLI, 302, 350.]

The Bolton men were :

	Age.	Stature.	Complexion.
Abel Baker,	21	5 ft. 9 in.	Dark.
Ebenezer Bailey,	27	6 "	Light.
Timothy Blair,	28	6 "	"
William Burges,	27	5 " 8 "	"
Samuel Moore,	25	6 " 2 "	"
Josiah Sawyer, Jr.	20	5 " 11 "	"
William Sawyer, 3d,	28	5 " 9 "	"
Jesse Walcot,	44	5 " 9 "	" *rejected.*
John Whitcomb, Jr.	18	5 " 6 "	"

[Mass. Archives, Muster Rolls, XXVII, 136; XLI, 222.]

The Harvard men were :

	Age.	Stature.	Complexion.
Lysaias Blanchard,	29	5 ft. 8 in.	Dark.
Jonathan Crouch, Jr.	31	5 " 9 "	Light.
Harbour Farnsworth,	21	5 " 6 "	Dark.
George Leason [*Gleason*]	30	5 " 6 "	Light.
Europe Hamblin,	20	5 " 10 "	Dark.
William Parks,	28	6 "	Light.
Aaron Priest,	20	5 " 9 "	Dark.
Freedom Ramsdell,	20	5 " 8 "	Light.
Abraham Willard,	28	6 "	Dark.

[Mass. Archives, Muster Rolls, XXVIII, 135.]

The Leominster men were :

	Age.	Stature.	Complexion.
Shubael Bailey,	18	5 ft. 9 in.	Dark.
Asa Buttrick,	31	5 " 8 "	"
David Johnson,	18	5 " 7 "	"
Thomas Page,	48	5 " 10 "	"
Simon Perrey,	33	5 " 9 "	Light.
Joseph Stuart,	20	5 " 8 "	Dark.

[Mass. Archives, Muster Rolls, XXVIII, 136.]

At the town meeting May 18, 1778, the town clerk, Cyrus Fairbank — who, like his predecessor, Nathaniel Beaman, obviously owed his official position to the high order of his patriotism rather than to his literary abilities — records that the town —

Voted to Rais Four thousand and Fourty-nine pounds seven shilings For to pay Solgers that was hyerd for eight months and nine months that was to Join the Contenantal army for the present year.

Voted to see what methurds the town will Come into for to Rase thes men that wair sent for to Reinfors the Contenantal army.

Voted to Rase eighteen Contenantal men for nine months and pay them by the town and to asses s[d] town for the same as they have in all other town taxes in tim past.

Voted and Chosen a Committe to Rase the eighteen men above Exprest and that the Committe Concist of the Commision officers of Each Compiney and the Selectmen and the Committe of Saftey for s[d] town.

Voted to Rais Fourteen men mor and to pay them by a town tax as the other above Exprest for to joine our armey.

Voted that the Comision officers of each Compiney in s[d] town with the Selectmen and Committe of Saftey be a Committe to hire money to pay the eighteen Contennatal men above Exprest upon the town's account.

October 26 1778. . . . .

Voted to Chus a Comitey to supply the Familey of thos that air Gon into the Contenantal army.

Voted and Chos Sollomon Jewet, Edward Newton, Josiah Kendal Jun. Elisha White, Daniel Rugg, William Tucker for s[d] Comitey.

The care of the soldiers' families was kept up for several years. At the town meetings above named were also discussed two important political questions : the acceptance of the State Constitution, and the division of the town.

May 18. . . . . Voted to Receive the new Form of Goverment and Constitution sent to us by the Great and General Corte; the number of pols that Voted to Receive it was one hundred and Eleven. Voted against Receive the Constitution, Forty-one.

Voted to Set of the Second Precinct in Lancaster as a Seprat Town.

January 4, 1779. . . . . .
Voted to Rase three hundred pounds to Supply the Famileys of those that air Gon into the Contenantal army.

March 1779. . . . . Voted and Choose Col. Joseph Reed, Cyrus Fairbank, Nathaniel White, Solomon Jewet, Luke Wilder committee of Inspection and Saftey.

May 17, 1779. . . . . . .
Voted to have new form of government and Constitution made; present at said meeting voting on the first article in the Court's direction to the Selectmen, 84 Yeas, 14 Nays.

Voted to accept the second article in the Court order Concerning a New Constitution with this addition. We do Impower our Representative to give his vote for Choosing a Convention for the purpose mentioned with Proviso that the Constitution Shall Return unto the hand of the people For their approbation or Disapprobation.

LANCASTER, June 28, 1779. . . . . .
3dly. Voted to raise the men sent for from the General Court (by the town).

4^{ly}. Voted to pay the men Required by the General Court by a town Rate.

5^{ly}. Voted to Chuse a Committee to Raise the men for the army.

6^{ly}. Voted that the Selectmen, Commissioned officers and Committee of Correspondence Be the above Committee.

7^{ly}. Voted and Impowered the Committee to hire the men for the most Reasonable sum and to pay in the produce of the land or in money.

8^{ly}. Voted to Impower the Committee to give the men 40/ pr. month to go into the army and pay at the price of the produce of the land at a price Eaqual to the above sum of 40 / pr. month.

LANCASTER, August 2, 1779. . . . . .
6. Voted that the Captains now in being of the Respective Companies make a Return at our next adjournment of what has been done by turnes or in money in the Services of their Country from the first of the war to this time.

At an adjourned meeting the captains presented their report, which was referred to an auditing committee, but not recorded. It probably met the fate of former attempts to equalize the burdens of patriotism.

. . . . . Nine months' men enlisted June 25, 1779, marched July 14.

	Age.	Height.		Age.	Height.
William Flud,	21	5 ft. 7 in.	Reuben Wilder,	18	5 ft. 10 in.
John Wyman,	17	5 " 2 "	Peter Putnam,	21	5 " 8 "
Elisha Woods,	20	5 " 7 "	William Kilburn,	17	5 " 3 "
Zimori Eveleth,	17	5 " 2 "	Julius Cæsar,	17	5 " 5 "
Samuel Sawyer,	30	5 " 10 "	Lemuel Shed,	17	5 " 3 "
Eber Sawyer,	25	5 " 10 "	Abijah Rice,	18	5 " 9 "
Jacob Sawyer,	23	6 " 1 "	Ephraim Fuller,	17	5 " 7 "
Abel Sawyer,	18	5 " 7 "	Levi Warner,	18	5 " 7 "
Calvin Sawyer,	18	5 " 7 "	James Houghton.		

[Mass. Archives, Muster Rolls, XLI, 352; XLII, 41; XXIX, 53..]

This detachment, it will be seen, included a larger proportion of youthful recruits, and those below the average stature, than Lancaster furnished at any other date. It would seem that the whole contribution of the state was similarly peculiar, for Washington, July 29, wrote to President Reed that he had received no re-enforcements since the last campaign, "excepting about four hundred recruits from the State of Massachusetts Bay (a portion of whom I am told are children, hired at above fifteen hundred dollars each, for nine months' service)."

The Bolton men enlisted for nine months, in 1779, were :

	Age.	Height.		Age.	Height.
John Barnard,	17	5 ft. 7 in.	Benj. Hastings,	17	5 ft. 9 in.
Gordon Goddard,			Rufus Moore,	19	5 " 10 "
Benjamin Haskell,			Samuel Moore,	27	6 " 2 "
Moses Haskell,			Paul Wilson,	21	5 " 8 "

Harvard men :

	Age.	Height.		Age.	Height.
Adam Amsden,	17	5 ft. 7 in.	Aaron Priest,	21	5 ft. 8 in.
Reuben Garfield,	25	5 " 10 "	Samuel Russell,	18	5 " 7 "
America Hamlin,	17	5 " 6 "	John Todd,	28	5 " 9 "
Jona. Houghton,	18	5 " 6 "	Reuben Willard,	23	6 "

Leominster men :

	Age.	Height.		Age.	Height.
Samuel Boutell,			Luther Marble,		
David Clark,	33	5 ft. 10 in.	Robert Motterhead,	24	5 ft. 6 in.
Samuel Houghton,	18	5 " 7 "	Calvin Oaks,	20	5 " 6 "
Samuel Jones.			Silas Perry.		
Abner Livermore,					

[Mass. Archives, Muster Rolls, XXIX, 55; XLI, 352.]

. . . . Captain Luke Wilder's Company in 2ᵈ Regt. Militia, Col. Samuel Denny, at Claverick in Continental Service, October 27 to December 11, 1779.

Luke Wilder, *capt.*	James Bellows,	Jonathan Newton,
Andrew Haskell, *lt.*	Stephen Cooledge,	Aaron Phelps,
John Daby, *lt.*	Thomas Davis,	John Prentice,
David Pike, *sergt.*	Jonathan Fairbank,	Ephraim Pike,
Wilder Chamberlain, *sergt.*	Joseph Fairwell,	Edward Prise,
Jacob Whitney, "	Leonard Fairwell,	Abel Priest,
Samuel Adams, *corp.*	David Fairwell,	Resolved Richardson,
Luther Stephens. "	William Farr,	Enoch Roper,
Abel Baker, "	Abial Holt,	Paul Sawyer,
Levi May, "	Oliver Haskell,	Oliver Wheelock,
John Wheelock, *drummer.*	Joseph Jewett,	John Willard,
John Priest, *fifer.*	John Hall,	Samuel Wright,
Joseph Beaman,	Oliver Hailes,	Elihu Wilder,
Roger Bartlett,	Thomas Henderson,	Phinehas Wilder,
Jonathan Bailey,	John Lacy,	Ephraim Whitney,
Ebenezer Burpee,	Abram Longley,	Joel Whitney,
Benjamin Bridge,	Ely Longley,	Amos Wetherby,
Jonathan Bush,	Robert Moor.	B. Whittemore Willard
Nathan Ballard,	Paul Mason,	Joshua Willard.
Amherst Bailey,	John Nichols,	59

[Mass. Archives, Muster Rolls, XXIV, 173.]

Residences are not recorded in the roll. The men were chiefly, if not all, from Lancaster, Bolton and Harvard.

2 : Voted and accepted of the proceedings of Committee with Regard to hiering soldiers.

3. Voted that the Committee be directed to pay the soldiers one month's pay Before they march for Claverack. . . . . . .

5. Voted that the Commission⁴ officers be directed to proceed to a draught upon the Respective Companies in case the Committee carn't hier the men as the town have voted the Remaining part of the soldiers that won't Inlist.

6 Voted that the Selectmen and the Captains be desired to stand as a Committee to hier soldiers for the service untill the estimation is Complyed with and Compleated. . . . . .

Voted to Raise the sum of £6381 to pay the soldiers for going into the service.

Voted that the assessors be directed to make the Rate for the above sum Emediately.

12

LANCASTER, March 6, 1780. . . . . . .

1. Voted and Chose James Richardson, Samuel Thurston, Thomas Gates, Capt. Luke Wilder and Capt. Benja. Richardson a Committee of Inspection and Correspondence. . . . . .

33^d. Voted to Choose a Committee to hire Soldiers for ye Future, when sent for by ye General Assembly.

March 8. . . . . .

8. Voted that the Field officers belonging to this Town with the Commanders of the respective companies, be for a committee to hire Soldiers for the future when sent for by ye General Court.

LANCASTER, May 2^d, 1780. . . . . . .

6. Voted that the Selectmen and Treasurer settle with ye Soldiers that have notes for Grain, upon the best Terms that they can.

In June, 1780, the government called upon Lancaster to furnish forty men for six-months' service, and at a town-meeting on the sixteenth of that month the town —

. . . . . 2. Voted to hire the men now sent for by the General Court by a Town Tax. . . . . .

4. Voted to Choose a Committee for the Purpose of hireing them as above. . . . . .

6. Voted and Chose Capt. Samuel Ward, John Prescott, Dea. Cyrus Fairbank, Capt. Nathaniel Balch, Samuel Thurston and Dea. Levi Moor of ye 1st Precinct and Thomas Brown, James Richardson, Nathaniel Houghton, Israel Moor, James Kendal Jr. and Jonas Wilder Jun. of ye 2^d Precinct for s^d Committee.

The sudden re-appearance of Captain Samuel Ward's name at the head of a Lancaster committee, when for nearly five years he had been almost excluded from town councils because his political utterances were not radical enough to suit the feverish times, is significant; and Joseph Willard, Esq., has explained the circumstances that brought him again to the front, where he naturally belonged. When the assembled voters began the consideration of ways and means to obtain the forty soldiers demanded by the General Court, Josiah Kendall, Jr., a prominent politician and inn-keeper of the second precinct, whose patriotism had hitherto been of an especially flamboyant character, arose, declaring it a hopeless task to try to induce so large a number to enlist, and seemed inclined to advocate refusal of obedience to the order. Captain Ward saw his opportunity, urged in a speech of great eloquence the duty of prompt compliance with the requisition, at any sacrifice, and moved the appointment of a committee to secure the men. Within twelve days the requisite number had been hired, received their bounty, and were on their way to the rendezvous. Their names will be given on the following page.

LANCASTER, June 23ᵈ. . . . . . .

On the 3ᵈ article in yᵉ Warrant, Voted to empower the Committee Chosen to hire the Men therein Mentioned on any Terms they think Proper, and if the sᵈ Committee or any of them shall contract with any Person to Do the Service Required by the Orders which are the occasion of this Vote, that the Town will in all Respects indemnify and make good to each one of sᵈ Committee severally all Monies, Damages and Expences which they or any of them shall incur by performing their sᵈ Contracts, and will also pay them their reasonable Expences and for their Trouble in and about the Premises.

June 26 at an adjournment—

Voted to Accept the following Report of the Committee viz : The Committee engage to each Man that will enlist 1400£ Lawˡ. Money, such Part as each Man may want to be paid Down, the Remainder, when paid, to be made as good as it now is; or 13£. 6ˢ. 8ᵈ Lawˡ Money to be paid in the Old Way in Corn, Beef and live Stock or any Produce as it formerly used to be sold, or the value thereof in Continental Money. The above Sum offerᵈ is a Bounty from the Town in Addition to the Wages alowᵈ. by the Court. And furthermore the Committee Engage that the Money which may be Due from the State for the Six Months Service the Town will get for each Man that will produce proper Certificates.

Descriptive List of 6 mos. men raised to re-enforce the Continental army, 1780.

	Age.	Height.		Age.	Height.
Ebenezer Flagg,	24	6 ft. 1 in.	John Brooks,	21	5 ft. 7 in.
Andrew Haskell,	33	5 " 11 "	John Parker,	21	5 " 9 "
Samuel Phelps,	23	5 " 11 "	Abel Richardson,	19	5 " 7 "
Samuel Johnson,	22	6 "	William Kilburn,	17	5 " 4 "
Joshua Phelps,	19	5 " 7 "	Elijah Burpee,	19	5 " 5 "
Daniel Willard,	25	5 " 9 "	Samuel Snow,	17	5 " 5 "
Jonathan Tenney,	21	5 " 9 "	Ephraim Pike,	20	5 " 7 "
Jotham Woods,	28	5 " 6 "	Jonathan Whitcomb,	17	6 "
Reuben Wilder,	20	5 " 11 "	Ichabod Garey,	30	5 " 5 "
Samuel Corey,	19	5 " 4 "	Ebenezer Burpee,	19	5 " 8 "

	Age.	Height.		Age.	Height.
Jonathan Barnard,	17	5 ft. 2 in.	Enoch Roper,	21	5 ft. 9 in.
Abel Sawyer,	19	5 " 8 "	William Pike,	16	5 " 8 "
Ezra Moore,	16	5 " 4 "	John Winn,	20	5 " 9 "
Jeduthan Sawyer,	17	5 " 4 "	John Dunsmore,	35	5 " 9 "
Thomas Moore,	18	5 " 10 "	John Willard,	19	5 " 9 "
Oliver Glazier,	17	5 " 8 "	Paul Sawyer,	21	5 " 11 "
Samuel Wright,	17	5 " 5 "	Jacob Allen,	22	5 " 11-"
Ephraim Houlton,	19	5 " 11 "	Aaron Willard,	22	5 " 8 "
John Putnam,	17	5 " 6 "	Philemon Allen,	22	5 " 9 "
Benjamin Roper,	29	5 " 7 "	Oliver Wheelock,	19	5 " 8 "
James Wilder,	18	5 " 9 "			

Besides the above, the names of sixteen other Lancaster soldiers are found in various rolls, serving for six months during 1780:

Nathaniel Brooks,	William Flood,	Levi Phelps,
Ebenezer Burditt,	John Green,	Rawson Phelps,
Stephen Corey,	Thomas Hammond,	John Sergeant,
Pardon Dolbee,	Ephraim Larkin,	Jacob Simonds,
John Drewmore,	John Parker,	Hosea Sprague.
Isaac Eveleth.		

[Mass. Archives, Muster Rolls, XXXV, 195; XXV, 230; IV, 125, etc.]

These men were paid their bounty in various ways and with a generous consideration of their individual preferences. Joseph Willard, Esq., narrates that John Dunsmoor promised to enlist if given a certain lot of land belonging to Deacon Levi Moore of the town's committee. "Take it," said the deacon, "take it; I'd rather part with that land, although 'tis the best I own, than lose the whole by any neglect in aiding the cause of my country."

Descriptive list of the six-months' men of Bolton, Harvard, and Leominster, raised for the Continental army in 1780.

BOLTON MEN.

	Age.	Height.		Age.	Height.
Nathaniel Oaks,	18	5 ft. 7 in.	John Barnard,	17	5 ft. 9 in.
Abel Priest,	20	5 " 8 "	Matthew Atherton,	19	5 " 6 "
Eli Longley,	18	5 " 6 "	John Burnham,	20	5 " 10 "
Rufus Houghton,	16	5 " 4 "	Ebenezer Bailey,	31	6 " 1 "
Nathan'l Whitcomb,	18	5 " 3 "	William Ross,	33	5 " 9 "
Moses Haskell,	20	5 " 7 "	William Bigelow,	35	5 " 6 "
Stephen Coolidge,	18	5 " 11 "			

HARVARD MEN.

	Age.	Height.		Age.	Height.
John Oaks,	22	5 ft. 5 in.	Salmon Whitney,	20	5 ft. 7 in.
Jonathan Stearns,	17	5 " 7 "	Jonathan Houghton,	19	5 " 8 "
John Atherton,	18	5 " 9 "	John Warner,	18	5 " 7 "
Simeon Conant,	18	5 " 7 "	John Scollay,	17	5 " 7 "
Thaddeus Brown,	18	5 " 6 "	Benjamin Bridges,	20	5 " 9 "
Benjamin Hale,	16	5 " 2 "	Oliver Haskell,	22	5 " 4 "
Jonathan Whitney,	21	5 " 6 "	Abijah Cole,	17	5 " 9 "
David Stone,	18	5 " 7 "	Manasseh Stow,	23	5 " 7 "
America Hamlin,	18	5 " 8 "	Joel Whitney,	17	5 " 10 "
Nathaniel Hazeltine,	16	5 " 6 "			

LEOMINSTER MEN.

	Age.	Height.		Age.	Height.
Silas Perry,	17	5 ft. 8 in.	Jacob Simons,	19	5 ft. 9 in.
Samuel Boutell,	18	5 " 10 "	Ephraim Johnson,	17	5 " 8 "
Benjamin Brown,	22	5 " 7 "	Silas Hale,	20	5 " 7 "
Levi Blood,	23	5 " 7 "	Joel Hale,	18	5 " 9 "
Otis Lincoln,	20	5 " 9 "	Samuel Barrett,	26	5 " 7 "
Benjamin Stearns,	31	5 " 8 "	Joseph Stuart,	21	5 " 8 "
Levi Phelps,	20	5 " 10 "			

May 13, 1780, at a town meeting . . . . . .

1. Voted to Receive yᵉ Constitution or Form of Government as it now stands — 103 for it and 7 against it.

2. Voted to impower ye Delegates at ye next Session to agree upon a Time when this Form of Government shall take Place without returning ye same again to the People, provided that two-thirds of ye Male Inhabitants of the age of twenty-one years and upwards voting in the several Town and Plantation Meetings shall agree to the same, or ye Convention shall Confirm it to the sentiments of two-thirds of the People as afore sd.

LANCASTER, July 3ᵈ, 1780. . . . . . .

1. Voted to Choose a Committee to Hire the Ten Contenental Men last sent for by the General Court.

2. Voted and Chose Moses Smith, Capt. Thomas Gates, Ebenʳ. Allen, John Brown, Dea. Joel Houghton and Josiah Kendall for ye above Committee.

3. Voted to Choose a Committee to Hire the 48 Militia men now sent for by ye General Court.

4. Voted and Chose Mr Ebenʳ. Bradish, Capt. Epᵐ. Carter, Dea. Benj. Houghton, Capt. John White Jun. Josiah Kendall Jr. Micah Harthan, Caleb Whitney and Thomas Sawyer for sᵈ Committee.

Monday, July 3, 1780. . . . . . .

Voted to Raise the sum of one Hundred and fifty Thousand Pounds for the Purpose of Hireing Soldiers for the Army paying their Mileage etc.

. . . . . Captain Nath¹. Wright's Co. Sept. to Nov. 18, 1781, *Col. Drury's Regt. of Militia.* [*At West Point.*]

OF LANCASTER AND STERLING.

Capt. Nathaniel Wright,	Ephraim Houghton,	Jacob Sawyer,
Corp. Levi Priest,	Stephen Houghton,	Samuel Snow,
John Clark,	Jacob Kilburn,	Jonathan Whitcomb,
Samuel Corey,	Enoch Roper,	Levi White,
Ebenezer Harris,	Reuben Ross,	Aaron Willard.
Abel Houghton,	Eber Sawyer,	Artemas Willard.

BOLTON MEN.

Sergt. Daniel Harris,	Nathaniel Holman,	Rufus Moore,
Matthew Atherton,	James Houghton,	Beriah Oaks.

HARVARD MEN.

Simeon Conant,	America Hamblin,	Benjamin Warner,
Jacob Fairbank,	Samuel Hutchins,	Phineas Warner.
Israel Hale,	David Stone,	

[Mass. Archives, Muster Rolls, XXIV, 119–120.]

The second precinct, during the revolution, grew more rapidly than the first, and in 1780 outnumbered and outvoted the older part of the town. It was finally set off from Lancaster, April 25, 1781, and named Sterling (with not unusual carelessness of orthography), in honor of the brave General William Alexander, the putative Earl of Stirling, with whom Lancaster men fought at Long Island and Monmouth.

At a town meeting in Lancaster, July 13, 1781, ...

8. Voted to raise the three and five-months' men agreeable to General Court Order.

9. Voted to Chuse a Committee to procure the said men.

10. Voted and Choose Josiah Ballard, Jeremiah Haskell and Joshua Fletcher as the above Committee.

LANCASTER, July 23, 1781. . . . . . .

2. Voted to raise two hundred and seventy five pounds to pay the three and five months men. . . . . . .

LANCASTER, September 3, 1781. . . . . . .

7. Voted that the constable be directed to proceed imediately to collect the money asses^d. on the town to pay the soldiers their money for the three months service and particularly their marching money.

LANCASTER, Sept. 10, 1781; Voted to desire the several Captains to Call their Companies together on Fryday next at 9 o'Clock A. M, at the meeting house in s⁴ town and the several constables are directed to exert themselves to Collect as much money in Silver as possible for paying the soldiers their advance pay.

Many of the soldiers that served for three months in 1781 may be found in the Rhode Island rolls given upon previous pages.

GUARDS.

Besides the frequent calls upon the militia for troops to go beyond the state line upon sudden alarms, or during some temporary emergency, there were constant details for guard duty within the state; and among the papers of company commanders in the revolution are found many requisitions like the following:

HARVARD, March 21, 1778.

To Capt. David Nurse. Sr. in consequence of orders I Rec⁴ from Gen¹¹ Warner he having Rec⁴ orders from the General Court of this State' Baring Dait the 9 of this Instant and I am ordered to Detach 46 men out of my Regᵗ. non-commisioned officers and privit soldiers to Do duty at or near Boston till the 2 day of July next unless Sooner Discarged : your cota is fore men which you are to Detach from your company without Delay, s⁴ men to be Equiped with arms and amonition acording to law and to be at head-qurters at Boston on the 2 Day of April next with out fail ther to Recᶜ further order & it is Resolved that if any noncommissoned officer or privit soldier so drafted as afores⁴ shall Neglect or Refuse to march in consequence heirof he shall hire an able bodyed man in his Rome or pay a fine of Ten pounds within twenty-fore hours, or shall be considered as a soldier in that detachment, and yᵉ Capt or commanding officer of the company shall cause others to be drafted in stead of those who pay their fines; or other men to be hired with said fines and you make Return of your doings and the names of the men so Drafted.

You are ordered to view the arms of both Lists and their acotrements & see that they are Compleet according to Law and at a minits warning and make Return of the number you have on Both Lists of men : and ther arms and ther Equipments : these Returns must be made to me by the 20 Day of this Instant without fail.

Yours to Serve.   J. WHITNEY *Coll.*

A Pay Roll of Capt. John White's Company in Colo Abijah Stearns' Regiment of Militia in the State of Mass. Bay. Doing Duty at and near Boston from the first Day of April Untill the Second Day of July 1778.

LANCASTER MEN.

John White, *captain.*	Elisha Phelps,	Oliver Wheelock,
Nath¹. Beaman, *lieut.*	Ephraim White,	Phinehas Wilder,
Samuel Snow, *sergt.*	Ebenezer Burditt,	Reuben Ross,
Samuel Johnson, *corp.*	John Wheelock,	Thomas Moore,
Abel Sawyer,	James Wilder,	Samuel Brown,
Abel Allen,	Jonathan Whitcomb,	Abraham Headley.
Elisha Woods,	Levi Robbins,	. . . .

LEOMINSTER MEN.

Sergt. John Low,	Joseph Johnson,	Phineas Carter,
Benjamin Johnson,	Josiah Whitcomb,	Samuel Boutwell,
Benjamin Stearns,	Nathaniel Joslin,	John Kidder.

There were sixty-nine men in the company, those omitted here being of Ashburnham, Princeton and Lunenburg.

[Mass. Archives, Muster Rolls, xxiv, 49.]

In Colonel Nathan Sparhawk's regiment, Captain James Mirick's company, near Boston, September to December, 1778, were :

OF LANCASTER.

Solomon Fleeman,	Benjamin Hale,	Phineas Phelps.
Reuben Gates,	Elisha Johnson,	

OF BOLTON.

William Coolidge,	Richard Townsend,	Abel Wilder.
Barnabas Sawyer,		

OF HARVARD.

David Baldwin,	Daniel Page,	Ephraim Whitney,
America Hamlin,	John Parker,	Stephen Whitney.
Oliver Haskell,	Walter Pollard,	

[Mass. Archives, Muster Rolls, xxi, 125.]

Extensive barracks were built at Rutland, and the English regiments of General Burgoyne's troops, prisoners of war, were removed thither from Cambridge, at which place they were thought too easily accessible if the British forces, by sudden raid from Newport, should attempt their release. The transfer was made during April, 1779. The guards employed were many of them boys, old men, and others unfit for field service.

Continental Pay Roll of Capt. Elias Pratt's Co. of Guards doing duty at Rutland. [April to July, 1779.]

Jabez Fairbank, *lieut.*	Samuel Brooks,	Walter Pollard,
Stephen Nowel, *sergt.*	Rufus Carter,	Abiah Rice,
John Atherton, "	Jonas Chase,	Daniel Rice,
Benjamin Buss, "	John Divol,	Silvester Roper,
David Wheelock, "	Samuel Foster,	John Scollay,
John Roper, *corp.*	Samuel Hoar,	David Stone,
Samuel Barnard, "	Abel Houghton,	Amos Tenney,
Nathan Adams,	Jonas Johnson,	James Thompson,
Samuel Allen,	Elias Joslin,	Hananiah Whitney,
Jonathan Barnard,	Reuben Lipenwell,	Luther Wilder,
John Blanchard,	Rufus Moore,	etc. . . . . .

[Mass. Archives, Muster Rolls, XXV, 123.]

Continental Pay Roll for Capt. Ephraim Hartwell's Company Doing Duty at Rutland Oct. 1779 to April 1780.

Sergt. John Persons,	Calvin Greenleaf,	Walter Pollard,
Nathan Adams,	Daniel Greenleaf,	Samuel Prentice,
Gideon Beaman,	Daniel Hazeltine,	Jonathan Tucker,
Benjamin Carter,	Samuel Kilburn,	Luther Wilder,
Zimri Eveleth,	Joseph Larkin,	Reuben Wilder,
Jacob Fairbank,	Jonathan Moore,	Daniel Willard,
Peter Fletcher,		etc. . . . .

[Mass. Archives, Muster Rolls, XXV, 120.]

MARINE SERVICE.

Lancaster furnished a few volunteers for the privateers that did efficient service on the coast, but the names of two only have come down to us. Reverend Timothy Harrington records their deaths thus :

Joseph Wilder, Junr. of ye Small Pox at sea.
Joseph Phelps, died of his wounds in a sea fight.

VI. CONTINENTAL ARMY.

The returns of enlistments for three years or during the
war, made by the towns in obedience to an order of General Court passed February 3, 1778, are found in Massachusetts Archives, XLII.   At that time few towns had filled
their quotas under the first call, which required one-seventh
of the males above sixteen years of age :

Lancaster. No. of males 672. One seventh 96. In service 91. Wanting 5.
Harvard.   "   341   "   49   "   48   "   1.
Bolton.   "   299   "   43   "   42   "   1.
Leominster.   "   216   "   31   "   32   "   0.

The terms of service of these "Continentals" mostly
ended in the spring of 1780, when new levies were called
for.   Ten men were sent from Lancaster at that time.
The third requisition came at the close of the same year.

*Return of men procured, agreeable to Resolve of 2ᵈ Dec. 1780, taken
from the Superintendent's Returns as well as from the Returns made
by the Several Towns* :

Lancaster,   35 men demanded, 34 procured.
Bolton,   16   "   16   "
Leominster,   13   "   13   "
Harvard,   15   "   15   "

In March, 1782, a call was issued under which Lancaster's quota was seven.   The sum of Lancaster's three-
years quota was therefore 148 ; and the records prove that
the requisitions were filled, although at last enormous
bounties were in a few cases paid to hireling substitutes
and "bounty-jumpers ;" and numerous contentions arose
between towns over their rival claims to particular soldiers.
The three-years' men were all volunteers, recourse being
had to a draft only in case of short-service calls.

. . . . Resolve, to stop proceedings on Execution vs. assessors of Lancaster issued by mistake by late Treasʳ. Gardner for not assessing a class,
for the raising one of the 3 years men for Continental army 1781 : it appears that the town had raised their full quota of men and that they had
actually joined the army when the Execution was issued.

[Court Records, XLIV, 244 ; Nov. 2, 1782.]

On pet^n. of Hon. Jno. Sprague on behalf of Lancaster for the abatement of a fine and allowance of a bounty to sd. town for reasons set forth in sd. petition — Resolved, that the fine be abated and bountyal lowed, the town having procured the whole of the men required by the resolve.

[A deficiency of one man had been reported under resolve of Dec. 2, 1780.]

[Court Records, XLV, 58.]

. . . . . the Class in Lan^r. of which Jabez Fairbank was the head, hired a soldier for the Continental army for 3 years and liberated him from jail at expense of 100£, supposing they had an undoubted right to s^d soldier, but afterwards he was challenged and by muster-master determined to belong to Rutland, and thus this class is deficient and liable to the fine annexed. Rutland was ordered to return 90£ to J. F. whose class is allowed 30 days to procure another man and execution is staid meanwhile, but to issue if they neglect to procure and muster a soldier and march him to Springfield and procure a receipt therefor, beyond the town.

Court Records, XLIII, 292; Feb. 20, 1782.]

In accordance with a custom of the period, the town had been divided into as many "squadrons" or "classes" as there were soldiers required for the quota — thirty-five ; and each class was expected to furnish a volunteer for three years. The amount of bounty paid was regularly assessed upon the citizens of the class, and by law was collectable like any other rate, the constable taking the body of the debtor if the assessment was not speedily forthcoming. If no person could be found willing to serve for such sum as the class would agree to pay, lots were cast to decide which member of the class should go. The man upon whom such lot fell had to enter the army for the remainder of that year, or supply a substitute.

The records of the continental soldiers serving for Lancaster, or residents of the town, 1777–1780, will be given in order of regiments, with dates of enlistment, names of captains under which they served, and such other facts of interest as have been ascertained. No representative of the town is found in the First or Ninth Massachusetts Continental regiments. The service was for three years unless specified. Nearly all the Massachusetts regiments participated in the battles that caused the surrender of Burgoyne, and were, during their remaining terms of service, for the most part stationed along the Hudson.

SECOND MASSACHUSETTS, COLONEL JOHN BAILEY.

Joseph House, lieutenant, Jan. 1, 1777, to August 1, 1778; resigned.
Perley Rogers, a negro, corporal, March 18, 1777, Capt. Hugh Maxwell.
Charles Stuart, a mulatto, deserted May 20, 1777.   "   "

THIRD MASSACHUSETTS, COLONEL JOHN GREATON.

Joseph Bailey, Jan. 1, 1777, Capt. Samuel Foster.
Jabez Beaman, Feb. 4, 1777, Capt. Charles Colton; *claimed by Harvard*.
Eleazar Priest, Jan. 17, 1777, Capt. Job Sumner; "with Qr. Mr. General."

FOURTH MASSACHUSETTS, COLONEL WILLIAM SHEPARD.

James Battels, Jan. 31, 1777, Capt. George Webb; *claimed by Leominster*.
John Battels, April 1, 1777;   "   "   "   "

FIFTH MASSACHUSETTS, COLONEL RUFUS PUTNAM.

This regiment was prominent in the battles of Stillwater and Saratoga.

In Captain Job Whipple's Company:

Cornelius Baker, corporal, Feb. 1, 1777.
Abel Bigelow, drummer, Feb. 10, 1777.
Jonas Carter, Jan. 10, 1777; a Lunenburg man, hired.
Joshua Johnson, May 10, 1777.
Jacob Kilburn, corporal, Feb. 10, 1777; promoted sergeant.
William Prentice, May 26, 1777.
John Wheeler, March 26, 1777.
Peter Willard, June 1, 1777.

In Captain Jonathan Goodale's Company:

James Sawyer, June 20, 1777; discharged March 9, 1779; hired by Princeton.

(Lemuel Shed and David Fleeman enlisted in this regiment but "never joined." For *Shed*, see Tenth regiment.)

SIXTH MASSACHUSETTS, COLONEL THOMAS NIXON.

This regiment was present in battles of Stillwater, Saratoga, etc.

Zimori Eveleth, drummer, Dec. 19, 1779, Capt. Benjamin Heywood.
Aaron Glazier, Feb. 12, 1777; served 46 m. 19 d.; Capt. Adam Wheeler.
Gershom Flagg, May 26, 1777, Capt. Simon Learned.
Abijah Phillips, Feb. 22, 1779, Capt. Samuel Flowers.
Burpee Prouty, Dec. 19, 1779, Capt. Japheth Daniels.
Paul Sawyer, Jan. 1, 1777; served four years; Capt. William Toogood.

SEVENTH MASSACHUSETTS, COLONEL ICHABOD ALDEN, *killed*; LT.COL-
ONEL JOHN BROOKS.

Jacob Allen, 1781, Capt. Eliphalet Thorp.
Shubael Bailey, 1781, Capt. Rufus Lincoln; *claimed for Leominster.*

EIGHTH MASSACHUSETTS, COLONEL MICHAEL JACKSON.

Timothy Wilder, Aug. 1, 1777, Captain James Varnum.

TENTH MASSACHUSETTS, COLONEL THOMAS MARSHALL.

This regiment was engaged in battles of Stillwater, Saratoga, etc.

In Captain Samuel King's Company:

John Hewitt, lieutenant, Jan. 1, 1777, to Nov. 1, 1778.
Samuel Blodget, enlisted 1777, by town returns; *not found in pay certifi-
cates.*
Philip Corey, sergeant, January, 1777; sergeant-major; ensign, Decem-
ber, 1780; lieutenant; served four years.
Samuel Corey, fifer, Jan. 1, 1777.
Elijah Dole, corporal, Jan. 1, 1777; died July 30, 1778.
Peter Franklin, a negro, died April 21, 1777.
Ephraim Fuller, July 7, 1779, aged sixteen.
Gideon Georges, a negro, Aug. 10, 1777, aged 17; *claimed by Bolton.*
Job Lewis, a negro, Jan. 1, 1777; "on wagon service."
Abel Moor, Jan. 1, 1777, died April 1, 1777; *claimed by Bolton.*
Jacob Lyden Parker, enlisted 1777, by town returns; *not found in pay
certificates.*
Jacob Phelps, sergeant, Jan. 1, 1777.
John Priest, wounded and discharged, Feb. 27, 1778.
James Russeil, sergeant, Jan. 1, 1777.
Robert Skinner, Jan. 1, 1777, died April 14, 1779; *claimed by Bolton.*
Cornelius Tigh, Jan. 1, 1777; a substitute; *claimed by Boston, etc.*
David Whitcomb, Jan. 1, 1777; died April 28, 1778.
Francis Whitcomb, Jan. 1, 1777; invalided because of wound.
Asa Wyman, March 1, 1780, aged seventeen.
John Wyman, corporal, July 10, 1779, aged seventeen.

In Captain William Parks' Company:

Julius Cæsar, a negro, Nov. 26, 1779, aged nineteen.
Robert Richardson, Oct. 7, 1779.
Lemuel Shed, Oct. 23, 1779.

In Captain William Warner's Company:

Edom London, a negro slave, Jan. 1, 1777; *claimed by Winchendon.*
Levi Priest, March 22, 1777.
John Warner, corporal, Jan. 27, 1777; promoted sergeant, April 1, 1779.

In Captain Josiah Smith's Company:

Samuel Herring, corporal, Jan. 17, 1777.

ELEVENTH MASSACHUSETTS, COLONEL EBENEZER FRANCIS, *killed;* COLONEL BENJAMIN TUPPER.

Lazarus Batherick, Feb. 28, 1780; in town returns, "enlisted with Capt. Ezra Lunt for Col. Henley."

Stephen Thompson, by town returns, "enlisted in Captain Steele's company, Colonel Francis;" *not in pay certificates.*

TWELFTH MASSACHUSETTS, COLONEL SAMUEL BREWER; LIEUT.-COL. EBENEZER SPROAT.

John Whiting, ensign, promoted to lieutenant, July 5, 1779.

Abiah Rice, corporal, Jan. 1, 1780, Capt. John Pray.

THIRTEENTH MASSACHUSETTS, COLONEL EDWARD WIGGLESWORTH; LIEUT.-COLONEL CALVIN SMITH.

In Company of Capt. Peter Page, successor to Capt. Matthew Fairfield.

Winslow Phelps, ensign, Jan. 1, 1777; resigned Dec. 26, 1777.

Benjamin Ballard, sergeant, Feb. 19, 1777.

Samuel Ballard, Feb. 20, 1777; *bounty paid by Bedford.*

John Dollerson, March 15, 1777; served 45 m. 16 d.; *claimed by Bolton and Stow.*

Peleg Rodman, Feb. 12, 1777; died June 2, 1778.

In Company of Captain Christian Woodbridge:

Thomas Wright, March 1. 1780; deserted Oct. 2, 1780.

FOURTEENTH MASSACHUSETTS, COLONEL GAMALIEL BRADFORD.

In Captain Zebedee Redding's Company:

Jonathan Sawyer, lieutenant, Jan. 1, 1777; killed by Indians, July 19, 1777.

Samuel Bennett, corporal, Jan, 1, 1777; discharged December, 1778,

Nathan Easterbrooks, corporal, Jan, 9, 1777.

Isaac Eveleth, April, 1777, re-enlisted 1781; aged forty-seven.

William Eveleth, Feb. 2, 1777; died Oct. 6, 1779.

Luther Fairbank, sergeant, Jan. 10, 1777; discharged Nov, 20, 1777.

Abel Fairbank, Jan. 9, 1777; died Nov, 26. 1777.

George Richardson, corporal, Jan. 30, 1777.

Benjamin Wheelock, April 4, 1777.

Jonathan Wheelock, drummer, Jan. 2. 1777; promoted to drum-major.

Joseph Wheelock, Feb. 4, 1777; died March 10, 1778.

James Willard, Feb. 12, 1777.

Samuel Woods, May 26, 1777; taken prisoner; discharged 1781.

Daniel Wyman, Jan. 30, 1777; died Aug. 16, 1778.

In Captain Isaiah Stetson's Company:

Jabez Brooks, sergeant, Jan. 1, 1777.

FIFTEENTH MASSACHUSETTS, COLONEL TIMOTHY BIGELOW of Worcester.

This regiment was engaged in battles of Stillwater, Saratoga and Monmouth; and stationed at Verplank's Point, Robinson's Farms, N. J., Peckskill, Valley Forge, West Point.

Henry Haskell, lieutenant-colonel, Jan 1, 1777, to July 1, 1779; mustered out as supernumerary; died at Lancaster, June 10, 1807.

Ephraim Sawyer, Jr., lieutenant, Jan. 1, 1777, resigned Oct. 1, 1777, to accept captaincy in Sixteenth Massachusetts.

In Captain Joseph Hodgkins' Company:

James Armstrong. July 22, 1777.

Philip Branscomb, drummer, April 26, 1780; deserted; *credited to Lancaster on pay certificates.*

Thomas Cleland, corporal, April 3, 1777; promoted sergeant; served 44 m. 28 d.

Asa Farrar, May 27, 1777.

Stephen Frost, March 11, 1777; discharged February, 1778.

Ebenezer Glazier, May 20, 1777.

Joshua House, by town returns enlisted 1777; *not found in pay certificates.*

Reuben Kendall, a negro, Sept. 10, 1777.

Israel Manning, corporal, April 1, 1777.

Judah Piper, April 21, 1777.

Luther Rice, Feb. 25, 1777.

Abner Sawyer, Sept. 1, 1777: died Nov. 10, 1777.

Onis Simes, Sept. 1, 1777; died Dec. 1, 1777.

Aaron Willard, May 2, 1777.

Levi Wilder, May 24, 1777.

Abel Wright, March 25, 1777; died July 2, 1778.

In Company of Captain Sylvanus Smith:

John Dresser, March 10, 1777; died June 29, 1778.

Elihu Goss, May 20, 1777; died July 6, 1778.

Matthias Larkin, sergeant, May 20, 1777; died April 13, 1778.

Levi Larkin, Sept. 3, 1777.

Edmund Milligen, enlisted 1777, by town returns; *not found in pay certificates.*

Nathan Osgood, Sept. 1, 1777; discharged April 2, 1779.

Seth Ross, drummer, May 2, 1777.

Asa Rugg, enlisted 1777, by town returns; *not found in pay certificates.*

Caleb Whitney, Sept. 1, 1777; died Dec. 10, 1777.

In Company of Captain William Gates — Joseph Pierce's, later:

Artemas Maynard, sergeant, May 29, 1777.

Matthew Wyman, May 16, 1777; *credited to Lunenburg.*

Joshua Whitney, sergeant, Aug. 10, 1777.

In Company of Captain Edward Munroe, (Bowen, in town returns):
William Boardman, May 15, 1777; re-enlisted 1781.
Thomas Grant, March 7, 1781, aged 52; *hired by Princeton.*

Elisha Houghton, sergeant, May 1, 1777, Capt. Joshua Brown; *claimed by Harvard.*
Joseph Jones, Nov. 10, 1777, Capt. Paul Ellis.

SIXTEENTH MASSACHUSETTS, COLONEL HENRY JACKSON.

This regiment was formed in April, 1779, by combining the three battalions of Colonels David Henly, William R. Lee and Henry Jackson, organized under a call for sixteen continental regiments in addition to the original eighty-eight formed early in 1777. None of the sixteen regiments were filled, and they were finally consolidated in spite of the great dissatisfaction caused both among men and officers. Among those enlisted especially for Colonel Henly, were many soldiers from the army of Burgoyne, then prisoners of war. These for the most part deserted as soon as opportunity offered. Colonel Jackson's regiment was in the expedition against the British force at Newport in 1778.

Ephraim Sawyer, Jr., captain, Dec. 26, 1777; supernumerary April 9, 1779.
William Harris, pay-master, died Oct. 30, 1778.

Serving in Company of Captain Thomas Turner:
Alixus Bear, Jan. 21, 1779; deserted April 25, 1779.
Nathaniel Brown, May 11, 1780; *claimed by Leominster.*
Nicholas Brune, May 27, 1777; deserted April 1, 1779.
John Kilburn, July 13, 1777; enlisted by Capt. Ezra Lunt for Col. Henley.
John Newman, fifer, Jan. 1, 1779; *claimed by Bolton.*
William Staples, May 26, 1777; deserted April 17, 1779.
William Taylor, Sept. 27, 1777: deserted Oct. 25, 1779; enlisted by Capt. Lunt for Col. Henley.
Peter Tew, Dec. 8, 1777; deserted April 1, 1779.
Isaac Warren, Sept. 24, 1777; enlisted by Capt. Lunt for Col. Henley.

MASSACHUSETTS ARTILLERY, ARTIFICERS, ETC. COL. HENRY KNOX (BRIG. GENERAL); COL. JOHN CRANE; LIEUT.-COL. DAVID MASON.

Enlisted in Capt. John Bryant's Company of Artificers:
John Baker, March 1, 1777; also with Capt. Benjamin Frothingham.
Joseph Bennett, March 30, 1777;   "   "   "
Josiah Bowers, Sept. 20, 1777; re-enlisted Feb. 2, 1781; also with Capt. Benjamin Frothingham.

Ebenezer Flagg, sergt., Jan. 17, 1780; also with Capt. Benj. Frothingham.
Gershom Flagg, Jr., March 8, 1777;   "   "   "
Ichabod Garey, March 22, 1777; re-enlisted March 3, 1781; also with
      Capt. Benjamin Frothingham.
Thomas Goodwin, matross, March 24, 1777.
Lemuel Gates, gunner, March 4, 1777; served 45 m. 27 d.; also with
      Capt. David Cook.
Samuel Gates, gunner, March 4, 1777; served 45 m. 27 d.; also with
      Capt. David Cook.
Jacob Wilder, Sept. 20, 1777; also with Knox's Artificers.

In other Companies :

William Campbell, 1781, with Capt. Thomas Jackson.
John Fuller, 1777, by town returns, with "Captain [David] Bradley,
      Colonel [Thomas] Crafts."
Cain Lewis, a negro, Aug. 17, 1777, with Capt. Thomas Wells; deserted
      January, 1778.
John McCoy, bombardier, Jan. 1, 1777, with Capt. Nathaniel Donnell;
      served four years.
Gilbert McIntyre, April 14, 1777; served three years with Capt. Benjamin
      Frothingham.
Jacob Stiles, Jan. 1, 1780; with Captains Thomas Patten and Phineas
      Parker; also in Capt. William Howe's Artificers at Springfield.
John Wilder; served under same captains as Jacob Stiles.

DRAGOONS.   COLONEL ELISHA SHELDON.

John Priest, corporal, March 22, 1777, Capt. Nathaniel Crafts.

FIRST NEW HAMPSHIRE, COLONEL JOSEPH CILLEY.

William Shaw, 1777, with Capt. William Scott.

UNKNOWN, *from town returns, etc.*

Jotham Woods, 1777; re-enlisted 1781.
John Wheelock, 1777; "Capt. Oaks."
Timothy Whiting, Jr., aide of Quarter-Master-General U. S. A.

At a town meeting, January 2, 1781, the following action
was recorded :

7.   Voted to raise our Quota of Men to serve in the Continental Army
for three years or during ye War, agreeable to the Resolve of the General
Court.

8.   Voted to Choose a Committe of twelve Men to hire the above men.

9.   Chose Israel Moor, Samuel Thurston, Natha^l. Beaman, Cyrus
Fairbank, Jonas Wyman, Josiah Kendall Jun., Capt. Samuel Sawyer,
Capt. Ephraim Wilder, Eben^r. Allen, Josiah Ballard, Dea. Joel Houghton,
Thomas Brown for s^d Committe.

13

LANCASTER, January 8, 1781. . . . . .

3. Voted that above Committe Chosen to hire the Men for 3 years service be impowered in every Respect, as the Committe Chosen ye last year to hire ye 40 Men sent for by the General Court.

4. Voted to Dismiss Leut. Ballard from serving in the above Committe and Chose Maj: Gardiner Wilder in his Room.

LANCASTER, January 11, 1781. . . . . .

1. Voted to make an addition of Six to ye above Committe for hireing of Soldiers.

2. Chose Capt. Nathaniel Balch, Capt. Samuel Ward, Capt. Timothy Whiting, Wm Dunsmoor, Esq., James Richardson and Capt. Fortunatus Eager for s^d Addition.

3. Chose Jabez Fairbank as one of the above Committe in the Room of Thos Brown who was Excused.

LANCASTER, Jany. 28, 1781. . . . . . .

1. Voted to Raise ye Sum of Six Thousand five Hund^d and Sixty two Pounds ten Shillings New Emission Currency to hire ye Soldiers for the Army.

2. Voted that the above sum be Assesed and Collected as soon as may be.

LANCASTER, February 5, 1781. . . . . .

2. Voted to See if the Town will Class in Order to get ye Men for ye Army and it pass^d in ye Negative.

LANCASTER, February 8th, 1781. . . . . . .

1. Voted to See if the Town would Class for ye Purpose of geting ye Men for ye Army and it Pass^d in ye Negative.

LANCASTER, February 19, 1781. . . . . .

1. Voted to See if the Town would Class and it pass^d in ye Negative.

2^d Voted to make an Addition of Seventeen to ye Committee for hiring Men.

3^d Voted and Chose for s^d Addition ye following Persons viz: Capt. David Osgood, Capt. Edward Newton, Nathaniel Houghton, Dea. Levi Moore, Dea. Benjamin Houghton, John Brown, Capt. Ephr. Carter, Silas Howe, James Kendal Jun., Joseph Reed, Levi Wilder, Heman Kendal, Capt. Thos. Gates, Joseph Sever, Capt. Nathl Sawyer Jun., Capt. John White Jun., Gershom Flagg.

4. Voted, that the town be divided into 35 Squadrons.

5. Voted, that the Assessors Divide ye Town as equal as they can into the above Squadrons.

6. Chose Aaron Sawyer for a Committee Man instead of Silas How.

March 16, ... Voted and Chose Dea. Eben^r Buss, Capt. Benj^a Richardson, Capt. Ephr^m Carter, Committee of Inspection and Correspondence.

The two first named belonged to Sterling; after the division of the town, Joshua Fletcher and Deacon William Willard were chosen in their places.

LANCASTER, April 2, 1781. . . . . . .
Voted to acknowledge what the Assessors have done with Regard to Classing the Town as being agreable to ye Act of Court.

April 25, 1781, Governor Hancock signed the act which created from Lancaster territory the town of Sterling.

DESCRIPTIVE LIST OF ENLISTMENTS, 1781.

	Age.	Height.	Complexion.	Occupation.	Date enlisted.	
Clarck Gibbs,	51	5 ft. 9 in.	light.	farmer·	July 5,	for 3 yrs.
Paul Kilborn,	25	6 "	dark.	joiner.	March 2,	"
Andrew Haskell,	33	5 " 11 "	dark.	farmer.	July 5	"
Ephraim White,	20	5 " 6 "	light.	farmer.	July 6,	"
Jeduthan Sawyer,	18	5 " 7 "	light.	farmer.	July 4,	6 mos.
Ephraim Larkin,	18	5 " 11 "	dark.	tarmer.	July 2,	"
Thomas Grant,	52	5 " 9 "	light.	weaver.	March 7,	3 yrs.
Samuel Barret,	18	5 " 4 "	light.	farmer.	July 20,	"
John Carter,	30	5 " 10 "	black.	farmer.	March 7,	"
Nathaniel Parkins,	26	5 " 6 "	light.	farmer.	Jany 21,	"
Wm. Gould,	16	5 " 6 "	dark.	farmer.	March 29,	"
Seth Sampson,	34	5 " 7 "	light.	farmer.	Feby. 11,	"
Beckes Boston,	28	5 " 5 "	black.	farmer.	April 7,	"
Isaac Payne,	24	5 " 9 "	light.	farmer.	Sept. 24,	"
Nathll. Books,	21	5 " 10 "	dark.	farmer.	Sept. 29,	6 mos.
Micah Ross,	22	5 " 11 "	light.	"	March 27,	3 yrs.
Jonathan Barnard,	17	5 " 4 "	light.	"	March 28,	"
Patrick Neef,	45	5 " 9 "	light.	"	June 19,	"
James Dunton,	21	5 " 4 "	light.	"	March 1,	"
–Ephrm. Whitcomb,	33	5 " 8 "	light.	"	May 1,	"
Chederhomr Collins	17	5 " 3 "	dark.	"	June 21,	"
Eli Lewis,	17	5 " 2 "	light.	"	June 21,	"
Josiah Bowers,	27	5 " 11 "	"	"cordwinder"	Feb. 20,	"
Isaac Eveleth,	47	5 " 8 "	"	farmer.	Feb. 12,	"
James Pratt,	42	5 " 5 "	"	"	May 27,	"
George McBride,	20	5 " 7 "	"	"	Feb. 20,	"
William Flud.	22	5 " 7 "	"	"	March 26,	"
Peter Zwear,	25	5 " 11 "	"	"	March 28,	"
Jesse Wyman,	48	5 " 8 "	"	"dish-turner"	April 27,	"
Ichabod Gary,	37	5 " 5 "	"	farmer.	March 3,	"
Calvin Piper,	18	5 " 5 "	"	tanner.	March 15,	"
Topsal Woodard,	16	5 " 4 "	black.	farmer.	Feb. 27,	"

	Age.	Height.	Complexion.	Occupation.	Date enlisted.	
Roger Bartlett,	41	5 ft. 8 in.	light.	farmer.	March 5,	3 yrs.
Nathan Tafft,	22	5 " 9 "	"	saddler.	Feb. 13,	"
Case Whitney,	37	5 " 5 "	black.	farmer.	March 5,	"
Jotham Woods,	40	5 " 4 "	dark.	"	March 8,	"
Lemuel Shed,						
Asa Knowlton,	23	5 " 11 "	dark(1 eye) "		March 5,	" 38

[Mass. Archives, Muster Rolls, XXXIII, 333–6; 386–8.]

A list of "recruits unfit for service" includes of the above :

Clark Gibbs, 60 years old.   Rheumatic and decrepid with age.
Lemuel Shed, infirm.
Jotham Wood, 41, bodily deformed.

Of the seven enrolled for three years to fill the quota of Lancaster under the final call, made March 1, 1782, William Deputin is the only one whose name is found, his enlistment being attested by the following :

WORCESTER, May 10th, 1782.
Received of Lt. Amos Allen, Chairman of Class No. — for the town of Lancaster, the sum of Fifty-Four pounds L. Money as a Bounty to serve in the Continental army for the term of three years.   Witness my Hand.

WILLIAM DEPUTIN.

The chief acts of the great revolutionary drama, after the first year's battles, were outside of New England, and Lancaster soldiers are more frequently found therefore in the six and nine-months' expeditions—in the defence of Rhode Island and Boston—in the re-enforcements sent upon emergencies to various points along the Hudson— among the guards over prisoners of war at Cambridge or Rutland.   Hence the recorded deaths upon the battle-field are comparatively few, while suffering and death from small-pox and wasting camp fevers form the text of many a sad petition during and after the long contest.   As time went on and volunteers grew more reluctant, and persuasive bounties became larger, new names were brought into Lancaster rolls ; and, as is often the case with hireling soldiery, against such names is sometimes set down the disgrace of desertion.   Of these, some were probably Burgoyne's soldiers, many of whom enlisted with intent to escape.

It is not claimed that the catalogue of nearly six hundred names in the foregoing pages gives a completely accurate enumeration of the men sent out by Lancaster in various patriotic service during the Revolution; although it is a labored compilation from scores of volumes of muster-rolls and other manuscript records in the state archives and various libraries. Many rolls, especially of militia for brief terms of service, are undoubtedly lost. Pay-rolls very commonly omit all mention of residence; and among the final pay certificates of Massachusetts soldiers for 1777–1780, forming twenty volumes, in the Massachusetts Archives, there are hundreds of names with no local habitation attached. A few of these names have been found to be undoubtedly Lancastrian. The valuation return of 1771, which practically is a census of tax-payers, has given authority for claiming some; petitions and militia rolls have led to the discovery of others. Several Lancaster soldiers are found serving for the credit of other towns. Moreover, so close was the connection of families in the villages that had grown out of or about Lancaster, and so frequently does the same christian name occur in those families, that biographical research is continually running against stumbling blocks in attempting to assort the re-duplicated Jacobs, Johns, Josephs and Jonathans. In short, the difficulty of making a roster pretending to anything like completeness has been very great, requiring much time and patience. The result, however imperfect it may be, is an astonishing one, exceedingly honorable to the town. It proves that almost every male citizen of military age must have served at some period of the war, either personally or by substitute; and that fully one-fourth of the whole male population above the age of sixteen were kept constantly in the army during the most trying years of the conflict. Nor was this exceptional, probably, for the Marquis de Chastellux, travelling through New England in 1780, says: "Among the men I have met with above twenty years of age, of whatever condition, I have not found two who have not borne arms, heard the whistling of balls, and even received some wounds."

The scant and unsystematic records extant, afford us the names of thirty Lancaster soldiers, who laid down their lives for their country between the date of the battle of Bunker Hill and the close of the year 1779. There were doubtless others unrecorded. Neither the causes of death, nor wounds received, are often mentioned in the rolls, and only five of the above thirty are known to have been killed in action.

Those who for various reasons could not bear arms, stinted no exertions, no sacrifices in the common cause. In the absence of the more stalwart breadwinners, the wives and daughters took up their burdens with hands already accustomed to toil, and the food harvest knew little diminution. The town fathers systematically cared for the needy families of those in service, and this care was continued to the widows and orphans after the close of the war, such expenditure being refunded by the state. In the schedule of dues to the towns "for supplies to soldiers' families," from 1781 to 1785, contained in Massachusetts Archives, xxxi, 66, Lancaster is credited with 1852£,,1ˢ,,4ᵈ. expended.

BOLTON CONTINENTAL SOLDIERS, 1777-9.

FIRST REGIMENT.

Moses Buck, under Capt. Belcher Hancock.
James Campbell,   "   "   "
William Coolidge, under Capt. Jeremiah Miller.
Michael Ferrin, under Capt. Jeremiah Hill; deserted.
York Ruggles, under Capt. Moses Ashley; a slave hired.
Joseph Salt, under Capt. Jeremiah Hill; deserted.

THIRD REGIMENT.

John French, corporal, under Capt. Abraham Watrous; a "stroller" hired.

FOURTH REGIMENT.

Moses Hudson, under Capt. Simon Learned.

FIFTH REGIMENT.

William Bigelow, sergeant, under Capt. Job Whipple.
Jeremiah Burnham,   "   "

TENTH REGIMENT.

In Captain Samuel King's Company:

Josiah Goddard,   Andrew McWain,
George Gideon, claimed for Lancaster.
Abel Moore,   "   "   Died April 1, 1777.
Robert Vaughan, credited to Westminster.
Robert Skinner, "a hired stroller;" died April 14, 1779; credited to Lancaster.

TWELFTH REGIMENT.

John Chowen, mulatto, under Capt. Elisha Brewer; *not found in pay certificates.*

THIRTEENTH REGIMENT.

Benjamin Bailey, under Capt. Ebenezer Smith.
James Bridge, under "Capt. White," in town reports.
John Dollerson, under Capt. Peter Page; claimed for Lancaster.
Reuben Moore,   "   "   "   "

FOURTEENTH REGIMENT.

In Captain Zebedee Redding's Company:

Isaac Buck,	Joseph Houghton,	Joseph Pratt,
John Hastings,	Abner Moore,	James Snow.

FIFTEENTH REGIMENT.

In Captain Daniel Barnes's Company:

John Barnard, Jr.,	John Burnham,	Edward Johnson, Jr.,
Abraham Brigham, sergt.,	James Crosman,	Jonas Johnson,
Benjamin Bruce.	Elijah Foster, Jr.,	Solomon Jones,
Daniel Bruce, corp.,	Asa Johnson,	Job Priest,
		Joseph Woods, corp.

Edward Howard, sergt., in Capt. Monroe's Co.; of Concord, hired.

SIXTEENTH REGIMENT.

Richard Joy, drummer, under Capt. Langdon.
Daniel McDonald,   "   "
John Newman, fifer, under Capt. Thomas Turner.
Antony Theron, under Capt. Thomas Hunt; a Frenchman, hired.

COLONEL JOHN CRANE'S ARTILLERY.

William Whybert, under Capt. Thomas Wells.

ENLISTED 1781, FOR THREE YEARS.

Jonathan Ball,	Levi Hazard,	Jonathan Munger, sailor,
William Bigelow,	John Hill,	Plato Negro,

Timothy Curtis,	Rufus Houghton,	Abel Priest,
Haran Eager,	James McIntire, sailor,	Thomas Wassels,
Moses Haskell,	John Moore,	John Whitney.

HARVARD CONTINENTAL THREE-YEARS SOLDIERS, 1777-79.

SECOND REGIMENT.

John Oaks, in "8th company."
Aaron Sampson, *not found in pay-rolls.*

THIRD REGIMENT.

Jabez Beaman, under Capt. Charles Colton; claimed for Lancaster.
Elias Warner, under Capt. Job Sumner.
James Willis,   "   "   "

FIFTH REGIMENT.

Jacob Davis, corporal, under Capt. Job Whipple; died Oct. 23, 1779.

SIXTH REGIMENT.

Jeremiah Bridge, in Capt. Adam Wheeler's company.

EIGHTH REGIMENT.

In Captain Benjamin Brown's Company:

Sergt. Jabez Keep,	Ezekiel Cox,	Jonathan Hutchins,
Corp. Phineas Whitney,	Jonathan Farnsworth,	Jabez Keep, Jr.
Samuel Atherton,	Israel Hale,	Jonathan Stearns,
Simon Blanchard,	William Harris,	Luther Topliff,
Thomas Burges,	Joseph Frye, died February 1, 1778.	
Daniel Burt,	Abraham Munroe, died March 11, 1778.	
	William Stone, killed July 17, 1779.	

TENTH REGIMENT.

In Captain Samuel King's Company:

| Thomas Chamberlain, | Reuben Dodge, ensign, | Isaac Sanderson. |
| Reuben Conant, sergeant. | Samuel Finney, corporal. | |

TWELFTH REGIMENT.

Francis Saussure, under Capt. John Pray.

FIFTEENTH REGIMENT.

In Captain Joshua Brown's Company:

Samuel Barret,	Levi Farnsworth,	William Proctor,
Zadock Burnham,	Manasseh Farnsworth,	Consider Turner, corp.
Titus Coburn,	Samuel Farnsworth,	John Whitney,
Elnathan Daby,	Jesse Lund,	Benjamin Willard, sergt.
Jonas Davis,	Eleazar Parkers,	Samuel Worcester.

Elisha Houghton, sergeant; claimed for Lancaster.

In Captain Sylvanus Smith's Company:

Thomas Burnham, corporal.   Joseph Longley, corporal.
David Parker, under Capt. Edmund Monroe.

COLONEL JOHN CRANE'S ARTILLERY.

Joseph Swaughtridge, under Capt. Benjamin Frothingham; credited to
Boston.

ENLISTED FOR THREE YEARS, IN 1781.

Joel Atherton,	Nath¹. Hellaston [Hazletine]	John Scollay,
John Atherton,	Jabez Keep,	Titus Tuttle,
Jonas Davis,	Daniel Knight,	Elias Warner,
John Dudley,	Asa Mead,	Edmund Wentworth,
Benjamin Hale,	Jason Mead,	Phineas Whitney.

LEOMINSTER CONTINENTAL THREE-YEARS SOLDIERS. 1777-9.

FOURTH REGIMENT.

In Captain George Webb's Company:

James Battles, claimed for Lancaster.   John Battles, claimed for Lancaster

FIFTH REGIMENT.

In Captain Job Whipple's Company:

Nicholas Durham,	Joshua White,	Joshua Peirce,
Richard Patten,	Abel Wilder, sergt.	Luke Wilson, corporal.
Benjamin Stuart,	Daniel Darling, died December 13, 1777.	
David Stearns,	Joshua Prouty, died May 15, 1778.	
	Samuel Rogers, sergt., died July 24, 1777.	

Joseph Hoar, under Capt. Haffield White; deserted.
Ebenezer Winship, drummer, under Capt. Benjamin Gardner; claimed by
Salem.

TENTH REGIMENT.

In Captain William Warner's Company:

Luke Aldridge, drummer.	John Joslin,	Joseph Robbins,
Levi Blood,	Levi Page,	Thomas Robbins,
John Buss, corporal.	Asa Priest,	
Silas Carter,	Pomp Cuffreer, died July 14, 1778.	
Nathaniel Evans, corporal.	Micah Nichols, died July 12, 1778.	
Silas Sharon, a servant, died July 14, 1778.		

TWELFTH REGIMENT.

Luther Marble, in Capt. John Pray's company.

COLONEL THOMAS CRAFT'S ARTILLERY.

In Captain John Gill's Company:

William Carpenter,	Elisha Davis,	Isaac Sollendine.
Daniel Colburn,		

ENLISTED FOR THREE YEARS, 1781.

Shubael Bailey,	David Johnson,	James Smith,
Levi Blood,	Ephraim Johnson,	Josiah Whitcomb,
Asa Buttrick,	David Joslin,	Caleb Wood,
Elisha Davis,	Job Priest,	Samuel Wood.
	Phineas Rice,	

VII. LANCASTER LOYALISTS.

The outburst of rebellion against British tyranny through-out Massachusetts was so universal, and the controversy so hot with the wrath of a people politically wronged, that the term *tory* comes down to us in history loaded with a weight of opprobrium not legitimately its own. After the lapse of a hundred years the word is perhaps no longer synonymous with everything traitorous and vile, but in it a national hate has been embalmed, and when it is desirable to suggest possible respectability and moral rectitude in any member of the conservative party of Revolutionary days, it must be done under the less historically disgraced title,—loyalist. In fact, in 1775, as always, two parties stood contending for principles to which honest convictions made adherents. If among the conservatives were timid office-holders and corrupt self-seekers, there were also of the Revolutionists, blatant demagogues and bigoted parti-sans. The logic of success, though a success made possi-ble at last only by foreign aid, justified the appeal to arms, begun in Massachusetts before revolt was prepared or thought imminent elsewhere. Now, to the careful student of the situation, it seems among the most premature and rash of all the great rebellions in history. But for the pre-cipitancy of the uprising, and the patriotic frenzy that fired the public heart at news of the first bloodshed, many ripe scholars, many soldiers of experience, might have been saved to aid and honor the building of the republic, instead of being driven into ignominious exile by fear of mob vio-lence and imprisonment, and scourged through the century in story as enemies of their country. In and about Lancaster the loyalists were an eminently respectable minority. At first, indeed, not only those naturally conservative by reason of wealth, or pride or birthright, but the majority of the intellectual leaders, both ecclesiastic and civilian, deprecated revolt as downright suicide. They denounced the Stamp Act as earnestly, they loved their country, in which their all was at stake, as sincerely as did their radical neighbors. Some of them, after the bloody nineteenth of April, acquiesced with such grace as they could in what they now saw to be inevitable, and tempered with prudent counsel the blind zeal of partisanship; thus ably serving their country in her need. Others would have awaited the issue of events as neutrals; but such the committee of safety, or a mob, not unnaturally treated as enemies.

On the highest rounds of the social ladder stood the great-grandsons of Major Simon Willard, the Puritan commander in the war of 1675. These three gentlemen had large possessions in land, were widely known throughout the Province, and were held in deserved esteem for their probity and ability. They were all royalists at heart, and all connected by marriage with royalist families. Abijah Willard, the eldest, had just passed his fiftieth year. He had won a captaincy before Louisbourg when but twenty-one, and was promoted to a colonelcy in active service against the French; was a thorough soldier, a gentleman of stately presence and dignified manners, and a skilful manager of affairs. For his first wife, he married Elizabeth, sister of Colonel William Prescott; for his second, Mrs. Anna Prentice; he had recently married a third partner, Mrs. Mary McKown, of Boston. He was the wealthiest citizen of Lancaster, kept six horses in his stables, and dispensed liberal hospitality in the mansion inherited from his father, Colonel Samuel Willard. By accepting the appointment of councillor — qualifying himself by the requisite oath August 15, 1774 — he became at once obnoxious to the patriots, and, on the twenty-fourth of the month, when visiting Connecticut on business connected with his large landed interests there, he was arrested by the citizens of the town of Union, who the next day conveyed him to Brimfield. There a mob of four hundred persons, after an informal trial, condemned him to imprisonment in the nearest jail, and began the march thither, having first tarred and feathered Captain Davis of Brimfield, whose indiscreet words had especially angered them. Whether their wrath became somewhat cooled by the colonel's bearing, or by a six-mile march, they released him upon his signing a paper dictated to him, of which the following is a copy, printed at the time in the Boston Gazette and other papers:

STURBRIDGE, August 25, 1774.

Whereas I *Abijah Willard*, of *Lancaster*, have been appointed by mandamus a Counsellor for this Province, and have without due Consideration taken the oath, do now freely and solemnly declare that I am heartily sorry that I have taken the said oath, and do hereby solemnly and in good faith promise and engage that I will not sit or act in the said Council, nor in any other that shall be appointed in such manner and form, but that I will, as much as in me lies, maintain the Charter Rights and Liberties of this Province; and do hereby ask the forgiveness of all honest, worthy Gentlemen that I have offended by taking the abovesaid oath; and desire this may be inserted in the publick prints.

Witness my hand. ABIJAH WILLARD.

[American Archives, IV, I, 731.]

From that time forward Colonel Willard lived quietly at home until the nineteenth of April, 1775; when, setting out in the morning on horseback to visit his farm in Beverly, where he had planned to spend some days in superintending the planting, he was turned from his course by the swarming out of minute-men at the summons of the couriers bringing the alarm from Lexington, and we next find him with the British in Boston. He never saw Lancaster again. It is related that, on the morning of the seventeenth of June, standing with Governor Gage, in Boston, reconnoitring the busy scene upon Bunker Hill, he recognized with the glass his brother-in-law, Colonel William Prescott, and pointed him out to the governor, who asked if he would fight. The answer was: "Prescott will fight you to the gates of hell!" or, as another historian more mildly puts it: "Ay, to the last drop of his blood." Colonel Willard knew whereof he testified, for the two colonels had earned their commissions together in the expedition of 1755.

An officer of so well-known skill and experience as Abijah Willard was deemed a valuable acquisition, and he was offered a colonel's commission in the British army; but refused to serve against his countrymen, and at the evacuation of Boston went to Halifax, having been joined by his own and his brother's family. In 1778, he was proscribed and banished. Later in the war he joined the royal army, at Long Island, and was appointed commissary; in which service it was afterwards claimed by his friends that his management saved the crown thousands of pounds. A malicious pamphleteer of the day, however, accused him of being no better than others, alleging that whatever saving he effected went to swell his own coffers. Willard's name stands prominent among the "Fifty-five," who, in 1783, asked for large grants of land in Nova Scotia as compensation for their losses by the war. In a letter dated August 9, 1784, Justice Peter Oliver writes: "Colonel Willard, with a thousand refugees, I hear, is embarking for Nova Scotia." He chose a residence on the coast of New Brunswick, near St. John, which he named *Lancaster* in remembrance of his beloved birthplace, and there died in May, 1789, having been for several years an influential member of the provincial council. His family returned to Lancaster, recovered the old homestead, and, aided by a small pension from the British government, lived in comparative prosperity. The son Samuel died on January 1, 1856, aged ninety-six years and four months. His widowed sister, Mrs. Anna Goodhue, died on August 2, 1858, at the age of ninety-five. Memories of their wholly pleasant and beneficent lives, abounding in social amenities and Christian graces, still linger about the old mansion.

Levi Willard was three years the junior of Abijah. He had been collector of excise for the county, held the military rank of lieutenant-colonel, and was justice of the peace. With his brother-in-law, Captain Samuel Ward, he conducted the largest mercantile establishment in Worcester county at that date. He had even made the voyage to England to purchase goods. Although not so wealthy as his brother, he might have rivalled him in any field of success but for his broken health; and he was as widely esteemed for his character and capacity. At the outbreak of hostilities he was too ill to take active part on either side, but his sympathies were with his loyalist kindred. He died on July 11, 1775. His partner in business, Captain Samuel Ward, cast his lot with the patriot party; but his son, Levi Willard, Jr., graduated at Harvard College in 1775, joined his uncle Abijah, went to England and there remained until 1785, when he returned, to die five years later.

Abel Willard, though equally graced by nature with the physical gifts that distinguished his brothers, unlike them chose the arts of peace rather than those of war. He was born at Lancaster on January 12, 1732, and was graduated at Harvard College in 1752, ranking third in the class. His wife was Elizabeth Rogers, daughter of the loyalist minister of Littleton. His name was affixed to the address to Governor Gage, June 21, 1774, and he was forced to sign, with the other justices, a recantation of the aspersions cast upon the people, in that document. He had the distinction of being claimed as a personal friend by the leading statesman of the Revolution, John Adams. So popularly esteemed was Abel Willard, and so well known his character as a peacemaker and well-wisher to his country, that he might have remained unmolested and respected among his neighbors, in spite of his royalist opinions; but, whether led by family ties or natural timidity, he sought refuge in Boston, and quick-coming events made it impossible for him to return. At the departure of the British forces for

Halifax he accompanied them, and reached London in July, 1776. A letter from Edmund Quincy to his daughter, Mrs. Hancock, dated Lancaster, March 26, 1776, contains this reference to him :

. . . . . I'm sorry for poor Mrs. Abel Willard, your Sister's near neighbour & Friend. She's gone we hear with her husband and Bro. and sons to Nova Scotia, p'haps in such a situation and under such circumstances of Offense respecting their Wos'ʳ Neighbours as never to be in a political capacity of returning to their Houses unless wᵗʰ power & inimical views wᶜʰ God forbid should ever be the case.

In 1778, the act of proscription and banishment included Abel Willard's name. His health gave way under accumulated trouble, and he died, as recorded in the diary of Peter Oliver, "of a slow fever in London the first week in Novʳ. 1781." The estates of Abijah and Abel Willard were confiscated. In Massachusetts Archives, CLIV, 10, is preserved the anxious inquiry of the town authorities respecting the proper disposal of the property they abandoned :

To the Honourable Provincial Congress now holden at Watertown in the Province of the Massachusetts Bay :

We the subscribers do request and desire that you would be pleased to direct or Inform this province in General or the town of Lancaster in Partickeler what is best to be done with the Estates of those men which are Gone from their Estates to General Gage, and to whose use they shall Improve them whether for the province or the town where sᵈ Estate is.

EBENEZER ALLEN,
CYRUS FAIRBANK,
SAMᴸᴸ. THURSTON,

LANCASTER, June 7 day, 1775.   *The Selectmen of Lancaster.*

The Provincial Congress placed the property in question in the hands of the selectmen and committee of safety to improve, and instructed them to report to future legislatures. Finally, Cyrus Fairbank is found acting as the local agent for confiscated estates of royalists in Lancaster, and his annual statements are among the archives of the State. His accounts embrace the property of "Abijah Willard, Esq., Abel Willard, Esq., Solomon Houghton,

Yeoman, and Joseph Moore, Gent." The final settlement of Abel Willard's estate, October 26, 1785, netted his creditors but ten shillings, eleven pence to the pound. The claimants and improvers probably swallowed even the larger possessions of Abijah Willard, leaving nothing to the Commonwealth.

Joseph Wilder, Jr., colonel, and judge of the court of common pleas of Worcester County — as his father had been before him — was prominent among the signers of the address to General Gage. He apologized for this indiscretion, and seems to have received no further attention from the committee of safety. In the extent of his possessions he rivalled Abijah Willard, having increased a generous inheritance by the profits of very extensive manufacture and export of pearlash and potash; an industry which he and his brother Caleb were the first to introduce into America. He was now nearly seventy years of age, and died in the second year of the war.

Joseph House, at the evacuation of Boston, went with the army to Halifax. He was a householder, but possessed no considerable estate in Lancaster. In 1778, his name appears among the proscribed and banished.

Samuel Stearns, a pensioned loyalist, who died in 1810 at Dummerston, Vermont, was a native of Lancaster, born in 1747, though not there resident at the breaking out of the revolution. He is noted as having published the first nautical almanac ever printed in the United States, December, 1782. The famous astronomer, William Herschel, F. R. S., was his personal friend, and married his sister. Dr. Stearns lived for several years in England, and obtained the degrees of M.D. and L.L. D. in some foreign college. Besides his almanacs, he published other scientific works. William Lincoln, in his history of Worcester, speaks of him as an "astrologer, almanac manufacturer and quack by profession." During the Shay's Insurrection a number of the insurgents at Worcester, became alarmingly nauseated after imbibing freely of a favorite stimulant. They at once declared themselves poisoned; and Dr. Stearns, then of Paxton, professed to detect "antimony and arsenic" in the dregs of their cups. This naturally raised a furious clamor, and bloody vengeance was threatened, when a local physician discovered that the pretended deadly drug was nothing but snuff, which had accidentally got mixed with the brown sugar used in the toddy and raised an insurrection of its own in the stomachs of the topers.

The following advertisement by the Lancaster Committee of Correspondence appeared in the Massachusetts Spy for Wednesday, August 16, 1775, and proves that though the word *boycott* may be modern, the principle thus designated is revolutionary:

LANCASTER, July 17th, 1775.

Whereas Nahum Houghton being complained of as being an enemy to his Country, by officiating as an unwearied Pedlar of that baneful herb TEA, and otherwise rendering himself odious to the inhabitants of this Town, and notwithstanding being warned, he did not appear before the Committee that his political principles might be Known. This therefore (agreable to a vote of said Town) is to caution all friends to the Community, to entirely shun his Company, and have no manner of dealings or connections with him, except acts of common humanity.

JOHN PRESCOTT, *Chairman.*

To this, reply was made in the Spy for September 6, which is given at length as illustrating well the methods of the patriot committees, and some curious customs of the times:

Mr. Thomas, A PIECE having appeared in your paper under the signature of John Prescot, in which I am complained of as an enemy to my country, by officiating as an unwearied pedlar in that baneful herb tea, and otherwise rendering myself odious to the inhabitants of this town; and also for not appearing before the committee to make known my political principles when requested so to do; I beg leave by a plain account of the matter, to let the public see how well their complaints are founded.—I sold tea about a twelve month ago; the people assembled and told me they were dissatisfied with me for selling it, notwithstanding nearly a quarter part of that assembly had bought tea of me. I settled the affair with them at that time by agreeing not to sell any more untill there should be an

14

alteration in the towns; nor have I counteracted the resolve of the Continental Congress in buying or selling tea at any time. How I have rendered myself in any other way odious to the inhabitants of this town I know not, and till an instance of that kind is pointed out it cannot be expected that I should make any reply to that complaint. With regard to my not appearing before the committee agreable to their warning, I would observe, that I was warned to appear the very day on which I had engaged to set out on a journey to take the small pox; when I returned I threw myself in the way of the committee and went before them; they demanded of me satisfaction for my past conduct. I asked them in what particular; they said on account of my not appearing before the committee when ordered. I told them the reason of my not appearing before them was on account of my going to take the small pox &c. Then one of the committee asked the chairman whether I should hear what the others had consented to, meaning those whom they had examined for supposed tories; they put it to vote, and it passed in the negative. Then they gave me leave to make my own declaration, and I wrote what follows:

Gentlemen of the Committee, I am called before you this day to make known my political principles, to answer for my past conduct; what you have against me I am not able to say, but as you insist upon something from me I make this declaration viz: I am willing to stand by charter rights and privileges granted us by King William and Queen Mary, and to take up arms in the defence of my country when thought proper, and as for treating the committee ill when I went to have the small pox I had no such design.

Now I appeal to the public whether in justice I ought to be deemed as an enemy to my country, and thus held up to public odium, for conducting as above.   NAHUM HOUGHTON.

LANCASTER, August 28th, 1775.

In the Boston Gazette for March 9, 1778, is the following communication:

With the troops that surrendered with General Burgoyne in October last, was a certain —— Atherton (now provost-master in the British service on Prospect Hill), born in Lancaster, in the county of Worcester; has been in the service of the United States and having deserted that service, joined the British forces at or near Skenesborough and continued to act against his country until made prisoner as aforesaid; he still continues his traitorous inveteracy against the United States, threatening the lives of the good people, and branding them with the epithet, "damn'd rebels," and damning their rebel army; notwithstanding this is notoriously known, he has been permitted for three months past daily to pass and repass from Prospect Hill to Weston, about twelve miles distance, where he quarters with a profest enemy to the liberties of America, surrounded by an infamous junto of tories, one of which has lately made a very private journey to Albany, North River, or as likely New York. . . . .

A special town meeting was called on June 30, 1777, chiefly "to act on a Resolve of the General Assembly Respecting and Securing this and the other United States against the Danger to which they are Exposed by the Internal Enemies Thereof, and to Elect some proper person to Collect such evidence against such Persons as shall be demeed by authority as Dangerous persons to this and the other United States of America." At this meeting Colonel Asa Whitcomb was chosen to collect evidence against suspected loyalists, and Moses Gerrish, Daniel Allen, Ezra Houghton, Joseph Moor, and Solomon Houghton, were voted "as Dangerous Persons and Internal Enemies to this State." On September 12 of the same year, apparently upon a report from Colonel Asa Whitcomb, it was voted that Thomas Grant, James Carter, and the Reverend Timothy Harrington, "Stand on the Black List." It was also ordered that the selectmen "Return a List of these Dangerous Persons to the Clerk, and he to the Justice of the Quorum as soon as may be." This action of the extremists seems to have aroused the more conservative citizens, and another meeting was called, on September 23, for the purpose of reconsidering this ill-advised and arbitrary proscription, at which meeting the clerk was instructed not to return the names of James Carter and the Reverend Timothy Harrington "on the Black List till after Next Meeting on the first Monday in November."

Thomas Grant was an old soldier, having served in the French and Indian War, and, if a loyalist, probably condoned the offence by enlisting in the patriot army; his name is on the muster-roll of the Rhode Island expedition in 1777, and in 1781 he was mustered into the service for three years. He was about fifty years of age, and a poor man, for the town paid bills presented "for providing for Tom Grant's Family."

Moses Gerrish was graduated at Harvard College in 1762, and reputed a man of considerable ability. Enoch Gerrish, probably a . brother of Moses, was a farmer in Lancaster who left his home, was arrested and imprisoned in York County, and thence removed for trial to Worcester by order of the council, May 20, 1778. The following letter uncomplimentary to these two loyalists is found in Massachusetts Archives, CXCIX; 278 :

Sir. The two Gerrishes Moses & Enoch, that ware sometime since apprehended by warrant from the Council are now set at Libberty by reason of that Laws Expiring on which they were taken up. I would move to your Hon^ra a new warrant might Isue, Directed to Doc^r. Silas Hoges to apprehend & confine them as I look upon them to be Dangerous persons to go at large. I am with respect your Hon^rs. most obedient Hum. Ser^t.

GROTON 12 of July 1778. JAMES PRESCOTT.
To the Hon^e Jereh. Powell Esq.

An order for their re-arrest was voted by the council. Moses Gerrish finally received some position in the commissary department of the British army, and, when peace was declared, obtained a grant of free tenancy of the island of Grand Menan for seven years. At the expiration of that time, if a settlement of forty families with schoolmaster and minister should be established, the whole island was to become the freehold of the colonists. Associated with Gerrish in this project was Thomas Ross, of Lancaster. They failed in obtaining the requisite number of settlers, but continued to reside upon the island, and there Moses Gerrish died at an advanced age.

Solomon Houghton, a Lancaster farmer in comfortable circumstances, fearing the inquisition of the patriot committee, fled from his home. In 1779, the judge of probate for Worcester County appointed commissioners to care for his confiscated estate.

Ezra Houghton, a prosperous farmer, and recently appointed justice of the peace, affixed his name to the address to General Gage in 1775, and to the recantation. In May, 1777, he was imprisoned, under charge of counterfeiting the bills of public credit and aiding the enemy. In November following he petitioned to be admitted to bail (see Massachusetts Archives, ccxvi, 129), and his request was favorably received, his bail bond being set at two thousand pounds.

Joseph Moore was one of the six slave-owners of Lancaster in 1771, possessed a farm and a mill, and was ranked a "gentleman." On September 20, 1777, being then confined in Worcester jail, he petitioned for enlargement, claiming his innocence of the charges for which his name had been put upon Lancaster's black list. His petition met no favor, and his estate was duly confiscated. [Massachusetts Archives, clxxxiii, 160.]

At the town meeting of the first Monday in November, 1777, the names of James Carter and Daniel Allen were stricken from the black list, apparently without opposition. That the Reverend Timothy Harrington, Lancaster's prudent and much beloved minister, should be denounced as an enemy of his country, and his name placed even temporarily among those of dangerous persons, exhibits the bitterness of party feeling at that date. This town-meeting prosecution was ostensibly based upon certain incautious expressions of opinion, but appears really to have been inspired by the spite of the Whitcombs and others, whose enmity had been aroused by his conservative action several years before, during the church troubles known as "the Goss and Walley war," in the neighboring parish of Bolton. The Reverend Thomas Goss of Bolton, Ebenezer Morse of Boylston, and Andrew Whitney of Petersham, were classmates of Mr. Harrington in the Harvard class of 1737, and all of them were opposed to the revolution of the colonies. The disaffection which, ignoring the action of an ecclesiastical council, pushed Mr. Goss from his pulpit, perhaps arose more from the political ferment of the day than from any advanced views of his opponents respecting the abuse of alcoholic stimulants, with which sin he was charged. For nearly forty years Mr. Harrington had doubtless never omitted from his fervent prayers in public assemblies the formal supplication for divine blessing upon the sovereign ruler of Great Britain. It is not strange, although he had yielded reluctant submission to the new order of things, and was anxiously striving to perform his clerical duties without offence to any of his flock, that his lips should sometimes lapse into the wonted formula, "bless our good King George." It is related that on occasions of such inadvertence, he, without embarrassing pause, added : "Thou knowest, O Lord, we mean George Washington." In the records of the town-clerk, nothing is told of the nature of the charges against Mr. Harrington, or of the manner of his defence. Two deacons, Benjamin Houghton and Cyrus Fairbank, were sent as messengers "to inform the Revd Tim^o Harrington that he has something in agitation Now to be Heard in this Meeting at which he has Liberty to attend." Joseph Willard, Esq., in 1826, recording probably the reminiscence of some one present at the dramatic scene, says that when the venerable clergyman confronted his accusers, baring his breast, he exclaimed with the language and feeling of outraged virtue : " Strike, strike here with your daggers ! I am a true friend to my country !"

Among the manuscripts left by Mr. Harrington there is one prepared for, if not read at, this town-meeting, containing the charges in detail, and his reply to each. It is headed : "Harrington's answers to ye Charges &c." It is a shrewd and eloquent defence, bearing evidence, so far as rhetoric can, that its author was in advance of his people and his times in respect of Christian charity, if not of political foresight. The charges were four in number : the first being that of the Bolton Walleyites alleging that his refusal to receive them as church members in regular standing brought him "under ye censure of shutting up ye Kingdom of Heaven against men." To this, calm answer is given by a review of the whole controversy in the Bolton church, closing thus :

Mr. Moderator, as I esteemed the Proceedings of these Brethren at Bolton Disorderly and Schismatical, and as the Apostle has given Direction to mark those who cause Divisions and Offences and avoid them, I thought it my Duty to bear Testimony against ye Conduct of both ye People at Bolton, and those who were active in settling a Pastor over them in the Manner Specified : and I still retain yᵉ sentiment and this not to shut the Kingdom of Heaven against them, but to recover them from their wanderings to the Order of the Gospel and to the direct way to the Kingdom of Heaven. And I still approve and think them just.

The second charge, in full, was as follows :

It appears to us that his conduct hath ye greatest Tendency to subvert our religious Constitution and ye Faith of these Churches.—In his saying that the Quebeck Bill was just—and that he would have done the same had he been one of ye Parliament— and also saying that he was in charity with a professed Roman Catholick, whose Principles are so contrary to the Faith of these churches.—That for a man to be in charity with them we conceive that it is impossible that he should be in Charity with professed New England Churches. It therefore appears to us that it would be no better than mockery for him to pretend to stand as Pastor to one of these churches.

To this, Mr. Harrington first replies by the pointed question : "Is not Liberty of Conscience and ye right of judging for themselves in the matters of Religion one grand professed Principle in ye New England Churches ; and one Corner Stone in their Foundation?" He then explicitly states his abhorrence of "the anti-Christian tenets of Popery," adding : "However on the other hand they receive all the articles of the Athanasian Creed — and of consequence in their present Constitution they have some Gold, Silver, and precious stones as well as much wood, hay, and stubble." He characterizes the accusation in this pithy paragraph : "Too much Charity is the Charge here brought against me, — would to God I had still more of it in ye most important sense. Instead of a Disqualification, it would be a most enviable accomplishment in ye Pastor of a Protestant New England Church." A sharp *argumen-*

tum ad hominem for the benefit of the ultra-radical accuser closes this division of his defence.

But, Mr. Moderator, if my charity toward some Roman Catholicks disqualifieth me for a Protestant Minister, what, what must we think of ye honorable Congress attending Mass in a Body in ye Roman Catholic Chapel at Philadelphia? Must it not be equal mockery in them to pretend to represent and act for the United Protestant States? . . .

The third charge was that he had declared himself and one of the brethren to "be a major part of the Church." This, like the first charge, was a revival of an old personal grievance within the church, rehabilitated to give cumulative force to the political complaints. The accusation is summarily disposed of; the accused condemning the sentiment "as grossly Tyrannical, inconsistent with common sense and repugnant to good order;" and denying that he ever uttered it.

Lastly came the political charge pure and simple.

His despising contemning and setting at naught and speaking Evil of all our Civil Rulers, Congress, Continental and Provincial, of all our Courts, Legislative and Executive, are not only subversive of good Order: But we apprehend come under Predicament of those spoken of in 2 Pet. II. 10, who despise government, presumptuous, selfwilled, they are not afraid to speak evil of Dignities &c.

Mr. Harrington acknowledges that he once uttered to a Mr. North this imprudent speech : "I disapprove abhor and detest the Results of Congress whether Continental or Provincial," but adds that he "took the first opportunity to inform Mr. North that I had respect only to two articles in said Results." He apologizes for the speech, but at the same time defends his criticism of the two articles as arbitrary measures. He also confesses saying that "General Court had no Business to direct Committees to seize on Estates before they had been Confiscated in a course of Law," and "that their Constituents never elected or sent them for that Purpose," but this sentiment he claimed that he had subsequently retracted as rash and improper to be spoken. These objectionable expressions of opinion, he asserts, were made "before ye 19th of April 1775."

It is needless to say that the Reverend Timothy Harrington's name was speedily erased from the black list, and,
to the credit of his people be it said, he was treated with
increased consideration and honor during the following
eighteen years that he lived to serve them.   In the deliber-
ations of the Lancaster town-meeting, as in those of the
Continental Congress, broad views of national independence based upon civil and religious liberty, finally prevailed
over sectional prejudice and intolerance.   The loyalist pastor was a far more consistent republican than his radical
inquisitors.

VIII. STATISTICS, AND SOCIAL ANNALS.

The census of 1765 gives brief statistics of the towns
formed from the territory originally granted to Lancaster,
which can be conveniently tabulated as follows :—

	Lancaster.	Harvard.	Bolton.	Leominster.
Houses,	301	153	145	104
Families,	328	173	155	107
Inhabitants under sixteen, males,	514	276	234	186
" " " females,	421	270	225	199
Inhabitants over sixteen, males,	505	272	225	173
" " " females,	532	296	239	180
Inhabitants, colored, males,	12	7	1	2
" " females,	14	5	1	3
" Indians,	1	French Neutrals, 6		
Total Population,	1999	1126	931	743

[Massachusetts Archives, LXXXVIII.]

A very notable fact in this enumeration is the marked
preponderance of male children above the female, while the
male adults are far outnumbered by the other sex.   Thus
nature made compensation for the waste of human life by
war.   The average size of the family was then over six
individuals.   In the census of 1885 the average of the four
thousand four hundred and sixteen families composing the
population of the seven towns shaped from the above four,
is but four and one-half persons.   Omitting Clinton, of

whose population nearly forty per cent is foreign-born, and
the average is but four and one-fifth persons. The colonial census of 1776 gives Lancaster — which included the
Chocksett Precinct, now Sterling, as well as the territory
now Clinton, and part of the Boylstons — a population of
2746. The returns of polls and estates required by the
government in 1769, 1770, 1771, 1781, 1784 and 1786
afford a fuller exhibit of the physical and financial ability
of the town during the outbreak and progress of revolution,
when every resource of the land was called into service.
The following compilation from the valuation returns of
1771, 1781 and 1784 will show the growth of the town
during an important decade, and afford data for a comparison of the two precincts of Lancaster at the time of their
final separation :

	1771.	1781.	1784. Lancaster.	1784. Sterling.
Polls,	595	646	307	440
Dwellings,	339	360	174	179
Shops and Stores,	61	126	45	19
Tanneries,		1	1	5
Pot and Pearlash Works,			2	5
Barns,		330	167	150
Grist, Saw and Fulling Mills,	17	24	7	6
Horses,	383	358	231	251
Oxen,	529	513	231	248
Other Neat Cattle,	1124	1428	883	1074
Sheep,	2310	3848	745	1073
Swine,	623	475	290	347
Pasturage, acres,	3581	4484	1411	2861
Tillage, acres,	1983	2207	1029	885
Grain, bushels,	26,905	24,946		
Cider, barrels,	2689	2456	1271	1942
English mowing, acres,	2264	1806	720	971
English hay, tons,	1578			
Meadow, acres,	1957	2192	435	1085
Meadow hay, tons,	1463			
Slaves between 14 and 45,	6			

[Massachusetts Archives, XXXIII, CLXII and CLXIII.]

Flax, hemp, hops, tobacco, potatoes, turnips and other
roots, though not included in the valuation, were very im-

portant items in the farmers' crops. During this period but seventeen towns in Massachusetts had a larger population than Lancaster, ten of which were in Essex county. It was the most populous town in Worcester county, Brookfield standing second in rank, and Sutton third. The number of shops and mills enumerated in the valuation indicates that Lancaster was then not only a commercial centre for the sparsely settled towns at the west, but that its citizens had turned their attention largely to manufactures and the mechanic arts. A letter and the reply, found in Massachusetts Archives, CLXXIII and CXLVI, of Council Records, afford other confirmation of this:

LANCASTER, July 15, 1777.

Gentlemen, We the selectmen of Lancaster, have been informed by W^m. Dunsmore Esq. who represents the town aforesaid, that there is a Quantity of Gun Locks for the use of this state at the board of War; we in behalf of said town make application for a Number of said Locks, as there is a number of good Gun Smiths in this town who cannot pursue that important branch of business for want of Locks, therefore we desire that we may have what you think Necessary for said town of Lancaster & Gentlemen you will obliege your most humble servants in Complyance with the above request.

Selectmen	{	EPH^M. WILDER,
of		W_M. GREENLEAF,
Lancaster.		SAMUEL SAWYER,
		SOLOMON JEWETT,
To the Gentlemen of the Board of War.		NATH. BEAMAN.

State of Massachusetts Bay, Council Chamber, July 17, 1777.

Ordered that the Board of War be, and they hereby are directed to deliver to Doc. William Greenleaf & Mr. Samuel Sawyer and other Selectmen of Lancaster four hundred wg^ht Lead, one thousand Flints and six Doz. Gun Locks for the use of said Town, they paying for the same.

A true extract from the Minutes of Council.

Attest JNO. AVERY, *Dpt. Secy.*

The manufacture of potash and pearlash had attained great importance here, the brothers Caleb and Levi Wilder sometimes exporting within a twelve-month seventy-five tons of potash and double that weight of pearlash. The slate quarry in the north part of the town was worked in a

modest way, and near by it was a furnace for the casting
of hollow ware. The cooper was one of the busiest of
men in every village. But, although boasting a larger
capital invested in trade and manufactures than any of the
towns about it, agriculture was the almost universal occupation of its people. Almost ten bushels of grain, chiefly
Indian corn, were annually harvested for every man,
woman and child of its population. In 1885 less than three
bushels of cereals per inhabitant were raised in the same
territory, and less than six within Lancaster's present
bounds. Even if we add the great root crop of these
later years, it will not bring the food product per individual
so high as the grain crop alone averaged in the days of the
Revolution. The supply of beef, mutton and pork upon
the hoof was then very much greater per inhabitant than
now. In short, the community, after supplying its own
wants, had a large surplus of food for sale. The following
bill is interesting in this connection, giving the prices of
various provisions during the siege of Boston. It was
found among some loose files in the Massachusetts
Archives:

The Coliney of the Masachusets Bay Detor to the town of Lancaster
for Provisions that was sent Down to the armey at Cambrig for the use of
the solders there is as followeth. Viz:

	L.	S.	D.	Q.
the Poork 2129 Pounds and ½ at 6ᵈ Pr Pound	52 –	0 –	7 –	0
to 180 and one ½ of Veal comes to	5 –	15 –	2 –	0
to 1372 Pounds of Bread at 3ᵈ Pr Pound comes to	5 –	14 –	0 –	0
to 145 Pound of Cheas at 4ᵈ Pr Pound comes to	2 –	8 –	4 –	0
to three bushels and 6 Quarts of beans at 6ˢ Pr bushel comes to		19 –	0 –	0
to seven bariels Sider at 7/8 Pr bariel	2 –	13 –	8 –	0
to 6 bushels Indian meal at 3 shillings	0 –	18 –	0 –	0
to 50 bushels of Potatoes at 1/4 Pr bushel	3 –	6 –	8 –	0
to 14 Pounds of Mutton comes to	0 –	2 –	4 –	0
to 47 Pounds of Salt Beaf comes to	0 –	12 –	1 –	0
to 30 bushels and ½ bushel of Rey meal 4ˢ	6 –	2 –	6 –	0
to 8 Pounds of Butter	0 –	4 –	11 –	0
to 6 Bariels to Carry Don sd Provisions in	0 –	5 –	4 –	0
to 181 Pounds of Flower at 2ᵈ Pr Pound	1 –	10 –	2 –	0

	L.	*S.*	*D.*	*Q.*
to 6 teames men and Expences and time to convey said Provisions to Cambrig	11	11	6	0
to a team and man and Expences to Convey a Great Gun by order of Congres to Cambrig	5	16	0	0
to Joseph Wheelock 3 Days and Expences to Gard Powder from Bolton to Brookline	0	9	0	0
to the mending of a Gun that was Lent to a Poor Solder & Brook on his Returning home from head Quaters	0	12	0	0
to Joseph Wheelock's son 3 Days and Expences to asist in Careing the Great Gun to head Quaters	0	9	0	0
to a man and hors to Carey cloathing to Cambrig and expences	0	6	0	0
	£94	12	3	0

To the Honble Committee on accts : the Dates of the above accts will appear by the a Vouchers sent herewith

A true acct. errors excepted.

W^M. Dunsmoor,
Cyrus Fairbank,
Sam^L. Thurston,
David Osgood,
Daniel Robbins,

March 1, 1776.   *Selectmen of Town of Lancaster.*

The continuous and rapid decrease in the purchasing power of the paper currency, both state and continental, worked severe and universal hardship. Just before the revolution Massachusetts was in an enviable financial condition. The debt incurred in the last war had been paid, and a stable metallic medium of exchange had been established ; both silver and gold, though chiefly of foreign coinage and not very abundant, were sufficient for trade purposes. Such was the variety of coins in circulation, and so frequently were these clipped, that traders kept scales to determine by weight the value of pieces received. By the spring of 1780, it required forty dollars in paper to purchase one of silver, and upon that basis of values a new emission of bills was made to replace the old paper currency. During the next year the new paper money became practically worthless. Not only was the depreciation embarrassing in business, but confidence was further impaired by the circulation of numerous well executed counterfeits. Forged paper well calculated to deceive was even manufactured in the British camps, and presumably with the sanction of the commander-in-chief. We often find town officials asking allowance for bad money received in their collections of taxes or fines. In the warrant for town-meeting in March, 1778, two articles are of this nature :

8thly. to see if the town will allow Mr Joshua Fletcher a Consideration in Regard of the Counterfeit Bills he Recd. at Worcester of Mr Curtis as fines of those Persons that was Drafted to go to the Jersies under Capt. Eager. . . . . .

14thly. to see if the town will allow Jonas Wyman what Counterfeit Money he Recd. for Rates 1777 . . . .

The most innocent persons were at times accused of passing counterfeit money.

On Tuesday the 24th. ult. came on the trial of Capt. Samuel Ward of Lancaster before the Hon. Superior Court then sitting in this town ; he was charged with uttering and passing three counterfeit 60ᵃ bills or notes, of the State of New Hampshire, knowing them to be counterfeit, and after a fair and impartial hearing of the cause, he was acquitted. It clearly appeared from the testimony of a great number of witnesses, as well on the part of the State, as of Capt. Ward, that his misfortune was that of many other respectable merchants, who innocently received and paid large quantities of the same kind of bad money. Two other persons were tried at said Court for passing counterfeit paper money and were found guilty.

[Massachusetts Spy, May 4, 1780.]

The Council, November 20, 1778,—

Ordered, that a warrant be drawn on the Treasury for Twenty pounds in favor of Ephraim Carter in full of the bounty allowed by the General Court for detecting Manasseh Divoll in passing counterfeit money, as appears by a certificate signed by Manchester Smith, clerk of the Superior Court.

The clergy, teachers, and others dependent upon salaries for their means of living, were especial sufferers from the depreciation. The first donation party in Lancaster of which we have any record is thus described by a correspondent of the Massachusetts Spy, July 15, 1779 :

A respectable number of ladies in the first parish in Lancaster assembled at the pastor's and presented him with 208 skeins of linen yarn and other valuable donations; and in the evening a worthy number of gentlemen assembled also and in wool and cash presented to the amount of 239 dollars; all which were gratefully accepted by the said pastor.

The fluctuation in the regular medium of exchange made time contracts difficult, and trade became as much a matter of barter as it had been in the earliest days of the colony. An example of ingenious avoidance of risk of loss from a debased currency is found in the following promissory note given to a hired soldier:

We the subscribers belonging to Bolton in the County of Worcester do promise to pay unto John Whitney of Harvard in said County or order in consideration of his Engageing into the Continental Service for three years for us, Eighteen Calves, Ten whereof are to be Heifers and Eight Steers to be Delivered to him within six weeks after his Discharge from the Continental Service (provided it be within three years) viz: if he be Discharged in one year after Date he is to Receive Said Stock at one year and Six weeks old and so for a longer or Shorter time according to the Same Rule. N. B. said Stock is to be Six weeks older when he Receives them than the time he is in the Service provided it be no longer than three years. Said Stock is to be of the midling Size, in witness whereof we have hereunto Sett our hands and Seals this Tenth Day of April A. D. 1781.

A true Coppy of the Obligation Signed by Nathaniel Holman John Whitney and Simon Houghton to me on account of my Engageing into the Continental Service for three years for a Class in Bolton to which they belong.

[Captain David Nourse's Papers.]

Each of the sixteen three-years men forming the quota of Harvard in the Continental army, under the call of 1781, signed a receipt similar to the following:

HARVARD 7, 1781.

Received of the Committee for Class No. 4 in sᵈ Town nine hard Dollars and ½ of a Dollar and Twenty-five hundred paper Dollars and an obligation for eighteen head of three year old Horned Cattle as encouragement for Inlisting and serving three years in the Continental army.

SAMUEL ATHERTON.

Through private hoarding and exportation by merchants, the precious metals soon totally disappeared from the ordinary channels of trade. A rapid increase followed in the prices of those commodities which wealthy or shrewd speculators could so monopolize as to forestall the market.

Thereupon, as is usual at such epoch, plausible financiers, patriotic but purblind, re-invented the device of legislating that prices should remain fixed, and be forever independent of the fickleness of supply and demand, and of the downward sliding values of a printed legal tender professing no certain day of redemption. An interesting list of official prices current at the close of the second year of the war, is found in the town records beautifully engrossed:

REGULATING ACT, 1777.

The Selectmen & Committee for the town of Lancaster having mett agreeable to the order of the General Court, proceeded to sett the price of the Necessary & Convenient Articles of Life as Follows, (Viz):

Farming Labour in the Summer Season June, July & August.		3/p day
September.		2/2 p day
October & November.		1/10 Do
December January & February.		1/6 Do
March & April.	·	1/10 Do
May.		2/2 Do
Wheat good marchantable.	@	6/8 p bushel
Rye marchantable.	@	4/6 Do
Indian Corn good Do.	@	3/ Do
Sheeps' wool Do.	@	2/ p pound
Poork fresh, well fatted.	@	4^d p Do
Ditto. Salt without bone.	@	8$^d_2$ Do
Beef grass fed.	@	2½$_4$ Do
Ditto stall Do.	@	3¾ Do
Raw Hides.	@	3^d Do
Calve Skins.	@	6^d Do
Salt according to Court Act	@	10/ p bushel
Rum Sugar Molasses Chocolate and Coffee according to Court Act		
Cheese good new milk	@	6^d p pound
Butter by the single pound		9^d Do
Peas good & Clean	@	6/8 p bushel
Beans	@	5/4 Do
Potatoes in Winter & Spring	@	1/6 Do
at all other seasons in proportion		
Good stokings, men's yarn	@	6/ a pair
Shoes according to Court Act	@	8/ Do
Pork & beef salt, by the barral as directed by Court Act		
Cotton & Oates see Court Act		
Shoes for women ware, either Cloth or Leather	@	5/8 a pair

Flax good, well dressed	@	1/ p pound
Tow Cloth good yard wide	@	2/3 p yard
Flannel good yard wide	@	3/6 Do
And all other wedths &c in proportion		
Good yard wide all wool Cloth striped or Checked	@	3/ pr yard
And all other wedths in proportion		

Good blue wool Cloth well fulled and Dressed ¾ yard wide @ 9/ pr yard
and all other fulled cloth in proportion

Wood good & Green delivered at the buyer's Door eight
    feet Long   @   6/ pr Cord

Good Charcoal delivered at the Shop Door   @   3½d. pr bushel

Tanned Hides   @   1/3 pr pound

Curried Leather in usual proportion

Cotton Cloth according to Court Act.

Mutton & Veal   @ 3d pr pound

Lamb under six months' old   @ 2d pr pound

Wheat Flour manufactured in this state   @ 20/ pr hundred

Imported Flour according to Court Act

Milk in the Winter   2d pr Quart

Horse Keeping for a Night or for 24 hours with English hay   1/2

& for a yoak of Oxen same manner as the Horse   @ 1/4

Teaming Work 1/6 for every ton Weight a mile

Milk in Summer Spring & fall   @ ½d Quart

English Hay of the best Quality in the winter and spring @ 3/ p hundred

and in Hay time &c   @ 2/   Do

all other hay in proportion

Good merchantable white pine boards fitt for Inclosing @ 29/ a thousand

Pitch pine for Do 26/8 Do. & other boards of Superior Kind in proportion

Shoeing a horse round steeling   6/4

Shoeing one yoke of Oxen steel &c   11/

Good narrow ax well steeled   10/6

and all other smithing in proportion

Carpenters', House Joiners' & Masons' each of them   3/4 p day

To keeping & boarding, a man 7 days finding washing & Lodging 6/

Dinner roast & boiled 1/, & all other meals in proportion–

Lodging one Night   3½d

Flip made of New England rum, Half a pint of rum in a mugg 9d a mugg

Flip made of West India rum   1/ a mugg

To Cutting out a man's Coat   10d

To Do. Jackett & briches   5d

Making a man's Coat Lined & full trimmed   8/

Making a man's Jackett with sleeves   3/6

Making   Do   cloth breeches   4/

Making   Do   Buckskin Do   6/

& all other Tayloring in proportion
    15

To one good Desk maid of Cherrytree	3£ 10/
To one Case of Draws	4£
Common Colour^d Chairs	3/4 a piece
One four feet Table	1£ 4/
& all other Shop Joinery in proportion	
Spinning yarn warp wool	2½^d a skain
Spinning filling for Ditto	2^d
Spinning Linnen 5 skain yarn 14 Knotts @	4^d p skain
and all other spinning in proportion	
To weaving wool or yard wide Linning	4^d a yard
and all other weaving in proportion	
To making men's shoes at their shop	3/
To Do Women's Do	2/8 p pair
To Specking shoes for men finding all	2/
To Do Women's Do	1/4 a pair
and all other making and mending in proportion	
Bricks well burnt Common Size	13/4 Thousand
Barral staves best kind	25/ a Thousand
and all other Cooper Staves in proportion	
To a heart barral 3/4. sap Do 2/8 other coopering in proportion	
To making a pair of Cart Wheeles	1£ 6ˢ 8^d
For a good seed plough 6/. & other ploughs in Proportion	
To a good Fire arm Compleat with bayonet	4£
and all other Gun Smithing in proportion	
A Good well made Man's Sadle	2£ 10/
A Good bridle with Common bitts	6/
and all other Saddler's work in proportion	
Iron hollow ware @	3^d p pound
Hard ware and all other Cast Iron Ware in proport^on	
Good old Cyder	8/ p barral
To a yoke of Oxen one day in Summer	1/6
To a Draft Horse one day in Summer	1/
and both in proportion in other seasons of the year	
Hemp well Dressed	8^d p pound
Sawing pine boards & Chesnutt	10/ a thousand
Do. Oake	11/ Do
and all other sawing in proportion	
Flax seed fitt for oil mill	3/6 p bushell
Flax seed fitt for sowing	5/ p bushell
Good barly malt	3/6 p bushell
Good Rye Do.	4/6 Do
Grammer School Master	£2..8/ a month
Good pair boots made of neat's Leather	1£ 6..8
Good Wool Hatt	8/

Good tryed tallow	7½ᵈ p pound
Rough tallow	3ᵈ Do
Riding Horse	2ᵈ p mile
A Woman to spin by the week	3/

Doctor's fees. Vomitt 1/. purge 1/. to a miles travel 8ᵈ. pull-
  ing tooth 8ᵈ. a Visit 8ᵈ. and all other Doctring in proportion

Good oake or pine plank three Inch thick   4£ a thousand

A true Coppy signed by Joseph Kilburn, Daniel Robbins, Joel Houghton, Samuel Thurston, Jonathan Wilder, Ebenezer Allen, Wᵐ Dunsmoor,
Cyrus Fairbank, Joshua Fletcher, Josiah Kendall, Junʳ. and Jabez Fairbank, Selectmen and Committee.

  For the town of Lancaster-   LANCASTER, Feby 28ᵗʰ. 1777.
    Examined and Entered by me.

                          Wᴹ GREENLEAF, *Town Clerk*.

The attempt to fix immutably the value of a promise-to-
pay based upon no security but hopes of future prosperity,
met the fate historic of such financial schemes.   Now and
then the scale of prices had to be re-adjusted.   May 17,
1779, the town voted to choose " four persons as Inspectors
of the markett," and David Osgood, William Dunsmoor,
Esq., Nathaniel Beaman and Captain William Putnam
were elected.   June 28, the town in solemn conclave,—

11. Voted that the price of the comodityes of the farmer and any
other article do Not Rise any hier than at this time.

12. Voted to Chuse a Committee to assertain the prices of every
article of Life. . . . . . .

14 Voted and Chosen Nathaniel Balch, Wᵐ Dunsmoor Esq, Josiah
Wilder Esq, Nath. Beaman, Capt. Wᵐ. Putnam, Joel Houghton, Aaron
Sawyer and Thomas Brown as the above Committee.

LANCASTER, July 12, 1779. . . . . .

9 Voted and Chosen Joseph Reed Esq. and Mr Ebenezer Allen to
attend at Concord the 14. Instant as deligates to set in a State Convention . . . . . .

LANCASTER August 2 1779 . . . . .

2 Voted and accepted the proceedings of the Convention lately held
at Concord . . . . . .

5 Voted that Joseph Reed Esq. and Ebenezer Allen be the Gentlemen
to attend upon the Convention to be holden at Worcester the second Tuesday of August.

Colonel Joseph Reed was chairman of this convention at Worcester, August 3, 1779, which met —

for the purpose of carrying into effect the several interesting and important measures first recommended by Congress to the inhabitants of the United States, and since to the inhabitants of this State by a Convention of their Delegates at Concord on the 14th ult.

The convention adjourned to August 11, when thirty towns of the county were represented, and several resolves were passed, the chief being to fix the prices at which merchandise and country produce should be sold.

LANCASTER August 16, 1779 . . . . .

1. Voted and accepted the proceedings of the Late County Convention held at Worcester.

2. Voted that the proceedings of the above Convention be posted at Phelps', Sawyer's Mills, Thomas Gates', Pope's, Elisha White's and Josiah Kendall's taverns.

3. Voted to Chuse a Committee to Regulate prices within the town and see the Proceedings of the late County Convention held at Worcester be carried into execution.

4. Voted to make an addition of ten persons to the standing Committee.

5. Voted and Choose Josiah Wilder, Samuel Thurston, Thomas Gates, Peter Larkin, Thomas Brooks, Nathaniel Balch, Jabez Brooks, Stephen Holman, Samuel Wilder Jr. and John Brown to be added to the standing Committee for the above purpose.

On the first of September the convention for forming the constitution of the state met at Cambridge, wherein Lancaster was represented by William Dunsmoor, Esq , Captain Ephraim Wilder and Captain William Putnam. On the first Wednesday in October another convention met at Concord to revise the price list again, and Lancaster sent the same delegates as before.

LANCASTER Novr 8th 1779 . . . . .

1 Voted and accepted the proceedings of the late Convention at Concord.

2ly. Voted to Chuse a Committee to see the Regulations of the Convention Complyd with within this town . . . .

4ly Voted and Choose Dea. Cyrus Fairbank, Capt. Nathaniel Balch, Ebenezer Allen, Capt. Jonathan Wilder, John Prescott, Capt. Benja. Richardson, Joseph Reed Esq, Capt. David Osgood, and Dea. Levi Moor as above Committee.

5ly Voted to Chuse a Committee to state the prices within the town that have Not been stated by Convention . . . . .

7ly Voted and Choose Dea. Benjamin Houghton Jabez Brooks, Samuel Thurston Nathaniel White and Josiah Kendall Jun. as the above Committee.

LANCASTER March 6, 1780 . . . . .

Voted that the price of Men's Labour be 6 pounds pr Day till ye first of August, Horses Oxen and Utensils to be in Proportion.

The tenth article in a warrant summoning a town-meeting for February 16, 1781, was:

To see if the Town will enquire for ye Reasons why ye new Emission Currency is sunk almost one half of the Value of what it was when first Emitted, and to show their Minds respecting paying the hard Money Tax, or act or transact any thing Relative thereto; agreable to ye Request of Caleb Whitney and others.

No action was taken upon this by the town, but at the March meeting it was voted to raise fifteen thousand pounds "old emission," for the year's appropriation to roads and bridges; and the pay of workmen upon the highways was fixed at twelve pounds per day till the first of September. The next town-meeting raised this to fifteen pounds per day. After this date the town estimates and appropriations are no longer reckoned in the values of paper currency, and September 3 the town voted —

. . . . . that the Constables and Collectors be directed not to Receive the Old Continental money for taxes untill further orders,—town or Precinct;—[for] which the town agree to endemnify said Constables and Collectors.

Perhaps nothing can better illustrate the ubiquity of the tax collector, and the depreciation in "fiat" values, than the annual summaries of the assessors:

An Accompt of the Moneys assessed on the Town of Lancaster by the Assessors of sd. Town for the year 1779 *viz*:

May 14 Assessed a Continental State Tax of	£7604..11.. 4
June 18 Assessed a Town Tax of	5800.. 0.. 0
" Also a Highway Tax of	1200.. 0.. 0

August 27	Assessed a Continental Tax of	£22219..11.. 3
"	A Town Tax of	11176.. 3.. 0
"	A County Tax of	178..12..10
Feb. 3	Assessed a State Tax of	19991..13.. 4
"	A Town Tax of	6381.. 0.. 0
"	A County Tax of	296.. 2..11
		£74847..14.. 8

An Accompt of the Moneys assessed on the Town . . . 1780.

Feby 10	a Town Rate of	£165000.. 0..0
" 22	a County Rate of	888.. 2..0
" "	a State Rate of	43607.. 6..8
Sept. 30	a State Rate (silver)	570.. 0..0
	a Town Rate (Highway)	5000.. 0..0
Nov. 4	a Town Rate (New Emission)	750.. 0..0
Dec. 4	a State Rate	44333.. 6..8
	a County Rate	2073.. 1..7
Feby. 5	a Town Rate (New Emission)	1500.. 0..0
	a Town Rate do.	6562..10..0

The credit of the continental currency had, during 1779, reached so low an ebb that the army commissaries could not purchase sufficient food for the soldiers, and Congress invented the expedient of requiring each state to supply its proportionate share. Therefore in the warrant for a town-meeting, October 24, 1780, appears this article:

2. To see what method the Town will come into respecting ye Resolution of the General Court, concerning the raising by a Tax or otherwise a Quantity of Beef, or act or transact any thing relative to s^d Resolution.

The town chose to purchase the beef, and elected as purchasing committee, Captain David Osgood, Captain Ephraim Carter and Nathaniel Houghton; raising seven hundred and fifty pounds for the purpose. David Osgood became the commonwealth's agent.

LANCASTER November 14. 1780.

Received of the Town of Lancaster by the Hands of Nathaniel Houghton and Ephraim Carter, Junr. Nineteen Thousand w^t of Beef, being the whole of what was sett in the Sch'dule by ye great and general Court.

DAVID OSGOOD, *Agent.*

. . . Second Day of January A. D. 1781 . . .

2dly. Voted to raise the Town's Proportion of Beef sent for by the General Court.

3dly. Voted & Chose Capt. David Osgood, Joseph Carter, Nathaniel

Houghton, Capt Solomon Jewett and Capt Ephraim Carter for a Committee to purchase s^d Beef.

4^{ly}. Voted to raise the Sum of Fifteen Hundred Pounds in ye New Emission to purchase said Beef.

LANCASTER January, 1781.

Received of this Town by the Hands of the Committee thirty-six Thousand 4 Hundred and 94 w^t of Beef being their full Quota as order^d by ye General Court Decb^r. 4, 1780.

DAVID OSGOOD *Agent*

LANCASTER July 13, 1781 . . . .

3. Voted to Comply with the General Court's orders Respecting beef for the army.

4. Voted to Chuse a Committee for purchasing beef as above. . . .

6. Voted and Choose Thomas Gates and Daniel Rugg as a Committee.

7. Voted to Raise two hundred pounds for procuring the above beef.

In matters of dress, which had greatly deviated from Puritanic simplicity, in the larger towns at least, a rigid economy became generally compulsory from scarcity of the materials as well as their cost. Silas Rice, however, continued to advertise in the Spy that he made and sold "silver shoe and knee-buckles at his shop near the second parish meeting-house." The census shows that every farmer kept his little flock of sheep, there being nearly four thousand in the town. The cultivation of hemp and flax was everywhere urged as a patriotic duty. By every fire-side the spinning-wheels busily hummed, twirled by the hands of the young, and the knitting needles constantly clicked in the deft fingers of the aged. Ephraim Carter in his tannery, Peter Thurston in his hat shop, Micah Harthan in his fulling mill, Thomas Grant with his loom, and many skilled and strong-handed helpers wrought at their crafts industriously. Yet the soldiers often went half clad, and among the bare-footed men whose steps stained with blood the snows of Valley Forge, were several of Lancaster and vicinity. When the knowledge of their pressing need came home to their neighbors, the town-meeting waited for no formality of requisition, but, February 5, 1778,—

4^{thly}. Voted, that the Selectmen and Committee estimate the Cloathing Collected for the Soldiers and to be made a town charge with the transporting.

5^{thly}. Voted, that the above Cloathing be sent to the Continental Soldiers in the Service for three years Belonging to this town.

6^{thly}. Voted, that the Selectmen and Committee Provide a man or men to transport the above Cloathing to the Soldiers.

Joshua Houghton served the town as express messenger, and was in due time paid 13£. 13ˢ. 10ᵈ for such service. At a town-meeting May 18, 1778 :

. . . 9^{thly}. Voted to allow the Selectmen seven pound fifteen shillings for Clothing they Found for the Solgers that Flead out of York in year 1776.

Massachusetts, from the beginning of the conflict, had adopted the policy of requiring each town to furnish its proportion of the clothing demanded for the soldiery, its quota being determined not by the number of men it had sent, but by its financial ability. In 1775, Lancaster was required to supply one hundred and sixteen coats. During the siege of Boston she was called upon for thirty-three blankets. In February, 1777, a requisition for clothing was made, based upon one-seventh of the male population above sixteen years of age. The following undated bill probably indicates the call made upon Lancaster :

State of Massachusetts Dr. to the Selectmen of Lancaster,

for sixty-four Summer Shirts at 40/, thirty-one Woolen Ditto

at 50/	£207 – 10ˢ
ninty-six pairs of Stockings	125 – 16
ninty.six pairs of Shoes	186 – 8
By or. of Selectmen	521 – 14

EBENEZER ALLEN
JOSHUA FLETCHER, Selectmen
WILLIAM PUTNAM, of
LEVI MOORE Lancaster
ISRAEL MOORE,

[Mass. Archives, Muster Rolls, XLI, 192.]

The assessment of clothing for the army in 1780, was :

Lancaster		40 pairs of Shoes, 41 Shirts, 26 pairs of Hose, 17 Blankets.					
Bolton	18	do.	15	do.	20	do.	0
Harvard	28	do.	10	do.	27	do.	0
Leominster	22	do.	22	do	22	do.	11

[Massachusetts Archives, CXL, 272-4.]

In 1781, Lancaster was required to supply sixty of each of the same articles of clothing.

Imported sweets, spices, and many articles of diet now thought necessities of daily domestic use, became so costly that every housekeeper was exercised in discovering substitutes for them among home products. Corn-stalks were ground, and the expressed juice boiled down to make molasses; the maple yielded sugar and the bees their more luscious manufacture. The cinnamon, nutmeg and ginger of the tropics were no longer to be had, and sassafras bark, caraway and coriander ill supplied the want of them. Salt often became scarce, and for that there was no equivalent. Tea had been in use in Massachusetts for over fifty years. The taste for it had become a passion with many, and manifold were the attempts to find in some infusion of native herbs all the cheering fragrance of the Chinese leaf. In 1768 the patriots generally resolved to abjure the use of foreign tea, and its buyers and sellers were equally proscribed. Nevertheless considerable quantities were secretly used, and the attempt to substitute for it the Labrador tea, *ledum latifolium*, met little favor with the female portion of the community, and royalists. But soon even the possession of the imported luxury was a crime against country. The ladies of this vicinity were however congratulated by no less an authority than the Massachusetts Spy, upon the discovery that their favorite beverage was easily attainable without sin.

. . . . It is with pleasure we can inform such of the fair sex, who are attached to Bohea Tea, that a shrub, supposed by many to be the same that produces the tea we have from the East Indies, grows in this town. Large quantities have been cured, and it is scarce known by smell or taste from the real Bohea.   [September 6. 1775]

This much vaunted shrub,—*ceanothus Americanus*,—continues to bear its revolutionary name, "Jersey tea;" but its virtues are purely historic. Another substitute for the bohea that had grown so politically poisonous, one quite popular among patriotic New England women, was "hyperion," a beverage made of the dried leaves of the raspberry. In more southern latitudes the same purpose was served by the flowers of the sassafras and the foliage of the yupon,— *ilex glabra*,—a shrub akin to that which furnishes the Paraguayan *yerva* or *maté*. Even garden herbs and mints were regularly utilized to appease the craving for the imported stimulant. Coffee was far more satisfactorily replaced by various home-made preparations.

From a series of probate inventories filed in colonial days can be got very suggestive pictures of the indigence or ascetic frugality of the pioneers, the slow accretion of household comforts, and the gradual changes in dress, social habits and domestic life. In the times specially under consideration we no longer find such items as the following, taken from some of the earliest property schedules of Lancaster's deceased yeoman: "the bedstead in the parlour"—"aucker of strong waters in cellar"—"a pair of querns"—"a posnet"—"a dozen trenchers"—"one dozen alcomy spoons"—"a satinisco and a red taminy petticoat" "a green say apron"—"a red serge hood"—"a fire slice" "matchlock"—"halbert"—"joint stools"—"a tumbril"— "thatching tools." In testamentary disposition of estates, "the great bible" or "one silver spoon" is not so frequently the sole bequest to a favorite daughter, and the eldest son no longer receives a double portion as his birth-right. But we continue to note a stinted supply and scant variety in the utensils of domestic economy, even among families esteemed well-to-do; and always find sundry chattels, the names or utility of which have long become unfamiliar, such as the following: spinning-wheels, brake, swingle, hetchel, wool-cards, loom, fire-steel and tinder box, cob-irons, basting ladle, fire-fork, cottrel, trammels, pot-hooks, peel, brander, trivet, iron and brass skillets, locker, settle, flock-bed, warming-pan, cheese-vat, brewing tub, malt-mill, powdering tub, piggin, noggin, keeler, rundlet, porringer, pewter platters, tankards, buckskin breeches, serge gowns and waistcoats, linsey-woolsey petticoats, pillion, pannel, saddle-bags, froe. Hoops and furbelows, saffron-hued lace, cocked hats, high-heeled satin shoes, ruffles and powdered perukes, we know there were from traditions that come down to us, but about them Lancaster administrators are silent.

In 1676, when savage hordes swept down from Wachu-set, and with fire and tomahawk drove the settlers from the Nashua valley to seek shelter in the bay towns, several of the homeless pioneers found hospitable doors open to them in Boston and Charlestown. Nearly one hundred years had elapsed and five thousand poor people of Boston, flee-ing from the insults of British soldiery and the sufferings incident to siege, were asking refuge and food. Thus Lancaster had her opportunity to repay tenfold what she had received. Of five hundred and thirty-nine poor of Boston assigned by the Provincial Congress to the charity of Worcester county, it was Lancaster's lot to provide for one hundred and three. Bolton was expected to care for forty-eight, Harvard fifty, and Leominster thirty-eight. To the quota of Lancaster were added thirty Charlestown exiles. The actual number who finally sought refuge here can never be known, for all attempts at a systematic distri-bution of the needy naturally failed in the confusion of the time. No lists of the names of the beneficiaries, and but few references to them are found. Some became sufficiently attached to their rural asylum to remain permanent resi-dents. Among these was a lame youth of fifteen years, the grand-nephew of Benjamin Franklin. This was Josiah Flagg, whose plain handwriting adorned the records of Lancaster for thirty-four years, 1800–1836. His father, William Flagg, remaining in the beleaguered city to pro-tect his personal effects, succumbed to hardship and dis-ease, leaving his crippled son dependent upon others. When past the allotted age of man, 'Squire Flagg, as the veteran town-clerk was generally called, was wont to tell of the hardships he endured as a boy in revolutionary days, and to show with honest pride the following testimonial :

This is to certify whom it may concern that Josiah Flagg has hired with me near Five Months, being employ'd as a Clerk and Accountant, and has behav'd in his Employment with great Ability, Diligence and Fidelity, so as to give me perfect Satisfaction.

This Testimony is given unask'd.   PHILADELPHIA Sept. 4, 1786
B. FRANKLIN.

The schoolmaster of Charlestown, William Harris, flee-ing on foot with his family of little ones to escape the devastating storm of flame in which his humble home was soon after swept away, by chance found friends and a refuge here. He became paymaster in the regiment of Colonel David Henley, died of fever Oct. 30, 1778, and was buried with military honors in the Second Precinct cemetery. The eldest of his children, a boy of ten when orphaned, through years of struggling with penury, rose to distinction— Thaddeus Mason Harris, S. T. D., A. A. S., etc.

John Newman, a "clock and watch maker," set up his shop near the store of Captain Samuel Ward, and there his descendants of two generations made steel tools of so excellent workmanship that they were sought for in all the country around.

The following documents tell of a family brought hither for temporary residence :

Massachusetts Bay to Oliver Pollard   Dr.
1775 July 17 bringing Richard Cartwright and family 7 persons to Lancaster as per certificate   2 - 3 - 0

LANCASTER Sept. 11 1775

Then Rec⁴ by the hand of David Moor Rebeccah Cartwright & a Grandchild of hers 7 years old who was not expressed in the stificat. This family was brought from Malden 42 miles. N. B. said Moor pad 1ˢ/4 for expence for said Cartwright.

CYRUS FAIRBANK ⎫ *The*
SAMLL. THURSTON ⎪ *Select*
EBENEZER ALLEN ⎬ *men*
DAVID OSGOOD ⎭ *of*
Lancaster

The Boston refugees who came "to share the homely banquet of peace" in the Nashua valley, were not all crafts-

men, nor of the impoverished class. Daniel Waldo bought
and occupied a farm upon the easterly side of the Neck,
and thither came the future lieutenant-governor, Levi Lincoln, to woo and wed Martha Waldo. Edmund Quincy,
Esq., another Boston merchant, one of whose daughters
was the wife of Governor John Hancock, came to reside
with a second daughter who had married Sheriff William
Greenleaf. Edmund Quincy's letter book, now the property
of the Massachusetts Historical Society, contains copies of
sundry epistles to Governor Hancock and other noted patriots, dated at Lancaster, in which he ably discusses the
gravest questions of state. Unfortunately there is little of
local color in these letters "*apud sylvas Lancastricnscs.*"
One he begins thus: "Among y⁰ exiles of Boston I am
here about forty miles from that formerly happy seaport,
now a strong fortress held under direful circumstances by
ye enemies of Great Britain and America." He often mentions the great scarcity of wool, and urges the encouragement of hemp culture, to supply a substitute. He pictures
the "Wonderful Flow of people into Cambridge and its
vicinage, for ye purpose of Common Curiosity," during the
weary months of siege. March 18, 1776, a rumor reached
Lancaster that Abel Willard, Esq., had been killed in Boston by a cannon ball from the patriot batteries, and Quincy
writes: "If ye news prove true I shall pity ye relict widow
for whom Dolly and her sister K. have a good value, and
who manifested much reluctance at going to Boston."

A sojourner even more noted at the time, made his home
in a house which stood in rear of the site now occupied by
Mrs. Elizabeth Frances Dix; one who, from his intimate
social relations with the first president of the Provincial and
Continental Congresses, had much influence with his
ardent whig neighbors, and, it is said, ever swayed them
towards justice and humanity; often moderating the patriot
rage towards those suspected of lukewarmness or toryism.
Nathaniel Balch had a shop on the west side of Washing-

ton, near and north of School street, in Boston, where he retailed hats, and original witticisms, which won him more than urban renown.   He became so marked a favorite with, and so inseparable a companion to Governor Hancock, that his rival town wits fastened upon him the title of "the Governor's Jester."   His name is prominent in the war committees of Lancaster in 1776.

In spite of the public anxiety and private distress, the arts were not banished, nor did the graces languish from neglect, on the Nashua.

THE French Gentleman who taught DANCING and the FRENCH LANGUAGE grammatically, in *Worcester* the last Winter and in LANCASTER the Spring ensuing, begs leave to inform the Publick that he has again opened a SCHOOL in LANCASTER, near the Meeting-House for the same purpose : Where he will pay the greatest attention to every Lady or Gentleman who will honour him with his or her presence.

[Massachusetts Spy, Thursday, November 15, 1781.]

Hasty inference drawn from a comparison of the often illiterate manuscript of the town's officials during the revolution with that of the pioneers in Lancaster, might lead to the assumption that there had been a decadence in popular education.   The enforced costly sacrifice of material interests during long years of warfare prevented generous expenditure for public schools, but the old custom was continued of annually hiring some college graduate to preside over the grammar school, usually for two terms.   Among the more noted of those thus employed were : Joseph Warren the patriot, who taught in 1759 and 1760, and Joseph Willard, later to become president of Harvard College, who was a teacher here in 1762.   After 1767 the orders for "schooling" were issued in favor of various townsmen acting as "prudential men" for the several squadrons into which the town was divided—the town treasurer no longer paying the teachers directly, and their names being therefore seldom found in town records.   The names of "school dames" first appear in these records about the close of the revolution.

The two ministers of Lancaster were ripe classical scholars, and were wont to eke out their scant stipends by receiving students preparing for college. At least ten Lancaster boys, under their tuition probably, sought matriculation at Harvard during the twenty years next preceding 1785, and a Lancaster graduate, Samuel Locke, was president of that institution during four years, 1770–1773. The two resident lawyers of the revolutionary period, Abel Willard and John Sprague, were men of collegiate education, as were also two of the several physicians of the town, Israel Atherton and Josiah Wilder.

Books were too costly to be abundant, but inventories of the period prove that every family possessed a few, mostly of a religious character. Of the working libraries of professional men we possess no full catalogue. The books of Reverend John Prentice were, at his death in 1748, appraised worth 53£ 8ˢ. 3ᵈ. After this collection was scattered, there was perhaps none rivalling it until the founding of the Lancaster Library by an association of citizens in 1790. Reverend Timothy Harrington's books, as listed in the inventory of his estate, 1795, were as follows :

McKnight's Harmony of the Four Gospels — Doddridge's Family Expositor in six volumes — Doddridge's Lectures — Bailey's Dictionary — Ball's Power of Godliness — Watts' Sermons — Bennet's Christian Oratory — Gordon's Geography — Latin and Hebrew Psalms, two volumes — Trumbull's Moral Philosophy — Grove's Lord's Supper — Prideaux's Connection of the History of the Old and New Testaments, four volumes — Annerson's Remonstrance — Calvin's Institutes of Religion — Kennett's Roman Antiquities — Bion's Works — Cicero's Orations — Trail's Sermons — Homer's Iliad — Simplicius's Commentary — Fuller's Worthies of England — Region of Parnassus — Theological Works in Latin, two volumes — Cruden's Concordance — Confessions of Faith and Moral Essays — Horace — Salmon's English Nobility — Euclid's Elements — Dialogues on Eloquence — Gulliver's Memoirs — Juvenal — Parable of Ten Virgins — Dr. Mayhew's Sermons — Dr. Whitby's Natural Religion — Trap's Trinity — Chauncy's State of Religion — Latin Bible — Latin Grammar — Greek and Latin Testament — Prince's Chronology of New England — Flavel's Works — Scott's Christian Life — Willard's Body of Divinity — History of Church of Scotland — Perkins's Works — Lord Chesterfield's Exposition — Pole's Synopsis, Latin, five volumes.

Doctor William Dunsmoor, a man of marked ability, the most prominent of Lancaster's patriots in 1775, had inherited his father's "hats and wiggs, and one Bible, and all his Physicall Books and Chirurgical Instruments." At his decease in 1784, the following volumes composed his little library :

A large Folio Bible with cuts — Henry Moore against Deism — Robert Morse's Sermons, five volumes — Burns's Justice, abridged — Bailey's Dictionary — Perry's Theatre of Physic, two volumes — Huxam's Essay on Fevers — Brown's Art of Physic — Allen's Synopsis Medicinæ — Shaw's Practice of Physic — Salmon's Practical Physic — The Marrow of Surgery — John Dayreel in Vindication of the Church—Snake in the Grass, three volumes — Tate and Brady's Psalms — A Bundle of Magazines and Pamphlets — Yorrick's Sermon's, two volumes — Humphrey Clinker, three volumes — The Devil on Two Sticks — Mrs. Chapone's Letters.

From time to time various paroled prisoners were quartered in and about Lancaster, occasional glimpses of whose impatience under restraint and consequent collision with local authority have come down to us. An incident which doubtless caused some stir for the day, was the passing through the town of a company of prisoners, as narrated in a journal kept by James Stevens of Andover, a soldier in the detachment of thirty-three men under Captain Joseph Baker, Jr., sent from Cambridge in charge of those captured July 31, 1775, during an attack upon Light House Island :

Tuesday August 1 ; this morning there was thirty-for prisnors a going to Woster, twenty-two regelers and twelve tories, we started for Woster a bout noon. We went to Concord and staid all night, we put the prisnors into jail, we got our super and sot sentry.

Wensday 2ᵈ ; this morning we got a dram & set of ; we marcht about ten mile and then went to brekfast to won Gilbards in little town, we marcht to Lanchester and staid al night, the town's people stod sentry over them.

Thursday 3ᵈ ; this morning we got a dram & set of, we marcht to Shusbury and there went to brekfast, & we started and went to Woster, we marcht through the town, the tories with there hats under there arms, and we returned them to the prison, the tories went in to the dungeon, we got some vitls and then sot of for home, we went to Shusbury we staid al night.

Friday, this morning we got our brekfast and started and through Lanchester and then went to little town & staid al night. . . . . .

June 17, 1776, the transports Anabella, Lord Howe and George, seven weeks from Glasgow, were captured in Nantasket Roads, having entered the harbor in ignorance that the blockade of Boston had been raised. Upon these vessels were two battalions of the Seventy-first Highlanders under command of Lieutenant-Colonel Archibald Campbell. After brief confinement in the Worcester jail, five Highland officers —Captain Lawrence Robert Campbell, Lieutenant Archie McLean and Lewis Colquhon, with volunteers Duncan Campbell and James Flint, were sent to Lunenburg on their parole not to go outside the limit of six miles from the residence assigned for their use. Each was allowed a Highland soldier as servant, for whose conduct he was responsible. If we may judge from the following pathetic complaint, these five Highlandmen and their gillies not only made Turkey Hills temporarily a very lively place indeed, but managed to endanger the safety of the United States by their un-Puritanic escapades :

To the Grate & General Court of the State of the Massachusetts Bay.

The Committee of Inspection &c for the Town of Lunenburg beg Leave to Inform your Honours of the conduct of the prisoners of war Residing in this Town & likewise our proceedings had thereon, & in the first place we would Inform you that some time since the sᵈ prisoners Requested the Commᵗᵉᵉ that they might Remove from where they ware stationed to the House of Capt. Ebenezar Robinsons (who is a professᵈ. Enemy to his country & under confinement) but we Refused to grant their Request, notwithstanding which & in contempt of our authority they Did without our knowledge Remove themselves and effects to sd. Robinsons but we soon Removed them from there to another place, since which they do frequently Visit sd. Robinson. Notwithstanding they are forbid so Doing, they frequently Visit the publick Houses & sometimes to stay very late at night to the Disturbance of the Inhabitants. Some of their servants have assalted one of our Inhabitants on the evening in the Highway & threatened to take away his life; further one of the officers passing by a number of School Boys in the street one of them observing his Dress to be in the Highland mode, asked his fellow if he did not think that Highlanders was a-cold, the officer hereing the speech Returned to them, threatened their

16

lives, calling them Dem^d Bastards, swearing by God if ever he heard them
say so again he would split their heads to attoms, therefore we think it our
Duty & for the safty of the United States that some Restraint be laid on
them, accordingly we have Restricted them to the limmits of twenty Rodes
from their lodgings untill further order.

Wᴹ Stearns	
Joseph Hartwell	*Committee*
Benjᴺ Redington	*of*
Josiah Stearns	*Inspection*
Daniel Gardner	*&c*

Lunenburg Jany. 21, 1777.

In Council Jany 24, 1777.   Read & Committed to John Whitcomb &
John Taylor Esq. to consider the same & report what is proper to be done
thereon.   John Avery *Dept. Secy*

The committee advised :

. . . . that in case the aforesaid Prisoners Do not observe the orders &
Direction of said Committy that they be Fourthwith sent by said Committy
to the Gould in Taunton in the County of Bristol, and committ them to
the costada of the keeper of said Gould.

[Massachusetts Archives, CLXXXII, 72.]

In the adjoining town of Harvard were rusticated two
gentlemanly Britons, Captain Edward Barron of the King's
Own, and Surgeon Walter Cullen of the Seventy-second
Foot or Royal Fencibles. They also got into temporary
disagreement with their custodians by once wandering beyond the limits assigned them, and were remanded to jail ;
but petitioning to return to the purer air of their country
quarters, their request was allowed.

Of those whose residence in this neighborhood during
the Revolution was compulsory, the most noteworthy per-
sonage was an eccentric bachelor tory. There lived in
South Lancaster, but a stone's throw apart, a sister and a
daughter of Judge John Chandler, "the honest Refugee"
of Worcester. They were the wives respectively of Levi
Willard, Esq., and Captain Samuel Ward. Mr. Willard
died in the first year of the war, and there came to reside
with these estimable and accomplished ladies an elder
brother of Mrs. Ward. He was about thirty-two years of
age, peculiar in person, habits and dress. Among other
oddities of apparel, he was partial to bright red small-

clothes.   His tory principles and singularities called down
upon him the gibes of the patriots among whom his lot was
temporarily cast, but his ready tongue and caustic wit were
sufficient weapons of defence.   In 1774, as town-clerk of
Worcester, he had recorded a protest of forty-three royalist citizens against the resolutions of the patriot majority.
This record he was obliged in open town-meeting to deface,
and when he failed to render it sufficiently illegible with
the pen, his tormentors dipped his fingers into the ink and
used them to perfect the obliteration.   He fled to Halifax,
but after a few months returned, and was thrown into Worcester jail.   The reply to his petition for release is preserved
in Massachusetts Archives, CLXIV, 205 :

> Colony of the Massachusetts Bay. By the Major part of the Council
> of said Colony.   Whereas Clark Chandler of Worcester has been Confined
> in the Common Prison at Worcester for holding Correspondence with the
> enemies of this Country and the said Clark having humbly petitioned for
> an enlargement and it having been made to appear that his health is greatly
> impaired & that the Publick will not be endangered by his having some
> enlargement, and Samuel Ward, John Sprague, and Ezekiel Hull having
> Given Bond to the Colony Treasurer in the penal sum of one thousand
> Pounds, for the said Clark's faithful performance of the order of Council
> for his said enlargement, the said Clark is hereby permitted to go to Lan-
> caster when his health will permit, and there to continue and not to go out
> of the Limits of that Town, he in all Respects conforming himself to the
> Condition in said Bond contained, and the Sheriff of said County of Wor-
> cester and all others are hereby Directed to permit the said Clark to pass
> unmolested so long as he shall conform himself to the obligations afore-
> mentioned.   Given under our Hands at ye Council Chambers in Water-
> town the 15 Day of Dec. Anno Domini 1775.
>
> By their Honors' Command. . . . . .
>
> PEREZ MORTON, *Dept. Secry.*

The salubrious air of Lancaster in time grew oppressive
to this loyalist bachelor, as is disclosed in his lengthy petition—to be found in Massachusetts Archives, CLXXIII, 546
—wherein he begs for a wider range, and especially for
leave to visit the sea-shore.   The medical certificate of a
local practitioner accompanies it, and affords confirmation
of the statement made by the Marquis de Chastellux, that

"the physicians in America pay much more attention than ours to qualities of the atmosphere, and frequently employ change of air as an effectual remedy."

LANCASTER, Oct. 25, 1777.

This is to inform whom it may Concern that Mr Clark Chandler, now residing in this Town, is in such a Peculiar Bodily Indisposition as in my opinion renders it necessary for him to take a short Trip to the Salt Water in order to assist in recovering his Health.

JOSIAH WILDER *Phn*

Chandler was permitted to visit Boston, and thereafter to wander at will within the bounds of Worcester county. He lived at Worcester until his death, in 1804. His "Peculiar Bodily Indisposition" proved highly infectious, and the whole community became so inoculated with it that descendants of the third and fourth generations periodically migrate seaward to test the prescription of Dr. Josiah Wilder.

Occasionally evidence is found, like that in the following advertisement, to prove that the spirit of independence had no "color line" in Lancaster:

Whereas Cæsar my negro man has absented himself from me, and is employed by several persons, without my consent: This is to caution all persons from harbouring or employing said negro, or trusting him on my account, from the date hereof. Those who entertain him, may expect to be dealt with according to Law.

LANCASTER, May 7, 1781.   JAMES WILDER.

Cæsar doubtless had read the Declaration of Rights with a clearer understanding than James, and knew that all men had been "born free and equal" in Massachusetts more than six months before. In September, 1777, the selectmen reported thirteen male "Negros" in Lancaster above sixteen years of age. Presumably these were mostly free, for in the valuation return of 1771, there were recorded but six "Servants for life between fourteen and forty-five years of age;" one each being credited to Doctor William Dunsmoor, Captain Hezekiah Gates, Peter Green, Samuel Joslin, Josiah Moore, and David Osgood. Free negroes and slaves fought at Bunker Hill, and are frequently found

in the rolls of the Provincial troops, although by the letter
of the militia law excluded from enrolment.   In October,
1775, both the Continental and Provincial councils formally
forbade the enlistment of the colored race ; but the royalists were not so scrupulous, and, before the close of the first
year of contest Washington found it necessary in general
orders to authorize the employment of negroes in the militia service.   Thereafter, throughout the continuance of
hostilities, they are found, north and south, fighting in the
ranks of both armies.   At least fourteen colored men appear in the revolutionary rolls, claimed as serving for Lancaster :

Peter Ayres,	Peter [Franklin?]	Job Lewis,
Becky's Boston,	Gideon Georges,	Edom Loudon,
Julius Cæsar,	Charles Henry,	Perley Rogers,
John Carter,	Reuben [Kendall?]	Charles Stuart,
	Cain Lewis,	Topsal Woodard.

The record of these men will be found on previous
pages.   One, Franklin, died in service ; two, Cain Lewis
and Stuart, deserted.   Edom Loudon was distinctly claimed
in Captain Daniel Goss's return of February, 1778, among
Lancaster's continental enlistments.   He was a slave owned
by Daniel Goodridge of Winchendon, who ran away from
a former master, and, enlisting, fought at Bunker Hill.
He died a pauper in Winchendon, and became noted as the
cause of the famous "Massachusetts Slave Case" of 1806–
7, Winchendon vs. Hatfield.

Upon the re-establishment in July, 1775, of a postal
system independent of royal authority, under the direction
of Benjamin Franklin, the office at Cambridge, and later
that at Worcester, were those most convenient to Lancaster, and so remained for several years.   In the lists of un-
called-for mail published in the New England Chronicle
and Massachusetts Spy, letters for her citizens are often
found advertised as remaining in both these offices.   The
first post-office in Lancaster was established April 1, 1795.
The postage upon letters was five and one-fourth pence for

each one-fourth ounce, for distances less than sixty miles; eight pence for distances between sixty and one hundred miles, and one shilling for distances over one hundred and less than two hundred miles. There were but twenty-eight post-offices in the whole country in 1776. The delivery of the mail to owners distant from the offices depended much upon neighborly courtesy or the news-carriers, who rode over their established routes once a week. Silent Wilde, or his partner, Isaac Church, started from Boston on Mondays, passing "through Lancaster, Rutland etc. to Northampton, Deerfield etc." In the New England Chronicle for "Oct. 19 to Oct. 26, 1775," is this advertisement by him:

SILENT WILDE
News-carrier to Deerfield &c.

BEGS Leave to inform his Customers, that the Time of his last Engagement ends on the 9th Day of November next, when he earnestly hopes for punctual Payment at the usual Places of receiving their Papers. He likewise earnestly desires hereby to give publick Notice, that he proposes, on suitable Encouragement to ride weekly, his usual Road for the term of six months next ensuing the said 9th Day of November and to supply each Subscriber with one of the publick News-Papers at One Dollar each, provided each Subscriber shall at the beginning of the said six Months pay the one Half of said Dollar. He would likewise take this Opportunity to call upon those who are in Arrears with him for past services, kindly to Consider that he stands in great Need of what is due to him.   SHUTESBURY, October 16, 1775.

Joshua Thomas was the post rider from Worcester through Shrewsbury, Lancaster, etc., to Londonderry, during the Revolution, and advertised to take pay for his services in produce and paper-rags. There seems to have been no public conveyance for travellers between Boston or Worcester and Lancaster until some years later, although an advertisement in The Boston Gazette, September 20, 1773, indicates that the enterprise was contemplated:

To the PUBLIC

The Concord Stage Coach sets out on Tuesday & Friday Mornings at 7 O'Clock from Common Street near Liberty Tree. The Price 4.s. The

Stage to be continued to Lancaster if suitable encouragement.   All Favors gratefully acknowledged, By their humble Servant.

NATHANIEL RUSSELL.

In modern days, at any public loss or signal victory won, the thrill of sorrow or joy runs through the nation almost universally coincident with the event that causes it, however far distant.   During the war for independence, neither bad, nor the best of good news travelled much more than fifty miles in twenty-four hours, and rarely was it less than five days creeping from New York to Boston. It was a fortnight's journey from New York to Virginia, but the glad tidings of the capture of Yorktown, however, which set the church bells ringing throughout the land because of its eloquent promise of national freedom, reached Lancaster in about a week, coming by vessel to Newport. The festivities consequent were at last reported a month after the surrender of Cornwallis.

LANCASTER, November 19, 1781.

On Thursday morning last, a considerable number of the most respectable inhabitants of this place assembled at the Sun Tavern to celebrate the capture of Cornwallis, when after mutual congratulations on this happy event, the company conducted by William Greenleaf Esq. formed and marched in procession through the principal streets of the town preceded by an advance guard, field piece, and band of musick with American colours displayed ; having fired sundry salutes followed with three huzzas, the company returned to the Sun, where an elegant dinner was provided for them, and such gentlemen from the neighbouring towns as were pleased to favour them with their company ; after dinner the following toasts were drank each being followed by a discharge of a field piece with three cheers.
  . . . . . .

Thirteen patriotic toasts then succeed, but are of no especial interest now; the last was the following snarl of metaphors :

May peace, liberty and uninterrupted commerce, break the jaws of tyranny, and be wafted by the Gods through the realms of Neptune to the welcome shores of the new world.

In the evening, Mason's Hall was beautifully illuminated ; the greatest harmony, concord, sociability and good friendship were preserved through the whole and crowned the festal day and evening.

[Massachusetts Spy, Nov. 22, 1781.]

With what the festive libations were poured we are not told, but neither the Sun Tavern nor "the most respectable inhabitants" were noted for thin potations on occasions like this.

This jubilation of the people over the victory that presaged honorable peace near at hand, was the first of many recorded. The date of the annual festal commemoration soon, however, became that of the Declaration of Independence. But at intervals the militia companies of the region around were wont to organize a celebration of the surrender of Yorktown ; when a motley army of spectators gathered from far and near, regaled themselves with unlimited gingerbread, spruce beer or more exciting beverages, derived amusement from the evolutions of grotesquely caparisoned troops in a sham fight, and indulged in effervescing jollity of various descriptions.

The last "Cornwallis" in the vicinity of Lancaster was held upon Burditt Hill, October 19, 1853, when the time-worn farce was re-enacted with a scenic display that outshone all traditions. Nine uniformed companies of militia were present, one each from Berlin, Clinton, Groton, Leominster, Marlborough, Oakdale, Sterling, West Boylston, and Westminster. An equal number of Continental companies un-uniformed, in all manner of dress, came from Bolton, Clinton, Harvard, Lancaster, Leominster, Marlborough, Rock Bottom, Shirley and Westminster, and a tribe of Indians from Berlin. Captain Jeremiah Barnard was in command of the Continentals, Sewall Richardson of Leominster enacted the role of General Washington, and Colonel Upton of Fitchburg, that of Cornwallis. The general parade of the troops occupied the morning hours, and a collation was partaken of at noon by fifteen hundred soldiers. After lunch the two armies were drawn up for battle on the hill, the British lines being half-way up the slope. The Continentals charged from Union street over the valley, and with more smoke and noise than that locality will probably ever experience again, carried the opposing works by storm, and marched their prisoners to the common, where the ceremony of surrender took place with military formality.

Forty years elapsed from the time the United States were acknowledged among independent nations, and the thirteen members of the original confederacy had become twenty-four, when an event occurred in Lancaster which revivified all the fading memories of the war for liberty, and inspired a day of festivity not equalled in enthusiasm of rejoicing by any that preceded it, nor surpassed by any of later years. One by one the general officers who served in the revolution had been borne to their graves, until Thomas Sumpter alone survived in America. In a foreign land, another, of exalted rank, "the high priest of cosmopolitism," one who with chivalric generosity gave up the comforts of a splendid home, and left wife and children to aid with his wealth and genius the Americans struggling for freedom—a major-general before he had seen his twentieth birthday—still lived, the most romantic figure of his age. The sixty-seventh and sixty-eighth anniversaries of his natal day were celebrated during his visit to the United States.

Thursday, September 2, 1824, the hero whose name is oftenest coupled with that of Washington in the memory and speech of Americans, set out from Boston, through highways thronged by a grateful people invoking with tearful eyes and swelling hearts blessings upon his head. It was arranged that he should spend the first night of his journey in Bolton, at the mansion of Sampson V. S. Wilder, whom he had known in France. Elaborate and tasteful preparations had been made within and without the house for welcoming the nation's guest. Over the entrance was a triumphal arch, the inscription upon which was characteristic of the eccentric owner: "The Great Jehovah, Washington and Lafayette." For a long time after this was quoted in the vicinity as "Wilder's trinity." The mansion and grounds were brilliantly illuminated. The Bolton Rifle Company, in their new green uniform, stood guard over the house all night. Lafayette could but be delighted with the beautiful homestead and his reception, and he is reported to have complimented his graceful hostess at departure by pledging his lifelong memory of "the fairy mistress of the enchanted castle." At the early hour of half-past six, Friday morning, Lafayette, escorted by a company of cavalry and accompanied by his son, M. Levasseur, a committee from Worcester, Generals Jewett, Gregory and staff, proceeded to the Lancaster line, over the turnpike road. The turnpike gate was covered with flowers and evergreen, and bore a legend, "The Free welcome the Brave." Here a national salute was fired by the artillery. Nearly opposite the meeting-house an arch thirty feet in height, and of nearly the same width, had been erected, and elaborately decorated. Upon it was the greeting :

WELCOME LA FAYETTE.

The American Eagle in triumph shall wave
Its pinions of Glory to welcome the Brave.

This arch, with its inscription, is yet preserved in the attic of the Brick church. The Leominster Artillery and the Lancaster Infantry had joined the escort. Passing through long lines of people — an immense concourse having assembled from all the country around —the general and his suite came to the arch, where they were met by the town's committee and conducted to a platform upon the green. There he was addressed by Doctor Thayer, as follows :

General Lafayette.—In behalf of the inhabitants of Lancaster, I offer you their cordial congratulations on your arrival in a country whose wrongs you felt and resented ; whose liberties you valiantly defended ; and whose interests and prospects have always been dear to your soul.

We all unite with the few surviving veterans which were with, loved and respected you on the high places of the field, in giving you a welcome to this village, once the chosen residence of savages, and the scene of their most boasted triumph; and rejoice that you visit it under the improvements of civilized life, in prosperity and peace.

It gladdens us that we and our children may behold the man, whom we have believed, and whom we have taught our children to believe, was second only to his and our friend, the immortal WASHINGTON. We participate in your joy, on beholding our institutions in vigor, our population extended, so that since you left us, from a little one we have become millions, and from a small band a strong nation; that you see our glory rising, our Republic placed on an immovable basis, all of which are in part, under Providence, to be ascribed to your sacrifices, dangers and toils.

We wish you health and prosperity. We assure you that wherever you shall go, you will be greeted by our fellow countrymen as one of the chief deliverers of America, and the friend of rational liberty and of man. It is especially our prayer, that on that day in which the acclamations and applauses of dying men shall cease to reach or affect you, you may receive from the Judge of character and Dispenser of imperishable honors, as the reward of philanthropy and incorruptible integrity, a crown of glory which shall never fade.

Lafayette, conquering with difficulty the emotion which the eloquence of the venerable pastor had excited, replied nearly as follows:

Accept my thanks, sir, for the kind welcome you have here offered me in the name of the inhabitants of Lancaster. In returning to this country after so long an absence, in receiving such proofs of gratitude and affection wherever I go, in witnessing the prosperity of the land, a prosperity you are pleased to say I have been instrumental in promoting, I feel emotions for which no language is adequate; in meeting again my former friends, in seeing the children and grandchildren of those who were my companions in the war of our revolution, I feel a gratification which no one can express. I beg you to accept, sir, and to offer to these people my acknowledgments.

One who witnessed the inspiring scene and recorded the address and reply, continues thus:

The surviving soldiers of the revolution dwelling in town were then introduced to the general, who received them in the most cordial and touching manner. He expressed himself highly gratified with the interest which the ladies discovered, pressing forward with eagerness to greet this distinguished friend of mankind. After remaining on the platform fifteen minutes receiving the various attentions and reciprocating the heartfelt delight experienced by the assembly, he returned to his carriage amid cordial huzzas and the discharge of a national salute from the artillery.

At Sterling he was met by the artillery companies of that town and Princeton, and escorted to the triumphal arch which bore the inscription :

WELCOME LAFAYETTE

America's adopted son,
Brother and Friend of Washington,
Our Land in trouble found a Friend in thee,
We'll not forget thee in prosperity.

He here replied to a brief address from Isaac Goodwin, Esq., referring in terms of kindly remembrance to Lord Stirling — in whose honor the town received its name — and amid the booming of cannon and the acclamations of the multitude, rode on towards Worcester.

A correspondent from Lancaster is quoted in the Columbian Centinel of Saturday, September 11, 1824 :

. . . . . The ceremonies here were not intended for idle display, nor was it wished to vie with those towns which have greater means at command. The preparations were few and simple. It was a moral spectacle of no ordinary interest, to see so large a collection of the well dressed and intelligent yeomanry of the county deeply interested in the proceedings of the occasion, offering the spontaneous homage of their hearts to him who stood by their country in the hour of her distress and weakness. There was not an individual unmoved by what was passing before him, during the short visit of the General — and you might see in every part of the crowd many of both sexes, and of all ages, whose moistened eyes told forth the strong feeling they neither wished nor were able to suppress. Such genuine heartfelt emotions have never before been so extensively excited amongst us. The praise of Lafayette swells in every heart, and is heard from every tongue.

The enthusiasm has no limit but that of good order and decency. It is the overflowing of full hearts — the strong expression of gratitude for services and sacrifices we can never repay. It gives me pleasure to be able to state that the General fully appreciated the feelings his presence occasioned. On his way to Sterling he repeatedly expressed to Mr. S. V. S. Wilder, who accompanied him from Boston to Worcester, the pleasure he felt at the reception he met with in Lancaster, and mentioned in the strongest terms how deeply he was affected with the address of Reverend Doctor Thayer. Nor was he insensible to the beautiful scenery in Lancaster — it came in for a full share of his praise. . . . . .

V.

SHAYS' INSURRECTION.

1786–1787.

WHEN peace had come and national independence was assured, and Massachusetts had time to count the cost of her tremendous exertions in behalf of liberty, she found herself weighed down by an enormous debt — nearly fifteen million dollars. She resolved to keep her credit free from reproach by revenues derived from direct taxation; but the people, groaning under personal sacrifices and sorrows — legacies of long years of war — became restive when additions to their burdens began to be made in the name of government. Many, maddened by what they deemed oppressive levies, refused tithe, and sought by mob violence to restrain the courts from enforcing the laws respecting debt. The ignorant could not discriminate between the wrongs they had suffered under monarchical rule and the discomforts, deprivations and burdensome taxes consequent upon the contest that had made them free citizens of a republic. The grievances of the rebellious were, however, too real not to find abundant sympathy. The merchants' and attorneys' wives and daughters flaunted their foreign silks, feathers and laces, while the farmer's crops, though luxuriant, filled his barns, not his purse, and could with difficulty be bartered for the commonest clothing and domestic necessities. Many an owner of valuable estate in land, who had sought by temporary mortgage to enjoy wonted luxuries, and hold his acres also, found himself bankrupt by a forced sale. Complaint and petition pressed the legislature for relief, but resolves could not

avail to make the indolent industrous, to give employment
to the artisan, to instruct the ignorant in political economy,
to bestow farms upon the landless, or to fill with silver the
pockets of the impecunious. Disappointment of exaggerated hopes increased agrarian discontent. Demagogic
agitators noisily advocated the turning of everything topsy
turvy—the charlatan's cheap panacea for setting right
times out of joint. Discussion and convention multiplied
dissatisfaction, and finally degenerated into organized insurrection. Then the common sense of the people asserted
itself. The first signs of disaffection presaging the storm
appeared even before the signing of the treaty of peace.
The warrant for a town-meeting summoned April 1, 1783,
contains this article :

3. To see if the Town will chuse one or more persons to meet at a
Convention to be held at Worcester the 2ᵈ Tuesday of April next at 9
O'Clock in the Morning, there to take into consideration the many Greiv-
ances the good people of this county at present Labour under, and to petition the general Court for Redress, and to act or transact any thing relative
thereto.

The town sent as delegates to this county convention
Captains Timothy Whiting and Ephraim Carter, and Whiting was chosen its secretary. Thirty-four delegates were
present from twenty-six towns, and after passing a series
of resolutions recommending certain instructions to the
representatives in General Court, which were ordered
printed in the Spy, the convention adjourned to the second
Tuesday in May, when a larger representation of the people assembled, and more resolves were published. The
next convention in August and meetings subsequent were
not reported in the newspapers, nor in Lancaster town-
meetings. When the town was represented, it was by the
delegates first chosen. The Committees of Correspondence, Inspection and Safety were regularly elected in 1782
and 1783, with other town officers, at the March meeting.
In 1782 this committee consisted of Timothy Knight, Daniel Rugg, and Jeremiah Haskell ; in 1783, of Captain

Timothy Whiting, Deacon Cyrus Fairbank, and Doctor Israel Atherton.

The following circular letter gives indication of one form which the general unrest of the times took, a year or two later :

LUNENBURG, May 23ᵈ, 1785.

To the Selectmen of the Town of Bolton.

Gentlemen, We have to acquaint you that on the nineteenth of May Instant in Pursuance of a Circular Letter from the Town of Leominster, Delegates from the following Towns viz : Townshend, Shirley, Ashby, Lancaster, Harvard, Lunenburg, Leominster, and Fitchburg convened at Mr Whitney's in this town, to take into Consideration the Expediency of applying for a new County to be erected in this Quarter of the Goverment, where it was voted unanimously that it is highly Convenant that a New County be erected, and that a Committe be Chosen to write to the Towns of Groton, Dunstable, Littleton, Westford, Pepperel and Boxboro and Bolton, Berlin, Sterling, Princeton, Westminster, Ashburnham and Winchendon, to inform them of the Proceedings of the Convention, and to Request them to join Herein at the adjournment which is to be held on the third Tuesday of June Next at Nine o'Clock in the morning at Mr Whitney's Tavern in this town. We are Gentlemen

Your most obedᵗ and very Hᵘˡᵉ: Servᵗˢ:

GEORGE KIMBALL ⎱ *Committee*
SAMᴸ. DEXTER ⎰

At a town-meeting held August 12, 1786, Ebenezer Allen was chosen "to represent the Town at the proposed County Convention to be holden at Leicester the 15ᵗʰ Inst.," and a committee consisting of Captain Timothy Whiting, Moses Smith, John Sprague, Esq., Deacon William Willard, Deacon Benjamin Houghton, Michael Newhall, and Captain Samuel Ward were elected "to prepare instructions for the said Allen, and lay the same before the Town."

LANCASTER, August 14, 1786 . . . . . .

The Committee appointed by the Town to prepare Instructions for the Delegate to Convention laid the same before the Town and the same being read Paragraph by Paragraph, and the Question being put to see whether the Town would adopt them, and it Passed in the affirmative.

LANCASTER, August 21, 1786.

The report of the Delegate from Convention being read and no objection being made thereto the Town then voted to adjourn to the first Monday in October next at 3 O'Clock P. M.

The instructions of the town to its delegate have not been discovered. The convention adjourned from Leicester, where thirty-seven towns appeared by delegates, to Paxton, at which place forty-one towns were represented, and a petition to the General Court was agreed upon, which Lancaster's delegate reported to the adjourned town-meeting.

LANCASTER, October 2, 1786 . . . . . .

Then the Town went into the Consideration of the doings of the Convention and after accepting such articles in the Petition to the General Court, and rejecting others, as the Town thought proper, (which are noted in the margin of the sd. Petition), then voted to adjourn. . . . . .

The proceedings of this town-meeting were more fully reported in the Worcester Magazine for the second week in October, 1786:

We hear from Lancaster on the 2ᵈ inst. the delegate to convention laid before the town for its consideration the petition agreed upon by that body, which was then examined article by article. On reading the 2ᵈ article the delegate was asked what convention intended by "*a portable representation of property*" and received no very satisfactory answer; they passed the article with an exception "*but no paper money be made.*" On the 4ᵗʰ article the delegate was called on to inform what officer of the government was therein alluded to; the delegate informed it was the Attorney General; the town were of the opinion that the office of Attorney General should be expressly named which would more probably cause an explanation of a motion not accurately understood and perhaps heal a sore in the political body that otherwise might remain festering for a long time. The last clause in the 8ᵗʰ article which says "the grant of the supplementary fund we conceive inconsistent with republican principles and very grievous to this people," the town would not adopt. The 11ᵗʰ article respecting registry of deeds in the several towns in the county, was disapproved by a great majority. The 13ᵗʰ and last article viz: the scheme for revising and amending the constitution (as it was termed,) was unanimously rejected. The town having thus avowed the constitution, were inclined to instruct their Representative rather than petition the General Court through the instrumentality of Convention; and accordingly directed the Clerk to forward the doings of the town to Capt. Carter the Representative, by the earliest opportunity, as the instructions of his Constituents.

After adjournment from November 20 and December 11, at which meetings no business offered, on January 4, 1787,

. . . . The address from the General Court was then read and Considered, and thereupon voted to choose a Committee of seven to draw up instructions for the representative, and thereupon voted and chose Sam¹. Ward, Capt. Tim⁰. Whiting, Jun', John Sprague, Esq. Mr. Moses Sawyer. Mr. Jonathan Wilder, Deacon Cyrus Fairbank and Capt. Daniel Goss as a Committee for the above purpose.

This committee reported at the adjournment of the meeting, January 22, 1787 ;

. . . . and the said instructions being presented, read and considered paragraph by paragraph were voted and accepted by the Town ; also voted that the instructions be printed in the Worcester newspaper. . . . . also to receive the report of the delegate to convention which being heard thereupon voted to discontinue the said Delegate to the County Convention.

To Capt. Ephraim Carter, Jun.

Sir. The law is the will of the state, and those laws seem most perfect which are the most equitable and convenient adjustments of the sentiments and interests of the whole people; it is therefore the duty as well as the right of constituents to furnish their Representatives with their essential ingredients of legislation ; and no one will doubt that the General Court are the only body to make the adjustments we now express. Your town have paid due attention to the late address to the people ; the submission of our publick affairs, and the doings of the General Court to the inspection and examination of the people we think a laudable and truly republican measure and is an evidence of the integrity as well as ability of the members of that honourable body, and could they have complied with some instructions to their members, which they have not yet done, we conceive they would have still further served the interest of the commonwealth. Your constituents are of opinion that in the ensuing session, it will be indispensably necessary to attend to the enacting of such laws as may alleviate the present distresses of the people, reconcile their jarring opinions, and restore tranquility to the state ; we therefore instruct you to attend particularly to the following articles.

1ˢᵗ. The present mode of taxation has become so burthensome to the farming interest, that if continued in the same degree, it will as we think, not only totally discourage the industrious husbandman (on whom this commonwealth will probably ever depend for its greatest strength,) but fail of affording so large a revenue as the state of our publick affairs may require. If the abilities of the people of this commonwealth could be placed in a fair point of view, we presume good policy would dictate that the greatest part of our revenue should be raised by duties. Such a mode, in our opinion would divide the burden more equally, and better answer

17

the requirements of government. Import and excise, we suppose, might be much further extended to the ease of the people in general, and we wish the legislature to consider if the following articles &c. &c, may not be proper subjects for such an extension :—Clocks, time-pieces, watches, silver plate, spermaceti candles, tallow consumed in every family above a certain number of pounds, cyder, painted sleighs, glass windows beyond a certain number of squares in each house, commissions for a justice of peace, and dogs.

2^d. That you endeavor the total abolition of the Courts of Common Pleas and General Sessions of the Peace ; and that their jurisdiction be transferred to the Supreme Judicial Courts, and that all processes originated there, excepting some part of the business of sessions, may be transacted by their Justices of the peace quorum unos ; this indeed will make it necessary to increase the judges of the Supreme Judicial Court, and instead of their clerk's office being kept in Boston, it must be kept in the several courts ; Such a change in that office we conceive, would be highly beneficial to the people ; nor will the increase of the number of Judges be a great increase of expense if two judges be made a quorum on the circuit, and compared with the present expense of the Courts of Common Pleas and General Sessions of the Peace, will be a saving worthy our attention, and by a power of reviewing or granting a new trial, in certain cases no great failure of Justice can be feared ; to make every necessary change in the above transfer of jurisdiction, would be to furnish a bill rather than instructions, and improper here.

3^d. While we are burthened with so large a debt, we think the abilities of the people of this commonwealth will not admit of supporting that courtly dignity, which in more affluent circumstances might be thought necessary. Would it not therefore become us to consider our chief magistrate, as a state officer, under no further obligations to expense but what arises from the discharge of his official duties : if our opinion in this respect is admissible you will use your endeavours to have the Governour's, and all other salaries, set as low as justice will admit of.

4th. The demands against the commonwealth for services are generally made with avidity. You are therefore particularly instructed against grants which heretofore have been too often made without due caution, have exceeded the value of the service done, and have been a matter of offence and a burden to the people.

5. It has been suggested by some, that government ought to call in their securities, at their present depreciated value ; We think that such an attempt would be inconsistent with justice and good policy ; nevertheless we presume that if such as have loaned monies to government would realize the present burden, the difficulties of collecting monies by taxation, the importance of supporting our credit with foreign nations, and the necessity of supporting our federal government, they would not complain

if government should delay even the payment of their interest for the present, especially when they reflect, that what they have thus loaned them has been, and probably will be free from taxation--and we cannot think that any one who has become a creditor to government, by purchasing its securities, could complain of such a measure with a good grace, if he calls to mind the amazing disproportion there is between the property he parted with, and the claims he has on government. If necessity ever had a right to claim indulgence, we think considering the circumstances of the people, government are entitled to it; therefore we expect you will oppose the appropriating any part of our revenue to the discharge of either the principal or interest of the domestic debt, excepting the necessitous circumstances of the original creditors of government shall require it.

6th. You are to endeavour that many fines which have heretofore been otherwise appropriated, be paid into the state treasury.

7th. Although we are persuaded that great advantages may be derived from a well regulated commerce, yet we think the commercial interest of this commonwealth ought never to engross so much of the attention of the legislature as to prevent their giving every due encouragement to our own manufactures.

8th. The proportion of the taxes now laid on the polls is a burden that the poorer part of the people can very illy support, you are therefore directed to endeavour a change in that proportion, and that it be made much lighter.

9th. The sitting of the General Court in the town of Boston is a matter which the citizens of this commonwealth are not generally satisfied with — We therefore wish further attention may be paid to that subject, and that the Court may be removed to some other town, until the propriety of that question may be determined from experience.

10th. The late outrageous and treasonable opposition to government, demands the most serious attention, and greatest wisdom of the legislature. The late pardon to the insurgents was truly humane and benevolent; and although the conduct of those people thenceforth was a high aggravation of their former offences, yet, considering them as a part of the whole with us, we wish a further extension of mercy; but we assure the legislature that we are ready to support our government according to our Constitution; and while government is suppressing the insurrections of a wicked and deluded party, we wish that the right of the subject may be attended to, in all their exertions, and if any of the servants or forces of government have or shall unlawfully invade the person or property of any citizen, whatever may be his description, let such invader be punished with the same justice that ought to overtake the vilest traitor.

By order of the Committee.

SAMUEL WARD, *Chairman.*

LANCASTER, Jany. 22, 1787.

The convention of August 17, 1786, at Leicester, unanimously voted to "bear testimony against all riots and unconstitutional combinations;" but very soon thereafter the officers of various courts in the commonwealth found their path to the court-house obstructed by bayonets in the hands of rioters, led by the very men who inspired the action of that convention. The government had patiently conceded much to the real distress and to the misconceptions of the malcontents. Serious offences against the public peace were pardoned or ignored. Misunderstanding the quality of this mercy the offenders were emboldened to more open defiance of authority, and it became necessary, in self preservation, for the executive to resort to vigorous coercion. The danger which the weak and distracted legislature failed to meet, fortunately culminated when the state had a prudent and faithful governor, James Bowdoin, who, the instant the necessity came, put forth the strong arm of the commonwealth with such prompt vigor that the insurgents disappeared at mere sight of the coming blow.

LANCASTER, January 18th, 1787.

On Tuesday the 16th inst., Colonel Greenleaf waited on the two companies of militia in this town assembled agreeably to his orders, when he communicated to them with his usual propriety, the importance of shewing their disapprobation to the illegal measures which have been adopted by the insurgents, and the necessity of evidencing their attachment to the government. The propriety of supporting the present measures of government against every opposition was urged as being necessary to enable them with dignity to remove our present complaints. After some calm debates on the subject, the Col., in order to discover their minds, requested all who were friends to government to follow him, when, with very few exceptions, the whole turned after him. He then informed them that twenty-eight men were required of the two companies to support the Court to sit at Worcester the 23d. inst. and gave them opportunity to engage voluntarily under these restrictions, viz: whoever offers his services shall be held to march, or produce an able effective man to the acceptance of the officer in lieu of himself; when the following persons hereafter named answered the requisition, viz:

Col. William Greenleaf,	Jonas Lane,	Cephas Prentice,
Capt. Nathaniel Beaman,	Eli Stearns,	James Otis Prentice,
Capt. John Whiting,	James Capen,	David Smith,

John Sprague,	Elisha Phelps,	Jacob Fisher,
Josiah Wilder,	Peter Beaman,	Amos Pollard,
Ephraim Carter, Jun.,	Abel Wheelock,	William Bridge,
Cyrus Fairbank,	Samuel Wheelock,	Jonathan Wheelock, Jr.
Timothy Whiting, Jr.,	William Greenleaf, Jr.,	Thomas Richardson,
Gershom Flagg,	Merrick Rice,	James White,
Levi Willard,	Habijah Wheelock,	Abner Pollard, 31
Joseph Wales,		

[Massachusetts Centinel, January 27, 1787.]

Lancaster was the rendezvous for the troops from the eastern part of the county, and on January 24, five hundred men, forming a regiment under the command of Colonel Ephraim Stearns, marched to Worcester. The character of the Lancaster volunteers named above is good warrant for the credibility of the following statement in a letter written at the time:

They are as fine a body of men as were ever assembled, composed of the most respectable characters in the places where they were raised. A circumstance worth relating is: there are in this regiment fifty or sixty persons who have borne commissions, some of which to command regiments in the late continental army and militia, who do duty in the ranks and submit to the hardships attendant on a soldier's life in this inclement season, with a spirit of patriotism and cheerfulness which nothing but the cause they are engaged in could inspire.

One veteran soldier among these Lancaster volunteers had, during the revolution, served under Captain Daniel Shays, who now commanded the insurgents. Eli Stearns, in 1775, was an apprentice to a carpenter of Princeton by the name of Whittaker, who sent him as his substitute to join the army before Boston, and he was present at the battle of Bunker Hill. In 1777 he enlisted in Colonel Thomas Nixon's regiment. While serving on a scout commanded by Captain Shays, he was struck by a bullet from an Indian's gun, which entered his cheek, and passing through his head came out under his right ear. After many months of suffering, he recovered sufficiently to be employed in the commissary department until discharged in 1783. He married Mary, the daughter of Jonathan Whitney, in Lancaster, took up his residence there, became justice of the peace, and was unanimously chosen the town's representative during five years, 1806–1810.

Colonel William Greenleaf was sheriff of the county. On Wednesday the twenty-second of November, 1786, he had, from the court-house steps in Worcester, read the riot act and harangued an armed mob there congregated to prevent the sitting of the Court of General Sessions. One of the orators of the insurgents, in reply, took the occasion to state that among many grievances which they found too oppressive for human endurance, and from which they were resolved to have speedy relief, were the sheriff himself and his exorbitant fees. Colonel Greenleaf coolly rejoined: "If you deem my fees for execution oppressive, gentlemen, you need not wait longer for redress; I will hang you all for nothing, with the greatest pleasure."

Captains Nathaniel Beaman, Timothy and John Whiting had served as officers in the army of the Revolution, and the latter attained the rank of brigadier-general in the militia. Honorable John Sprague was at this time state senator. He served upon the staff of the commanding general.

The regiment of Colonel Stearns having joined the other state troops, under General Benjamin Lincoln, at Worcester, on the twenty-fifth of January marched against the insurgents, who, to the number of two thousand, were at Springfield, but retreated to Pelham upon the approach of the militia, January 27. Lincoln led his forces to Hadley, whereupon Shays judiciously and secretly changed his base to Petersham. Thither Lincoln promptly pursued, starting at eight o'clock on the evening of February 13, Colonel Stearns's regiment being in advance. From Hadley to Petersham, thirty miles, the troops marched that night, through an almost mountainous country, and during the last part of the way facing a violent storm. The drifting snow impeded their steps, and it grew so intensely cold that the majority of the force were frost-bitten. To the hardiest soldier, that terrible night's march was something to be remembered for life. Within twelve hours of the order to move, the advance guard of the army had reached their destination, it being then Sunday morning. Shays and his "regulators" were completely taken by surprise, and fled in hot haste, scattering in every direction. The insurrection was practically at an end. No one was punished for sedition, and three years later the vigorous financial policy of Alexander Hamilton silenced the majority of the grumblers. The first Federal Congress was persuaded to pass a funding bill, and to authorize the assumption of the state war debts by the national government. Taxes were correspondingly lightened ; trade revived ; manufactures were introduced and prospered ; numbers of the landless migrated to the valley of the Ohio ; and in April, 1791, Fisher Ames, writing of the people so lately distracted by the prospect of bloody civil war, says : "There is a scarcity of grievances. Their mouths are stopped with white bread and roast meat."

Lists of the men from Lancaster and adjoining towns, who served in the expedition against Shays, and in subsequent guard duty, follow. No residences are given in the original rolls, and an entirely accurate determination of them is not here possible :

Pay Roll of Captn. Nathl. Beeman's Comp^y, Col^o. Eph^m. Stearns's Regiment, for services rendered to Commonwealth of Mass^tts. in the months of Jany. and Feby. 1787.

[Chiefly men of Lancaster and Sterling ; serving from Jan. 15 to Feb. 21.]

Capt. Nathaniel Beeman,	Joshua Eveleth,	Amos Pollard,
Lieut. Timothy Brown,	Jacob Fisher,	Elisha Phelps,
Ensign Nathaniel Houghton,	Manasseh Fairbank,	J. Otis Prentice,
Sergt. Eli Stearns,	Salmon Godfrey,	Thomas Richardson,
" Aaron Willard,	John Gill,	Joshua Read,
'· Jonas Lane,	William Gibbs,	Jacob Read,
" Jacob Robbins,	Benjamin Holden,	Nathan Read.
Corp. Josiah Phelps,	Joseph Holden,	Artemas Richardson,
" Elias Farnsworth,	Andrew Haskell,	Phineas Richardson,

Corp. Joseph Reed,
" Artemas Maynard,
Drum^r. Zimri Eveleth,
Fortunatus Ager,
Ammi Brooks,
Peter Beeman,
William Bridge,
Silas Buss,
Ebenezer Burpee,
Joseph Baker,
James Capen,
Bartholomew Cheever,
Eliphas Copeland,
James Curtis,
Dunsmore Dole,
Joseph Eveleth,
Joseph Eveleth, Jr.,

Samuel Haynes,
Eli Houghton,
Abel Kendall,
Pearson Kendall,
Asa Knowlton,
John Littlejohn,
Seth Lyon,
Abel Moore,
Paul Mason,
Silas Mason,
Artemas Manning,
Asa Maynard,
Houghton Osgood,
Abijah Phelps,
David Phelps,
Abner Pollard,

Asa Rugg,
David Smith,
Manasseh Sawyer,
Jonas Stearns,
Richard Smith,
Israel Underwood,
Abel Wheelock,
Abijah Wheelock,
Samuel Wheelock,
James White,
Asa Whitcomb,
Joel Wilder,
Andrew Whitney,
Lewis Woolson,
Manasseh Wilder,
Asa Whitcomb,
Joseph Wyman,

[Massachusetts Archives, CXCI, 92.]

Pay Roll of Capt. Nathaniel Beaman's Company, Col. Newell's Regiment in the service of Government, inlisted for four months from the 23^d. of Febry. 1787. [Served to May 31.]

Capt. Nathaniel Beaman,
Lieut. Timothy Brown,
Ensign James Curtis,
Sergt. Jonas Stearns,
" Jacob Robbins,
" William Gibbs,
" Joseph Wyman,
Corp. Oliver Fullam,
" Artemas Maynard,
" Timothy Brigham,
" Reuben Kendall,
Drum^r. Augustus Kendall,
Fifer Joseph Chaplin,
Samuel Rice,
Phineas Richardson,
Abner Mitchell,
John Butler,
Mitchel Richards,
James Wade McDunn,
Jonathan Clark,

Benjamin Bailey,
William Bigelow,
John Ford,
Raymond Hunt,
Joseph Eveleth,
Abijah Hagar,
Abel Wood,
Abraham Eager,
Bartholomew Brown,
Daniel Mixer,
Ephraim Whitcomb,
Ephraim Adams,
Eliuda Bartlett,
Joseph Hoar,
Josiah White,
Joel Warren,
Jacob Brown,
Isaac Stearns,
Joseph Hasty,

James Moore,
John Harward,
John Haskell,
John Whitcomb.
Phineas Warren,
Roderick McKenzey,
Samuel Burbank,
Silvanus Holden,
Stephen Torrey,
Theophilus Page,
Thomas Cook,
William De Putrin,
William Barker,
Amasa Bigelow,
Daniel Cowden,
Ebenezer Fay,
William Boardman,
Thomas Walcot,
William Flood.

[Massachusetts Archives, CXCI, 93.]

Pay Roll of Capt. John Whiting's Company, of Colonel Ebenezer Lovell's Regiment in the service of the Commonwealth of Massachusetts, for wages and deficient rations.

[Service : January 30 to February 18.]

Capt. John Whiting,
Lieut. John Watson,
Ensign Israel Manning,
Clerk Elisha Rugg,
Sergt. Elihu Wilder,
" Job Spafford,
" Abel Baker,
" Jonathan Bush,
Corp. Joseph Prescott,
" James Ellis,
" Ebenezer Pike,
" Joshua Wilder, ✓
Drumʳ. Augustus Kendall,
Abel Allen,
Oliver Carter,
Samuel Carter, Jr.,
Jonas Carter,
Haran Eager,
Nathaniel Kendall,
John Maynard,
Joseph Hoar,

John Prescott,
Samuel Ward,
Levi Wilder,
John Wilder,
Daniel Garfield,
Joseph Haynes,
Elisha Hobbs,
Samuel How,
James Hunt,
Ephraim Myrick,
John Richardson,
Moses Thatcher,
Thomas Wyman,
Joseph Wilder,
Nathan Burpee,
Cyrus Belknap,
William Carter,
William Kilburn,
William Palmer,
✓ Andrew Petegrew,

Thomas Sawyer, Jr.,
Thos. Sawyer, *tertius*,
Joseph Willard,
Phinehas Wilder,
Reuben Ross,
James Atherton,
Lemuel Burnham,
Cyrus Hamblin,
Jonathan Houghton,
James Houghton,
William Woodbury,
Thomas Welch,
Coffin Chapin,
John Barnard,
Josiah Barnard,
Charles Holman,
Martin Cox Jones,
Isaac Moore,
Shadrach Priest,
Abijah Pratt.

[Massachusetts Archives, CXCII, 212.]

Capt. William Sawyer's Company, in Col. Stearns's Regiment.

[Of Bolton and Harvard, serving from January 23, to February 21.]

Capt. William Sawyer,
Lieut. Henry Powers,
Ensign Jonas Welch,
Clerk Rufus Moor,
Sergt. Eli Longley,
" Europe Hamlin,
" Eber Goddard,
" Manassah Fairbank,
Corp. James Britain,
" Silas Whitcomb,
" Thaddeus Brown,
" Stephen Nurse,
Fifer Jonathan Barnard,
Joshua Hemmingway,
William Bigelow,

Simeon Hemmingway,
Benjamin Hastings,
William Hastings,
David Whitcomb,
Asa Whitcomb,
Jonathan Holman,
Levi Townsend,
Calvin Bush,
Uri Sawyer,
Simeon Conant,
Joseph Houghton,
Ebenezer Moore,
David Nurse,
Gustavus Goss,
Jonathan Whitcomb,

Peter Atherton,
Eleazar Hamlin, Jr.,
Richard Bryant,
Stephen Cleverly,
Caleb Parker,
Joseph Hoar,
Caleb Fairbank,
Abel Hastings,
Sanderson Carter,
Henry Temple,
Moses Coolidge,
Benjamin How,
Silas Jones,
Silas Houghton,
Andrew Kittell,
William Ross.

[Massachusetts Archives, CXCI, 109.]

Capt. Levi Warner's Company, in Col. Stearns's Regiment.

[Of Leominster; serving January 20 to February 22.]

Capt. Levi Warner,
Lieut. John Leach,
Ensign John Billings,
Clerk Timothy Stearns,
Sergt. Thomas Legate,
"   Benjamin Stuart,
"   Nathaniel Joslin,
Corp. Samuel Kendall,
"   Oliver Carter,
"   Abiathar Houghton,
"   Levi Phelps,
Drumr Joseph Joslin,
Fifer Joseph Snow,
Robert Legate,
William Legate,
Jabez Fairbank,

Jonas Johnson,
Benjamin Milliken,
Noah Harrod,
Daniel McGregore,
Joseph Knight,
Daniel Carter,
John Boutel,
Heman Evans,
Levi Nichols,
William Boutel, Jr.,
Levi Joslin,
William Jepson,
John Shed,
William Warren,
Jesse Lincoln,
Thomas Lincoln,

Luther Houghton,
Luther Phelps,
Samuel Ruggles,
John Richardson, Jr.,
Jeremiah Chace,
Joseph Darling,
Jonas Jones,
Joshua Kimball,
Peter Wilder,
John Hills,
William Burrage,
Stephen Wood,
Abel Wood,
James Carter,
Benjamin Peirce.

[Massachusetts Archives, CXCII, 183.]

Of the field and staff officers of Colonel Stearns's regiment were: Lieutenant-Colonel Timothy Boutell, of Leominster; Quartermaster-Sergeant William Greenleaf, Jr., Drum-Major Jonathan Wheelock, and Surgeon's Mate Cephas Prentice, of Lancaster. John White and Gershom Flagg, of Lancaster, served with a detachment of artillery under Major William Stevens, from Jan. 15 to Feb. 9.

Capt. Andrew Putnam's Cavalry Company, in Col. Ebenezer Craft's Regiment.

[Serving January 23 to February 6.]

Capt. Andrew Putnam,
Lieut. John Whitney,
Lieut. John Ballard,
Cornet Robert Townsend,
Trumpr. John Lock,
Sergt. Jonathan Prescott,

William Hobart,
Peter Hunt,
Timothy Goldsmith,
Thomas Chace,
William Ballard,
Nahum Ball,

Israel Thayer,
Asa Warner,
Manasseh Knight,
William Putnam,
Samuel Sargeant,
Josiah Divol.

Edmund Heard was lieutenant-colonel of the regiment.

[Massachusetts Archives, CXCII, 45.]

The only person in the Lancastrian towns known to have been arrested on suspicion of treasonable complicity with the insurrection, was Brigadier-General Josiah Whitney of Harvard, whose services during the Revolution have been set forth in former pages.

In the Indian War of 1790–1794, upon the northwest frontier, but one of Lancaster's citizens is known to have served his country in the field, though there very probably were others.   Andrew Haskell, who commanded a company of his neighbors in the battle of Bunker Hill, and fought in various capacities, from captain to private, throughout the war of the revolution, enlisted in the little army which marched under General Arthur St. Clair against the Miamis, and was slain in the disastrous fight of November 4, 1791.   Haskell was a fearless and efficient soldier, but uneducated, rough in manners, and probably incapable of self-restraint.   Joseph Willard, Esq., records, doubtless from the authority of his companions in arms, that Haskell's conduct as an officer on June 17, 1775, would have entitled him to reward, but that he was "kept from promotion by his want of dignity and self-respect."   He is described as well proportioned, within an inch of six feet in height, with black hair and eyes.   At his death he was forty-three years of age.

VI.

WARS WITH ENGLAND AND ALGIERS.

1812 – 1815.

DURING the desperate conflict that raged in the first decade of the current century, between England and the Emperor Napoleon, neither belligerent was restrained by any respect for the rights of weaker nations, and neutrals suffered in their commercial interests almost equally with the combatants. Orders in council and imperial decrees threatened and obstructed the mercantile navies of the world, and the merchants of the United States, having built up an extensive and profitable carrying trade, were especially sufferers. In revolutionary days American patriotism had met Great Britain's arbitrary trade restrictions with the self-denying policy of non-intercourse. The same retaliatory measure approved itself to the Jeffersonian administration, and a general embargo was proclaimed. But in the changed conditions of the body politic the operation of this measure was now claimed to be sectional. It worked grievous distress to the Northern states. Ships soon lay rotting at the deserted wharves, and, although bread was abundant, mechanics grew gaunt with hunger because their labor would not purchase food. The Southern and Midland states, chiefly devoted to agriculture, controlled the government by virtue of slave representation. With them the embargo was popular for a time, and perhaps not the less so, that it struck a damaging blow at the prosperity

of their aggressive political foes, the New England Federalists. The grievances of the ruined merchant and the
unemployed workman found voice speedily in the resolutions of the New England town-meeting.

September 15, 1808, Lancaster voted to petition President Jefferson for the suspension of the embargo, and
Major Joseph Hiller, Honorable William Stedman and
Captain Samuel Ward were chosen to draft the document,
which was duly forwarded. William Stedman was at this
date representative in Congress:

The inhabitants of the Town of Lancaster in the Commonwealth of
Massachusetts, in legal town-meeting assembled, respectfully solicit the
attention of the President of the United States to the following representation:

It has been with an honest pride that we have viewed the rising glory
and wealth of our nation. We have cheerfully contributed by the "sweat
of our brow" to the support of the federal government, believing that
human wisdom could not devise a more perfect system for the protection
of our national rights and for encouraging us in the diligent use of the
means of subsistence and accumulation.

Trained up in the belief that Agriculture and Commerce are reciprocal
in their supports and inseparable in their interests, we cannot silently en-
dorse the long continuance of the Embargo, a measure calculated (as we
conceive) to sever those supports and interests; to check the spirit of
enterprise, and take away the hopes and rewards of industry.

When the embargo was laid by Congress, altho. we could not perceive
its necessity, we were induced to acquiescence by an habitual resolution to
respect the constituted authorities of our country and to obey the laws.
We frankly confess it has not been in our power to reconcile the reason
assigned, viz: "to keep in safety our vessels, our seamen, and merchandise from the dangers with which they are threatened on the high seas and
elsewhere, from the belligerent powers of Europe," with extending the
restrictions for Commerce to the safe and peaceable inland parts of the
community.

Seeing that by this measure, after an unexampled experiment, the chief
sources of our country's wealth are closed; sensibly feeling the injury, in
the depreciation of our agricultural products, and in the inevitable waste
of a proportion of them, for want of a market; finding also, that the imported articles without which we cannot comfortably subsist, have so risen
in value that we have no means to procure them, we are imperiously
urged to address the President of the United States for relief.

The evils we have recited are in comparison of little moment. We deeply lament, that by annihilating the customary incentives to virtuous industry and by multiplying the temptations to violate the laws and to commit fraud and injustice, a state of things may be introduced which can scarcely be equalled by the desolations of war. The changes which have recently taken place among the belligerent nations and the prospect some of them present, of emancipation from the dominion of the Common Usurper, and the consequent scarcity promised to the Commerce of the United States we presume are sufficiently apparent. The relaxation of the British orders in Council as respects neutral trade with those parts of Spain which are struggling for self government opens to the United States an extensive commerce. South America and the West Indian Islands also, offer safe and profitable markets for American produce. Indeed there appear to us many other sources of profitable trade, inviting the enterprise of the merchant, which to the President need not be mentioned. Could the commercial advantages they offer be engaged even under the restrictions the President is authorized to require, the labors of the husbandman and mechanic would again be encouraged and they rescued from those distresses which threaten to destroy that competency their industry has acquired, and those blessings which the wise policy of former measures had promised. We therefore earnestly entreat the President to exercise the power vested in him by Congress, to suspend the whole or in part the act laying an Embargo, and the several acts supplementary thereto, or to convene that honorable body as soon as may be, for the purpose of terminating the sufferings those acts have occasioned.   Septr. 3, 1808.

February 1, 1809, the town met—

. . . . . 2, To take into Consideration the alarming situation of our Public affairs, and to Petition or address the Legislature of this State on the subject of our grievances, or to do or transact any matter and things relative thereto which the town may deem expedient and necessary. . . .

The town voted — to commit the subject matter of the second article in the warrant to a committee of five.

Voted, and Chose: Joseph Hiller, Moses Smith, Jr., Jonathan Wilder, Samuel Ward, John Thurston, Committee.

The committee's report was accepted, but not recorded. The chairman of this and the before-named committee, Major Joseph Hiller, was a venerable ex-collector of Salem, who came to Lancaster to reside in 1804, and purchased the Wilder farm, so called, now occupied by the state's Industrial School for Girls. This place had for about fifteen years been in the possession of Burrill Carnes, Captain Benjamin Lee, and other English gentlemen, who had

lavished large sums upon it to give it the semblance of
an old-country baronial estate. The spacious three-story
mansion of brick, begun by Colonel Caleb Wilder in the
days of the revolution, had its milk cellar and wine closets,
spacious guest chambers, and all the appointments of an
elegant homestead. A semicircular corridor nine feet in
width and seventy feet long adjoined the house, and bounded a garden wherein grew English strawberries and other
small fruits, flowering plants and shrubs in great variety.
About it was a lawn of three acres adorned with choice
trees, and near at hand a farm house, extensive barns and
offices, and a fine coach house in which was kept the only
family coach in the town. The relics of a paled deer-park
also told of the taste and wealth of earlier owners. Joseph
Hiller was a jeweller by trade, Master of the Essex Masonic
Lodge, a thorough patriot and a public-spirited Christian
citizen. At the Lexington Alarm he led a company from
Salem to Cambridge, and served later in the Rhode Island
expedition. He was made major of the First regiment of
militia in 1778. Washington showed his esteem for him
by making him the first collector at Beverly and Salem.
In the custom house at the latter place hangs his portrait.
The major had an enthusiastic admiration for Washington,
and displayed it by wearing an agate seal upon which was
a portrait head of the father of his country, beautifully cut
in England for its wearer, at a cost of twenty guineas.
Having lost his wife, two accomplished daughters presided
over his home.

With these valued immigrants from quaint old Salem,
there came into the green meadows of Lancaster a spicy
perfume of East Indian commerce, a novel flavor of nautical romance breathing of "the mystery and magic of the
sea." Captain Richard J. Cleveland — one of Major Hiller's sons-in-law, and one of the most highly esteemed of
Lancaster's citizens — lost one ship and its valuable cargo,
unjustly confiscated by the rapacious English admiral,

Cochrane, under the pretence of authority derived from orders in council. He was soon after robbed of another vessel by Napoleon's agents. The dramatic narrative of Cleveland's daring commercial enterprises has been told by his own modest pen, and public interest in them has been quite recently renewed by a son's loving tribute to his father's memory, entitled: Voyages of a Merchant Navigator.

The friends of Jefferson's administration, the French party, as the Federalists stigmatized them, were very few in Lancaster. The most prominent of these were two brothers, Timothy and John Whiting, who, had they been of the political faith then dominant in the commonwealth, might have gained influence and fame proportionate to their ability. As boys of eighteen and sixteen years they marched beside their father—who was a veteran soldier and served Lancaster in 1755, at Lake George—at the head of the company of minute men who hurried from Billerica on the nineteenth of April, 1775, to take part in the pursuit of the British from Lexington. During the revolution the family came to Lancaster to reside. The elder son, Timothy, Jr., succeeded his father as tavern keeper upon the Old Common, was the second postmaster of Lancaster, holding the office for twenty-two years, 1803–1825, and like his brother, became associate justice of the Court of Sessions. At a special election, October 8, 1810, he was the Jeffersonian candidate for Congress, in place of William Stedman of Lancaster, who had resigned his seat; and again was the unsuccessful nominee for the same office at the regular election in November of the same year.

John Whiting served under Arnold and Gates in 1776, and displayed such military ability that he received the commission of ensign in the Twelfth Massachusetts Continental Regiment, and when but nineteen years of age was promoted to a first-lieutenancy, with which rank he served on staff duty during the war. He was highly esteemed in

Lancaster, being a favorite moderator at public meetings, and commonly one of the school-committee. At the age of twenty-nine he was chosen deacon, and was nearly always employed in some capacity in the management of the town's prudential affairs. Experienced and zealous in military matters, he soon rose to the rank of brigadier-general in the militia. In politics, however, he was less successful, being defeated at several successive elections when candidate for state senator or representative to congress, although his neighbors very generally waived their whig prejudices, attesting their sense of his manly worth by honoring him with a majority of the town's votes.

Politics then raged with a fervor never since exceeded, and partisans indulged in vituperation without restraint of decency; but political opponents found little in John Whiting's character to blame, and their attempts to throw ridicule upon him turned chiefly upon his polite manners. They acknowledged that he was early upon the first battle ground of the revolution, but—"only as a fifer." They credited him with being "a good deacon and a good bookbinder," but sneered about his ability to "enter and depart from a room with a genteel air." When his friends dilated upon his mastership of the English, Latin and French languages, and the breadth of his general scholarship, his political foes affected to discredit the depth of that scholarship, and would recognize no merit in him superior to that of his rivals, save that the general could undoubtedly "make the best bow." In 1808, General Henry Dearborn, secretary of war in Jefferson's cabinet, offered him a commission as lieutenant-colonel of the Fourth U. S. Infantry, which he accepted. He died at Washington, September 3, 1810, aged fifty years. General William Eaton says of him: "He was a most lovable Christian gentleman, a pure and good man."

Congress so far heeded the numerous complaints of the suffering people as, in March, 1809, to repeal the embargo,

18

substituting for it a milder non-intercourse act, which proved inefficient and unsatisfactory to both Democrats and Federalists. In brief, the administration was anxiously striving to preserve peace, but never pursuing the only peace measure that could win respect at home or abroad—diligent preparation for war. Both England and France persisted in insolent aggression ; but near the close of the year 1810, Napoleon revoked all decrees inimical to the United States. England, besides her plundering of defenceless American merchantmen under various pretences, added the grosser outrage of man-stealing under cover of the exercise of a right of search upon the high seas. No sailor upon an American vessel was safe from impressment and slavish service in the British navy, unless he could satisfactorily prove to the kidnappers that he was born on American soil. By the British naval officer—familiar with the unscrupulous methods of the press-gang and lacking able seaman—noble brawn and thoroughbred sea-dog bearing were too often held to be ample proof of allegiance due King George. A strange commentary upon the arrogant enforcement. in 1810, of this alleged right over neutral commerce, was the noisy wrath of Englishmen in 1861, when an United States naval commander arrested two traitors on board the Trent. There was also much reason to suspect that British influence was busily instigating the powerful Indian tribes both of the West and the South to begin hostilities. Submission to such insults and injuries had long dishonored the nation. Without navy or army, military leaders or financial resources adequate to the emergency, June 19, 1812, war was declared. The vote in Congress that decided the question was practically divided on geographic lines, and so fierce was the heat of political partisanship that the opponents of the administration universally protested against the war as suicidal and unnecessary, and declared that only office-holders, office-seekers, bankrupts and a Jacobin mob favored it.

On Wednesday, June 24, 1812, at a special town-meeting called in Lancaster to remonstrate against the declaring of war with England, Jonathan Wilder, Moses Smith, Eli Stearns, Jacob Fisher, Joseph Wales, Josiah Flagg and Jonas Lane were chosen a committee to present suitable resolutions. The report of this committee, made after an hour's adjournment, was read and accepted, one hundred and fifteen voting for, and fifteen against it. It was ordered that a copy should be transmitted to the President of the United States, and that it should be printed in the Columbian Centinel. In that paper it appeared as follows, in the issue of July 4:

At a numerous meeting of the Freeholders and other Inhabitants of the town of Lancaster legally convened for the purpose of considering the alarming state of the country,—The following REPORT of their Committee was almost unanimously adopted.

The right of expressing our opinion of public men and measures, is a privilege guaranteed and secured to us by our National as well as State Constitutions. And at this alarming crisis of national concerns when recent intelligence confirms the belief that we are now upon the eve of a British war it is impossible for good citizens anxious for their general welfare not to feel deeply interested in so great an event. And sensibly affected by that interest it is an indispensable duty to God and their country to give expression to their feelings and sentiments on a measure which involves everything dear and valuable in society. But although such a cause of procedure may have no immediate influence on the plans and measures now adopting by the General Government, yet when combined with similar expressions of other towns and sections of the country, it will evince to Congress and the world, that the great mass of the people, especially in the Eastern States, are utterly averse to a war, in the prosecution of which they are unable to discover anything but ruin to themselves and misery to their posterity. Were it probable in the view of government that this would have been the issue, good policy it should seem, would have dictated a state of preparation adequate to the exigency of the case — Against such a day of darkness and of danger a wise and prudent administration would have laid up something in store to have softened and alleviated the afflictions and distresses incident to such a state. But it is a melancholy consideration and one that must sicken and damp the courage of even the stoutly brave, that we are now to be plunged into a war with the most powerful maritime nation on the globe without any adequate means of attack or self defence.

From this concise view of the subject, and considering the defenceless state of the nation— the inadequacy of means to annoy the declared enemy — the want of resources to prosecute the war with effect— the uncertainty of its duration—and almost certainty of its terminating whether sooner or later in our own disgrace and ruin, a picture is presented fraught with scenes the bare imagination of which shock humanity and fill the soul with awful gloom. From these considerations connected with many others that naturally crowd upon our minds, and in compliance with the views and wishes of the patriotic town of Boston, your Committee are induced to recommend to the town for their discussion and adoption the following resolutions.

Resolved—as the sense of this town that although we deem it a duty to submit to the wise and wholesome laws of the government, still under existing circumstances we are constrained to declare that we consider a British War as neither founded in justice, necessity or good policy, and as calculated only to bring an endless train of evils upon ourselves, and involve our posterity in ruin and disgrace. That in the prosecution of a War against England we can discern nothing but a total destruction of the remnant of our maritime rights—a prostration of the agricultural and mechanic interests—an enormous increase of the public debt—unparalleled taxes and a host of tax gatherers following in the rear. In the event of such a war, we also perceive in the background an alliance with France, whose embrace experience of the past foretells will be our political death.

Resolved — That we consider it the true interest of our nation to maintain a neutral position, and pursuing the Washington policy not to depart therefrom without the most urgent necessity—That to suffer the nation to be drawn into the vortex of European politics, and of course participate in their contests and Wars, will inevitably prove the downfall of our infant republic.

Resolved—That if the interest or honor of the nation demanded a sacrifice of our lives and fortunes in carrying on an offensive War against either of the belligerents yet we can neither perceive the policy or justice in selecting England as the most suitable object of our resentment. That if the Decrees of France and the Orders in Council of England have operated an infringement of neutral rights, documents and facts abundantly show that England was not the first aggressor—And that it is an undeniable fact that England has uniformly declared her Orders in Council repealed whenever France should fully revoke her decrees.

Resolved — That we view the restrictive system, in all the forms it has assumed, as inconsistent with the genius and habits of the people,—as repugnant to the true spirit and meaning of the constitution—as tending to impoverish the nation and eventually, if persisted in, to weaken and finally destroy the government. That we deem it a solemn obligation imposed on every citizen by a true and genuine patriotism to use all fair and honorable means in the exercise of his elective franchise to produce a speedy change in the Administration of our National Government, and thereby save us from the horrors and calamities of war, and ere it be too late re-establish our common country in its wonted peace and happiness, its former rank and dignity among the nations of the earth.

LANCASTER, June 24, 1812.

The foregoing report being twice read and discussed voted to adopt the same.

Attest.

JOSEPH HILLER, *Moderator.*
JOSIAH FLAGG, *Town Clerk.*

The declaration of war met with very few sympathizers in New England. Like many of his brother clergymen, the pastor of Lancaster, Reverend Nathaniel Thayer, seized the opportunity of a day of "Publick Humiliation and Prayer, appointed by the National Government who had declared War against Great Britain," August 20, 1812, to preach a denunciatory sermon, in which he inveighed against what he esteemed the iniquitous policy of the administration, taking for his text Jeremiah iv, 19:

. . . . I am pained at my very heart; . . . . I cannot hold my peace, because thou hast heard, O my soul, the sound of the trumpet, the alarm of war.

Probably very few of his congregation but applauded the preacher's political sentiments, although it is related that Jacob Sweetser, indignant at some vehement arraignment of the administration, slammed his pew door behind him and marched out of the meeting-house, pounding his cane along the aisle as he went.

In the warrant summoning a town-meeting, February 21, 1814, the second article was:

To consider the propriety of petitioning the legislature of this Commonwealth to adopt such Constitutional Measures, as to them shall seem necessary relative to the oppressive operation of the late embargo law of the United States, as well as to ensure for the people of this Commonwealth their Rights as Citizens and as a State, or act anything relating thereto.

At the meeting a committee, consisting of Eli Stearns, Moses Smith, Jonathan Wilder, Jonas Lane and Doctor

Samuel Manning, were chosen, and the same day their report, which follows, was accepted:

The Committee appointed by the Town at the meeting held this day, for the purpose of Considering the second article in the Warrant, have attended to that subject and report that considering the present session of the General Court is near closing, and also the small glimmering prospect that a peace may take place, and the oppressive restrictions on commerce be removed: We therefore recommend to the Town to refer the further consideration of the Article to the first Monday in May next at 3 O'Clock in the afternoon.

The subject was not again agitated. During the summer the depredations of the British navy along the coast created great alarm throughout New England. When, on September 1, 1814, the force of Sir John Sherbrook captured Castine, fears of an attack upon Boston were awakened, and a proclamation was issued convening the legislature. Governor Strong also, in a general order dated September 6, called upon the militia to hold themselves in readiness to march at a moment's notice, and summoned the artillery and several light-infantry companies to report at Boston for immediate service. The appearance of the hostile fleet off Gloucester and Cape Cod, exacting heavy ransom from various towns, kept the public excitement at fever heat. Extensive earth-works were thrown up upon Noddle's Island and at South Boston, by volunteer working parties of the inhabitants of the city and adjoining towns. Benjamin Apthorp Gould, a native of Lancaster, was at that date master of the Boston Latin School, and one day led his flock of boys to be ferried over and aid in the work. More than fifty militia companies were encamped about the city before the end of the month. Among the first to arrive were the Light Artillery and a Light Infantry Company of Lancaster. The cannon and other military property of the state in this town were then kept at the North Village in a structure the origin of which is given in the orders of council, June 12, 1801:

. . . . . . One hundred and twenty dollars in favor of Captain Jacob Fisher commander of a Company of Artillery in the Town of Lancaster, in full for erecting a gun house for the depositing their field pieces and other military apparatus therein agreeably to the Resolves of the General Court.

This artillery company was commanded by Captain John Lyon, who, on Sunday, September 14, 1814, after a service at the church, led it to Cambridge. The tradition is that he returned to his home before the next morning. Certainly his official duties speedily devolved upon another. Several of the privates were temporary substitutes procured by those who were unable or unwilling to do duty as soldiers. The list of those who actually served for two months follows:

Roll of detached Company of Artillery of Captain Silas Parker from Lancaster and vicinity in Lieut. Col. Edward's Reg¹. in service at Boston, from Sept. 8th to Nov. 5th, 1814.

Silas Parker, Captain.   John Taylor, Lieut.   Abraham Mallard, Lieut·
Sergeants: Abijah Brown, Hannibal Laughton, Artemas H. Brown, Nathaniel Thayer.

Privates Edward Brown,	Gardner Maynard,	Israel Haskell,
Thomas Safford,	Apollus Osgood,	Benjamin S. Rice,
Samuel Damon,	Thomas Phelps,	Calvin Wheeler,
Jonathan Osgood,	Asa Goddard,	Prosper Randall,
Titus Wilder,	Samuel Mepec,	Alvin Randall,
Nathaniel Gould,	Odel Brown,	Ebenezer Wilder,
Josias Johnston,	Henry Houghton,	Robert Hewson,
Reuben Blood,	Liberty B. Moses,	John Lynn,
Samuel Churchill,	John Lynch,	Ebenezer Taylor,
William McLalen,	Ephraim C. Fisher,	George Phelps.
Ephraim Walden,	Phinehas Sawyer,	

The infantry company, having been ordered out through some misunderstanding, returned after an absence of less than a week. It was commanded by Captain Ezra Sawyer, but no roll of its men has been found.

Nathan Puffer served during the war as an artificer in the United States artillery. Among the death records of the town is the name of Henry Moore, "killed in a battle with British troops and Indians at Brownstown, August [4] 1812;" and Josiah Rugg, "in the army," died of fever, aged twenty-nine, November 22, 1813. Two sons of

General John Whiting, who attained distinction in their country's service, won their first military honors in the campaigns of 1812–1814. Henry Whiting was born in Lancaster, 1788, and died at St. Louis, September 16, 1851. His army record is as follows :

Cornet Light Dragoons 20 Oct. 1808; second-lieutenant Sept. 1809; first-lieutenant, 20 Aug. 1811 ; aid to Brigadier-General Boyd ; brevet captain, 17 March 1814, for meritorious service ; transferred to Fifth Infantry, 17 May, 1815; captain, 3 March, 1817; transferred to First Artillery. 1 June, 1821 ; brevet major, 17 March, 1824, for ten years faithful service ; brevet lieutenant-colonel, 30 June, 1834, for faithful and meritorious service ; major, quartermaster, 23 Feb., 1835 ; lieutenant-colonel, deputy quartermaster-general, 7 July, 1838 ; colonel, assistant quartermaster-general, 21 April, 1846; brevet brigadier-general, 23 Feb. 1847, for gallant and meritorious conduct at the battle of Buena Vista.

Fabius, a younger brother of Henry—born 1792, died May 16, 1842—has the following record :

Second-Lieutenant Artillerists, 10 Feb., 1812; in First Artillery March, 1812; first-lieutenant 20 June, 1813; transferred to Corps Artillery, 12 May, 1814; captain, 10 Sept., 1819; transferred to First Artillery, 1 June, 1821 ; brevet major, 10 Sept., 1829, for ten years faithful service in one grade.

Levi Whiting—son of Timothy, and cousin of Henry and Fabius—born in Lancaster, 1790, also won honorable rank in the regular army :

Second-lieutenant Artillerists, 10 Feby. 1812, in First Artillery, March 1812; transferred to Corps Artillery, 12 May, 1814; first-lieutenant, 14 June 1814; transferred to Fourth Artillery, 1 June, 1821 ; captain, 22 May, 1822; brevet major, 21 May, 1832, for ten years faithful service in one grade ; major First Artillery, 19 March, 1842; lieutenant-colonel 1 April, 1850. Died 3 August, 1852.

Other men of Lancaster, whose names are undiscovered, doubtless served either in army or navy. The brief, unpopular war ended in a treaty that did not pretend to adjust the grievances that caused it, and neither nation has cause to remember it with pride, save for the valor shown in the desperate contests upon the ocean and lakes. The proclamation of peace was received with universal joy. Soon

emigration began its westward march; manufactures, trans-
planted from France, England and Germany to the river-
sides of New England, showed healthy and vigorous
growth; and prosperity made bright the faces of farmer,
merchant and mechanic.

Most nations point with pride to some epoch in their
growth as the Augustan age of their history.   So not infre-
quently a town may boast, with sighs for subsequent decadence, an era when some intellectual coterie, some concurrence of choice spirits elevated the average tone of
thought, and stirred the neighborhood to loftier aims and a
nobler social life; a period when business activity sought
the honorable acquisition of the means of comfortable living, and was not, as now, a hurried, pauseless race for the
dazzling prizes in a lottery; when personal enterprise was
not synonymous with selfish greed, and hospitality had not
become offensive with ostentatious display.   The golden
age of Lancaster shone in the first third of the present
century.   Though not characterized by restless haste, it
was nevertheless a busy era.   Robert Stephenson had not
yet harnessed steam to the wheels of commerce, but a perpetual procession of heavily laden wagons drawn by horses
wore deep ruts in the highways that traversed the town from
west to east, bearing freights of country produce to the city
markets and returning with assorted merchandise to stock
the village stores.   These wagons, numbering about forty
per day, Sunday inclusive, averaged fully a ton of freight
each.   Coaches filled with travellers, drawn by four or six
horses, daily dashed into town, halted at the central inn
long enough to change the wheelers, exchange the mail
and pick up or set down a passenger or two, and then
dashed out of town again.   The incoming of the "mail
stage" was the most important daily episode in village life.
As the hour of its arrival drew near, a motley group of
young and old gathered about the store in which the post-
office was kept—the majority not so much because of any

expectation of private letters, but to stare curiously at the passengers and get an item of gossip from the city.

Until A. D. 1800, Lancaster was the terminus of the "Boston, Concord and Lancaster mail line," and Jonathan Whitney, its proprietor, sent the mail and chance passengers hence to Leominster and beyond by special conveyance. Not many years later the mail route was extended and made daily. The fare from Lancaster to Boston was two dollars, and each passenger was allowed fourteen pounds of baggage free. Taverns abounded, sometimes numbering one to the mile along the more frequented highways, and they were not too many for the hungry and thirsty wayfarers. Nightly there congregated in each bar-room a jolly company, and, in the cold season, around the blazing fire of logs that roared and crackled in the wide-throated chimney, many a merry catch was sung, many a tough yarn spun, many a laughter-provoking joke cracked. In the red coals upon the hearth lay the pokers conveniently hot for the brewing of flip, and the toddy stick beat continual tattoo upon the tumblers' bottoms. A grizzled revolutionary soldier often sat in the chimney corner— some veteran like William Deputron or Jacob Zwears, always ready to "fight his battles o'er," or accept a treat. Against his name upon the slate hanging behind the bar usually grew a lengthening score rarely wiped out; but for what he had been and done and suffered in "the days that tried men's souls," no one grudged the old soldier the warm nook by the fireside, and his maudlin repetitions of camp stories were patiently endured. The Ægis or Spy once a week opened for the landlord and his guests a glimpse of the world's progress. In these diminutive and ill printed sheets they by turn could con the "latest news" from Europe—two months old—and a "despatch just arrived from Washington"—dated a week previous to publishing day.

In the harvest season, husking bees brought together

young and old, male and female, and, with jovial din, quick
hands would clean the barn floor of a huge obstructive
mound of corn; then refreshed with unlimited pumpkin
pie and sweet cider, every Jack would find his Jill, and
responsive to the summons of some Fiddler John, the rustic
ball began, and joyous activity made amends for any lack
of cultured grace. Now and then a "raising" brought out
all the stout arms of the town to help in the setting up of a
new roof-tree, where the common thirst excited by much
hallooing and emulative lifting of heavy timber, was sated
with a compound fabricated with molasses, gin, and a
modicum of water, known as black-strap.

But an auction by administrator or sheriff was an event
of excelling interest in the community, for attendance at
which all ordinary duties were made to give way, and even
bar-rooms were deserted. At a public vendue, better than
at all other assemblages, were to be studied the quainter
specimens of Lancastrian eccentricity. There, rough dia-
monds jostling together threw out scintillations of rude,
sparkling wit. Thither came the "deacon's one horse
shay," nearly ripe for its logical catastrophe, drawn by a
worthy descendant of that veritable quadruped which, under the name of Rozinante, the genius of Cervantes has
immortalized. There might be seen every manner of
wheeled vehicle that had been invented in America before
A. D. 1800, in every stage of picturesque dilapidation.
Every fashion of dress known of Yankeedom had there its
votary. The 'squire and the minister, with pig-tail queues
tied with black ribbon, black breeches, silk stockings and
glittering paste buckles at the instep of their low shoes,
there took snuff with other clean-shaven gentlemen of the
old school, who wore their long hair clubbed, sported
ruffled shirt fronts and Hessian boots with tassels pendent
from the tops, and carried silver-headed canes. Yeomen, in leather breeches and coats made of a coarse
satinet that had been home-spun, home-woven and home-

dyed, chaffered with villagers clad in cassimere pantaloons, brass buttoned, blue broadcloth coats with swallow tails, and buff vests. Individualism had not then been crushed out by tyranny of fashion in dress, the dictation of social arbiters, or the averaging processes of compulsory education ; and queer folk were not as now segregated for show in cheap museums or hidden in lunatic asylums and hospitals, but walked about among their kin unabashed. Joviality reigned over the scene, and warming pans, tall clocks, brass andirons, flag-bottomed chairs, spinning wheels and blue crockery were knocked down to the dilatory bidders, at prices which no sane modern auctioneer would deign to accept as a first bid for such æsthetic heirlooms.

The mechanics of the town were widely known for their versatility and superior workmanship. People came from long distances to the whitesmith, Gowen B. Newman, for his conscientious work, and some of his tools even now remain to testify to his skill. Tanners, fullers and hatters plied their handicrafts, and every little village had its blacksmith, wheelwright, cobbler and cooper. Here and there would be found some ideal mechanical genius, a genuine Yankee jack-at-all-trades, like John Bigelow who played the violin in the choir on Sundays, and on week days developed such a knack for successfully tinkering refractory clocks and watches that he quite spoiled the business of the regular watch repairer, Major Jacob Fisher, and finally found his proper career at the head of a noted Boston firm of jewellers.

The story of the obscure shoemaker who made slippers for Parisian belles, deserves telling for its moral if nothing more. On a cross-road in the southern part of Bolton stood a humble cottage with a little unpainted shop near by, wherein lived and worked a Quaker cordwainer, by name Holder. He was no common cobbler. The surpassing excellence of his work gained the attention of the wealthier ladies of Lancaster and vicinity, and soon they would wear no shoes but those of his make. When Captain Cleveland went to Havana as vice consul, Mrs. Cleveland left the measure of her foot with Friend Holder, and every year packages of shoes went from his little shop to her, and certain Cuban friends of hers. While S. V. S. Wilder resided in Paris, Mrs. Wilder periodically sent orders to the Quaker expert; and not for herself alone, since several of her acquaintances, ambitious of being as well shod as their American friend, found no readier way than to become patrons of the rustic shoemaker thousands of miles distant, in a Bolton byway; and his handiwork often crossed the ocean to shame the skill of the Parisian Crispins.

To become a master carpenter in those days required a long apprenticeship, for everything that entered into the construction and fitting of a house for occupancy was laboriously fashioned from the rough lumber by hand. Of thoroughly educated and honest builders Lancaster had a goodly row, as the carpentry of certain old mansions can yet attest. For many years Eli Stearns stood at the head of these workers in wood. The Sprague house is perhaps the best example of his workmanship. When the Brick church was erected in 1816, he was chosen chairman of the building committee, being then sixty years of age ; and it is related that the workmen upon that edifice soon found that there was little use in trying to conceal any inferior work from his vigilant eye.

Game and fish were not only abundant, but some animals now rare anywhere, then haunted the wilder recesses of the extensive forests on the borders of the larger ponds. Now and then a deer or an otter was seen ; raccoons were common, and the lynx prowled about on his murderous errands. There still survived a few of that race of men now almost extinct in the older states, who possessed an instinct for hunting and trapping. They were not caparisoned with the outfit now deemed almost essential ; they carried neither double-barreled shot-gun nor breech-loader, nor split bamboo rod with invisible line and artificial bait. Their weapons were a flint-lock smooth-bore, home-wrought powder-horn and shot-pouch, home-made flax fishing lines, and traps fashioned by the owner. With an intelligence always alert, they had also an inborn faculty for acquiring an intimacy with the occult habits of beast and bird and fish, such as insures success in their pursuit; and their habits of observation were joined to such quickness of vision and hearing that if fortune had so directed they might have become famous naturalists.

Types of the better class of yeomany were common; men who daily delved with their own hands in all the arduous duties of the farm; legitimate sons of the soil, but no groundlings in the political or social theatre. As early in spring as the retreating frost left the fields mellow, they were seen barefoot, with trousers rolled to the knees, behind their oxen in the furrow; and all the months of summer and autumn their toilsome lives were a practical oration upon the dignity of labor. They were diligent readers, or students rather, of the few choice books attainable; thought much about the various problems of human life, and showed abundance of hard common sense in discussing the political or social questions of the period with their neighbors or the minister. At town-meeting often one of them, with shrewd, Socratic argument, would prick the bubble scheme of a demagogue, or pluck the palm of forensic victory from the 'squire himself.

From farming to the calculus seems a long step; but a majority of the farmers of the day had implicit faith in lunar influence upon most mundane matters, from the boiling of pork in the pot to the success of important enterprises; and the almanac took rank next to the Bible in the frequency with which its counsels were sought. The phases of the moon may almost be said to have governed the sowing of seed and the gathering of harvest. A local almanac-maker even was not wanting. Asa Houghton began publishing astronomical calculations about 1796, and for twenty years at least "The Gentlemen's and Ladies' Diary and Almanac" had an extended patronage. Houghton, in his annual address to the public, sometimes indulged in somewhat stilted rhetoric about the "awfully sublime ideas" inspired in the almanac-maker by "the study of that Divine and Heavenly Science, Astronomy;" but his mathematical deductions seem to have been sufficiently accurate, and his pages of miscellany of fully average interest and usefulness. A rival almanac was published for a few years in Harvard.

It was many years later that the use of lead or iron pipe for conducting water into dwellings became common here; but two acqueduct companies, one incorporated as early as 1797, utilized the famous springs of Quasaponikin and George Hills, bringing water to the inhabitants of the Neck and the village of New Boston in bored logs, specimens of which in perfect preservation occasionally even yet come to the surface.

Sectarian differences existed, but had not engendered bitterness in discussion, nor lessened the general harmony of social relations. There was but one meeting-house, one religious society; and the deservedly revered pastor, Nathaniel Thayer, was the prominent central figure of the town — its very centre of gravity. Nor was he prized by the community only as the competent public teacher of divine truth, and sought for as a benignant presence to bless occasions of rejoicing and to comfort in great sorrow. The prayer from his lips was the never-failing prelude to business at the town-meeting. The young bashfully, the old unreservedly confided their hopes, soul experiences, and troubles to him, assured of hearty sympathy and wise counsel. He was the repository of family secrets; the composer of neighborhood disputes; the ultimate referee in mooted points of taste and opinion; the universal arbiter.

Though hedged about with such native dignity as would become a prince, yet he was beloved of children, and his affability knew no difference between those who sat exalted in the choice pews and the humblest in the congregation. Before five o'clock in the summer mornings he could be seen tilling his own garden, and in the after part of the day he rode over his parish, stopping with every one he met for greeting and kindly inquiry.

To this era belongs the honor of founding the Latin Grammar School, long known as the Lancaster Academy. Captain Richard J. Cleveland and his accomplished wife, anxious about the education of their own sons, proposed its establishment, contributed liberally to its support, and at the recommendation of their friend, President Kirkland of Harvard College, secured the services of Jared Sparks as its instructor, in 1815. The experiment proved full of promise, as the following advertisement from the Columbian Centinel of April 26, 1817, gives evidence:

LANCASTER SCHOOL.

The Latin Grammar School in Lancaster will commence on the 22d May next, on an improved plan. A commodious house is erecting for the purpose, and an approved instructor is provided. Tuition is five dollars a quarter, and board may be had in respectable families near the school, at two dollars a week, including washing, fire, &c. Lancaster is a pleasant and healthy town, 34 miles from Boston, and combines as many advantages for a school of this description as perhaps any town in the country. A stage runs between this town and Boston every day. It is believed that parents designing to fit their sons for college or for active life in any employment, will find this school perfectly adapted to their wishes. For further particulars inquiry may be made of Rev. PRESIDENT KIRK-LAND, or of Mr. J. SPARKS Tutor at Cambridge, or of Dr. JACKSON, Summer Street, Boston.

This edifice of 1817 was a small, low walled, square structure of wood, painted red, with a hipped roof. In it the late George B. Emerson, LL. D., began his career as a teacher. The residence of the Clevelands was near by, a home rich in music, good books and pure taste. Mrs. Dorcas Hiller Cleveland would have been a queen in society wherever fortune had placed her; but she was much more than this. Although gifted with personal grace and beauty, educated in all the useful as well as ornamental accomplishments of a gentlewoman, and endowed with rare intellectual powers, the few living who knew and loved her remember best her moral attributes. She wrote papers upon religious topics which were considered admirable in tone and thought. She had given much study to the subject of female education, and contributed a series of essays to the Advertiser, which make us regret that her ideas upon this topic, which she was so competent to handle, were not elaborated for preservation in more permanent form. But the subtle influence of her opinions was doubtless far reaching in beneficent results, for in the genial domestic circle over which she presided, were often welcomed those scholarly young men who soon after laid the foundations of our present common-school system. While enjoying the charming hospitality of host and hostess, they heard discussed the writings of Pestalozzi and the theories of Joseph Lancaster; and there they formulated those advanced opinions respecting the teacher's mission and the pupil's needs upon which they subsequently organized the educational institutions of this commonwealth.

To Warren Colburn, Jared Sparks, George B. Emerson, Solomon P. Miles and James G. Carter, who in the most enthusiastic period of their life's work, sat at the hospitable board of the Clevelands and debated about the natural method of developing the reasoning powers in children, is due the honor of originating in Massachusetts the normal and graded school system, as much as to Horace Mann, who has won the chief renown. And today, studying moral and social results, it may well be doubted whether much of the gradual departure from their original, simple scheme of education, has not been in effect unfortunate.

At the beginning of the century common cotton cloth of English make was retailed at about thirty-three cents per

19

yard, and there were but two or three small cotton factories in New England. By the close of the war the same grade of cloth had more than doubled in price, and over fifty manufactories of textile fabrics had been organized in Massachusetts alone. The enterprise of a Frenchman had given promise of adding greatly to the material prosperity of Lancaster. In 1809, a dapper, bald-headed man, wearing a queue and carrying a gold-headed cane, appeared in town, investigating the merits of its various water-power privileges. Soon it was known that David Poignand, a native of the island of Jersey, and his son-in-law, Samuel Plant, an Englishman by birth, had purchased the site of the Prescott mill in the south part of the town ; and there they set up a cotton factory, one of the earliest successfully operated in the state. In recognition of the value, and difficulties of establishing, a new industry, Poignand & Plant's mill was temporarily exempted from local taxation. In peaceful later years this enterprise attained great prosperity. King Cotton had begun his long and arbitrary reign in America. The war of 1812 so stimulated manufactures that when peace again opened the market for cheap foreign merchandise, a protective tariff became a patriotic necessity. The revolution of 1775 ensured the United States political freedom ; the war of 1812 was the cradle of her industrial independence.

WAR WITH ALGIERS.

Hardly had the treaty of Ghent been consummated when the United States sent Commodore Stephen Decatur, with a powerful naval force, to visit Algiers with retributive justice for its insolent violations of neutrality during the war with England, and its piratical depredations upon American commerce. Accompanying Decatur, whom he admirably seconded by his diplomatic skill and personal daring in dealing with the barbarous court of Algiers, to which he was credited as consul general and chief commissioner, was William Shaler, for some years a citizen of Lancaster. In the year 1800, Captain Richard J. Cleveland and William Shaler met for the first time at the Island of Mauritius, being both young and akin in ambitious energy and manly worth. This casual meeting upon a foreign strand developed into commercial partnership, and ripened into a friendship that closed only with their lives. Mr. Shaler visited Captain Cleveland at his Lancaster home, and, charmed with the loveliness of the Nashua valley, purchased a house near his friend, in which, being a confirmed bachelor, he installed a widowed sister, with her children, about 1820. He was rich in all those personal gifts that mark the natural rulers of men ; a man whom those who could boast his friendship used to recall as the peer in social and physical graces of Daniel Webster in the fulness of his manhood. One who saw the first coming of this stately gentleman into the assemblage awaiting the opening of the mail at the post-office one day, was wont to describe the tableau thus : "Why, they opened right and left, and shrunk out of his way as though a desert lion had walked in upon them."

Upon a wall of the English church in the Moorish capital has been placed a memorial tablet in honor of "Mr William Shaler Consul-General of the United States, who during all the troublous times preceding and subsequent to Lord Exmouth's operations, when the British consul was in chains, and when he and his family were subsequently expelled by the Dey, rendered most eminent service to them and to the British nation." In October, 1823, the Kabyles in the mountains revolted, and Hussein Pasha ordered that any and all members of that tribe should be seized, wherever found, and dragged to slavery or a dungeon. It so happened that many of them, the race being esteemed for their cleanliness and fidelity, were the domestic servants of the foreign ambassadors. The emissaries of the Dey, contemptuous of all protests, bore away their victims from the consular residences of other nations, but when they came to the American consulate they encountered upon its threshold, standing under the stars and stripes, sword in hand, the stalwart consul himself; and as he told them that they should take his servants from the protection of that flag only by passing over his body, the look of stern resolution in his grey eye spoke more forcibly than words even. The scowling barbarians quailed, and finally withdrew, foiled of their prey. William Shaler, returning from Africa to Lancaster, published an octavo volume, entitled "Sketches of Algiers," which was favorably received. He had deserved so well of his country that, although a thorough whig in political faith, he was in 1829 selected by Andrew Jackson for the post of consul at Havana, then, with the exception of Liverpool, the most remunerative diplomatic position in the president's gift. The United States had hitherto been represented in Cuba only by a commercial agent, and to gain Shaler's acceptance, this office was raised to the rank of that held by him at Algiers.

Before leaving Lancaster he purchased the Cleveland estate, and Captain and Mrs. Cleveland accompanied him to Cuba. In the spring of 1833, Havana was visited by a fearful epidemic. The cholera in a single day numbered five hundred victims. About five o'clock one evening, William Shaler came in from the street and took to his bed. At seven the next morning he was dead.

GENERAL G. SHEPLEY

VII.

THE REBELLION.

1861 – 1865.

THE constitution of the United States, as ratified in 1787, was a compromise. Of the patriotic statesmen who framed it, many signed their assent with misgiving, and even with protest. Some, esteeming it too democratic, predicted the dismemberment of the confederation, sooner or later, because of the lack of a sufficiently strong central power. Others were disturbed by forebodings of monarchial possibilities, and insisted that by its provisions the sovereign states were called upon to surrender too much to congress and the executive. A phrase or two of elastic significance, admitted for the purpose of harmonizing local prejudices at the time, became later a fertile source of acrimonious debate. The bitterest apple of discord was the provision which protected property in human beings, at the same time recognizing these so called chattels as three-fifths human, and allotting to the proprietors of them in several states a proportionate political representation in national councils. This sanctioning of sectional and aristocratic privilege in a government claiming to be based upon the principle of natural democratic equality, at once gave birth to an "irrepressible conflict" between North and South — oligarchist and republican. From the outset this antagonism was, by the wise, foretold to be inevitable. It began with the first congress and grew more fierce and ungovernable year by year. Washington, himself a slave-holder, in prophetic spirit wrote to a friend: "I can clearly foresee that nothing but the rooting out of slavery can per-

petuate the existence of our Union, by consolidating it in a
common bond of principle." Disruption, often threatened,
was long evaded by concession and subterfuge; but the
insolence and usurpations of the privileged oligarchists
finally culminated in open rebellion. Beaten at the ballot-
box, they appealed to the sword. That appeal resulted in
emancipation, radical amendment of the constitution, and
—logically consequent upon the political and military victory of free labor—a revolution in the moral sentiment of
the nation, even yet not fully consummate. A brief sketch
of the part taken by Lancaster in this struggle for national
integrity, and a roster, reasonably complete and correct, of
Lancastrians who rallied round the insulted flag, is all that
is contemplated in the following pages.

No sooner was it known throughout the nation that
Abraham Lincoln had been constitutionally elected President, than the "political hacks and bar-room bullies," who
led, or seemed to lead, public sentiment in the states south
of Mason and Dixon's line, plied all their arts and energies
to work destruction to the government which Southern
policy had largely controlled, until that day, during three-
fourths of a century. The North, slow to wrath, remained
for a time almost apathetic, scornfully believing the boast-
ful threats and military preparations of the southern "fire
eaters" to be "full of sound and fury, signifying nothing."
The cannon of Sumter proclaimed the audacity of the con-
spirators and patriotism awoke to the imminent danger.
Treason, sagaciously planned and boldly led, efficiently
armed and equipped at the nation's cost, was already on
the march to the capital, and must be met. The free states
were all unready for the encounter. Massachusetts was
almost singular in possessing a militia organized and capable of speedy mobilization. On Monday, April 15, 1861,
the President called for seventy-five thousand volunteers to
serve for three months. Four days later, on the anniversary of the battles of Lexington and Concord, the Massa-

chusetts Sixth Regiment shed the first blood of the war in
the streets of Baltimore. It was the first volunteer military
organization to reach the Capital, already in great peril.
In this regiment was one soldier of Lancaster, Henry
Jackson Parker. The bloody outbreak of a secessionist
mob in Baltimore, soon known in every village, intensified
the previous excitement. The bitterness of barbarous war
had begun. Monday evening, April 22, a mass-meeting
of the citizens of Lancaster, at the town hall, considered
the grave dangers threatening the foundations of the republic. Dr. J. L. S. Thompson was chairman of the
meeting, and Henry C. Kimball, A. M., secretary. The
patriotic enthusiasm of the assemblage did not need to be
kindled with flaming oratory. Earnest feeling broke forth
in impassioned speech, and many lips became unwontedly
eloquent under the inspiration of the occasion. It was
determined to call a legal meeting of the town at the earliest day possible, and Jacob Fisher and Charles L.
Wilder were appointed a committee to report to such town-
meeting what action in the premises they might deem
necessary or desirable. Woodbury Whittemore and Christopher A. Pollard were appointed a committee to canvass
the town for volunteers to a company to be raised for the
defence of the Union. During the evening thirty names
were enrolled. It was also resolved to organize a company
of "home guards." Suitable resolutions were offered by
Honorable Francis B. Fay, and unanimously adopted by a
rising vote amid "tumultuous applause."

The warrant calling a town-meeting, April 29, 1861,
contained these articles:

. . . . 2. To see what action the Town will take in reference to the
present state of the country, and act thereon.

3. To see if the Town will raise money to defray the expenses of an
outfit for the Lancaster Volunteer Company now being raised to tender
their services to the Government for the defence of the Union, and for the
purpose of granting aid to the families of said Volunteers in their absence,
or act anything relating thereto.

On the designated day the voters filled the town hall, and elected as presiding officer, Solon Whiting, Esq., brother of two noted soldiers whose record has been given in previous pages. The committee appointed at the citizens' meeting of April 22, presented their reports:

Report of Committee on Business.

The Committee would recommend that a Committee of seven be chosen by the Town to have charge of such funds as may be voted by the Town, and that said Committee have full power to expend any portion, or all of such appropriation for the above purpose as they may deem expedient.— That the Town pay each Volunteer from the time called for until discharged thirteen dollars per month, in addition to Government pay, and one dollar per day for each day devoted to drill not exceeding thirty days, and not less than six hours to be considered a day.—That the Town Treasurer is hereby authorized to borrow on behalf of the Town, any sum that may be needed for the above purpose not exceeding Five Thousand Dollars, subject to the order of the above Committee, and that George W. Howe, George Dodge, John M. Washburn, John Bennett, Anthony Lane, J. L. S. Thompson and J. Marshall Damon constitute said committee.

Respectfully submitted,

C. L. WILDER,
JACOB FISHER.

After the reading of the Report the several parts were separately considered and the report unanimously adopted, Jacob Fisher and C. L. Wilder being added to the committee.

Report of Committee on Outfit for Volunteers.

Outfit for forty men :

2 Shirts apiece ; 80 shirts, at 1.50, ...	$120 00
2 Flannel Waistcoats ; 80 waistcoats, at 1.00, ...	80 00
40 Woollen Blankets, lined with brown drill, ...	160 00
40 Rubber Blankets, at 1.50, ...	60 00
80 pr. Socks, at .50, ...	40 00
40 light colored soft Felt Hats, at 2.00, ...	80 00
	$540 00

HENRY C. KIMBALL, *for Committee.*

Report of Committee on Volunteer Company.

Your committee appointed on Monday, the 22d inst., to inquire into the practicability of raising a company of Volunteer Militia, and to take

such measures for so doing as they may deem necessary, respectfully beg
leave to offer the following report: That they have canvassed the town
with a roll of enlistment and the result is that about forty names of steady
and able bodied young men have been enrolled to serve in the Volunteer
Militia, with the understanding that they are liable at any moment to be
called into active service.

Your committee further report that they have conferred with a similar
committee of the citizens of the town of Sterling, with a view to unite
with said town in raising an efficient company for immediate service ; and
that the committee of the town of Sterling have given assurance that they
would appear to make all necessary arrangements for a union company at
or immediately after the present town-meeting.

Your committee would respectfully recommend that the town of Lancaster raise and equip for active service one-half of said union company,
and that an armory be obtained free of expense to the state, as a deposi-
tory of the arms of the Lancaster members of said company.

All of which is respectfully submitted, by

W. WHITTEMORE,
C. A. POLLARD,
for Committee.

After listening to the patriotic speeches of several citizens, upon the importance of making every sacrifice for
the support of government, the meeting adjourned.

A legal meeting, June 8, Henry C. Kimball being moderator, heard a verbal report from the committee of nine,
and after some discussion, deeming no instructions necessary, left the committee to take such further action as they
might deem advisable. At the town-meeting of November
14, a report was presented by the committee, showing that
they had expended for outfit of the volunteers the following sums:

```
Paid for drilling — Volunteers,  . . . . . . . . . . . $357 00
  "   Drill-master, . . . . . . . . . . . . . . . . .    20 00
  "   E. Ballard, for printing, . . . . . . . . . . . .     2 50
  "   Cobb, Whittemore, Burbank, for swords, . . . . .    60 00
  "   Committee of ladies, . . . . . . . . . . . . . .    31 42
  "   George Dodge, for towels, . . . . . . . . . . .     7 74
  "   F. B. Fay, for cash advanced, . . . . . . . . . .   250 00
Balance due at expiration of 90 days, . . . . . . . . .   241 50
                                                         ‾‾‾‾‾‾‾
                                                         $970 16
```

An independent military company, organized in May, 1853, well drilled and equipped, existed in Clinton, called the Clinton Light Guard, several members of which, and all the officers, were natives of Lancaster. This company at an early date offered its services to the government, and it was understood would be attached to a Worcester county regiment, to be commanded by Colonel Charles Devens, Jr., and called the Fifteenth Massachusetts Infantry. It was resolved to use the forty men enlisted in Lancaster as the nucleus of a second company to be raised for the same regiment. Bolton and Harvard joined Lancaster in its formation, and the organization received the name, *Fay Light Guard*, in respect for Honorable Francis Ball Fay. At an election of officers and non-commissioned officers, Thomas Sherwin, Jr., then principal of the Houghton School in Bolton, was chosen captain. The company, recruited to the number of seventy-eight men, after three weeks' diligent drill in Lancaster, went to Camp Scott, at Worcester, and was joined to the Fifteenth Massachusetts as Company I. For some reason never satisfactorily explained to those most deeply interested, Sherwin was denied a commission as commander of the company, and Alfred F. Walcott of Salem was appointed its captain. If, as then believed by the volunteers, Governor Andrew was inspired with distrust of Sherwin's fitness for that office by a secret communication unfavorable to him, from some citizen of Lancaster, the war record of that gallant officer, in connection with the Twenty-second Massachusetts Infantry, of which he became lieutenant-colonel, was a significant reproach for such unwise meddling. His men indignantly refused to be sworn into service unless given the officers of their choice, in accordance with promises made and the general custom of that time. They proved persistent in this resolve, and had to be disbanded. Several of the Lancaster volunteers at once enlisted in the Clinton Light Infantry, known as Company C, and nearly all sooner or later did their country good service in other organizations. The roll of Company I, July 6, 1861, here follows, his subsequent enlistment, if any known, being noted after each soldier's name :

Captain Thomas Sherwin, Jr.; teacher. Lieutenant-Colonel Twenty-second Mass. Infty.

1st Lieutenant Woodbury Whittemore; shoemaker. Twenty-first Mass Infty.

2d Lieutenant William L. Cobb; pocketbook-maker. Thirty-fourth Mass. Infty.

3d Lieutenant Levi E. Brigham; farmer.

4th   "   Calvin W. Burbank; teacher. Not in service.

1st Sergeant J. Curtis Ayres; farmer. Fifty-third Mass. Infty.

2d   "   Christopher A. Pollard; jeweller. Not in service.

3d   "   Joseph H. Sawyer of Bolton; clerk. Thirty-sixth Mass. Infty

4th   "   George Lyman Stratton. Not in service.

1st Corporal George K. Richards; farmer. Sixteenth Mass. Infty.

2d   "   Edwin F. Field. Twenty-first Mass. Infty.

3d   "   Stephen H. Hunting; hostler. First Heavy Artillery.

4th   "   Silas H. Holman of Bolton; student. Twenty-third Artillery.

Drummer George E. Burgess of Bolton. Twenty-first Mass. Infty.

Armorer Francis Henry Fairbank; pump-maker. Fifteenth Mass. Infty.

Private Henry O. Adams of Townsend; mechanic. Fifteenth   "

  "   Galen P. Atherton of Harvard; farmer. Twenty-first   "

  "   Thomas E. Barker of Bolton; farmer. Twenty-first   "

  "   Jacob M. Barnard of Bolton; mechanic.

  "   George Albert Barnes; mechanic. Sixteenth   "

  "   Willard A. Bowers of Bolton; mechanic. Twenty-first   "

  "   Lawrence H. Braman.

  "   Henry F. Brigham of Boylston; miller. Twenty-first   "

  "   Charles H. Burgess of Harvard; mechanic. Fifty-sixth   "

  "   James E. Burke; farmer. Twenty-first   "

  "   Victor Censer of Clinton; comb-maker.

  "   William Cohen of Clinton. Twenty-first   "

  "   George W. Cutler; mechanic. Fifteenth   "

  "   Isaac N. Cutler; farmer. Fifteenth   "

  "   Daniel W. Dickinson of Harvard; farmer. Fifteenth   "

  "   John W. Dickinson of Harvard; farmer. Fifteenth   "

  "   Edward B. Ellis; mechanic. Served in a Vermont regiment.

  "   Warren Ellis; mechanic. Fifteenth   Mass. Infty.

  "   Franklin H. Farnsworth : farmer. Fifteenth   "

  "   Charles B. Flagg; farmer. Thirty-fourth   "

  "   William L. Fox; sailor. Twenty-first   "

Private Charles E. Gould; mechanic.
   "   James M. Gray; pump-maker. Fifteenth   Mass. Infty.
   "   Gilbert W. Greene; mechanic. Fifteenth   "
   "   George H. Hardy; farmer. Twenty-first   "
   "   Thomas Hastings of Berlin; mechanic. Fifteenth   "
   "   Charles R. Haven of Bolton; mechanic. Twenty-first   "
   "   Henry H. Hosley; painter. Fifteenth   "
   "   Albert C. Houghton of Bolton; mechanic. Sixteenth   "
   "   Emory H. Houghton; mechanic.
   "   W. W. Ingerson of Harvard; farmer. Twenty-first   "
   "   John James; farmer. Fifty-third   "
   "   William E. Johnson; mechanic.
   "   James Kennedy of Bolton; mechanic. Twenty-first   "
   "   Joseph W. Kingsbury; farmer. Fifteenth   "
   "   George C. Mann; mechanic. Fifteenth   "
   "   Charles H. Maynard of Sterling; mechanic. Thirty-fourth "
   "   James Montgomery of Harvard; farmer. Twenty-first "
   "   Rolla Nicholas of Bolton; farmer. Thirteenth   "
   "   Henry J. Nourse of Marlborough; mechanic. Fifteenth "
   "   Oliver L. Nourse of Bolton; mechanic. Sixteenth   "
   "   Luke Ollis; farmer. Twenty-first   "
   "   Nelson Pratt of Bolton; mechanic. Fifteenth   "
   "   John Quinn of Clinton; mechanic. Twenty-first   "
   "   Thomas W. Reid of Clinton; mechanic. Fifty-third "
   "   Eben W. Richards; mechanic. Twenty-first   "
   "   Henry H. Rugg; farmer. Fifteenth   "
   "   James Ryan; mechanic. Thirty-fourth   "
   "   William H. Savage of Harvard; farmer. Fifteenth   "
   "   William Schumaker; mechanic. Fourth U. S. Cavalry.
   "   Patrick Shanley.
   "   Charles H. Sinclair; mechanic. Twenty-first   "
   "   Francis E. Smith of Clinton; manufacturer. Fifteenth "
   "   Jonas H. Spencer of Clinton; manufacturer. Fifteenth "
   "   John B. Stanley of Bolton; mechanic. Fifth U. S. Cavalry.
   "   William Stone of Bolton; student. Nineteenth   Mass. Infty.
   "   William Thompson; teamster. Sixteenth   "
   "   John Whalen of Clinton.
   "   Harrison Willard; farmer.
   "   George Willis of Stow; farmer.
   "   John S. Williams of Bolton; mechanic. Fifteenth   "
   "   Oliver M. Wise; store-keeper. Died 1861.
   "   Archibald D. Wright of Clinton; mechanic. Fifteenth "

Before the close of August, 1861, nearly forty volunteers representing the town were in the debatable land, mostly serving in the Fifteenth, Sixteenth and Twenty-first Massachusetts regiments. Amid huzzas and the waving of handkerchiefs and silken banners they went forth, singing as they marched, their faces flushed with hope, believing the Lord on their side and dreaming little of the trials before them. Before October ended, four of those in the Fifteenth slept their last sleep in graves upon the banks of the Potomac; and their surviving comrades were writing home details of the hair-breadth escapes and trying experiences of their first battle—the crushing defeat of Ball's Bluff. These earliest martyrs of Lancaster were George Wright Cutler, Willard Raymond Lawrence, James Gardner Warner and Luther Gerry Turner. The captain of the Clinton and Lancaster company, and several of his men, were prisoners of war. The first-lieutenant, Andrew L. Fuller, had reached home but a few days before, having resigned because physically unable to perform military duty. He immediately returned to the regiment, bearing words of cheer and substantial comforts, and brought home a detailed report of the casualties and condition of the survivors. The war that to the community had hitherto seemed far away—a formless, dark shadow in the horizon —became thenceforward a perennially present and defined horror.

The excitement at this period was intense, and military enthusiasm took form during November in the organization of a company of home guards, which intrenched itself behind the formidable name of "The Lancaster Independent Phalanx." One hundred names were enrolled, of old and young, and meetings for drill were held every Monday evening at the town hall, each member bringing his own arms. Hon. F. B. Fay was the first captain elect, and Solon Whiting, Esq., the second in command. Upon their declining office, Dr. Reuben Barron was made commander, and Lyman Moore lieutenant. On the first of March, 1862, Thomas B. Warren succeeded Doctor Barron. The platoons of the Phalanx, after the first few meetings, were rarely of a length unmanageable in the hall, the older members becoming very irregular in attendance. The motley outfit and style of drill at times called up amusing recollections of the annual May Training under the old militia law, when the street evolutions of the "Slambangs" were the only visible relic of military glory left to inspire the rural patriot. At these drill meetings, however, many a volunteer, who afterwards did good service in the field, received his first lessons in the school of the soldier.

December 2, 1861, a citizens' meeting, of which G. F. Chandler was chairman and J. Prescott Wilder secretary, after discussing the needs of the soldiers in the winter's campaigning, chose a committee to ascertain and provide for their wants. This committee was organized as follows:

Miss Mary G. Chandler,	Dr. J. L. S. Thompson,
Mrs. Emily Leighton,	G. F. Chandler,
Mrs. Joseph H. Dudley,	Spencer R. Merrick,
Miss Mary T. Humphrey,	Horatio D. Humphrey,
	George Dodge.

The selectmen and town-clerk, after correspondence with officers in the Fifteenth and Twenty-first regiments, reported that about thirty Lancaster men were in the field, many of whom were in need of warmer clothing. The committee at once collected by popular subscription the sum of one hundred and sixty-six dollars, with which under-garments and other articles of apparel were purchased, and forwarded together with numerous special donations. After the town's men were well supplied, a surplus remaining was transferred to the Sanitary Commission. A list of the articles contributed is preserved:

20 pairs boots,	15 flannel shirts,	23 pairs mittens,
30 blankets,	18 pairs drawers,	25 towels, etc.
14 quilts,	51 pairs stockings,	

July 8, 1862, a public meeting, called to plan measures for the relief of the sick and wounded, organized by the

choice of George W. Howe, chairman, and Dr. J. L. S.
Thompson, secretary. A committee, consisting of Caleb
T. Symmes, G. F. Chandler and George A. Johnson was
chosen to solicit contributions of money and hospital supplies, and the following week reported that they had received three hundred and sixty dollars and seventy-three
cents, and forwarded to the Sanitary Commission two hundred dollars in money and the following articles, chiefly
the handiwork of the women of Lancaster:

171 sheets,	2 dressing gowns,	12 coats,
161 pillow-cases,	63 shirts,	4 vests,
102 towels,	36 pairs drawers,	2 pairs pantaloons,
49 napkins,	5 pairs slippers,	6 boxes lint,
17 handkerchiefs,	6 neckties,	

besides quilts, stockings, bandages, bundles of linen, etc.

The governors of eighteen states having officially advised large increase of the army in order to a more vigorous prosecution of the war, President Lincoln, on the first
of July, 1862, issued a call for three hundred thousand
three years troops. Under this call seventeen men were
required of Lancaster. To secure prompt enlistments the
stimulation of a bounty was thought necessary. At a
meeting of the people July 14, Reverend Amos E. Lawrence, Reverend Milo C. Stebbins, George A. Johnson,
Calvin W. Burbank and Eli E. Howe were chosen to act
with the selectmen as a recruiting committee. Supported
by pledges from gentlemen of means, this committee was
able to guarantee a bounty of one hundred dollars to each
volunteer. At the meetings of July 14 and 23, much enthusiasm was awakened, and the fervid appeals of prominent citizens were rewarded with loud applause, while at
the successive enlistment of several young men, the assemblage was almost frantic in its demonstrations of approval.
In general the persuasive counsels of those, the unselfish-
ness of whose patriotism was attested by silvered locks or
personal sacrifice, bore fruit as well as won respect. Occasionally the *ad captandum* harangue of some "self-consti-

tuted exempt" provoked broad hint that the eloquence of service far outshines that of words. Very few, however, shirked or attempted to evade their proper share in the grave responsibilities of the hour, and the active patriotism of the young and stalwart only kept step with the generosity and self negation of those whom sex, the burden of years, or infirmity, or apparent duty, held at home. Those enlisted at this date entered the Thirty-fourth Massachusetts Infantry, organizing at Camp Wool. The action of the town at a legal meeting July 23, 1862, is thus recorded :

Voted, that the selectmen be a committee to pay each recruit, when sworn into the United States service, the sum of One Hundred Dollars.

Voted, that recruits at Camp Wool who shall be accepted by the Adjutant General as a part of the quota of seventeen required from this town, be paid the sum of one hundred dollars.

Voted, that the committee chosen at a citizen's meeting be requested to act with the selectmen in procuring recruits.

The following day a citizens' meeting elected George W. Howe, Dr. J. L. S. Thompson and Christopher A. Pollard a committee to provide for the families of those absent as soldiers, and look after the gathering of their crops and other farm work in proper season. On August 4, was proclaimed a call for three hundred thousand militia to serve for nine months, and soon after Lancaster received notice that her quota was twenty-one men. August 25, 1862, action was taken by the town as follows :

Voted, that the town pay to each volunteer, one hundred dollars, provided the full quota (21) for nine months is furnished.

Voted, that the above sum be paid whenever said volunteers are mustered into the United States service.

Voted, that the selectmen and treasurer be authorized to borrow such sums as may be necessary to pay volunteers, and the state aid to families.

Previous to this date the women of Lancaster had been indefatigable in labors for their fellow townsmen absent fighting the battles of freedom, and in the name of the existing charitable societies of the two churches, had forwarded to them Bibles, money, and several boxes filled with blankets, clothing, reading matter, and miscellaneous comforts. August 27, 1862, the Soldiers' Relief Association was organized. Its officers were : Mrs. Harriet W. Washburn, president; Miss Mary Anderson, Miss Mary Ann Thayer and Miss Mary Whitney, vice-presidents : Miss Elizabeth P. Russell, secretary and treasurer. It soon became a branch of the New England section of the Sanitary Commission. Its weekly meetings were uniformly well attended. From month to month, under its auspices, public entertainments of varied character were given in furtherance of its Christian aims. A vast amount of beneficent work of incalculable value was quietly accomplished by these true and tender-hearted laborers, neither seeking nor reaping any recompense, save the grateful prayers of thousands maimed, sick and dying — prayers mostly inaudible to human senses, but all recorded above.

September 10, a citizens' meeting considered the need of systematic aid for soldiers and their families, and especially for those sick or wounded. It was decided to establish a Soldiers' Relief Fund, to be used by a committee composed of the selectmen and such others as they might select to assist, at their discretion, for the comfort of the town's soldiers, and those dependent upon them, when found in want or distress. A subscription was opened and five hundred dollars were pledged at once. The selectmen soon after organized the committee, calling to their aid the following citizens : Nathaniel Thayer, Hon. Francis B. Fay, George Stratton, Charles L. Wilder, George Cummings, Rev. M. C. Stebbins, Dr. J. L. S. Thompson, Charles J. Wilder. At subsequent weekly meetings the fund was increased by the liberality of various contributors to the sum of twelve hundred and ninety-one dollars, and, by additions of interest and dividends upon investments, to sixteen hundred and sixty-six dollars and twenty-seven cents, including expenditures. Ultimately the purpose of this local relief fund was subserved by state aid, the expen-

20

diture of the town being refunded under established regulations from the treasury of the commonwealth. Upon the treasurer of the committee, George W. Howe, Esq., devolved the care and judicious disbursement of the contributions, a duty often onerous and perplexing, but cheerfully performed without recompense. January 5, 1872, a meeting of the contributors recorded their thanks for Mr. Howe's faithful service, and transferred the balance remaining in his hands, the sum of eight hundred dollars, to the trustees of the Lancaster Charitable Fund.

At two of the meetings held during September, the Reverends Merrill Richardson of Worcester, George Putnam, S. T. D., of Roxbury, and Mr. Edward R. Washburn of Lancaster, gave addresses noteworthy for their patriotic eloquence. Mr. Washburn was at this time engaged in recruiting for the Fifty-third Massachusetts Infantry, and was successful in enlisting from his neighbors enough men to fill the town's quota for the nine months' service, going himself as their captain. The shorter term of enlistment gave popularity to the call of August, and several more than the quota demanded went from Lancaster in this and other nine months' regiments. The vote of August 25, only authorizing the payment of bounty to the twenty-one required, a special town-meeting October 15, 1862, voted "to pay a bounty of One Hundred Dollars to those who have enlisted and who shall be mustered and accepted into the United States service."

As in quick succession came news from the battlefields of New Berne, Shiloh, Fair Oaks, Chantilly, Antietam, Fredericksburg, Chancellorsville and Port Hudson, Lancaster knew that her sons were doing their duty, and family after family mourned their unreturning brave.

Under date of October 17, 1863, a call was issued by the President for three hundred thousand men for three years. Lancaster's quota was established as fourteen. The government bounty offered for volunteers was now four

hundred dollars to veterans and three hundred for recruits.
At an extra session of the Massachusetts legislature in
November it was voted to pay an additional bounty of three
hundred and twenty-five dollars to each man enlisting in
the state, or, at his option, fifty dollars in hand and twenty
dollars per month for actual service, over and above the
legal wages. The citizens of Lancaster, assembled to devise ways and means for meeting the new demand, November 23, 1863, voted to seek the aid of popular orators from
Worcester and Fitchburg to reanimate the somewhat jaded
enthusiasm, and on December 3, Rev. Merrill Richardson
spoke to a large audience. The same night a recruiting
committee of twenty-one was chosen :

Lieut. William L. Cobb,	Jonas Goss,	Levi P. Wood, Jr.,
George Cummings,	James Childs,	Levi Farwell,
Rev. Milo C. Stebbins,	Lieut. John C. Ayres,	Barney S. Phelps,
Hon. Francis B. Fay,	Benjamin B. Otis,	Sewell Day,
George F. Chandler,	Thomas Laughton,	G. C. Colburn,
Rev. Marcus Ames,	Calvin W. Burbank,	Charles L. Wilder,
Charles J. Wilder,	Calvin Holman,	Samuel Rugg.

This committee, their energy inspired and sustained by
the universal determination to avoid a draft, addressed
themselves to the difficult task assigned them. The common laborer now commanded unprecedented wages, and
skilled mechanics could earn four or five dollars per day,
while the private soldier was paid thirteen dollars a month,
besides clothing and rations. It was finally found expedient to promise for every accepted recruit a town bounty of
one hundred dollars in addition to the national and state
bounties, thus raising the total premium upon enlistment to
the sum of seven hundred and twenty-five dollars. Again
the subscription lists were borne from house to house
throughout the town, and one thousand and twenty dollars
were pledged by individuals. The fourteen volunteers
were soon after obtained, and joined their brethren in the
field, most of them being assigned to the Thirty-fourth
and Thirty-sixth Massachusetts Infantry.

On February 1, 1864, a draft for five hundred thousand men, to serve three years or during the war, was ordered to take place on the tenth of March; but this number included the three hundred thousand called for October 7, 1863. On the fifteenth of March, 1864, came a call for two hundred thousand men, to be raised by volunteering or draft; and on the fourth of July the President summoned five hundred thousand more to enlist, for one, two or three years, as they might elect. This human avalanche from the North soon began its crushing progress southward, down the valleys of Georgia and Virginia.

The town, at its legal meeting April 4, 1864,—

Voted, that the town pay the sum of one hundred and twenty-five dollars for each man required to fill the quota [15] of Lancaster under the last call of the President.

Voted, that the Assessors be authorized to abate the poll taxes of nine-months men assessed in 1863.

The legislature had recently established the maximum bounty that could be offered by town or city at one hundred and twenty-five dollars. On the same day that the above votes were passed, at an adjournment of the March meeting, it was—

Voted on motion, that the selectmen and treasurer be authorized to borrow or appropriate any money in the treasury not otherwise appropriated, and pay the sum of one hundred and twenty-five dollars for each man under the present or any future call before the first of March, 1865.

Voted, that they pay the same sum to any enrolled man who shall send an alien substitute on any quota between the first of March, 1864, and the first of March, 1865; provided, that in the opinion of the selectmen such substitute shall be good for the quota of the town.

June 7, 1864, at a special town meeting, of which George W. Howe was moderator, it was—

Voted, that the selectmen be instructed to procure the necessary number of men which, in their opinion, may be required to fill the anticipated call for more troops, on the best terms possible.

Voted, that the selectmen and treasurer be authorized to borrow a sum not exceeding three thousand dollars, to be used by the selectmen for recruiting purposes.

October 6, 1864, at a meeting of voters desiring the re-election of Abraham Lincoln to the presidency, the organ-ization of a Union Club was perfected. Doctor John L. S. Thompson was chosen its president, and twelve vice-presidents were elected. Meetings were held on Wednes-day and Saturday evenings of each week. The members were pledged

> . . . . to support, sustain and defend the Government as at present ad-ministered, to prosecute the war against traitors, and not to relax our efforts until treason and rebellion are conquered, the union restored and freedom vindicated.

From time to time speakers were procured by the direc-tion of the club to address the public upon the topics of the period. October 24, Rev. Merrill Richardson of Worces-ter spoke; November 2, Rev. Mr. Fairchild delivered an address upon Sherman's campaign; and November 3, Hon. Edwin Bailey of Boston spoke effectively upon the issues of the election pending.

At a legal meeting June 22, 1864, the action of the previous town-meeting was rescinded, and it was —

> Voted, that the selectmen and treasurer be authorized to borrow the sum of two thousand dollars for the purpose of refunding the money con-tributed by individuals for the purpose of filling the quota of the town under the calls for troops made by the President on October 17, 1863, and February 1, 1864; provided such money shall be put in the hands of the recruiting committee for the purpose of procuring more troops.

The re-enlistment of eleven veterans, who, having served their country three years, did not falter but held up their hands to be counted again as soldiers for Lancaster during the war, greatly assisted in meeting the demands upon the town. Three other residents enlisted for the war, and, Congress at length having recognized the grave in-justice done in refusing to allow enlistments in the navy to stand on a par with those in the army, four sailors were added to Lancaster's credit. Half a dozen citizens of the town joined the regiments sent to Washington for garrison duty in July, 1864, to serve one hundred days. These last, however, though exempted from the operation of the draft, were not credited to the town's, or the state's, quota. It was seen to be hopeless to expect further avoidance of conscription. Should the quota not be filled by September 5, the law made personal service obligatory upon those that chanced to be drafted. Until that date a money commutation of three hundred dollars relieved the conscript from military duty save by substitute. Accordingly on July 18, 1864, a lot decreed that ten of Lancaster's citizens should join the army or buy exemption. Each of the ten paid the required fee, and fought by proxy. This was the only draft in Lancaster. A few non-residents were hired to serve the town, and all national calls upon its patriotism were much more than satisfied.

The first president of the Soldiers' Relief Association in Lancaster, who had lost two gallant sons, stricken down in the front of battle, sought early in 1865 to be relieved from the post she had honored, and Mrs. Mary G. Ware was chosen to the office. Mrs. Jane Humphrey became vice-president, succeeding Miss Mary Anderson. The society despatched its last invoice of hospital stores on May 10, 1865, but retained its organization until August 30, when, having completed the third year of its nobly beneficent existence, it was reorganized as a branch of the New England Freedmen's Aid Society, retaining the old officers. The following summary of the work of the Relief Association is derived from the quarterly reports of its secretary, Miss Elizabeth P. Russell, to whose enthusiasm and unremitting energy much of its efficiency was due :

Proceeds of ten public entertainments, ... $1,292 37
Donations from individuals, ... 217 38
Obtained by sale of sundry articles, ... 45 61

Total cash receipts $1,555 36
Total expenditures for materials, etc., ... 1,185 30

Balance in treasury, transferred to Freedmen's
Aid Society, ... $370 06

The materials bought—often more than doubled in value through the labor expended upon them by the skilful needlewomen who, once a week, met for the purpose in the ante-rooms of the town hall—were packed in boxes and barrels, together with the many special contributions of citizens, and promptly forwarded. The Lancaster contribution of sanitary goods for the benefit of the wounded at. Antietam was the first to reach the Boston office. There were sent to the Sanitary Commission, forty-seven boxes and barrels chiefly laden with clothing, six boxes containing wine, jellies, etc., thirty-two barrels of potatoes and fruit, and two barrels of reading matter; to the Christian Commission, one box of clothing; to the Massachusetts agent at Washington, one box of hospital goods and clothing; to the Fifty-third Massachusetts Infantry, one box of clothing; to the Thirty-seventh Massachusetts Infantry, one box of hospital goods; to Mrs. C. P. Russell at Washington, D. C., for distribution, two boxes of hospital goods. A schedule of the various articles included in the above follows:

Pocket handkerchiefs,	1144	Eye shades,	39
Stockings, pairs,	344	Compresses,	258
Shirts—cotton,	202	Bandages,	933
flannel,	117	Boxes of lint,	27
Drawers—cotton,	228	Fans,	24
flannel,	295	Bundles of old cotton and	
Coats, chiefly linen,	23	linen,	20
Vests,	12	Reading matter, barrels,	2
Pantaloons,	8	" " bundles,	15
Dressing-gowns,	25	Potatoes, barrels,	25
Mittens, pairs,	7	Apples, barrels,	2
Neckties,	13	Dried apple, barrels,	5
Caps—sleeping,	44	" " packages,	39
Slippers and moccasins, pairs,	188	Wine, home-made, bottles,	63
Boots and shoes, pairs,	18	Cider, bottles,	12
Housewife bags, needle-books,		Jellies and preserves, jars, etc.,	38
etc.,	68	Dried currants, packages,	4
Quilts (160 made by S. R. A.),	170	Lemon syrup, bottles,	4
Sheets,	56	Blackberry syrup, bottles,	27
Blankets,	2	Pickles, bottles,	4

Pillow-cases,	112	Condensed milk, cans,	3
Towels,	178	Tea, coffee, cocoa, chocolate,	
Napkins,	298	packages,	19
Table-cloth,	1	Farina, arrowroot, corn starch,	
Pillows and cushions, sundry		gelatine, sago, tapioca,	
kinds,	271	Irish moss, etc., packages,	64
Arm slings,	24		

The generous givers who helped our loyal women-workers to achieve such remarkable results need not be enumerated, for the list of them would be but a census of the families of Lancaster; all in unity of spirit bestowing their mites or lavish bounties, according to ability. The war historian of the commonwealth records the contributions of the Lancaster women to the Sanitary Commission as in value about three thousand five hundred dollars. This certainly, at war prices, was not too liberal an appraisal. The lady associates, in continuing their charitable labors after the return of peace, had specially in view the maintenance of a teacher of freedmen. Miss Abigail Jane Knight, one of their own circle, a lady well qualified by her attainments and heartfelt sympathy for the cause, taught for four years under the auspices of the society, at Edisto Island, South Carolina. Including the sum which it inherited at the start, the society raised and expended in support of Miss Knight's school, the sum of two thousand three hundred and forty-six dollars and sixty-two cents, most of which was derived from series of entertainments, embracing concerts, fairs, readings and lectures by home and foreign talent, dancing parties, etc.

Accurately to classify or sum such expenditures of the town in its corporate capacity as were strictly chargeable to the war, would be difficult, if not impossible. The yearly payments to the needy soldiers and their families, refunded as "state aid," were given by the state's historian as follows:

1861	1862	1863	1864	1865
$327.02	$1,839.14	$2,756.02	$2,545.00	$1,550.00

The selectmen's books, however, differ from this, showing a total of $10,036.62. The total of military expenses other than this aid has been stated at $18,719.70 by one authority, and at $20,864.06 by another. The latter is probably not an exaggerated estimate.

Upon the executive and financial officers of the town during the civil war, novel and perplexing duties devolved, and labors for which their unaided strength would have been wholly insufficient; but seconded by the committees hereinbefore mentioned, they performed the varied work entrusted to them by the confidence of the public, with such earnestness and fairness as to receive general commendation. These officers were:

Selectmen.

1861. James Childs, Jeremiah Moore, Warren Davis.
1862-3. Jeremiah Moore, Jonathan Buttrick, Spencer R. Merrick.
1864. George W. Howe, Jonathan Buttrick, Spencer R. Merrick.
1865. Jonathan Buttrick, Spencer R. Merrick, Levi W. Farwell.

Assessors.

1861 and 1862. Warren Davis, Solon Whiting, Silas Thurston.
1863. Warren Davis, Stedman Nourse, Charles Safford
1864. Warren Davis, Sewell Day, Jeremiah Moore.
1865. Stedman Nourse, Sewell Day, Charles J. Wilder.

Town Clerk.

J. L. S. Thompson, M. D., 1861-1865.

Treasurers.

1861. John M. Washburn. Died December 26, 1861.
1862-4. Christopher A. Pollard. Died.
1865. Solon Wilder.

DESCRIPTIVE ROSTER OF SOLDIERS OF LANCASTER,

INCLUDING NATIVES AND RESIDENTS OF THE TOWN, AND
THOSE HIRED FOR HER QUOTA.

SECOND MASSACHUSETTS INFANTRY.

Under the call for five hundred thousand additional three years troops, made by President Lincoln, October 17, 1863, and February 1, 1864, several non-resident substitutes were hired for the town, and received a state bounty of three hundred and twenty-five dollars each. Six of these are found mustered as recruits for the Veteran Second Massachusetts, then commanded by Colonel William Cogswell, attached to the Army of the Cumberland, and engaged in the Atlanta campaign.

Company A.

John Dupee, aged 36; mustered in, July 2, 1864; transferred from 33 M. V. I., June 1, 1865; mustered out, July 14, 1865.

Company G.

John Mayo, 24; July 2, 1864; deserted August 10, 1864.

Company I.

Joseph Clinton, 22; May 7, 1864; mustered out July 14, 1865.

Unassigned.

David H. Tracy, 29; July 2, 1864. Never joined regiment.
George Watson, 32; July 2, 1864. " "
Peter Zahn, 24; May 7, 1864. " "

FIFTH MASSACHUSETTS INFANTRY. 9 Months [Militia].

This regiment, George H. Pierson, colonel, left Boston in transports for New Berne, N. C., October 22, 1862. Kinston, Whitehall and Goldsboro are inscribed upon its banner. A history of the regiment, by Frank J. Robinson, was published in 1879.

Company E.

Benjamin F. Wyman, 23; Sept. 16, 1862; mustered out July 2, 1863.

Company I.

William D. Pierce, 23; Sept. 16, 1862; mustered out July 2, 1863. Enlisted from Bolton, but born and bred in Lancaster. Brother of Frank E. Pierce of 21 M. V. I.

Eben C. Mann (not a resident of Lancaster until after the close of the war) was a corporal in Company B of this regiment.

FIFTH MASSACHUSETTS INFANTRY. 100 Days.

This regiment was stationed at Fort Marshall, in the vicinity af Baltimore, Maryland, Colonel George H. Pierson commanding. A bounty of seventy-six dollars sixty-six cents was paid each soldier.

Company E.

Thomas Augustus Hills, sergeant, 23; July 23, 1864; mustered out Nov. 16, 1864. Credited to Leominster; served previously in Company C, 53 M. V. I., for Lancaster.

Adrian T. Nourse, 21; July 22, 1864; mustered out Nov. 19, 1864.

Roscoe H. Nourse, 23: July 22, 1864; mustered out Nov. 16, 1864. Served previously in Co. C, 53 M. V. I. Brother of foregoing.

Frederick Fordyce Nourse, 21; July 22, 1864; died at New Brunswick, N. J., on his way home, Sept. 13, 1864. Brother of Frank E. Nourse of 51 M. V. I.

[The three last named soldiers are credited to *Leominster* in Mass. Records, erroneously.]

Company I.

Cyrus E. Coburn, 21; July 19, 1864; mustered out Nov. 16, 1864. Brother of George B. Coburn. 34 M. V. I.

Sumner W. Keyes, 21; July 19, 1864; mustered out Nov. 16, 1864. Brother of Stephen A. Keyes, 53 M. V. I.

SIXTH MASSACHUSETTS INFANTRY. 3 Months.

This regiment was the first sent to Washington from Massachusetts, and is noted for its conflict with the Baltimore mob, April 19, 1861. Colonel Edward F. Jones, commander.

Company B.

Henry Jackson Parker, 25; June 19, 1861; mustered out Aug. 2, 1861. Served subsequently in 33 M. V. I. Resident of Townsend, but born and bred in Lancaster.

Seventh Massachusetts Infantry.

This regiment. under Colonel Darius N. Couch, reached Washington July 15, 1861.

Company B.

William Harrison Farnsworth, 20; June 15, 1861; deserted Sept., 1862, at Alexandria, Virginia.

Ninth Massachusetts Infantry.

Henry Holton Fuller, M. D., who had been resident of Lancaster for three years, was commissioned assistant surgeon of this regiment, July 7, 1862, having served with it in camp for a time, but declined commission.

Eleventh Massachusetts Infantry.

Abner Wheeler, 25; June 13, 1861; deserted June 23, 1862. This man, a teamster, in the Records of Massachusetts Volunteers is credited to Lancaster. He may have been a temporary resident here, but does not appear in the town's quota list.

Fifteenth Unattached Company, Massachusetts Infantry. 100 Days,

Nine companies of one hundred days men were recruited for garrison duty in forts on the coast. This company was commanded by Captain Isaac A. Jennings.

Bartholet Fahay, 21; July 28, 1864; mustered out Nov. 15, 1864. Received a bounty of sixty-four dollars sixty-six cents. [*Bartlett Fay, in Mass. Records.*]

Fifteenth Massachusetts Infantry.

This regiment, commanded successively by Colonels Charles Devens, Jr., George H. Ward, and George C. Joslin, left Camp Scott, Worcester, where it had been stationed about six weeks, August 8, 1861. It met with severe loss in the unfortunate battle of Ball's Bluff, October 21, 1861; was in the battles of Fair Oaks, Savage Station, Antietam and Fredericksburg during 1862; Chancellorsville, Gettysburg, Bristoe Station and Robertson's Tavern in 1863; the Wilderness, Spottsylvania, Petersburg, etc., in 1864.

Company A.

Thomas H. Davidson, 25; July 12, 1861; discharged for disability April 25, 1862. He died of consumption shortly after the close of the war.

Fordyce Horan, 20; Dec. 24, 1861; enlisted Nov. 17, 1862, in First U. S. Artillery, Co. I; died insane in hospital at Washington, Nov. 3, 1864.

Joseph W. Kingsbury, 18; Aug. 1, 1861; taken prisoner; discharged for disability Nov. 27, 1862.

Henry T. Taylor, 27; July 12, 1861; discharged on account of rheumatism, April 25, 1862. Died Oct. 18, 1868.

Company C.

Nathaniel Alexander, 40; Dec. 17, 1861; discharged for disability, Oct. 15, 1862.

Charles H. Balcom, 33; Dec. 14, 1861; transferred to Veteran Reserve Corps, April 15, 1864. [*Balcomb* and *Balam* in Mass. Records.]

Henry Bowman, captain, 26; Aug. 1, 1861; captured Oct. 21, 1861, at Ball's Bluff, Va., and held in Libby Prison, Richmond, as hostage for Confederate privateersmen condemned for piracy, he with twelve others having been selected by lot for this purpose, Nov. 12, 1861; paroled Feb. 22, 1862; exchanged August, 1862; commissioned major 34 M. V. I., Aug. 9, 1862; colonel 36 M. V. I., Aug. 22, 1862. He was a citizen of Clinton, but born and bred in Lancaster.

George W. Cutler, 22; July 12, 1861; shot through the head at Ball's Bluff, Va., Oct. 21, 1861. Brother of next, and of Henry A., 53 M. V. I., and Francis B., 35 N. Y.

Isaac N. Cutler, 20; July 12, 1861; severely wounded in left ankle at Antietam, Sept. 17, 1862; discharged for disability, March 20, 1863.

Francis Henry Fairbanks, 25; July 12, 1861; discharged on account of asthma, April 10, 1862; re-enlisted in 34 M. V. I. Brother of Charles T., 1 N. H. Cav. [Mass. Records report Fairbanks *killed at Fair Oaks.*]

Franklin Hawkes Farnsworth, 19; July 12, 1861; shot through the body and killed at Fair Oaks, May 31, 1862. Brother of John E. and George W., 34 M. V. I.

Andrew L. Fuller, first-lieutenant, 37; Aug. 1, 1861; resigned Oct. 7, 1861, on account of feeble health, and died of consumption, Sept. 10, 1867. He was a manufacturer, of Clinton, but born and bred in Lancaster.

James M. Gray, 23; July 12, 1861; discharged for disability, Feb. 16, 1863, being lame. [Mass. Records say *Feb.* 11.] Brother of Stephen W., 34 M. V. I.

Henry H. Hosley, 18; July 12, 1861; enlisted Nov. 12, 1862, in First U. S. Artillery, Co. I, known as "Flying Artillery."

Adelbert W. Johnson, 23; July 12, 1861; discharged for rheumatism, May, 1862; re-enlisted in 53 M. V. I.

Sumner Russell Kilburn, 18; July 12, 1861; re-enlisted as veteran, Feb. 18, 1864. He received two or three wounds in the battle of the Wilderness, May 6, 1864, and died at Fredericksburg, May 16, 1864. [Mass. Records say *June* 10, an error.]

Solomon Kittredge, 42; Dec. 17, 1861; transferred, because of rheumatism, to Veteran Reserve Corps, May 1, 1862; re-enlisted as veteran.

Willard Raymond Lawrence, 28; July 12, 1861; shot through the abdomen and killed at Ball's Bluff, Va., Oct. 21, 1861.

Robert Roberts Moses, 24; Dec. 17, 1861; shot through the lungs at Antietam, Sept. 17, 1862, and died Oct. 3, 1862. [Mass. Records say Oct. 5.]

George F. Osgood, 21; Aug. 12, 1862; taken prisoner at Antietam, Sept. 17, 1862; killed at Gettysburg, July 3, 1863. A soldier of Clinton, but born in Lancaster.

Henry H. Rugg, 21; July 12, 1861; shot in shoulder at Ball's Bluff, Va., Oct. 21, 1861; discharged because of wound, May 1, 1862; re-enlisted later in the 53, and 42, M. V. I.

Luther Gerry Turner, 23; July 12, 1861; wounded in right arm at Ball's Bluff, Va., Oct. 21, 1861, and died Nov. 1, 1861, mortification having supervened. Buried in church-yard at Poolesville, Md.

James Gardner Warner, 31; July 12, 1861; killed by bullet, or drowned, at Ball's Bluff, Va., Oct. 21, 1861.

Edwin H. Willard, 23; July 12, 1861; mustered out July 28, 1864.

Company D.

Joseph Copeland, 21; April 29, 1864; July 27, 1864, transferred to 20 M. V. I. A non-resident hired; bounty $325.

Company F.

Warren Ellis, 20; July 12, 1861; wounded at Antietam, Sept. 17, 1862; transferred to U. S. Signal Corps, Oct. 27, 1863. [Mass. Records say *Veteran Reserve Corps*; an error.] Died July 21, 1880, of consumption, at Fitzwilliam, N. H.

George C. Mann, 21; July 12, 1861; taken at Ball's Bluff, Oct. 21, 1861, and in prison at Richmond until February, 1862; wounded in right leg at Gettysburg, July 2, 1863; mustered out July 28, 1864. Died 1887.

Gilbert W. Greene, 18; July 12, 1861; discharged for disability, Jan. 17, 1863. A member of Fay Light Guard in Lancaster, but enlisted for Leominster when that company was disbanded. Re-enlisted in 4 Mass. Cavalry.

George C. Shean. This man was enlisted, according to Lancaster Records, in the Fifteenth Massachusetts, but the name is not found in muster-rolls of that or other regiment.

SIXTEENTH MASSACHUSETTS INFANTRY.

This regiment, under Colonel Powell T. Wyman, left for the front August 17, 1861, and for several months was stationed at Fortress Monroe, Va. It joined the Army of the Potomac June 13, 1862, and participated in the battles of Fair Oaks, Glendale, Malvern Hill, Second Bull Run, Chantilly and Fredericksburg in 1862 ; Chancellorsville, Gettysburg and Locust Grove, 1863 ; Wilderness, Spottsylvania, Cold Harbor and Petersburg, 1864.

Company B.

Albert G. Hunting, 19 ; July 2, 1861 ; killed at Fair Oaks, June 25, 1862. Served for Holliston, as did his brother, J. W. Hunting, the Hunting family having moved from that place to Lancaster a short time before the war.

Joseph W. Hunting, 22 ; July 2, 1861 ; mustered out July 27, 1864. Died not long after.

William Thompson, 18 ; July 2, 1861 ; shot in the face, the ball passing through the head, May 10, 1862, at Spottsylvania Court House, Va., but survived, and was mustered out July 27, 1864. Shot and killed in Connecticut, 1877. Brother of George, 53 M. V. I.

Company C.

George A. Barnes, corporal, 20 ; July 2, 1861 ; shot through the foot in the second battle of Bull Run, Va., and taken prisoner, Aug. 20, 1862 ; discharged because of wound, Oct. 10, 1862

Frank W. Barnes, 18 ; enlisted July, 1862, but not mustered, and enlisted in U. S. Navy, Sept. 15, 1862. Brother of foregoing.

George K. Richards, 39 ; Nov. 25, 1861 ; transferred Aug. 11, 1863, to Veteran Reserve Corps ; re-enlisted veteran.

NINETEENTH MASSACHUSETTS INFANTRY.

This regiment left the state August 28, 1861, commanded by Colonel Edward W. Hinks. It took part in the battles of Ball's Bluff, Fair Oaks, Savage Station, the second Bull Run, Malvern Hill, Antietam, Fredericksburg, Chancellorsville, Gettysburg, Wilderness, and the various battles before Richmond and Petersburg.

Company F.

Asa Whitman Green, 22; Jan. 30, 1862; wounded Dec. 13, 1862, at Fredericksburg, Va., in left leg; transferred Sept. 26, 1863, to Veteran Reserve Corps. Enlisted in Haverhill; native of Lancaster, and brother of the following; died 1885.

Franklin Webster Green, 21; Jan. 25, 1862; wounded June, 1862, in left leg, during the seven days fighting before Richmond; discharged because of wound, Feb. 19, 1863. Credited to Clinton.

TWENTIETH MASSACHUSETTS INFANTRY.

This regiment was led successively by Colonels William R. Lee, Francis W. Palfrey, Paul J. Revere and George N. Macy; and was engaged at Ball's Bluff, Fair Oaks, Savage Station, Glendale, Malvern Hill, Chantilly, Antietam and Fredericksburg, 1861–2; Chancellorsville, Gettysburg, Bristoe Station, 1863; Wilderness, Spottsylvania, Cold Harbor, Petersburg, etc., 1864.

John Louis Moeglen, "36;" Aug. 29, 1861; discharged for disability, April 29, 1862; served later in Co. M, 2 Mass. Cavalry. A Prussian resident of Lancaster, probably over fifty years of age.

Company D.

Thomas E. Burditt, 22; Sept. 4, 1861; mustered out Sept. 14, 1864.

Company E.

Joseph Copeland, 21; April 29, 1864; transferred from Co. D, 15 M. V. I., July 27, 1864, to complete term of enlistment; died a prisoner at Salisbury, N. C., Dec. 21, 1864. Non-resident employed by Lancaster; bounty $325.

Unassigned.

Charles Wilkinson, 30; July 18, 1863; mustered out June, 1865. A boatman, non-resident, hired substitute for George E. P. Dodge.

TWENTY-FIRST MASSACHUSETTS INFANTRY.

This Worcester County regiment left camp August 23, 1861, commanded by Colonel Augustus Morse, and was for four months stationed at Annapolis, Md. Its battle experience was as follows: Roanoke, New Berne, Camden, Second Bull Run, Chantilly, South Mountain, Antietam,

Fredericksburg, during 1862 ; Blue Springs, Tenn., Siege of Knoxville, 1863 ; Wilderness, Spottsylvania, Coal Harbor, Petersburg, etc., in 1864. A history of the regiment by Bvt. Brig.-Gen. Charles F. Walcott was published in 1882. All but twenty-four of the regiment re-enlisted December 29, 1863, and came home on veteran furlough, January 8, 1864. August 19, 1864, the surviving veterans of this organization were transferred to the 36 M. V. I.

Company A.

William H. Robbins, 39 ; Aug. 23, 1861 ; member of band, and discharged by a special order of War Dept., Aug. 11, 1862, mustering out all regimental bands.

Company B.

Dennis Mahar, 21 ; Aug. 23, 1861 ; discharged for disability Jan. 16, 1863. Credited to Clinton.

Company D.

George H. Hardy, corporal, 21 ; Aug. 23, 1861 ; wounded in leg at Roanoke Island, N. C., Feb. 8, 1862, and again in body before Petersburg, June, 1864 ; re-enlisted for Leominster, Jan. 2, 1864, and transferred to 36 and 56 M. V. I. Station agent at Lancaster, when enlisted.

Daniel W. Rugg, 32 ; July 19, 1861 ; discharged for disability Dec. 20, 1862. Lancaster born and bred, but resided in Fitchburg when enlisted. Died 1876. Brother of James, 53 M. V. I.

Company E.

William W. Bigelow enlisted, but was rejected by surgeons ; he afterwards enlisted for West Boylston in 25 M. V. I.

James E. Burke, 26 ; Aug. 23, 1861 ; killed at Chantilly, Sept. 1, 1862.

Edwin F. Field, 29 ; Aug. 23, 1861 ; sergeant ; promoted to second-lieutenant Dec. 18, 1862 ; resigned May 8, 1863.

William L. Fox, 19 ; Aug. 23, 1861 ; corporal ; wounded in arm at Chantilly, Sept. 1, 1862 ; promoted to sergeant ; re-enlisted Jan. 2, 1864 ; discharged as supernumerary sergeant, Sept. 24, 1864.

Charles E. McQuillan, corporal, 20 ; Aug. 23, 1861 ; wounded at Antietam, Sept. 17, 1862 ; transferred to 2 U. S. Cavalry, Co. K, Oct. 30, 1862 ; re-enlisted veteran. Also in Hancock's U. S. Vet. Vols., Dec. 9, 1864, to Dec. 9, 1865. Found in Mass. Records as *Maquillon*, *Macquillen* and *Magwilliam!*

Luke Ollis, 19 ; Aug. 23, 1861 ; transferred to 2 U. S. Cavalry, Co. K, Oct. 23, 1862. Re-enlisted.

Frank E. Pierce, 20 ; Aug. 23, 1861 ; transferred to 2 U. S. Cavalry, Co. K, Oct. 23, 1862. Brother of W. D. Pierce, 5 M. V. I.

21

Ebenezer Waters Richards, 35; Aug. 23, 1861; killed at Fredericksburg, Va., Dec. 13, 1862, by a shell.

Oliver B. Sawyer, 21; Aug. 23, 1861; discharged for disability resulting from small-pox, June 30, 1862. Served again as sergeant, Co. B, 40 M. V. I.

Charles H. Sinclair, 21; Aug. 23, 1861; shot in head and killed, at New Berne, N. C., March 14, 1862. Of Leominster, resident in Lancaster when enlisted.

Woodbury Whittemore, 33; Aug. 21, 1861; second-lieutenant; promoted first-lieutenant, March 3, 1862; captain, July 27, 1862; resigned October 29, 1862. When enlisted, was foreman of the shoe manufactory in Lancaster.

Twenty-third Massachusetts Infantry.

Colonel John Kurtz commanded this regiment when it left the state, November 11, 1861. After remaining encamped for two months at Annapolis, Md., it was attached to the Burnside Expedition, and took part in battles of Roanoke, New Berne and Rawle's Mills, 1862; Kinston, Goldsboro, Wilcox's Bridge and Winton, 1863; Drewry's Bluff, Cold Harbor, etc., 1864.

Company H.

Sewell T. Lawrence, 31; Oct. 5, 1861; discharged for disability, Aug. 11, 1862.

Caleb Wood Sweet, 23; Sept. 28, 1861; re-enlisted Dec. 3, 1863; wounded and taken prisoner at Drewry's Bluff, Va., May 16, 1864. His wound was in the flesh of left arm, but gangrene supervened, and he died at Richmond, Aug. 3, 1864.

Twenty-fourth Massachusetts Infantry.

The six Lancaster men in Company G of this regiment were transferred to it from Company H of the Thirty-fourth, June 14, 1865, to complete their terms of enlistment, after the latter organization had been mustered out at the end of three years' service.

Charles E. Blood; mustered out Jan. 20, 1866.

Joseph N. Day; transferred to Veteran Reserve Corps, May 2, 1865.

David W. Matthews.

George W. Matthews; discharged for disability, June 1, 1865.

Patrick Sheary; mustered out Jan. 20, 1866, with the regiment, at Richmond, Va. [*Shary* and *Sherry* in Mass. Records.]

George E. Wiley; discharged because of wound, June 26, 1865.

TWENTY-FIFTH MASSACHUSETTS INFANTRY.

Colonel Edwin Upton of Fitchburg led this regiment from the state. October 31, 1861. It formed a part of the Burnside Expedition to North Carolina, and participated in the battles of that campaign, 1862 and 1863. In 1864, being re-enlisted as a veteran regiment, it was engaged at Arrowfield Church, Drewry's Bluff and Cold Harbor. See "Wearing the Blue in the 25th Mass. Volunteer Infantry," by J. Waldo Denny.

Company C.

Jonas H. Beard, 25; Sept. 28, 1861; re-enlisted Dec. 18, 1863; wounded in hip, June 3, 1864, at Cold Harbor, Va.; mustered out, July 13, 1865. [*James* H. Beard in Mass. Records and History of regiment.]

Company D.

William W. Bigelow, 21; Sept. 27, 1861; enlisted for West Boylston; taken prisoner; discharged for disability, March 18, 1863.

TWENTY-SIXTH MASSACHUSETTS INFANTRY.

At the date of muster of the two Lancaster recruits for this regiment, it was with General Sheridan in the Shenandoah Valley. Each received $325 bounty.

Company E.

Charles Puffer, 41; Aug. 9, 1864; mustered out Aug. 26, 1865.

Unassigned.

Charles L. Souveur, 21; May 7, 1864. A non-resident hired. [*Le Souvenir* in quota list.] No further record found.

TWENTY-EIGHTH MASSACHUSETTS INFANTRY.

A large proportion of this regiment were Irishmen by birth. It was in the battles of Second Bull Run, Chantilly, South Mountain, Antietam and Fredericksburg, 1862; Chancellorsville, Gettysburg, 1863; Wilderness, Spottsylvania, Cold Harbor, Petersburg, etc., 1864. Colonels: William Montieth, Richard Byrnes and Richard W. Cartwright. The Lancaster men in this regiment, except the brothers True, were non-resident substitutes.

Company A.

William Atchinson, 22 ; Aug. 10, 1863 ; mustered out June 30, 1865. A boiler-maker, hired substitute for Charles L. Wilder, Jr.

George H. True, 21 ; Oct. 8, 1861 ; member of band; discharged by special order of War Dept., Aug. 17, 1862. Died in Ohio, Aug. 30, 1863.

James G. True, 25 ; Oct. 8, 1861 ; member of band; discharged by special order of War Dept., Aug. 17, 1862. Died in California, Nov. 27, 1863, of consumption contracted in service.

Company D.

John Smith, 23 ; May 7, 1864 ; mustered out, June 15, 1865 ; bounty $325.

Unassigned.

Michael O'Brien, 23 ; May 7, 1864 ; bounty $325. No further record.

William Smith, 25 ; May 7, 1864 ; bounty $325. No further record.

TWENTY-NINTH MASSACHUSETTS INFANTRY.

Two non-resident substitutes, recruits to the Thirty-fifth M. V. I., were transferred to this regiment, June 9, 1865, to complete the unexpired terms of their enlistments.

Edward Pierce. Dropped as a deserter.
John Krum. Deserted June 6, 1865.

THIRTIETH MASSACHUSETTS INFANTRY.

In this regiment, John Edwin Dudley, credited to Boston, was a native of Lancaster. He had previously served as sergeant in the First California Vols. He was commissioned second-lieutenant, December 7, 1864; first-lieutenant, December 8, 1864 ; captain, April 21, 1865 ; mustered out July 5, 1866. His brother, Nathan A. M. Dudley, colonel of this regiment, and brevet brigadier-general, though not born in Lancaster, lived here in boyhood.

THIRTY-SECOND MASSACHUSETTS INFANTRY.

Company D.

William F. Murphy, 22 ; Sept. 7, 1863 ; transferred May 3, 1864, to U. S. Navy. A non-resident, substitute for Elbridge W. Hosmer.

THIRTY-THIRD MASSACHUSETTS INFANTRY.

Colonel Adin B. Underwood, who succeeded Colonel Albert C. Maggi in the command of this regiment, published in 1881, "The Three Years Service of the Thirty-third Mass. Infantry Regiment." It went to the front Aug. 14, 1862, and was engaged at Fredericksburg, Chancellorsville and Gettysburg while in the Army of the Potomac ; and at Lookout Mountain, Missionary Ridge, Resaca, Cassville, Dallas, Kenesaw, Atlanta, etc., after joining the western army under General William T. Sherman.

Company E.

Roswell Atherton, 30 ; Aug. 5, 1862 ; discharged for disability, Nov. 30, 1862. Born and bred in Lancaster, enlisted in Groton.

John Dupee, 36 ; July 2, 1864 ; transferred to 2 M. V. I., June 1, 1865, to complete term of service. A hired substitute ; bounty $325.

Henry Jackson Parker, 27 ; Aug. 5, 1862 ; first-sergeant ; sergeant-major Feb. 18, 1863 ; second-lieutenant, March 29, 1863 ; first-lieutenant, July 16, 1863 ; killed at Resaca, Ga., May 15, 1864, while commanding skirmish line. He served in the "old Sixth" three months. Resident of Townsend, but born and bred in Lancaster.

THIRTY-FOURTH MASSACHUSETTS INFANTRY.

This regiment left the state August 15, 1862, commanded by Colonel George D. Wells. Its second in command, Colonel William S. Lincoln, in 1879 published a history of the regiment. It participated in the Shenandoah Valley campaign of 1864, being in the battles of Newmarket, Piedmont, Lynchburg, Snicker's Gap, Martinsburg, Halltown, Berryville, Winchester, Fisher's Hill and Cedar Creek. In March. 1865, it was joined to the Army of the James, and fought at Hatcher's Run, and in the capture of Battery Gregg.

Henry Bowman, before named in 15 M. V. I., was commissioned major of this regiment, Aug. 6, 1862, but did not join it, being promoted to colonelcy of 36 M. V. I.

Company A.

Charles B. Flagg, corporal, 23 ; June 23, 1862 ; mustered out June 16, 1865. Brother of Albert, 53 M. V. I.

John Patrick Wise, 21; July 31, 1862; died at home of consumption, March 15, 1864; [*March* 16 in Mass. Records, by error.] Company clerk.

Company C.

Oren Hodgman, 19; July 31, 1862; taken prisoner May 15, 1864, at New-market, Va., and died at Charleston, S. C., September 30, 1864. Credited to Sterling.

Henry W. Willard, 21; Aug. 2, 1862; discharged for disability Feb. 26, 1863. Credited to Leominster.

Company F.

Edward M. Fuller. corporal, 20; Aug. 9, 1862; appointed captain in 39 U. S. Colored Troops, by S. O. 123, March 21, 1864. Credited to Clinton.

Horatio Elisha Turner, 18; Aug. 2, 1862; died a prisoner at Anderson-ville, Ga., Sept. 8, 1864. (Cenotaph in middle cemetery has *Sept.* 5, by error.) Credited to Clinton.

Company H.

Charles E. Blood, 21; Dec. 19, 1863; bounty $325; taken prisoner at Cedar Creek, Oct. 13, 1864, but escaped at night; transferred June 14, 1865, to Co. A, 24 M. V. I.

James Andrew Bridge, 18; Dec. 19, 1863; bounty $325; shot in forehead at Newmarket, Va., May 15, 1864, and died of wound.

Jonas H. Brown, 41; July 31, 1862; mustered out June 16, 1865.

Levi B. Burbank, 43; July 31, 1862; discharged for disability, Feb. 27, 1864.

Solon Whiting Chaplin, corporal, 38; July 31, 1862; killed at Piedmont, Va., June 5, 1864.

William L. Cobb, 22; July 18, 1862; second-lieutenant; first-lieutenant, Aug. 23, 1862; commissioned captain Feb. 18, 1865, but mustered out May 15, 1865, as first-lieutenant; wounded severely in forehead at Ripon, Oct. 18, 1863; Oct. 12, 1864, captured in Shenandoah Valley, he having voluntarily remained to aid Colonel George D. Wells, mortally wounded; in Libby and Danville prisons five months. Died May 17, 1879, at Hot Springs, Arkansas, of brain fever, resulting from his wound.

George B. Coburn, 18; July 31, 1862; shot himself through foot before Petersburg, and discharged for disability, May 16, 1865. Brother of Cyrus E., 5 M. V. I.

James Dailey, 18; July 31, 1862; mustered out June 16, 1865.

Daniel M. Damon, 25; July 31, 1862; first-sergeant; commissioned second-lieutenant, May 15, 1865, but mustered out as first-sergeant, June 16, 1865; taken prisoner at Winchester, Sept. 19, 1864.

Joseph N. Day, 22; Jan. 4, 1864; bounty $325; shot in the head Sept. 19, 1864, at Winchester; transferred to 24 M. V. I., June 14, 1865, and to Veteran Reserve Corps, May 2, 1865; discharged July 25, 1865.

James Dillon, 26; July 31, 1862; injured in back hurling shot in camp, and discharged for disability, April 7, 1863; died at home, of consumption, May 10, 1863.

Francis Henry Fairbanks, 26; July 31, 1862; died a prisoner at Salisbury, N. C., Jan. 4, 1865, having been captured at Cedar Creek, Oct. 13, 1864. [Jan. 5, in Mass. Records.] Served before in 15 M. V. I.

George W. Farnsworth, 18; Jan. 4, 1864; bounty $325; wounded in face at Piedmont, June 5, 1864; discharged for disability, June 8, 1865. Brother of John E. Farnsworth.

John A. Farnsworth, corporal, 18; July 31, 1862; wounded in arm at Piedmont, Va., June 5, 1864; discharged for disability, May 18, 1865.

John E. Farnsworth, corporal, 18; July 31, 1862; wounded in leg at Newmarket, Va., May 15, 1864; wounded in arm at Winchester, Sept 19, 1864; also slightly wounded in hip; mustered out June 16, 1865.

Michael Fury, 26; July 31, 1862; severely wounded in leg at Piedmont, Va., June 5, 1864; mustered out Aug. 5, 1865; died March 3, 1888.

Stephen Wesley Gray, 30; July 31, 1862; died of fever at Martinsburg, Va., April 2, 1864. Brother of James, 15 M. V. I.

Thomas A. G. Hunting, 45; July 31, 1862; shot through the body and taken prisoner at Piedmont, Va., June 5, 1864; discharged for disability, May 23, 1865. He had two sons in the 16 M. V. I.

David W. Matthews, 20; Sept. 19, 1863; bounty $50; transferred June 14, 1865, to 24 M. V. I. Brother of next.

George W. Matthews, 18; Sept. 19, 1863; bounty $50; wounded in leg at Newmarket, Va., May 15, 1864; taken prisoner at Liberty, West Virginia, June 19, 1864, and starved nearly to death in Andersonville prison, Georgia; discharged for disability, June 1, 1865, and died of consumption in Lancaster, Nov. 24, 1876.

William H. Mellor, 18; July 31, 1862; transferred to Veteran Reserve Corps, Jan. 19, 1865. [*Miller* in Mass. Records.]

Patrick Sheary, 28; Jan. 5, 1864; bounty $325; transferred to 24 M. V. I., June 14, 1865.

Charles E. Tisdale, 20; July 31, 1862; corporal; discharged for disability, Jan. 8, 1863.

George E. Wiley, 22; Jan. 1, 1864; bounty $325; wounded in arm at Fisher's Hill, Va., Sept. 22, 1864; transferred to 24 M. V. I., June 14, 1865, and discharged for disability, June 26, 1865.

THIRTY-FIFTH MASSACHUSETTS INFANTRY.

Two non-resident substitutes, hired for the town, were recruits for this regiment, received $325 bounty, and upon muster out of the organization after its three years' service had expired, were transferred to the 29th M. V. I., to complete their term of enlistment. Both deserted. Major Sidney Willard, who was shot through the body, being in command of the regiment, at Fredericksburg, Va., December 13, 1862, and died the next day, was the son of Joseph Willard, Esq., historian of Lancaster, and born in this town, A. D. 1831.

Company B.

Edward Pierce, 21 ; June 29, 1864.

Company K.

John Krum, 24; June 29, 1864.

Thirty-sixth Massachusetts Infantry.

Lieut.-Col. John W. Kimball of the 15th M. V. I., was to have received the command of this regiment. The War Department not consenting to his discharge, Henry Bowman was commissioned its colonel, he being then major of the 34th M. V. I. The regiment left the state September 2, 1862. It participated in the battles of Fredericksburg, 1862 ; Jackson, Miss., Blue Springs, Campbell's Station, Siege of Knoxville, Tenn., 1863 ; Wilderness, Spottsylvania, Cold Harbor, Petersburg, Hatcher's Run, etc., 1864–5. A history of the regiment was published in 1884.

Henry Bowman, 28; Aug. 22, 1862, colonel; resigned July 27, 1863; recommissioned in October, 1863, and chief of staff of General Wilcox at Cumberland Gap, Tenn., Nov. 21 to Dec. 25, 1863; rejoined the regiment Dec. 26, 1863, but unable to be mustered in as colonel, the regiment being below the minimum; appointed captain and assistant quartermaster of volunteers, Feb. 29, 1864, and on duty with Third Division, Ninth Army Corps; mustered out as brevet major, Aug. 15, 1866. Bowman commanded the Third Brigade of First Division, Ninth Army Corps, June and July, 1863. Brother of Lieutenant Samuel Mirick Bowman of 51 M. V. I.

Company G.

John Chickering Haynes, 29; Jan. 2, 1864; bounty $325; died of disease at Camp Nelson, Kentucky, March 19, 1864.

George Henry Patrick, 21 ; Oct. 14, 1864; bounty $202.66; transferred to 56 M. V. I., June 8, 1865. Credited to Worcester; served for Lancaster in 53 M. V. I.

Company I.

George H. Hardy, 23; Jan. 2, 1864; re-enlisted veteran in 21 M. V. I., from which he was transferred to 36 M. V. I., Aug. 30, 1864; transferred to 56 M. V. I., June 8, 1865. Credited to Leominster.

Unassigned.

Charles F. Burditt, 43; Dec. 26. 1863; rejected by surgeon, Jan. 2, 1864. A veteran soldier of the Seminole War.

Leonard H. Parker, 21; Dec. 29, 1863; bounty $325; mustered out June 8, 1865. Brother of Lieut. Henry J. Parker.

FORTIETH MASSACHUSETTS INFANTRY.

Company B.

Oliver B. Sawyer, sergeant, 22; Aug. 22, 1862; mustered out June 16, 1865. Credited to Stow. Served before for Lancaster in Co. E, 21 M. V. I.

FORTY-SECOND MASSACHUSETTS INFANTRY. 100 Days.

A history of this regiment was published in 1886.

Company E.

Henry H. Rugg, 24; July 22, 1864; bounty $73.33; mustered out Nov. 11, 1864. Served before in 15 and 53 M. V. I.

Company K.

Horace Worcester, 20; July 18, 1864; bounty $75 99; mustered out Nov. 11, 1864. Credited to Boston. Bred and died in Lancaster. Died of consumption engendered in service, May 22, 1866.

FORTY-FIFTH MASSACHUSETTS INFANTRY. 9 Months.

Company F.

Henry Maynard Putney, 20; Sept. 26, 1862; shot through the head at Dover Cross Roads, N. C., April 28, 1863. Credited to Framingham.

FORTY-SEVENTH MASSACHUSETTS INFANTRY. 9 Months.

Company K.

George D. Weld, 44; Oct. 31, 1862; mustered out Sept. 1, 1863. Killed in Lancaster, Dec. 1, 1865, being run over by his own team.

FIFTY-FIRST MASSACHUSETTS INFANTRY. 9 Months.

This regiment, commanded by Colonel A. B. R. Sprague, left the state November 25, 1862, by transport from Boston, and served in North Carolina.

Company A.

Samuel Mirick Bowman, sergeant, 25; Sept. 25, 1862; mustered out July 27, 1863. Credited to Clinton; born and bred in Lancaster. Served later in 57 M. V. I. Brother of Col. Henry Bowman, 36 M. V. I.

Company C.

Frank E. Nourse, 21; Sept. 25, 1862; mustered out July 27, 1863. Brother of Fred F., 5 M. V. I.

Edwin A. Otis, corporal, 19; Sept. 25, 1862; mustered out July 27, 1863.

Company E.

Simon M. Plaisted, 24; Sept. 25, 1862; mustered out July 27, 1863. Credited to Worcester. Served later in Co. F, First Battalion, Heavy Artillery.

FIFTY-THIRD MASSACHUSETTS INFANTRY. 9 Months.

This regiment was commanded by Colonel John W. Kimball of Fitchburg, and left Camp Stevens, near Groton, November 29, 1863. It was transported by steamer from New York to New Orleans, and was engaged in various severe marches and skirmishes in Louisiana. Its most important record was made during the siege of Port Hudson. In the assault upon that stronghold, June 14, 1863, it won much credit and experienced heavy loss. Each soldier of Lancaster in this regiment received a bounty of one hundred dollars from the town. The date of enlistment of the Lancaster men was September 2, 1862, in nearly every case.

Company C.

Thomas Augustus Hills, 21; Nov. 6, 1862; mustered out Sept. 2, 1863. Credited to Leominster; clerk in Lancaster. Served later in 5 M. V. I., 100 days.

Adelbert W. Johnson, 24; Nov. 6, 1862; wounded in knee at Port Hudson, La., July 11, 1863, and died at Baton Rouge about three weeks later. Credited to Leominster. Had served Lancaster in 15 M. V. I.

George Thompson, 21; Nov. 6, 1862; died of disease at Brashear City, La., May 30, 1863. Credited to Leominster, but Lancaster born and bred. Brother of William, 16 M. V. I.

Company I.

John G. Albee, 18; Oct. 18, 1862; taken prisoner at Thibodeaux, La., and held in rebel prison for a month; mustered out Sept. 2, 1863.

John Curtis Ayers, 25; sergeant, Oct. 18, 1862; appointed second-lieutenant May 22, 1863; first-lieutenant July 2, 1863; mustered out Sept 2, 1863.

Walter Andrew Brooks, 25; corporal, Oct. 18, 1862; died of disease in hospital at Memphis, Tenn., Aug. 22, 1863.

George Edwin Chafee, 35; Oct. 18, 1862; taken prisoner at Brashear City, La., June 20, 1863, and paroled; mustered out Sept. 2, 1863.

Frank W. Chandler, 18; Oct. 18, 1862; mustered out Sept. 2, 1863.

Henry Albert Cutler, 18; Oct. 18, 1862; died of chronic diarrhœa, July 9, 1863, at Baton Rouge, La.

William H. Fisher, 18; Oct. 18, 1862; mustered out Sept. 2, 1863.

Oscar Frary, 30; Oct. 18, 1862; died of chronic diarrhœa and homesickness at Baton Rouge, La., July 28, 1863. [Mass. Records say *June* 28.] Company cook.

Harris C. Harriman, 33; Oct. 18, 1862; wounded in assault at Port Hudson, La., June 14, 1863, a piece of shell passing through calf of leg; mustered out Sept. 2, 1863; died Feb. 4, 1888, in Chicago.

David W. Jackson, 33; Oct. 18, 1862; mustered out Sept. 2, 1863.

John James, 21; Oct. 18, 1862; mustered out Sept. 2, 1863; killed May 25, 1884.

Joseph B. Moore, 38; Oct. 18, 1862; wounded in head May 27, 1863, at Port Hudson, La.; mustered out Sept. 2, 1863.

Byron H. Nourse, 24; sergeant, Oct. 18, 1862; promoted to first-sergeant Jan. 22, 1863; mustered out Sept. 2, 1863.

Roscoe H. Nourse, 22; drummer, Oct. 18, 1862; mustered out Sept. 2, 1863. Served again in 5 M. V. I. Brother of Byron H.

George Henry Patrick, 19; Oct. 18, 1862; mustered out Sept. 2, 1863. Served again in 36 and 56 M. V. I.

Walter C. Rice, 45; Oct. 18, 1862; mustered out Sept. 2, 1863. Served chiefly as company cook and hospital attendant; died in Lancaster, July 30, 1867.

Edwin Sawtell, 24; Oct. 18, 1862; mustered out Sept. 2, 1863.

Walter S. H. Turner, 18; Oct. 18, 1862; mustered out Sept. 2, 1863.

Edward Richmond Washburn, 26; first-lieutenant Oct. 18, 1862; promoted captain Nov. 8, 1862. In the assault upon Port Hudson, La., June 14, 1863, his left thigh was shattered by musket ball and buck shot. Of this wound, after apparent recovery, he died at Lancaster, Sept. 5, 1864. Brother of Colonel Francis Washburn, 4 Mass. Cavalry.

Edmund C. Whitney, 26; corporal, Oct. 18, 1862; clerk in quartermaster and commissary departments Dec. 16 to Jan. 20, 1863; promoted sergeant July 14, 1863; wounded in right arm at Port Hudson, July 14, 1863; mustered out Sept. 2, 1863.

Charles H. Wilder, 42; Oct. 18, 1862; mustered out Sept. 2, 1863. Died Nov. 30 1885, in Lancaster.

Company K.

Albert Flagg, 18; Oct. 17, 1862; mustered out Sept. 2, 1863. Resident of Lancaster, but enlisted for Sterling.

Stephen Adams Keyes, 18; Oct. 17, 1862; died on transport while on the way homeward, and buried at sea, off Florida coast, Aug. 10, 1863. Brother of Sumner W., 5 M. V. I.

Henry H. Rugg, 22; corporal, Oct. 17, 1862; mustered out Sept. 2, 1863. Rugg had served before in 15 M.V. I., and enlisted later in 42 M.V.I.

James Rugg, 42; Oct. 17, 1862; mustered out Sept. 2, 1863. Brother of Daniel W., 21 M. V. I.

FIFTY-SIXTH MASSACHUSETTS INFANTRY.

Company G.

George H. Hardy was transferred June 8, 1865, from 36 M. V. I.; mustered out July 12, 1865. Credited to Leominster.

George Henry Patrick; transferred from 36 M. V. I.; mustered out Aug. 7, 1865. Credited to Worcester.

FIFTY-SEVENTH MASSACHUSETTS INFANTRY.

This regiment, under Colonel William F. Bartlett, left the state April 18, 1864. It was engaged in the battles of the Wilderness, Spottsylvania, Cold Harbor, Petersburg, Hatcher's Run, etc.

Company C.

Samuel Mirick Bowman, 26; first-lieutenant, Dec. 26, 1863; terribly wounded in body and limbs by fragments of a shell, when in his tent before Petersburg, Va., July 24, 1864, and died two days after. He had before served in 51 M. V. I. Credited to Worcester. His name is inscribed upon the memorial tablets of Lancaster, Clinton and Worcester.

Frank B. Leroy, 18; Feb. 18, 1864; bounty $325; mustered out June 22, 1865. A non-resident hired for the town.

Edwin Sykes, 29; Feb. 18, 1864; deserted July 1, 1864. A non-resident hired for the town; bounty $325.

FIRST MASSACHUSETTS CAVALRY.

Francis Washburn, 24; second-lieutenant, Dec. 26, 1861; promoted to first-lieutenant March 7, 1862; transferred to 2 Mass. Cavalry as captain, Jan. 26, 1863. Brother of Capt. Edward, 53 M. V. I.

Company G.

Charles A. Robinson, 21; Oct. 5, 1861; discharged for disability Feb. 6, 1863. Native of Lancaster, enlisted for Lowell.

Second Massachusetts Cavalry.

This regiment, commanded by Colonel Charles R. Lowell, Jr., left the state May 11, 1863, and was in the Department of Washington during that year. During 1864 it was chiefly in the Army of the Shenandoah, and conspicuous in numerous engagements.

Francis Washburn, 25; captain, Jan. 26, 1863; promoted lieutenant-colonel 4 Mass. Cavalry, Feb. 4, 1864.

Company H.

John Coyle, 22; May 7, 1864; deserted Feb. 15, 1865. Non-resident hired; bounty $325. [*Coye* in Mass. Records.

William Ross, 27; May 7, 1864; deserted May 12, 1864. Non-resident hired; bounty $325.

Company L.

John Goodwin, 18; Sept. 13, 1864; deserted Dec. 1, 1864. Non-resident hired; bounty $50.

Company M.

John Louis Moeglen, 43; Feb. 2, 1864; died Sept. 28, 1864, of bullet wound received in Shenandoah Valley campaign. A Prussian, resident of Lancaster, who had served before in 20 M. V. I. Credited to Boston in Mass. Records; bounty $325.

Unassigned.

John Bell, 25; May 7, 1864; bounty $325; non-resident hired. No further record.

James Langley, 22; May 7, 1864; bounty $325; non-resident hired. No further record.

John Monyer, 35; Dec. 27, 1864; bounty $325; non-resident hired. No further record. [*Mongen* in Mass. Records.]

Third Massachusetts Cavalry.

Company A.

William S. McKay, 24; sergeant, April 8, 1864; bounty $325; promoted sergeant-major July 26, 1865: mustered out Sept. 28, 1865. Non-resident substitute.

Unassigned.

Albert Bergmann, 26; July 2, 1864; bounty $325; a hired substitute, of Jersey City.

FOURTH MASSACHUSETTS CAVALRY.

This regiment was organized by consolidation of the Third Battalion of the First Massachusetts Cavalry with two battalions of veterans recruited in the spring of 1864. Colonel A. A. Rand was its first commander. The Second Battalion served with the Army of the South; the First and Third participated in the military operations before Richmond, and the guidons of Companies E and H were the first Union colors raised upon the capital of that city, April 3, 1865. The desperate charges of Companies I, L and M, at High Bridge, Va., led by Colonel Francis Washburn, delaying the advance guard of Lee's retreating army, essentially hastened the final collapse of the Confederacy.

Francis Washburn, 25; lieutenant-colonel, Feb. 1, 1864; colonel, Feb. 4, 1865; wounded at High Bridge, Va., April 6, 1865, while leading a charge against a vastly superior force. Being engaged in a hand-to-hand encounter with a Confederate officer, he received a pistol shot in the face from another, and fell stunned from his horse. Lying on the ground, he was fatally wounded by a sabre stroke upon his skull, inflicted by a ruffian to whom, while engaged in despoiling his person, he made some motion of remonstrance. He died at Worcester, Mass., April 22, 1865. Brevet brigadier-general vols., April 6, 1865. [*See Appendix.*]

Company C.

Henry F. Ball, 24; Dec. 31, 1863; promoted hospital steward September, 1864; discharged Nov. 14, 1865. Credited to Clinton.

Company E.

William Schumaker, 21; corporal, Jan. 27, 1864; bounty $325; died a prisoner at Andersonville, Ga., Sept. 13, 1864. Credited to Southbridge.

Company F.

John Veret, 28; Jan. 5, 1864; bounty $325; mustered out Nov. 14, 1865. Enlisted as a farrier.

SEVENTH BATTERY MASSACHUSETTS LIGHT ARTILLERY.

Shortly after the Lancaster recruits joined this battery, it proceeded by steamer from Baltimore to the Department

of the Gulf, and was engaged in the siege operations at
Mobile.

George Walton Divoll, 37; Jan. 5, 1864; bounty $325; died at New Or-
leans, La., of disease, Sept. 21, 1864. Credited to Leominster.

Henry S. Priest, 25; Jan. 4, 1864; rejected recruit Jan. 9, 1864.

J. Prescott Wilder, 31; Jan. 4, 1864; bounty $325; mustered out June
8, 1865.

Eleventh Battery Massachusetts Light Artillery.

This battery left the state February 5, 1864, and was in
the engagements of the Wilderness, Spottsylvania, Cold
Harbor, Petersburg, etc. The three Lancaster recruits
were non-residents.

Thomas Fox, 18; Dec. 23, 1864; bounty $325; mustered out June 18, 1865.

John Toole, 18;   "   "   "   "

Joseph Valdez, 30;   "   "   "   "

Thirteenth Battery Massachusetts Infantry.

This battery served in the Department of the Gulf. Its
two recruits credited to Lancaster were non-residents.

George W. Davis, 23; April 6, 1864; bounty $325; mustered out July 28,
1865.

William Smith, 22; April 6, 1864; bounty $325; mustered out July 28,
1865.

First Battalion Massachusetts Heavy Artillery.

Company F.

Simon M. Plaisted, 25; Aug. 15, 1864; bounty $209.32; mustered out
June 28, 1865; served also in 51 M. V. I., nine months. Credited to
Grafton.

First Massachusetts Heavy Artillery.

This regiment, originally the Fourteenth Infantry, re-
enlisted in December, 1863, and was for six months in the
fortifications of Washington. Thence it marched to the
front, and as infantry fought in the several engagements
that ended in the fall of Richmond.

Company G.

John Ollis, corporal, 18; Dec. 3, 1863; bounty $325; wounded in foot by shell, at Petersburg, Va., June 22, 1864; mustered out as supernumerary July 31, 1865. Credited to Boston. Brother of Luke, 2 U. S. Cavalry.

SECOND MASSACHUSETTS HEAVY ARTILLERY.

This regiment was stationed in North Carolina during its full term of service. Companies B, C, F, I and M, under command of Lieutenant-Colonel A. B. R. Sprague, took part in the battle of Kinston, N. C.

Company A.

Frank Miller, 27; July 2, 1864; bounty 325; died May 12, 1865, at New Berne, N. C. Non-resident hired.

Louis Neu, 22; July 2, 1864; bounty $325; died Nov. 22, 1864, at Plymouth, N. C. Non-resident hired.

Company M.

Sanford B. Wilder, 24; Dec. 24, 1863; bounty $325; mustered out Sept. 3, 1865. Had enlisted before in 53 M. V. I., but illness prevented service with that regiment.

Unassigned.

John Kern, 22; July 2, 1864; bounty $325. No further records. Non-resident substitute. [*Jean Kern* in Mass. Records.]

THIRD MASSACHUSETTS HEAVY ARTILLERY.

Company L.

William McCarron, 23; May 30, 1864; bounty $325; discharged for disability Sept. 30, 1864. Non-resident.

VETERAN VOLUNTEER RESERVE CORPS.

Charles H. Balcom, 33; transferred from 15 M. V. I., Co. C, April 15, 1864; re-enlisted May 14, 1864, and credited to Randolph; mustered out Nov. 14, 1865.

Joseph N. Day, 22; transferred from 34 M. V. I., Co. H, and 24 M. V. I., Co. G, May 2, 1865; mustered out July 25, 1865.

Asa Whitman Green, 22; transferred from 19 M. V. I., Co. F, Sept. 26, 1863.

Solomon Kittredge, 42; transferred from 15 M. V. I., Co. C, May 1, 1862; re-enlisted veteran July 1, 1864; mustered out Nov. 14, 1865.

William H. Mellor, 18; transferred from 34 M. V. I., Co. H, Jan. 19, 1865.

Oliver W. Moore, 20; transferred from 15 M. V. I., Co. C, Sept. 8, 1863 re-enlisted for Lancaster, July 21, 1864; mustered out Nov. 17, 1865 Served the first three years for Lowell.

George K. Richards, 39; transferred from 16 M. V. I., Co. C, Aug. 11 1863; re-enlisted for Provincetown, Nov. 30, 1864; mustered out Nov. 14, 1865. Died March 17, 1879.

U. S. Veteran Volunteers, Hancock's Corps.

Charles E. McQuillan, 23; Dec. 9, 1864; bounty $240; mustered out Dec. 9, 1865. Served before in 21 M. V. I. and 2 U. S. Cavalry.

U. S. Colored Troops, Thirty-ninth Regiment.

Edward M. Fuller, 21; appointed captain by S. O. 123, transferred from 34 M. V. I., Co. F; wounded in head at Petersburg, Va., July 30, 1864; major U. S. C. T., June 1, 1865; mustered out December, 1865.

U. S. Signal Corps.

Henry H. Elden, 23; Dec. 2, 1864; bounty $325. A non-resident hired. [*Elder* in Mass. Records.]

Warren Ellis, 20; transferred from 15 M. V. I., Co. F, Oct. 27, 1863.

Second U. S. Cavalry.

Company K.

Charles E. McQuillan, 20; enlisted from 21 M. V. I., Co. E, Oct. 30, 1862. Served later in U. S. Veteran Vols., Hancock's Corps.

Luke Ollis, 19; enlisted from 21 M. V. I., Co. E, Oct. 23, 1862; re-enlisted veteran Feb. 29, 1864; wounded in arm when in pursuit of Early in the Shenandoah Valley, and died of wound Oct. 13, 1864.

Frank E. Pierce, 22; enlisted from 21 M. V. I., Co. E, Oct. 23, 1862; re-enlisted Feb. 29, 1864.

First U. S. Artillery.

Company I.

Fordyce Horan, 20; enlisted from 15 M. V. I., Co. A, Nov. 17, 1862; died insane, in hospital at Washington, Nov. 3, 1864.

Henry H. Hosley, 19; enlisted from 15 M. V. I., Co. C, Nov. 12, 1862; mustered out July 12, 1864.

22

U. S. Navy.

Frank W. Barnes, 18; Sept. 15, 1862; enlisted on receiving ship Ohio, at Charlestown; Oct. 1, 1862, transferred to supply steamer Rhode Island; January, 1863, on blockading frigate Minnesota; discharged Sept. 15, 1863.

John Gould; October, 1862, was on supply steamer Rhode Island. No other record found.

Ephraim Mackrell, 18; Aug. 26, 1863, enlisted at Charlestown; served one year, chiefly on the gunboat Nipsic, in blockading Charleston. Brother of following.

William J. Mackrell, 21; Aug. 12, 1862, enlisted at Charlestown; wounded by concussion of shell, causing contusion of thigh, Feb. 1, 1863, at Stono Inlet, S. C., and captured; paroled March 1, and sent north.

William F. Murphy, 22; May 3, 1864, transferred from 32 M. V. I. Non-resident substitute for Elbridge W. Hosmer.

Twentieth Connecticut Infantry.
Company F.

David Wilder Jones, 46; Aug. 11, 1862; enlisted at Newtown, Ct.; wounded at Chancellorsville, May 3, 1863, and died the same day. Native and long resident of Lancaster.

First Connecticut Heavy Artillery.
Company F.

James Homer Newman, 27; May 23, 1861; enlisted at New Haven; re-enlisted veteran, Dec. 10, 1863; mustered out Sept. 25, 1865. Born and bred in Lancaster.

Eleventh Rhode Island Infantry. 9 Months.
Company D.

Charles T. Wiley; enlisted at Providence, Oct. 1, 1862; mustered out July 13, 1863. Resident of Lancaster.

Company G.

James T. Fletcher; enlisted at Providence, Oct. 1, 1862; mustered out July 13, 1863. Born and bred in Lancaster. Dead.

First New Hampshire Infantry. 3 Months, etc.

Charles Timothy Fairbanks, 23; May 2, 1861, enlisted in Co. F, at Nashua; mustered out Aug. 6, 1861, and enlisted Sept. 15, 1862, in the New Hampshire Battalion of New England Cavalry, Co. M; shot through the body in a skirmish, June 18, 1863, and died the next day. Born and bred in Lancaster. Brother of Francis Henry, 15 and 34 M. V. I.

EIGHTH NEW HAMPSHIRE INFANTRY.

Frank Carter Bancroft, 17 ; Oct. 25, 1861, enlisted under the alias of Henry F. Colter, in Co. A, at Nashua, and served as drummer ; re-enlisted as bugler, Jan. 4, 1864, and transferred Jan. 1, 1865, to 8 Battalion N. H. Mounted Infantry; mustered out Oct. 28, 1865.

THIRTEENTH NEW HAMPSHIRE INFANTRY.

William Dustin Carr, 40 ; corporal ; Sept. 19, 1862, enlisted at Mason ; severely wounded by shell, May 13, 1864, and died at Point Lookout, Md., in hospital, June 20, 1864. [N. H. Records say *June 22.*]

NINTH VERMONT INFANTRY.

Frank O. Sawyer, 30 ; July 9, 1862, at Burlington ; commissioned first-lieutenant and quartermaster; appointed captain a. qm. U. S. vols., June 30, 1864 ; mustered out May 31, 1866. Born and bred in Lancaster.

TWELFTH VERMONT INFANTRY. 9 Months.

Thomas Henry Warren, 35 ; enlisted at Burlington, Vt., Aug. 23, 1862 ; mustered out July 14, 1863. He died Sept. 29, 1873, in Lancaster, and was resident here most of his life.

Nathaniel C. Sawyer was appointed from Vermont, major and paymaster, July 21, 1863, and mustered out July 20, 1866. Brother of Frank O. Sawyer.

THIRTY-FIFTH NEW YORK INFANTRY.

Francis B. Cutler, 25 ; enlisted in Co. A, at Elmira, N.Y., June 1, 1861 ; killed at Fredericksburg, Va., Dec. 13, 1862. He resided in Lancaster until manhood, and his three brothers, credited to Lancaster, were in 15 and 53 M. V. I.

FORTY-SECOND NEW YORK INFANTRY. Tammany Regt.

James Finnessey, 21 ; corporal ; enlisted in New York city, Aug. 9, 1861 ; from Lancaster. Sergeant, transferred to 59 N. Y.; mustered out Aug. 5, 1864 ; died Oct. 10, 1864.

SIXTIETH NEW YORK INFANTRY.

Martin Kelly, 20 ; corporal ; enlisted Oct. 17, 1861, in Co. H, at Ogdensburg, N. Y.; re-enlisted as veteran at Wauhatchie, Ala., Dec. 14, 1863 ; mustered out July 17, 1865.

Ninth Iowa Infty. and Third Battery L. Art.

Jerome Bradley, 28; September, 1861, commissioned junior second-lieutenant of the Dubuque Battery L. A.; promoted senior second-lieutenant same battery, called 3 Iowa, Feb. 28, 1862; promoted first-lieutenant and quartermaster 9 Iowa V. I., March 16, 1862, but declined commission; appointed captain and a. qm. U. S. vols., Feb. 19, 1863; resigned Jan. 9, 1865. From infancy to manhood, of Lancaster.

Richard Jeffrey Cleveland, 40; enlisted in Co. B, Jones county, Iowa, Oct. 9, 1861; discharged April 1, 1863. Born and bred in Lancaster.

Eleventh Illinois Cavalry.

This regiment fought in battles of Shiloh, Corinth, Iuka, Lexington, Vicksburg, etc.

Charles Lowell Bancroft, 34; of Farmington, Ill.; commissioned second-lieutenant Co. B, Dec. 20, 1861; promoted first-lieutenant July 6, 1862; mustered out Dec. 19, 1864. Slightly wounded in skirmish at Meridian, Miss. Born and lived until manhood in Lancaster. Died April 16, 1888, at Yankton, Dakota.

Thirteenth Illinois Infantry.

This regiment was in the Fifteenth Army Corps, and in battles of Chickasaw Bayou, Arkansas Post, Vicksburg, Jackson, and Missionary Ridge.

Edward Russell Joslyn, 21; enlisted in Co. B, at Sterling, Ill., May 24, 1861; died at St. Louis, Mo., April 13, 1865, from effects of starvation in military prison at Florence, Ala., having been taken prisoner May 17, 1864, in the Georgia campaign. Native of, and credited to Lancaster.

Fifty-Fifth Illinois Infantry.

A history of this regiment was printed in 1887. The two Lancaster men serving in it enlisted at Camp Douglas, Chicago, and enrolled themselves in aid of the quota of their native town. The regiment was of General W. T. Sherman's original division in the Fifteenth A. C., and lost in killed and wounded nearly forty per cent of its numbers engaged at Shiloh, its first battle. It participated later in the battles of Russell's House, Chickasaw Bayou, Arkansas Post, Champion's Hill, Missionary Ridge, Kenesaw,

Atlanta, Ezra Church, Jonesboro, Fort McAllister and Bentonville; and the sieges of Corinth, Vicksburg, Jackson, Atlanta and Savannah. It marched 3240 miles, and travelled during its four years of service, 11,965 miles.

Henry Stedman Nourse, 30; Oct. 23, 1861, began service as clerk of regiment; adjutant, March 1, 1862; captain of Co. H, Dec. 19, 1862; senior officer in command of regiment after battle of Jonesboro', Sept. 1, 1864; appointed commissary of musters Seventeenth A. C., Oct. 24, 1864; slightly wounded in leg at Shiloh, by shell; declining commission as lieutenant-colonel then due, mustered out at expiration of service, March 29, 1865.

George Lee Thurston, 30; Oct. 31, 1861, adjutant; promoted captain Co. B, March 1, 1862. Given leave of absence by Gen. Grant, July 1, 1862, on surgeon's certificate "that such absence is necessary to save his life." Died at Lancaster, Dec. 15, 1862, of consumption engendered by fatigue and exposure during battle of Shiloh, April 6 and 7, 1862. *See Appendix.*

Veteran Re-enlistments.

Charles H. Balcom, 15 M. V. I. and Veteran Reserve Corps.
Frank Carter Bancroft, 8 N. H. V. I.
Jonas H. Beard, 25 M. V. I.
William L. Fox, 21 M. V. I.
George H. Hardy, 21 M. V. I.
Martin Kelly, 60 N. Y. V. I.
Sumner R. Kilburn, 15 M. V. I.
Solomon Kittredge, 15 M. V. I. and Veteran Reserve Corps.
Charles E. McQuillan, 2 U. S. Cavalry and U. S. Vet. Vols.
Oliver W. Moore, 15 M. V. I. and Veteran Reserve Corps.
James Homer Newman, 1 Conn. Heavy Artillery.
Luke Ollis, 2 U. S. Cavalry.
Frank E. Pierce, 2 U. S. Cavalry.
George K. Richards, 16 M. V. I. and Veteran Reserve Corps.
Caleb W. Sweet, 23 M. V. I.

Of the commissioned officers, Bancroft, Henry Bowman, Bradley, Cobb, Fuller, Nourse, Sawyer and Francis Washburn served throughout the war.

Drafted July 18, 1864, and paid $300 for Substitutes.

Miron H. Brewer,	George E. P. Dodge,	Horatio D. Humphrey,
Oliver Warner Carter,	Josiah Harris,	Henry Stowe,
Henry C. Cutting,	Eli E. Howe,	Charles Lewis Wilder, Jr.
	Elbridge Warren Hosmer,	

SUMMARY.

The population of Lancaster, by census of 1860, was 1732
Its valuation in 1860 was $848,100
Lancaster's quota under all calls was 171
Credited to the town by state authorities, ... 181

     Surplus, ... — 10

Individuals named in preceding lists, ... 215
Of these, actual residents or natives were 168

  "   non-residents employed as substitutes 36
  "   drafted citizens paying $300, ... 10
  "   re-enlisted veterans for three years were 15
  "   serving in more than one organization, ... 24
  "   commissioned, ... 20
  "   killed in action or died of wounds, ... 27
  "   died of disease before 1867, ... 23
  "   wounded other than mortally (so far as recorded), ... 31

The Cutler family furnished four brothers to the Union
army, three of whom laid down their lives, the fourth being
severely wounded. Two fathers, Benjamin Farnsworth
and Jonathan Puffer Nourse, each sent three sons to the
war. One father, Thomas A. G. Hunting, gave two sons
and fought for the Union himself. Nineteen other families
had each two brothers in the service.

Several soldiers born in Lancaster, but whose birthplace
and residence were in that part of the town which in 1850
was incorporated as Clinton, will not be found named in
the preceding lists. Doubtless several other natives of the
town, not hereinbefore mentioned, fought during the civil
war to the credit of other places, where they had made for
themselves new homes; but the military experience of
such has not come to the knowledge of the writer.

Adjutant General Schouler, in his History of Massachusetts in the Civil War, says: "Lancaster furnished one
hundred and eighty-one men for the war, which was a surplus of ten over and above all demands. Six were commissioned officers." This statement coincides with the
original quota list of the selectmen, and from that it was
probably derived. It is, however, as the roster proves, an
undervaluation of the contribution of manhood made by

Lancaster for the suppression of the great treason. In the printed quota list some errors are noticeable; and the omission of several names of soldiers, known to be Lancaster born and bred, impelled the writer to attempt faithfully and patiently to make up from all records attainable —aided by the memories and diaries of fellow soldiers, and the fellow townsmen who keep freshly in mind the soul-stirring experiences of the civil war—a full and accurate roster of the men who represented this town in various military organizations during that momentous struggle. He cannot hope that the outcome of his honest endeavors, as set forth in the preceding pages, is free from mistakes; but it is hoped that these may not be found many nor inexcusable. The published Records of the Massachusetts Volunteers are far from being always reliable; indeed, the more searchingly they are examined, the more charity it requires to spare harsh terms in criticism of their inaccuracies. Whenever possible, statements of these Records have been verified or corrected by certified copy from original muster rolls, army letters, family records, and discharge papers. When discrepancies have been found in different authorities, and they were many, they have been used to eliminate error, and noted with comment when important or productive of uncertainty.

It is no part of the purpose of this chronicle to magnify individual prowess and success, or to excuse individual failure and misconduct; to eulogize, much less to underrate any one. It would have given the writer great pleasure to add to his pages by including the battle record of each soldier. But this, while honoring the few living and accessible, would unavoidably have resulted in injustice to the majority, dead or distant. The foregoing lists are therefore merely a catalogue of those soldiers in army or navy who can, for any reason, be considered of Lancaster, with a systematic statement of such facts in their war experiences as usually appear in regimental muster rolls.

To comrades and fellow townsmen, this effort to preserve in more full and convenient form than hitherto existed, honorable record of our active patriotism during a period of great national peril, is respectfully submitted by one proud to call himself a Lancaster soldier.

The army of the West, under Sherman, had swept down from Atlanta to the sea, and now, jubilant and invincible, was advancing northward, half way on its triumphal march towards Richmond. The army of the East had at last completely enveloped its stubborn antagonist in gigantic coils, and crushed it into submission. The joy of peace assured and the nation regenerated illumined the faces of the loyal millions. Suddenly a brief electric message flashed east, west, north, south, that hushed all voice of rejoicing, carried dismay and indignation everywhere, and saddened each northern home. For "Father Abraham" had become a household word, and the loss by tragic death of President Lincoln was felt even more as a private than a public grief, now that the great mission of his life had been brought to grand conclusion. At a meeting of the town convened May 20, 1865, resolutions expressive of its profound sense of this calamity were recommended for adoption, and it was unanimously voted that they be recorded in the town's book.

On July 4, 1865, the people of Lancaster celebrated the victory of free institutions, assembled *en masse* in the field and adjoining grove at the "Meeting of the Waters." Professor William Russell read the Emancipation Proclamation, and the minister of the First Parish made an address. It was in itself one of the brightest and most beautiful of days. It was an immortal date, "wearing a double crown of Providential honors, as the commemoration not only of the first, but of the second Birth of the Republic—not only

of the Declaration of the fathers, but of its re-affirmation
and practical confirmation for all time." Not the least
grateful duty of the occasion was to welcome so many as
had returned of those who went forth with the blessings
and prayers of the town upon them, to stand or fall in the
mighty struggle. Their ranks had been thinned by disease
and violent death. Some had not come back, and never
will — but they are not dead — for that which inspired them
dies not with the physical forms in which it was embodied.

> "Ah no! the life they gave
> Is not shut in the grave.
> The valorous spirits freed,
> Live in the vital deed!
> Marble shall crumble to dust.
>   *   *   *   *
> Broken and covered with stains,
> The crossed stone swords must yield;
> But the great deed remains."

A building commemorative of the patriotic self-sacrifice
of these "unreturning brave," begun in 1867, was completed and dedicated in the spring of the following year;
and extensive improvements upon it are going on as these
pages pass through the hands of the printer.

SOLDIERS OF THE REBELLION HAVING MEMORIAL STONES IN LANCASTER CEMETERIES—1889.

NORTH VILLAGE CEMETERY.

Charles Coolidge, Co. E, 21 M. V. I. Died March 29, 1862, aged 34.

Franklin Hawkes Farnsworth, Co. C, 15 M. V. I. Killed May 31, 1862,
aged 19. [Cenotaph.]

Henry M. Putney, Co. F, 45 M. V. I. Killed April 28, 1863, aged 20.

James G. True, Co. A, 28 M. V. I. Died November 27, 1863, aged 27.
[Cenotaph.]

William Dustin Carr, Co. G, 13 N. H. I. Died of wound June 20, 1864,
aged 40.

Edward R. Washburn, Co. I, M. V. I. Died of wound September 5, 1864,
aged 28.

George W. Divoll, 7 Battery M. L. A. Died September 21, 1864, aged
37. [Cenotaph.]

Francis Washburn, 4 Mass. Cav. Died of wound April 22, 1865, aged 26.
George D. Weld, Co. K, 47 M. V. I. Died December 1, 1865, aged 53.
Walter C. Rice, Co. I, 53 M. V. I. Died July 30, 1867, aged 45.
James Montgomery, Co. D, 21 M. V. I. Died January 22, 1870, aged 53.
William N. Spencer, Co. J, 98 N. Y. Vols. Died March 11, 1871, aged 22.
Joseph C. Stevens, Surgeon Washington hospital. Died August 7, 1871, aged 39.
George W. Matthews, Co. H, 34 M. V. I. Died November 24, 1876, aged 29.
Charles G. Stevens, Asst. Surgeon 19 Maine Vols. Died March 1, 1877, aged 33.
George K. Richards, Co. C, 16 M. V. I. Died March 17, 1879, aged 59.
George A. Foss, Co. I, 44 M. V. I. Died April 16, 1885, aged 43.

MIDDLE CEMETERY.

Ebenezer W. Richards, Co. E, 21 M. V. I. Killed December 13, 1862, aged 37. [Cenotaph.]
George Lee Thurston, Co. B, 55 Ill. V. I. Died December 15, 1862, aged 32.
Horatio Elisha Turner, Co. F, 34 M. V. I. Died September 8, 1864, aged 20. [Cenotaph.]
Fred Fordyce Nourse, Co. E, 5 M. V. I. Died September 13, 1864, aged 22.
Horace Worcester, Co. K, 42 M. V. I. Died May 22, 1866, aged 22.
Henry T. Taylor, Co. A, 15 M. V. I. Died October 18, 1868, aged 34.
Charles H. Wilder, Co. I, 53 M. V. I. Died November 30, 1885, aged 66.

OLD COMMON CEMETERY.

John James, Co. I, 53 M. V. I. Died May 25, 1884, aged 42.

EASTWOOD CEMETERY.

William L. Cobb, Co. H, 34 M. V. I. Died May 17, 1879, aged 39.
Harris C. Harriman, Co. I, 53 M. V. I. Died February 4, 1888, aged 59.

CAPTAIN GEORGE LEE THURSTON

APPENDIX.

I. JOHN PRESCOTT, THE FOUNDER OF LANCASTER.

1605 – 1681.

THE facts that have come down to us whereupon to build a biography of John Prescott are scanty indeed, but enough to prove that he was that rare type of man, the ideal pioneer. Not one of the famous frontiersmen, whose figures stand out so prominently in early American history, was better equipped with the manly qualities that win hero worship in a new country, than was the father of the Nashaway Plantation. Had Prescott, like Daniel Boone, been fortunate in the favor of contemporary historians to perpetuate anecdotes of his daily prowess and fertility of resource, or had he left grateful successors withal to keep his memory green, his name and romantic adventures would, like Boone's, adorn Colonial annals. Persecuted for his opinions, he went out into the wilderness with his family to found a home, and for forty years thought, fought and wrought to make that home the centre of a prosperous community. Loaded from his first steps with discouragements that soon appalled every other of the original copartners in the purchase of Nashaway from Showanon, Prescott alone held to his purpose, and death found him at his post. His grave is in the old burial field at Lancaster, yet not ten citizens can point it out. At its head stands a rude fragment from some ledge of slate rock, faintly incised with characters which few eyes can trace :

JOHN PRESCOTT DESASED

No date! no comment! That is his only memorial stone — his only epitaph in the town of which, for its first forty years, he was the very heart and soul. But this fair township—now divided among nine towns—and all it has been and is to be, may be justly called his monument. The House of Deputies in 1652 voted it to be rightly his, and marked it by incorporative enactment with his name— *Prescott.* Unfortunately, however, some years before this he had favored Doctor Robert Childe's criticisms of the Colonial system of taxation without representation; criticisms that grew, and bore good fruitage when the times were riper for individual freedom, when Samuel Adams and James Otis took up the peoples' cause where Sir Henry Vane and Robert Childe had left it. Therefore when, in 1652, what had been known as the Nashaway Plantation was fairly named for its founder in accordance with the petition of its inhabitants, some one of influence, whether magistrate or higher official, perhaps bethought himself that no Governor of the Colony even had been so honored, and that it might be well, before dignifying this busy blacksmith so much as to name a town for him, to see if he could pass examination in the catechism deemed orthodox at that date in Massachusetts Bay. Alas! John Prescott was not a freeman. Having a conscience and fixed religious convictions of his own, he had never given public adhesion to the established church covenant, and was therefore by law debarred from holding any civil office, and even from the privilege of voting for the magistrates. There was a year's delay, and, in 1653—just after the Rump Parliament had disappeared, fleeing the wrath of Cromwell and his musketeers—"Prescott" was expunged from the Court's grant, and *Lancaster* began its history.

As in the broad area of the township various centres of population grew into villages and were one by one excised and made towns, it would be supposed that each of them would have been eager to honor itself by adopting so euphonious and appropriate a name as *Prescott.* But no! The first candidate for a new designation, in 1732, was given the name of the generous Charlestown clergyman, *Harvard*, for no local reason now discoverable. Six years later another body corporate appropriated the Lancashire name — *Bolton*. Two years passed and a third district sought across the ocean for its title — *Leominster*. Then Woonksechocksett, forgetful of its benefactors and the sonorous Indian names of its hills and waters, borrowed the title of the putative Scotch earl who bravely fought for our independence ; and, in adopting, paid him the poor compliment of misspelling it — *Sterling*. The next seceder ambitiously chose the name of a Prussian city — *Berlin*. The sixth perpetuated its early admiration of the great small-pox inoculator — *Boylston* ; and the last was named — for a hotel. None so poor as to do Prescott reverence. But surely, it would be thought, banks and manufactories, halls or at least a fire company might with tardy respect have paid cheap tribute to his name by bearing it. Until recently only a short street, one having little connection, sentimental or real, with the pioneer, bore his name, even in the aspiring town, almost a city, of which John Prescott's old millstone is the visible foundation — *Clinton*.

I have stated that Prescott was an ideal pioneer. Not that there was in him anything of kinship to that class of frontiersmen now deployed along the outer verge of American civilization, like the thread of froth stranded along a beach outlining the extreme advance made by the last wave of the tide. The bibulous gamblers, reckless duellists, blasphemous savages of mixed blood, the curse of our frontier today, had no prototype in Colonial days ; for the human harvest then gathered to the stocks, the whipping-post and the gallows, was of a far less obtrusive class of offenders against morals and social decency. Prescott was a Puritan soldier, a seeker of liberty not license ; rebellious against tyranny, but no contemner of constituted authority or moral law. It was no accident that put him in the advance guard of Anglo-Saxon civilization, then just starting on its westward march from the shores of Massachusetts Bay. The position had awaited the man. When he set up his anvil and with skilful blows hammered out the first plough-shares to compel the virgin soil of the Nashaway valley to its proper fruitfulness, he was all unwittingly helping to forge the destinies of this great republic;—was in his humble sphere a true builder of the nation. His neighbors and friends, John Tinker, Ralph Houghton, and Major Simon Willard, doubtless excelled him in culture, but no neighbor surpassed him in natural personal force, whether physical, mental or moral.

Alas! no contemporary has with pencil or pen limned for us the personality of the Nashaway pioneers. Whether Prescott was by symmetry of form and comeliness of feature a fit figure to grace the pediment of a Grecian temple, or was moulded after a much more rugged northern type, we do not know. He is now a mere name, bereft by time even of ghostly shape and vesture. But his career makes us sure that his gifts and traits were those of a born leader of men; that he was well dowered with brain, thew and sinew; was masterful and stirred to restlessness by useful energies. We may therefore trust the tradition which fays with these facts, telling that he was of commanding stature, stern of mien and strong of limb, and had a heart devoid of fear, great physical endurance and an unbending will. These qualities his savage neighbors early recognized and bowed before in deep respect, and because of these no Lancaster enterprise but claimed him as its head. His manual skill and dexterity must have been great, his mental capacity and business energy remarkable, for we find him not only a farmer, trader, blacksmith and hunter, but a surveyor and builder of roads, bridges and mills. The records of the town show that he was seldom free from the conduct of some public labor. The greatest of his benefactions to his neighbors were his corn-mill erected in 1654, and his saw-mill in 1659. No event could rival in its vital interest to every family in that little hamlet the coming of the first millstone.   Until the miller announced his readiness to take toll of their grain, every grist had to be borne on horse-back to Watertown, nearly thirty miles away, or was prepared for bread by fatiguing labor at hand-quern and mortar, or made fit for human food by slow, crude processes copied from savage life.   Before the starting of his saw-mill, the rude houses must have been of logs, stone, and clay, for it was an impossibility to bring from the lower towns, on the existing "Bay road" and with the primitive tumbril, any large amount of sawn lumber.

We have the authority of Camden, the antiquary, writing in 1586, that in the northern counties of England many of the smaller towns gave names to families having freeholds therein.   Thus originated the Lancashire names so familiar among us: Atherton, Farnsworth, Houghton, More, Rigby and Prescott.   In West Derby Hundred, about eight miles to the eastward from Liverpool, is the very ancient town, Prescot, one of fourteen townships forming Prescot parish, wherein certain manorial rights were granted by Edward III, in 1333, to Sir William de Dacre, then its rector.   Its name is obviously compounded of two Anglo-Saxon words, *preost* and *cote*, hence meaning the priest's dwelling place. In the adjoining parish of Standish, John Prescott — the youngest son of Ralph and Ellen of the hamlet of Shevington, and the great-grandson of Sir James Prescot of the manor of Dryby — was baptized in 1604/5, the year famed in English history for the Gunpowder Plot.   It was about this time also that William Shakespeare, comedian to King James I, retired from the stage.   January 21, 1629, being then a land-holder of Shevington, Prescott was married to Mary Platts at Wigan.   Probably within the year he removed to Sowerby, Halifax parish, in the West Riding of Yorkshire, where he lived for about seven years.   It has often been alleged that he crossed the ocean to escape from prelatical tyranny, but this statement may rest upon infer-

ence or tradition only, no evidence being given in proof of
it. If indeed he fled from Anglican bishops, it was an
irony of fate that he soon found himself subject to the in-
quisitorial despotism of the Massachusetts Precisians. His
first haven was Barbadoes, where he is recorded as owning
lands in 1638. For reasons now unknown that prolific but
hurricane-swept island did not prove a satisfactory residence, and in 1640 Prescott landed in Boston. He at once
chose a home in Watertown, and became possessor of six
lots of land, aggregating one hundred and twenty-six
acres. In 1643 his name is associated with those of Thomas King of Watertown, Henry Symonds of Boston, and
others, the first proprietors of the Nashaway purchase.

Of Prescott's wife we know only her name ; but her
daughters were sought for in marriage by men of whom
we know nothing that is not praiseworthy ; and her sons all
honored their mother's memory by useful and unblemished
lives. His children were eight in number, and all were
married in due season. They were :

1. Mary, baptized at Halifax Parish, February 24,
1630, married Thomas Sawyer in 1648. The bridegroom
was fourteen years older than his young bride. The couple
selected their home lot adjoining Prescott's in Lancaster,
and there eleven sons and daughters were born to them.
The husband died September 12, 1706, his wife surviving
him several years.

2. Martha, baptized at Halifax Parish, March 11, 1632,
married John Rugg in 1655 ; and these twain began life
together in sight of her paternal home in Lancaster. She
died with her twin babes in January, 1656.

3. John, baptized at Halifax Parish, April 1, 1635,
married Sarah Hayward at Lancaster, November 11, 1668,
and had five children. He was a farmer and blacksmith,
lived with his father, and succeeded him at the mills.

4. Sarah, baptized in 1637, at Halifax Parish, married Richard Wheeler at Lancaster, August 2, 1658, and

lived in the immediate vicinity of those before named.
Wheeler was killed in the massacre of February 10, 1676,
and the widowed Sarah married Joseph Rice of Marlborough. By her first husband she probably had eight children.

5. Hannah was probably born at Barbadoes in 1639.
She became the second wife of John Rugg, May 4, 1660,
and had eight children. She lost her husband by death,
January, 1697, and was slain by the Indians in the massacre of September 11, 1697.

6. Lydia, born at Watertown, August 15, 1641, married Jonas Fairbank at Lancaster, May 28, 1658. He
owned the lands next south of Prescott's home. Fairbank
had seven children. In the massacre of February 10, 1676,
he and his son Joshua were victims. The widowed Lydia
married Elias Barron.

7. Jonathan — if twenty three years old in 1670, as an
unknown authority has noted, or "about 38," November 6,
1683, as stated in a deposition of that date — was probably
born in Lancaster between 1645 and 1647. He was a
blacksmith and farmer, and married first Dorothy, August
3, 1670, in Lancaster. She died in 1674, leaving a son
Samuel, noted in the town history as the unfortunate senti-
nel who, on November 6, 1704, killed by mistake his
neighbor, the beloved minister of Lancaster, Reverend
Andrew Gardner. Jonathan Prescott married second,
Elizabeth, daughter of John Hoar of Concord, who died
in 1687, leaving six children. Jonathan's third wife was
Rebecca Bulkeley, and his fourth Ruth, widow of Thomas
Brown. He did not reside in Lancaster after the massacre
of 1676, but became an influential citizen of Concord,
which he served as representative for nine years. He died
December 5, 1721. His grandson John was commander
of the Massachusetts men who served in the expedition
against Carthagena in 1740.

8. Jonas, born June, 1648, in Lancaster, married Mary

23

Loker of Sudbury, December 14, 1672. The marriage
took place in Lancaster, and here their first child was born
—they had twelve children in all—but later they removed
to Groton, where Jonas became captain, selectman and justice. He died in Groton, December 31, 1723. Of his
most illustrious descendants were Colonel William, and the
historian William H. Prescott.

In May, 1644, John Winthrop records that "Many of
Watertown and other towns joined in a plantation at Nashaway"—and Reverend Timothy Harrington in his Century
Sermon states that the organization of this company of
planters was due to Thomas King. The immediate and
final disappearance of this original proprietor has seemed
to our historians good warrant for charging that King and
his partner, Henry Symonds, were but land speculators,
who bought the Indians' inheritance to retail by the acre to
adventurers. I believe this an unjust assumption. At the
date when Winthrop recorded the inception of the Nashaway Company, Henry Symonds had already been dead
seven months. He was that energetic contractor of Boston
noted as the leader in the project for establishing tide mills
at the Cove, and was no doubt the capitalist of the trading
firm, Symonds & King, who set up their "trucking house"
as early as 1643 on the sunny slope of George Hill. Symonds's widow, a few months after his death, married Isaac
Walker, who in 1645 was active among the Nashaway proprietors. If King sold his share of the Indian purchase,
may it not have been therefore because, his senior partner
being dead, he had no means to continue the enterprise?
He too died before the end of the year 1644, not yet thirty
years of age. The inventory of his estate sums but one
hundred and fifty-eight pounds, including his house and
land in Watertown, his stock in trade, and seventy-three
pounds of debts due him from the Indians, John Prescott,
and sundry others. King's widow made haste to be con-
soled, and her second husband, James Cutler, soon appears
in the role of a Nashaway proprietor.

The direction of the company was at the outset in the hands of men whose names were, or soon became, of some note throughout the Colony. Doctor Robert Childe, a scholar who had won the degrees of A. M. and M. D. at Cambridge and Padua, a man of scientific acquirements, but inclined to somewhat sanguine expectations of mineral treasure to be discovered in the New England hills, seems to have been a leading spirit in the adventure; and unfortunately so, since his views about certain inalienable rights of man, which now live and are honored in the Constitution of the Commonwealth, naturally seemed vicious republicanism to the ecclesiastical aristocracy then ruling the Colony of the Massachusetts Bay; and the odium that drove Childe across the ocean, attached also to his companion planters, and perhaps through the prejudice of those in authority unfavorably affected for several years the progress of the settlement on the Nashaway. Certainly such prejudice found expression in all action or record of the government respecting the proprietors and their petitions. The ecclesiastical figure-head of the company — without which no body corporate could have grace with the Colony — was Nathaniel Norcross. Of him, if we can surmise aught from his early return to England, it may be said that he was not imbued with the martyr's spirit, and his defection was, some time later, more than made good by the accession of the beloved Rowlandson. But far more important to the enterprise than these two graduates from the English University — Childe the radical, and Norcross the preacher — were two mechanics, the restless planners and busy promoters of the company, both workers in iron — Steven Day the locksmith, and John Prescott the blacksmith. Steven Day was the first in America, north of Mexico, to set up a printing-press. The Colony had wisely recognized in him a public benefactor, and sealed this recognition by substantial grant of lands. He entered upon the Nashaway scheme with characteristic zeal and energy, if we may believe his own manuscript testimony; but Day's zeal outran his discretion, and his energy devoured his scant means, for in 1644 we find him in jail for debt, remonstrating piteously against the injustice of a hard-hearted creditor. He parted with all rights at Nashaway before many years, and finally delved as a journeyman at the press he had founded.

John Prescott, deserted by all his early co-partners, was sufficient for the emergency, a host in himself. He sells his one hundred and twenty-six acres and house at Watertown, puts his all into the venture, prepares a rude dwelling in the wilderness, moves thither his cattle, and chattels, and finally, mounting wife and children and his few remaining goods upon horses' backs, bids his old neighbors good-bye, and threads the narrow Indian trail through the forest westward. The scorn of men high in authority is to follow him, but now the most formidable enemy in his path is the swollen Sudbury River and its bordering marsh. We find the aristocratic scorn mingling with the story of Prescott's dearly bought victory over this natural obstacle, told in Winthrop's History of New England among what the author classes as remarkable special providences:

Prescot another favorer of the Petitioners lost a horse and his loading in Sudbury river, and a week after his wife and children being upon another horse were hardly saved from drowning.

That the kindly-hearted Winthrop could coolly charge the pitiable disaster of the brave pioneer to the wrath of God towards the Erastian liberality or suspected Presbyterianism of Robert Childe and his associate petitioners, pictures vividly the bigotry natural to the age and race, a bigotry which culminated in the horrors of the persecution for witchcraft. This Sudbury swamp was the lion in the path from the bay westward during many a decade. In 1645, an earnest petition went up to the council from Prescott and his associates, complaining that much time and means had been spent in discovering Nashaway and preparing for the settlement there, and that on account of the lack of bridge and causeway at the Sudbury River, the proprietors could not pass to and from the bay towns— "without exposing our persons to perill and our cattell and goods to losse and spoyle; as yor petitioners are able to make prooffe of by sad experience of what wee suffered there within these few dayes." The General Court ordered the bridge and way to be made "passable for loaden horse," and allowed twenty pounds to Sudbury, "so it be donne wthin a twelve monthe." The twelve months passed and no bridge spanned the stream. That the dangers and difficulties of the passage were not exaggerated by the petitioners is proven by the fact that more than one hundred years afterwards the bridge and causeway at this place, "half a mile long," were represented to the General Court as dangerous, and in time of floods impassable. Between 1759 and 1761, the proceeds of special lotteries amounting to twelve hundred and twenty-seven pounds were expended in the improvement of the crossing.

John Winthrop, writing of the Nashaway planters, tells us that "he whom they had called to be their minister [Norcross] left them for their delays," but omits mention of the fact recorded by the planters themselves in their petition, that the chief and sufficient cause of their slow progress was the inability or unwillingness of the Governor and magistrates to afford effective aid in providing a passable way, even for horsemen, over a small river.

Prescott, at least, was chargeable with no delay. By June, 1645, he and his family had become permanent residents on the Nashaway. Richard Linton, Lawrence Waters the carpenter, and John Ball the tailor, were his only neighbors; these three men having been sent up to build, plant, and prepare for the coming of other immigrants. But two houses had been built. Linton probably lived with his son-in-law, Waters, in his home near the fording place in the North Branch of the Nashaway, contiguous to the lot of intervale land which Harmon Garrett and others of the first proprietors had fenced in to serve as a night pasture for their cattle. Ball had left his children and their mother in Watertown, she being at times insane. Prescott's first lot embraced part of the grounds upon which the public buildings in Lancaster now stand, but this he soon parted with, and took up his abode a mile to the south-west, on the sunny slope of George Hill, where, beside a little brooklet of pure, cool water, which then doubtless came rollicking down over its gravelly bed with twice the flow it has today, there had been built, two years at least before, the trucking house of Symonds & King. This trading post was the extreme outpost of civilization; beyond was interminable forest, traversed only by the Indian trails, which were but narrow paths hard to find and easy to lose unless the traveller had been bred to the arts of wood-craft. Here passed the united trails from Washacum, Wachusett, Quaboag and other Indian villages of the west, leading to the wading place of the Nashaway River near the present Atherton Bridge, and so down the Bay Path over Wataquadock to Concord. The little plateau half way down the sheltering hill, with fertile fields sloping to the south-east and its never failing springs, was and is an attractive spot; but its material advantages to the pioneer of 1645 were far greater than those apparent to the Lancastrian of this nineteenth century in the changed conditions of life. With the privilege of first choice therefore, it is not strange that Prescott and his sturdy sons-in-law grasped the rich intervales, and warm, easily-tilled slopes, stretching along the Nashaway south branch from the meeting of the waters to John's Jump on the east, and extending west to the crown of George Hill — lands now covered by the village of South Lancaster.

In 1650 John Prescott found himself the only member of the company resident at Nashaway. Of the co-partners, Symonds, King and John Hill were dead; Norcross and

Childe had gone to England ; Cowdall had sold his rights
to Prescott ; Chandler, Davis, Walker and others had formally abandoned their rights ; Garrett, Shawe, Day, Adams, and perhaps two or three more, retained their claims
to allotments, making no improvements and contributing
nothing by their presence or tithes to the growth of the
settlement, thus becoming effectual stumbling blocks in the
way of progress. Prescott, very reasonably, held this a
grievance, and, having no other means of redress, asked
equitable judgment in the matter from the magistrates in a
petition which cannot be found. His answer was the following official snub :

Whereas John Prescot & others, the inhabitants of Nashaway pferd a
petition to this Ccurte desiringe power to recover all common charges of
all such as had land there, not residinge wth them, for answer whereunto
this Court, understandinge that the place before mentioned is not fit to
make a plantation, (so a ministry to be erected and mayntayned there,)
which if the petitioners, before the end of the next session of this Courte,
shall not sufficiently make the sey'd place appeare to be capable to answer
the ends above mentioned doth order that the pties inhabitinge there
shalbe called there hence, & suffered to live without the meanes, as they
have done no longer.

This dire threat of the closing sentence may have been
simply "sound and fury, signifying nothing," or Prescott
may have been able to prove to the authorities that Nashaway was fit and waiting for its St. John, but found none
willing for the service. In fact, its St. John was then a
junior at Harvard College writing a pasquinade to post
upon the Ipswich meeting-house, and Nashaway was "suffered to live without the meanes" waiting for him until 1654.

John Prescott retained ownership of his early home—
the site of the trucking house which he had purchased of
John Cowdall — as long as he lived, but did not reside there
many years. No sooner had the plantation attained the
dignity of a town under the classic name of Lancaster,
than its founder bent all his energies towards those enterprises best calculated to promote the comfort and prosperity
of its then inhabitants, and to attract by material advantages

a desirable and permanent immigration. His practical eye had doubtless long before marked the best site for a mill in all the region round about, and on the slope scarce a gun shot away he set up a new home, afterwards well known to friend and savage foe as Prescott's Garrison. Those who remain of the generation familiar with this region before the invention of the power loom made such towns as Clinton possible, remember the depression that told where Prescott dug his cellar. The oldest water mill in New England was scarce twenty years old when Prescott contracted to grind the corn of the Nashaway planters. His "Covenant to build a Corne mill" has been preserved through a copy made by Ralph Houghton, Lancaster's first Clerk of Writs, and is as follows:

Know all men by these presents that I John Prescott blackesmith, hath Covenanted and bargained with Jno. ffounell of Charlestowne for the building of a Corne mill, within the said Towne of Lanchaster. This witnesseth that wee the Inhabitants of Lanchaster for his encouragement in so good a worke for the behoofe of our Towne, vpon condition that the said intended worke by him or his assignes be finished, do freely and fully giue, grant, enfeoffe. & confirme vnto the said John Prescott, thirty acres of intervale Land lying on the north riuer, lying north west of Henry Kerly, and ten acres of Land adjoyneing to the mill; and forty acres of Land on the south east of the mill brooke and Nashaway riuer in such place as the said John Prescott shall choose with all the priuiledges and appurtenances thereto apperteyneing. To haue and to hold the said land and eurie parcell thereof to the said John Prescott his heyres & assignes for euer, to his and their only propper vse and behoofe. Also wee do couenant & promise to lend the said John Prescott fiue pounds in current money one yeare for the buying of Irons for the mill. And also wee do couenant and grant to and with the said John Prescott his heyres and assignes that the said mill, with all the aboue named Land thereto apperteyneing shall be freed from all com'on charges for seuen yeares next ensueing, after the first finishing and setting the said mill to worke.

In witnes whereof wee haue herevnto put our hands this 20th day of the 9mo. In the yeare of our Lord God one thousand six hundred fifty and three.

WILL^M KERLY SEN^R.	THOMAS JAMES
JNO PRESCOTT	LAWRENCE WATERS
JNO WHITE,	EDMUND PARKER
RALPH HOUGHTON	RICHARD LINTON,
JNO LEWIS	RICHARD SMITH
JACOB FARRER	JAMES ATHERTON
	WILL^M KERLY JUN^R.

In six months from that date the mill was done, and Prescott "began to grind corne the 23d day of the 3 mo, 1654."

The commissioners appointed by the General Court to oversee the prudential management of the town, met at John Prescott's, in 1657, and confirmed "the imunityes provided for" in the above covenant, specifying that they "should continue and remayne to him the said Jno. Prescott his heyres and assignes vntil the 23d of May, in the yeare of our Lord sixteen hundred sixty and two."

The corn mill was located a little lower upon the brook than the extensive factory buildings now utilizing its water power. The half-used force of the rapid stream and the giant pines of the virgin forest then shadowing all the region about were full of reproach to the restless miller. His busy brain was soon planning a new benefaction to his fellow-citizens, and, when his means grew sufficiently to warrant the enterprise, his busy hands wrought its consummation. As before, a formal agreement preceded the work :

Know all men by these presents that for as much as the Inhabitants of Lanchaster, or the most part of them being gathered together on a trayneing day, the 15th of the 9th mo, 1658, a motion was made by Jno. Prescott blackesmith of the same towne. about the setting vp of a saw mill for the good of the Towne, and yᵗ he the said Jno Prescott, would by the help of God set vp the saw mill, and to supply the said Inhabitants with boords and other sawne worke, as is afforded at other saw mills in the countrey. In case the Towne would giue, grant, and confirme vnto the said John Prescott, a certeine tract of Land, lying Eastward of his water mill, be it more or less, bounded by the riuer east, the mill west the stake of the mill land and the east end of a ledge of Iron Stone Rocks southards, and forty acres of his owne land north, the said land to be to him his heyres and assignes for euer, and all the said land curie part thereof to be rate free vntill it be improued. or any pᵗ of it, and that his saws, & saw mill should be free from any rates by the Towne, therefore know ye that the ptyes abouesaid did mutually agree and consent each with the other concerning the aforementioned propositions as followeth :

The towne on their part did giue, grant & confirme, vnto the said John Prescott his heyres and assignes for euer, all the aforementioned tract of land butted & bounded as aforesaid, to be to him his heyres and assignes for euer with all the priuiledges and appurtenances thereon, and therevnto belonging to be to his and their owne propper vse and behoofe as aforesaid, and the land and eurie part of it to be free from all rates vntil it or any pt of it be improued, and also his saw, sawes, and saw-mill to be free from all towne rates, or ministers rates, prouided the aforementioned worke be finished & compleated as abouesaid for the good of the Towne, in some convenient time after this present contract covenant and agreemᵗ.

And the said John Prescott did and doth by these psents bynd himself, his heyres and assignes to set vp a saw-mill as aforesaid within the bounds of the aforesaid Towne, and to supply the Towne with boords and other sawne worke as aforesaid and truly and faithfully to performe, fullfill, & accomplish, all the aforementioned p'misses for the good of the Towne as aforesaid.

Therefore the Selectmen conceiuing this saw-mill to be of great vse to the Towne, and the after good of the place, Haue and do hereby act to rattifie and confirme all the aforementioned acts, covenants, gifts, grants, & im'unityes, in respect of rates, and what euer is aforementioned, on their owne pt, and in behalfe of the Towne, and to the true performance hereof, both partyes haue and do bynd themselves by subscribing their hands, this twenty-fifth day of February, one thousand six hundred and fifty nine.　　　　　　　　　　　　　　　　JOHN PRESCOTT

The worke aboue menccened was finished according to this covenant as witnesseth　　　　　　　　　　　　　　　RALPH HOUGHTON

Signed & Delivrᵈ	THOMAS WILDER
In presence of	THOMAS SAWYER
	RALPH HOUGHTON

Monday, the seventeenth of February, 1659, "the Company granted him to fall pines on the Com'ons to supply his saw-mill."

In April, 1659, Ensign Noyes came to make official survey of the eighty square miles granted to the town, and John Prescott was deputed by the townsmen at their March meeting to aid him and "mark the bounds." Among his varied accomplishments natural and acquired, Prescott seems to have had some practical skill in surveying, the laying out of highways and the construction of bridges. In 1648 John Winthrop records: "This year a new way was found out to Connecticut by Nashua which avoided much of the hilly way." As appears by a later petition Prescott was the pioneer of this new path. In 1657 he was appointed by the government a member of a committee upon the building of bridges "at Billirriky and Misticke." In 1658 he, with his son-in-law Jonas Fairbank, was appointed to survey a farm of six hundred and fifty acres for Captain Richard Davenport, the western part of which is now the most densely peopled portion of West Boylston.

To the General Court which met October 18, 1659, the following petition was presented :

The humble petition of John Prescot of Lancaster humblye Sheweth That whereas yr petitioner about nine or ten yeares since, was desired by the late hon'red Governour Mr. Winthrop, wth other Magistrates, as alsc by Mr. Wilson of Boston, Mr. Shephard of Cambridge with many others, did lay & marke out a way at ye north syde of the great pond & soe by Lancaster, which then was taken by Mr. Hopkins & many others to bee of great vse ; This I did meerly vpon the request of these honored gentlemen, to my great detrim't, by being vpon it part of two summers not only my-selfe but hiring others alsoe to helpe mee, whereby my family suffered much : I doe not question but many of ye Court remember the same, as alsoe that this hath not laine dead all this while, but I haue formerly mentioned it, but yet haue noe recompence for the same ; the charge whereof came at 2^s p day to about 10^l ; it is therefore the desire of y^r petitioner y^t you would bee pleased to grant him a farme in some place vndisposed of which will engage him to you and encourage him and others in publicque occasions & y^r petitioner shall pray etc.

One hundred acres of land were granted him, and laid out near the Washacum ponds where now stand the railroad buildings at Sterling Junction.

We get very few glimpses of Prescott from the meagre records of succeeding years, but those serve to show that he was busy, prosperous and annually honored by his neighbors with the public duties for which his sturdy integrity, shrewd business tact and wisely directed energy peculiarly fitted him. He had taken the oath of fidelity in 1652. Such owning of allegiance was by law prerequisite to the holding of real estate. Refusing such oath he might better have been a Nipmuck so far as civil rights or privileges were concerned. He was not yet a member of the recognized church, however, and therefore lacked the political dignities of a freeman; although his intimate relations with Master Joseph Rowlandson, and his personal connection with the earlier cases of church discipline in Lancaster, sufficiently attest the austerity of his religious views. Doubtless Governor John Winthrop, in his hasty and harsh dictum respecting the Nashaway planters, classed John Prescott among those "corrupt in judgment." But it must be remembered that in the Puritan's visionary commonwealth — republican as it was in theory — there was no room for liberty of conscience. All were esteemed corrupt in judgment or even profane, whose religious beliefs, when tested all about by the ecclesiastic callipers, proved not to have been cast in the doctrinal mould prescribed by the self-sanctified founders of the Massachusetts Bay Colony. No known fact in any way warrants even the conjecture that Prescott was not a sincere Christian, earnestly pursuing his own convictions of duty without fear and without reproach. The doubts and dogmas by which his soul was bound are voiceless to us, and could they be brought to light would seem to the modern mind but dead ashes and dross.

Prescott's mechanical skill and business ability had more than a local reputation. In 1667, we find him contracting with the authorities of Groton to erect "a good and sufficient corne mill or mills, and the same to finish so as may be fitting to grind the corne of the said Towne." For the fulfilment of this agreement he received five hundred and twenty acres of land, and mill and lands were exempted from taxation for twenty years. Assistance towards the building of the mill was also promised to the amount of "two days worke of a man for every house lott or family within the limitts of the said Towne, and at such time or times to be done or performed, as the said John Prescott shall see meete to call for the same, vpon reasonable notice given." The covenant was fulfilled by the completion of a mill at Nonacoiacus, then in the southern part of Groton.

The mill site is now in Harvard. Prescott's youngest son, Jonas, was the first miller. The history of the old mill is obscured by the shadows of two hundred years, but a bright gleam of romantic tradition concerning the first miller is warm with human interest now. Perhaps at points the romantic may infringe upon the historic, but

Se non e vero,
E ben trovato.

Down by the green meadows of Sudbury there dwelt a bewitchingly fair maiden. the musical dissyllables of whose name were often upon the lips of the young men in all the country round about, and whose smile could awaken voiceless poetry in the heart of the most prosaic Puritan swain. There is little of aristocratic sound in Mary Loker's name, but her parents sat on Sunday at the meeting-house in a "dignified" pew, and were rich in fields and cattle. Whether pushed by pride of land or pride of birth, in their plans and aspirations this daughter was predestinated by them to enhance the family dignity by an aristocratic alliance. In Colonial days a maiden who added a handsome prospective dowry to her personal witchery was rare indeed, and Mary Loker had, coming from far and near, inflammable suitors perpetually burning at her shrine. From among these the father and mother soon made their choice upon strictly business principles, and shortly announced to Mary that a certain ambitious gentleman of the legal profession had furnished the most satisfactory credentials, and that nothing remained but for her to name the day. Now the fourth commandment was very far from being the dead letter in 1670 that it is in 1889, and it was matter for grave surprise to the elders that their usually obedient daughter, when the lawyer proceeded to plead, refused to hear and peremptorily adjourned his cause without day. Maternal expostulation and paternal threats availed nothing. The because of Mary's contumacy was not far to seek. A stalwart Vulcan in the guise of Antinous, known as Jonas

Prescott, had wandered from his father's forge in Lancaster down the Bay Path to Sudbury. Mary and he had met, and the lingering of their parting boded ill for any predestination not stamped with their joint seal of consent. With that lack of astuteness proverbially exhibited by parents disappointed in match-making designs upon their children, the vexed father and mother began a course of vigorous repression, and thereby riveted more firmly than ever the chains which the errant young blacksmith and his apprentice Cupid had forged. In due time, they perforce learned that love's flame burns the brighter fed upon a bread and water diet; and that confinement to an attic may be quite endurable when Cupid's messages fly in and out of its lattice at pleasure.

Finally Mary was secretly sent to an out-of-the-way neighborhood in the vain hope that the chill of absence might hinder what home rule had only served to help. But one day Jonas on a hunting excursion made the acquaintance of some youth, who, among other chitchat, happened to break into ecstatic praise of the graces of a certain fair damsel who had recently come to live in a farm-house near their home. Of course the anvil missed Jonas for the next day, and the next, and the next, while he experienced the hospitalities of his new-found friends—and their neighbors. It was time for a recognition of the inevitable by all concerned, but when, and with what grace Mary's stubborn parents yielded, if at all, is not recorded. But what mattered their consent? Old John Prescott installed Jonas at the Nonacoicus Mill and endowed him with all his Groton lands, and in Lancaster, December 4, 1672, Jonas and Mary were married. For over fifty years fortune smiled upon their union. Four sons and eight daughters graced their fireside, and the father was trusted and clothed with local dignities. In after time the memory of Jonas and Mary has been honored by many worthy descendants, and especially by the gallant services of Colonel William Prescott at Bunker Hill, and the literary renown of William Hickling Prescott, the historian.

In 1669, John Prescott was proclaimed a freeman. He may have been long a church member, or may not even at this date have yielded the conscientious scruples that had a quarter of a century earlier subjected him to Winthrop's reproach. The laws, in reluctant obedience to the letter of Charles II, dated June 28, 1662, were so modified by the General Court of 1664, that citizens, although not "members of some Church of Christ and in full Communion," if freeholders of a sufficient estate and guaranteed by the local minister "to be Orthodox in Religion and not vicious in their lives," might be admitted to the freedom of the commonwealth by a majority vote in the General Court.

Prescott had the true Englishman's love of landed possessions, and about this time added a large tract to his acreage by purchase from his Indian neighbors. This transaction gave cause for the following petition, in the terse, straight-forward diction and the dignified tone of which, we may, I think, read something of its author's character :

To the honorable the Govr. the Deputy Govr. magts & Deputyes assembled in the genrall Court :

The Petition of Jno Prescott of Lanchaster, In most humble wise sheweth. Whereas ye Petition[r] hath purchased an Indian right to a small parcell of Land, occasioned and circumstanced for quantity & quality according to the deed of sale herevnto annexed and a pt. thereof not being legally setled vpon mee vnlesse I may obteyne the favo[r] of this Court for the Confirmation thereof, These are humbly to request the Court's favo[r] for that end ; the Lord hauing dealt graciously with mee in giueing mee many children I account it my duty to endeauor their provission & setling and do hope that this may be of some vse in yt kind. I know not any claime made to the said land by any towne, or any legall right yt any other persons haue therein, and therefore are free for mee to occupy & subdue as any other, may I obteyne the Court's approbation. I shall not vse further motiues, my condition in other respecks & w[t] my trouble & expenses haue been according to my poor ability in my place being not altogether vnknowne to some of ye Court. That ye Lord's p'sence may be with & his blessing accompany all yo[r] psons, Counsells, & endeauo[r]s for his honor & ye weale of his poor people is ye pray[r] of

Yo[r] suppliant, JOHN PRESCOTT SEN[R]

This request was referred to a special committee composed of Edward Tyng, George Corwin and Humphrey Davie, who reported as follows:

> In Refference to this Petition the Comittee being well informed that the Pet^r is an ancient Planter and hath bin a vseful helpfull and publique spirited man doinge many good offices ffor the Country, Relatinge to the Road to Conecticott, marking trees, directinge of Passengers &c, and that the Land Petitioned for beinge but about 107 Acres & Lyinge not very Convenient for any other Plantation, and only accomodable for the Pet^r, we judge it reasonable to confirme the Indian Grant to him & his heyres if ye honored Court see meete.

This report was approved by the magistrates May 29, 1672. James Wiser *alias* Quanapaug, the Christian Nash-away chief who appears as grantor of the land, was a warrior whose bravery had been tested in the contest between the Nipmucks and the Mohawks, and was so firm a friend of his white neighbors at Lancaster, that when Philip persuaded the tribe with Sagamore Sam to go upon the war path, James refused to join them. He even served as a spy and betrayed Philip's plans to the English at great risk of his life, doing his utmost to save Lancaster from destruction. General Daniel Gookin acknowledged that Quanapaug's information would have averted the dire massacre of February 10, 1676, had it been duly heeded. The fact of the friendly relations existing between Prescott and the tribe whose fortified residence stood between the two Washacum ponds is interesting, and confirms tradition. It is related that at his first coming he soon won the respect of the savages, not only by his fearlessness and great strength, but by the power of his eye and his dignity of mien. They soon learned to stand in awe of his long musket and unerring skill as a marksman. He had no doubt seen some military service in England, for he came of a soldierly race, his great-grandfather having been knighted for gallantry in battle. He had brought with him from England a suit of mail—helmet and cuirass— probably such as were worn by the soldiers of Cromwell.

Clothed with these, his stately figure seemed to the sons of the forest something almost superhuman. One day some Indians, having taken away a horse of his, he put on his armor, pursued them alone, and soon overtook them. The chief of the party seeing him approach unsupported, met him menacingly with uplifted tomahawk. Prescott dared him to strike and was immediately taken at his word, but the rude weapon glanced harmless from the hemlet, to the amazement of the red men. Naturally the Indian desired to try upon his own head so wonderful a hat, and the owner obligingly gratified him, claiming the privilege, however, of using the tomahawk in return. The helmet proving a scant fit or its wearer neglecting to bring it down to its proper bearings, Prescott's vengeful blow not only astounded him, but left very little cuticle on either side of his head and nearly deprived him of ears. Prescott was permitted to jog home in peace upon his horse.

After hostilities began, it is said that at one time the savages set fire to his barn, but fled when he sallied out clad in armor with his dreaded gun; and thus he was enabled to save his stock, though the building was consumed. More than once attempts were made to destroy the mill, but a sight of the man in mail with the far reaching gun was enough to send them to a safe distance and rescue the property. Many stories have been told of Prescott's prowess, but some bear so close a resemblance to those credibly historic in other places and of other heroes, that there attaches to them some suspicion of adaptation at least. Such undoubtedly is the story that in the assault upon the town "he had several muskets but no one in the house save his wife to assist him. She loaded the guns and he discharged them with fatal effect. The contest continued for nearly half an hour, Mr. Prescott all the while giving orders as if to soldiers, so loud that the Indians could hear him, to load their muskets, though he had no soldiers but his wife. At length they withdrew, carrying off several of their dead and wounded."

24

In 1673 Prescott had nearly attained the age of three score and ten. The weight of years that had been full of exposure, anxiety and toil rested heavily upon even his rugged frame, and some sharp touch of bodily ailment warning him of his mortality, he made his will. It is signed with his mark, although he evidently tried to force his unwilling hand to its accustomed work, his peculiar J being plainly written and followed by characters meant for the other letters of his first name. To earlier documents he was wont to affix a simple, neat signature, and although not a clerkly penman like his friends John Tinker, Master Joseph Rowlandson and Ralph Houghton, his writing is superior to that of Major Simon Willard.

JOHN PRESCOTT'S WILL.

Theis presents witneseth that John Prescott of Lancaster in the Countie of Midlesex in New England Blaksmith being vnder the sencible decayes of nature and infirmities of old age and at present vnder a great deale of anguish and paine but of a good and sound memorie at the writing hereof being moved vpon considerations aforesaid togather with advis of Christian friends to set his house in order in Reference to the dispose of those outward good things the lord in mercie hath betrusted him with, theirfore the said John Prescott doth hereby declare his last will and testament to be as followeth, first and cheifly Comiting and Comending his soule to almightie god that gaue it him and his bodie to the comon burying place here in Lancaster, and after his bodie being orderly and decently buryed and the charge theirof defrayed togather with all due debts discharged, the Rest of his Lands and estate to be disposed of as followeth : first in Reference to the Comfortable being of his louing wife during the time of her naturall Life, it is his will that his said wife haue that end of the house where he and shee now dwelleth togather with halfe the pasture and halfe the fruit of the aple trees and all the goods in the house, togather with two cowes which shee shall Chuse and medow sufisiant for wintering of them, out of the medowes where she shall Chuse, the said winter pvision for the two cowes to be equaly and seasonably pvided by his two sons John and Jonathan. And what this may fall short in Reference to convenient food and cloathing and other nesesaries for her comfort in sickness and in health, to be equaly pvided by the aforesaid John and Jonathan out of the estate. And at the death of his aforesaid louing wife it is his will that the said cowes and household goods be equally deuided betwene his two sons aforesaid, and the other part of the dwelling house, out housing, pasture and orchard togather with the tenn acres of house

lott lying on Georges hill which was purchased of daniell gains to be
equaly deuided betwene the said John and Jonathan and alsoe that part of
the house and outhousing what is Convenient for the two Cowes and their
winter pvision pasture and orchard willed to his louing wife during her life,
at her death to be equaly deuided alsoe betwene the said John and Jonathan. And furthermore it is his will that John Prescott his eldest son
haue the Intervaile land at John's Jumpe, the lower Mille and the land belonging to it and halfe the saw mille and halfe the land belonging to it and
all the house and barne theire erected, and alsoe the house and farme at
Washacomb pond, and all the land their purchased from the indians and
halfe the medowes in all deuisions in the towne acept sum litle part at bar
hill wh. is after willed to James Sawyer and one halfe of the Comon Right
in the towne, and in Reference to second deuision land, that part of it
which lyeth at danforths farme both vpland and interuaile is willed to Jonathan and sixtie acres of that part at Washacom litle pond to James Sawyer and halfe of sum brushie land Capable of being made medow at the
side of the great pine plain to be within the said James Sawyers sixtie
acres and all the Rest of the second deuision land both vpland and Interuaile to be equaly deuided betwene John Prescott and Jonathan aformentioned. And Jonathan Prescott his second son to haue the Ryefeild and
all the interuaile lott at Nashaway Riuer that part which he hath in poses-
ion and the other part joyneing to the highway and alsoe his part of second deuision land aforementioned and alsoe one halfe of all the medowes
in all deuisions in the towne not willed to John Prescott and James Sawyer
aforementioned, and alsoe the other halfe of the saw mille and land belonging to it, and it is to be vnderstood that all timber on the land belonging to both Corne Mille and Saw Mille be Comon to the vse of the Saw
Mille. And in Reference to his third son Jonas Prescott it is herby declared that he hath Received a full childs portion at nonecoicus in a Corne
mille and Lands and other goods. And James Sawyer his granchild and
Servant it is his will that he haue the sixtie acres of vpland aforementioned
and the two peices of medow at bare hill one being part of his second
deuision the upermost peic on the brook and the other being part of his
third deuision lying vpon Nashaway River purchased of goodman Allin.
Prouided the said James Sawyer carie it beter than he did to his said granfather in his time and carie so as becoms an aprentic & vntil he be one
and twentie years of age vnto the executors of this will namly John Prescott and Jonathan Prescott who are alsoe herby engaged to pforme vnto
the said James what was pmised by his said granfather, which was to endeauor to learne him the art and trade of a blaksmith. And in Case the
said James doe not pforme on his part as is afor expresed to the satisfaction of the overseers of this will, or otherwise, If he doe not acept of the
land aforementioned, then the said land and medow to be equaly deuided
betwene the aforsaid John and Jonathan. And in Reference to his three

daughters, namly Marie, Sara and Lydia they to haue and Receive curie of them fiue pounds to be paid to them by the executors to curie of them fiftie shillings by the yeare two years after the death of theire father to be paid out of the mouables and Martha Ruge his granchild to haue a cow at the choic of her granmother, And it is the express will and charge of the testator to his wife and all his Children that they labor and endeauor to preserue loue and unitie among themselves and the vpholding of Church and Comonwealth. And to the end that this his last will and testament may be truly pformed in all the parts of it, the said testator hath and herby doth constitut and apoynt his two sons namly John Prescott and Jonathan Prescott Joynt executors of this his last will. And for the preuention of after trouble among those that suruiue about the dispose of the estate acording to this his will he hath hereby Chosen desired and apoynted the Reuerend Mr. Joseph Rowlandson, deacon Sumner and Ralph Houghton overseers of this his will; vnto whom all the parties concerned in this his will in all dificult Cases are to Repaire, and that nothing be done without their Consent and aprobation. And furthermore in Reference to the mouables it is his will that his son John have his anvill and after the debts and legacies aformentioned be truly paid and truly discharged by the executors and the speciall trust pformed vnto my wife during her life and at her death, in Respect of, sicknes funerall expences, the Remainder of the mouables to be equaly deuided betwene my two sons John and Jonathan aforementioned. And for a further and fuller declaration and confirmation of this will to be the last will and testament of the afornamed John Prescott he hath herevnto put his hand and seale this 8 of 2 month one thousand six hundred seaventie three. JOHN PRESCOTT

his *John* mark

Sealed signed owned to be the Last will and testament of the testator afornamed In the presence of JOSEPH ROWLANDSON
ROGER SUMNER

April 4 : 82. RALPH HOUGHTON
ROGER SUMNER }
RALPH HOUGHTON } Appearing in Court made oath to the above s⁰ will. JONATHAN REMINGTON, *Cleric.*

But John Prescott's pilgrimage was far from ended, and severer chastenings than any yet experienced awaited him. He had lived to see the settlement that called him father struggle upward from discouraging beginnings to become a thriving and happy community of over fifty families. Where at his coming all had been pathless woods, now fenced fields and orchards yielded annually their golden and ruddy harvests; gardens bloomed; mechanics plied their various crafts; herds wandered in lush meadows;

bridges spanned the rivers, and roads wound through the
landscape from cottage to cottage and away to neighboring
towns. All this fair scene of industry and rural content,
which he might in modest truth claim to be the fruit of his
care and toil, he lived to see in a single day made more
desolate than the wilderness from which it had been laboriously conquered. He was spared to see dear neighbors and
kindred massacred in every method of revolting atrocity,
and their wives and children carried into loathsome captivity by foes more relentlessly cruel than wolves. When
now weighed down with age and bodily infirmities, the rest
he had thought won was to be denied him, and he and his
were driven from the ashes of pleasant homes — about
which clustered the memories of thirty years' joys and sorrows — to beg shelter from the charity of strangers. For
more than three years his enforced banishment endured.
In October, 1679, John Prescott with his sons John and
Jonathan, his sons-in-law Thomas Sawyer and John Rugg,
his grandson Thomas Sawyer, Jr., and his neighbors John
Moore, Thomas Wilder and Josiah White, petitioned the
Middlesex Court for permission to resettle the town, and
their prayer was granted. Soon most of the inhabitants
who had survived the massacre and exile were busily building new homes, some upon the cinders of the old, others
upon their second division lands east of the rivers where
they were less exposed to the stealthy incursions of their
savage enemies. The two John Prescotts rebuilt the mills
and dwelt there. Whether the pioneer's life-long helpmate
died before their settlement, in exile, or shortly after the
return, has not been ascertained, but it would seem that he
survived her. Jonathan having married a second wife remained in Concord. For two years the old man lived with
his eldest son, seeing the Nashaway Valley blooming with
the fruits of civilized labor ; seeing new families filling the
woeful gaps made among the old by the warriors of Sho-
shanim and Monoco ; seeing children and grandchildren

grasping the implements that had fallen from the nerveless hold of the earliest bread-winners, with hopeful and pertinacious purpose to extend the paternal domain : seeing too, may we not trust, from the Pisgah height of prophetic vision the glorious promise awaiting this his Canaan ;— these softly rounded hills and broad valleys dotted with the winsome homes of thousands of freemen ; churches and schools, shops of artisans, and busy marts of trade clustered about his mill site ; and, above all, seeing the assertion of political freedom and liberty of conscience, which Governor John Winthrop had reproached him for favoring in the petition of Robert Childe. become the corner-stone of a giant republic.

No record of John Prescott's death is found ; but when upon his death-bed, feeling that the changed condition of his own and his son Jonathan's affairs required some modification of the will made in 1673, he summoned two of his townsmen to hear his nuncupative codicil to that document. The date of the affidavit here appended makes it certain that his death occurred about the middle of December, 1681 :

The Deposition of Thos: Wilder aged 37 years sworn say[th] that being with Jno: Prescott Sen[r] About six hours before he died he ye s[d] Jno: Prescott gaue to his eldest sonn Jno: Prescott his house lott with all belonging to ye same & ye two mills, corn mill & saw mill with ye land belonging thereto & three scor Acors of land nere South medow and fourty Acors of land nere Wonchesix & a pece of enteruile caled Johns Jump & Bridge medow on both sids ye Brook. Cyprian Steevens Testifieth to all ye truth Aboue writen.

DECEM. 20. 81. Sworn in Court. J. R. C.

Though three years short of fourscore at the time of his death, he was Lancaster's oldest inhabitant. His fellow pioneer, Lawrence Waters, who was the elder by perhaps a year, survived, though blind and helpless ; but he dwelt with a son in Charlestown after the destruction of his home, and never returned to Lancaster. John and Ralph Houghton, much younger men, were now the veterans of the town.

II. CAPTAIN SAMUEL WARD.

Born in Worcester, Sept. 25, 1739. *Died at Lancaster, Aug.* 14, 1826.

The death of SAMUEL WARD, Esq., late of Lancaster, at the advanced age of 87, has been noticed in several of the public prints. By that event society has lost one of its strong pillars, his town an active and liberal citizen, and his relatives and associates a long-tried and valuable friend. He was endowed with rare qualities both of mind and heart, and these he retained to the close of his life. We too often linger around the aged only in token of our remembrance of times and services which are past. But in the evening of his days his society lost little of its charm. Even then his faculties had much of their original brightness. His deep interest in the varying appearance of men and things was unquenched. His social powers were in full exercise. His venerable features greeted with a smile the old and the young, and all felt blessed by his presence. His speech literally distilled as the dew, for to the last it came richly fraught with entertainment and instruction. Seldom did any one leave him without something new and worth remembering.

He was born in Worcester, where he enjoyed the teaching of the late President ADAMS. He served for some time in the old French War, as it is called, and as a soldier, was firm and faithful in the service of his country. Though he was not of the number, who from the beginning were confident of the success of the Revolution, yet he cheerfully contributed of his treasure toward maintaining our rights. He was willing to leave to the just who would struggle for it the poor and hard-earned palm of political eminence, and therefore studiously avoided a public career. Most of the active portion of his life was devoted to mercantile pursuits. The last twenty years of it he spent in superintending an extensive farm, in reading and reflection, and in deeds of friendship and benevolence.

He was remarkable for a quick and accurate discernment of character. He seemed to read it in every line and every change of the countenance. Before him the mean might well quail, and the guilty tremble — for none ever saw more clearly than he the dark windings of their hearts. He had too the judgment and virtue to make the noblest use of his knowledge of man. He made it the foundation of an elevated and philosophic prudence, — that Christian prudence which is not bound up in self, but which sends forth its cheering and restoring influence to neighborhood, community, country ; building them up with holy caution and care.

His memory will long be revered for the liberality he manifested in all the relations of life. His substance was always ready at the call of deserving need — for upholding good government ;— and giving strength and efficiency to institutions. As the thought of *doing* good was to him satisfaction enough, he was ever anxious to veil his benefactions in silence. At his death he left a generous legacy to the Evangelical Missionary

Society of which he was a member, and to the poor of the town in which he lived.

And now he is gone — the many whose tears he has wiped away shall weep over his grave. They whose wants he has felt and supplied, will rise up and bless him. The strangers, who found a welcome shelter under the shades of his hospitable mansion will remember him. The companions, who were glad in his company will sigh for his cheering accents. And the Christian, who bowed as his venerable form entered the house of God, will while he mourns cherish the consoling hope, that his alms and all which was excellent in his life have gone up for a memorial in Heaven.

[Columbian Centinel, Wednesday, August 30, 1826.]

III. CAPTAIN GEORGE LEE THURSTON.

Born in Lancaster, January 16, 1831.   Died December 15, 1862.

Among the men of Lancaster who in 1861 girt themselves with the weapons of strife that the nation might have lasting peace, the one most experienced in the mimic warfare of the citizen soldiery, and apparently by nature the best equipped with taste and aptitude for arms, as well as inspired with that patriotic enthusiasm, fearlessness and ambition which deserve and win high command, was Captain George Lee Thurston. He was the son of Honorable John Gates, and Harriet Lee, Thurston. His father as adjutant of the old Lancaster regiment was noted for efficiency and soldierly bearing. George played soldier with the paternal accoutrements in his tender years, and always assumed command of the boy militia companies that were casually improvised at school, or noisily organized and paraded during vacations. In earliest manhood, wherever his business located him, he at once became a leading spirit in some independent military organization of the vicinity. At Boston he was a member of the "Tigers;" at Ogdensburg he was lieutenant in an infantry company; at Chicago he was sergeant in the famous "Light Guard." Returning to his birthplace shortly before the civil war, he joined the Clinton Light Guard, as lieutenant. Remunerative employment failing him in Massachusetts, during the winter of 1860 he accepted a situation as book-keeper in Chicago.

When drum and fife began to be daily heard in the city streets, as company after company of volunteers marched to the camps of instruction, Thurston felt all his pulses stirred with desire to join the first regiment starting for the front. But he was in precarious health and without money A wife and infant son were dependent upon his salary even for their daily bread. Advantageous offers of military position were made him which he felt compelled to decline : but in the early autumn of 1861 he yielded to his patriotic inclinations, took the post of adjutant at Camp Douglas, and was commissioned in the Fifty-fifth Illinois Infantry, with the promise of speedy promotion. Before reaching the seat of war he was made captain.

The prolific state of Illinois sent forth no better regiment than the Fifty-fifth, and its story of desperate and sanguinary service can hardly be surpassed by any in the records of either army. It first met the enemy Sunday April 6, 1862, at Shiloh, which battle Generals Sherman and Grant—as also the distinguished Confederate generals, their opponents—have publicly characterized as among the most terrific they ever witnessed. Captain Thurston, commanding the two flank companies of the regiment as skirmishers, met the first onset of Chalmers' brigade, which, consisting of five regiments and a battery, formed the extreme right of the attacking forces, and confronted Stuart's brigade of three regiments. This last brigade, without artillery, was posted in an isolated position at the extreme left of the Union army. The Fifty-second Tennessee Infantry, while coming into line, encountered such a withering fire from Captain Thurston's command that, according to the Confederate reports, it fled in wild dismay, and took little further part in the conflict. The fire of the hostile battery and the advance of overpowering numbers soon compelled the withdrawal of the skirmishers to the hastily but wisely chosen line of battle, where Stuart's little force was drawn up, on the crest of a deep ravine. One ill-officered regiment of his brigade, as the shells of the enemy began to burst over it and the minie bullets to hiss through its ranks, rapidly melted away into the forest-shadowed valley to the rear. The other two, as though each soldier fully understood that the safety of the whole Federal army depended upon a manly defence of this naturally strong position guarding its flank, fought stubbornly, desperately, against overwhelming odds. For over four hours from the firing of the first gun they struggled successfully, holding Chalmers' brigade in check until about three o'clock in the afternoon. Ammunition being entirely exhausted, even from the cartridge-boxes of the slain, and another brigade, Jackson's, having joined the Confederates, the survivors sullenly retired from the ridge now strewn with their dead comrades, and unpursued marched towards the steamboat landing for cartridges and orders.

Captain Thurston was conspicuously brave during the action. His company suffered more severely than any other of the Fifty-fifth. The total loss in the regiment was fifty-one killed, one hundred and ninety-seven wounded, and twenty-seven captured, out of much less than six hundred men in line of battle. Captain Thurston's company had nine killed outright and thirty-two wounded—one-sixth of the regimental loss. But one other Federal regiment engaged at Shiloh lost so great a number. In Grant's army were seventy regiments and twenty batteries, besides several thousand cavalry. The casualties in the Fifty-fifth Illinois were nearly one-thirtieth of the whole loss of that army in the two days' fighting. Captain Thurston, though untouched by bullet, was utterly exhausted by the labors of the day. He lay upon the ground that night among his men, drenched with the pouring rain that came down with the darkness upon the bloody field, unable to get food or other refreshment, debarred from sleep by excitement, the fierce thunder storm, and the roar of the heavy ordnance hurling from the gunboats every five minutes a huge shell almost over the heads of the beleaguered patriots, to crash through the trees and burst in the neighborhood of the Confederate bivouacs.

Early in the morning ammunition and rations were obtained, and the regiment received orders to advance again to the conflict. Captain Thurston walked at the head of his company for a while, but was suddenly seen to stagger, and had to be helped fainting to the wayside. He never recovered from the shock to his constitution, but until July remained with the advancing army, though unable to perform any military duty. General Grant then gave him leave of absence upon surgeon's certificate that such absence was necessary to save his life. His strength barely sufficed to enable him to reach Chicago. There, with the tender care of friends and quiet rest, he was in time sufficiently recuperated to endure the journey home, where, gradually growing weaker, he peacefully closed his honorable earthly career, December 15, 1862.

IV. COLONEL FRANCIS WASHBURN, FOURTH MASSACHU-
SETTS CAVALRY.

Born in Lancaster, July 6, 1838. Died at Worcester, April 22, 1865.

. . . . Companies I, L and M, commanded by Colonel Francis Washburn, marched to Burkesville, arriving on the night of the 5th of April. Early on the following morning, in compliance with orders received the night previous, Colonel Washburn, with two regiments of infantry, each about 400 strong, and a part of his own force of cavalry, numbering 13 officers and 67 men, started to destroy High Bridge, 18 miles distant, and of great importance to the retreating rebel army. The bridge was reached about noon, the enemy offering feeble resistance to his advance. The infantry were halted in the vicinity of the bridge, while the cavalry pushed on about two miles further, meeting a superior force of the enemy's cavalry with artillery. A short time before the bridge was reached, Brevet Brigadier-General Theodore Read arrived, with orders to hold and not destroy the bridge. He took command. The cavalry retired to the bridge, and found the infantry warmly engaged with another force of the enemy's cavalry, and showing signs of breaking. It was soon evident that the enemy was superior in numbers, and that a fight at long range could not be maintained until General Ord should be apprised of their situation, and should send infantry — the only troops he had — to their relief.

Thus situated between two forces of the enemy — the larger between him and the Army of the James — to charge and break through the enemy, if possible, seemed the only honorable course for General Read to take ; no other was suggested. Twice the cavalry charged, breaking through and dispersing one line of the enemy, reforming and charging a second, which was found in a wood too dense to admit of free use of the sabre. In vain, however ; eight of twelve officers engaged were put *hors de combat* ; three killed and five severely wounded. The little band was hemmed in and overpowered by two divisions of cavalry — Rosser's and Fitz Hugh Lee's — the advance of General Lee's army.

Colonel Washburn, whose intrepid bravery in this fight endears his name to his associates, and adds the crowning glory to a life elevated by the purest patriotism, died a few weeks afterwards from the effects of his wounds.

Because of the influence of the affair npon the results of the campaign, I have dwelt upon it.

"To the sharpness of that fight," says a rebel colonel, inspector-general on Lee's staff, to General Ord, "the cutting off of Lee's army at Appomattox Court House was probably owing. So fierce were the charges of Colonel Washburn and his men, and so determined their fighting, that General Lee received the impression that they must be supported by a large part of the army, and that his retreat was cut off." Acting under this impression, he halted his army, gave what the "inspector general" calls stampeding orders, and began to throw up the line of breast-works which were found there the next day. Three trains of provisions, forage and clothing which had been sent down from Lynchburg. on the South Side road, were sent back to prevent them from falling into our hands, and his army which was on third rations, and those of corn only, was thus deprived of the provisions, the want of which exhausted them so much.

Moreover, by the delay occasioned by the halt, General Sheridan was enabled to come up with Ewell's Division at Saylor's Creek. When Lee discovered his mistake, and that the fighting force in his front was only a small detachment of cavalry and infantry, General Ord, with the Army of the James, had already profited by the delay, and so closed up with him that a retreat directly south was no longer practicable ; he was obliged to make the detour by way of Appomattox Court House. General Rosser concurs in this opinion, and states that the importance of the fight has never been appreciated.

That Lieutenant-General Grant and General Ord appreciate its importance and confirm the principal facts stated above, is shown by the following extract from General Grant's Report of the Armies of the United States :

"General Ord advanced from Burkesville towards Farmville, sending two regiments of infantry and a squadron of cavalry, under Brevet Brigadier-General Theodore Read, to destroy the bridges. The advance met the head of Lee's column near Farmville, which it heroically attacked and detained until General Read was killed and his small force overpowered. This caused a delay in the enemy's movements, and enabled General Ord to get well up with the remainder of his force, on meeting which the enemy immediately intrenched himself. In the afternoon General Sheridan struck the enemy south of Saylor's Creek." . . . . .

. . . . . Colonel Washburn.—The death of this brave and gallant officer mentioned in the foregoing narrative was deeply felt, and the tribute of respect to his memory was universal. Lieutenant-General Grant, as soon as the intelligence of his death was received, paused amidst his vast labors, to write with his own hand, a letter to the family of the deceased expressive of his sympathy in their loss, and admiration for his gallant and heroic conduct. . . . . . .

[Report of the Adjutant-General of Massachusetts for 1865.]

The letter of the commanding general was as follows:

HEADQUARTERS ARMIES OF THE UNITED STATES,
WASHINGTON, D. C., May 21, 1865.

Mrs. HARRIET W. WASHBURN,
Lancaster, Massachusetts.

My Dear Madam :

I have just seen for the first time the obituary notice of your noble son who fell wounded at the "High Bridge" so gallantly leading his men. I had hoped his wound would not prove mortal and that he might be spared many long years to view with pride the work which he so bravely aided in consummating.

Allow me to express my sincere condolence for your bereavement, and to express the hope that in the blood of so many thousand martyrs our country has sealed her liberties and peace, at home, at least, for all time to come. Very truly yours,

U. S. GRANT, *Lt. Gen.*

. . . . Colonel Francis Washburn, of the Fourth Massachusetts Cavalry, wounded in the desperate engagement at High Bridge, Thursday, the 16th inst., arrived in Worcester on Friday last, and died the following night at the house of his brother, Mr. J. D. Washburn. Only a few months before, another brother, Captain Edward R. Washburn, well known to many of our citizens, had yielded his life under the wounds received at Port Hudson. Thus the experience of this war repeats itself— and thus these two at length meet again.

It was a pleasure, early in the war, to urge upon the governor that he should commission Frank Washburn as junior second-lieutenant in the

First Massachusetts Cavalry. The commission was cheerfully bestowed. It was all the young gentleman asked for. By the course of his studies and practice in Germany he had acquired peculiar fitness for the cavalry service, and seemed worthy of a higher rank, which was suggested to him; but he modestly declined, remarking that he preferred to stake the chances of his promotion on the merits of his service. He had returned from Europe at the first intelligence of the war, to offer himself to his country, as some others had done, and preferred to pass upward through the gradations of her service to the honors of the field, if he might win them. He was soon made captain in the Second Cavalry, all the while remaining at his post. When the Fourth Cavalry was organized, without solicitation, but not without reason, he was selected by the governor for the lieutenant-colonelcy. Upon the resignation of Colonel Rand of this regiment, Washburn was promptly promoted to his rank. That rank he distinguished in the eyes of all his men and his superior officers; and that saddle, save only a few days of furlough in which to witness the burial of his soldier-brother, he constantly filled until he fell from it to die. He fought in South Carolina and in Virginia; he led his men under Sheridan, in the presence of Ord and of Grant; and the best proof of his fidelity and his gallantry was in the special recommendation of the Lieutenant-General, forwarded to Washington after his last battle, and when his wounds were not supposed to be mortal, that he should be brevetted brigadier-general — which request was no doubt complied with before his death. At all times and on all fields he received the respect and confidence of his men for brilliant action, for kind and affectionate treatment. In all the engagements of three years and a half, he never received a wound until he received the last.

His fatal encounter was in that last critical battle which enforced the surrender of Lee. While endeavoring to destroy the High Bridge, over which it was feared Lee's army might escape, Colonel Washburn was surrounded by Rosser and F. H. Lee, and fought them till he fell, in the odds of eight men to one. He was conspicuous through the fight, and twice with impetuous charge broke through the rebel lines and threw them into confusion. He might at either of these times have passed on with his cavalry and escaped. But he refused to leave the infantry while their remained the slightest chance of rescuing them from their situation. Accordingly he made his third charge, and in this, while crossing sabres with a rebel officer whom he had nearly disarmed, he was shot in the head by another, *and after he had fallen* received a sabre cut upon the skull which finished his work. He was two days a prisoner, during which, notwithstanding the gallantry he had displayed, and which even the enemy affected to extol, they did nothing for his wounds, and robbed him of his horse, his sword and his money! . . . . . .

[Hon. Alexander H. Bullock, in the Worcester Spy.]

It should be said that Colonel Washburn was perhaps subjected to no worse treatment by the Confederates than their own wounded received, he being then in the midst of an ill-appointed and fleeing army. His sword, which had been taken by General Rosser, was recovered in due time, but his watch and the other articles of which he was despoiled have never been restored. The sabre stroke of a cowardly ruffian caused his death; but the pistol bullet, which, entering his cheek, passed down into his lungs, excited an irritation that in time would probably have proved fatal.

INDEX.

SUBJECTS AND PLACES.

INDEX OF PERSONS.

I. COLONIAL SOLDIERS OF LANCASTER.

II. Colonial Soldiers of Bolton (including Berlin).

III. Colonial Soldiers of Harvard.

IV. COLONIAL SOLDIERS OF LEOMINSTER.

V. LANCASTER SOLDIERS IN REVOLUTION.

VI. BOLTON SOLDIERS IN REVOLUTION.

VII. HARVARD SOLDIERS IN REVOLUTION.

VIII. LEOMINSTER SOLDIERS IN REVOLUTION.

IX. Soldiers in Shays' Insurrection serving for Lancastrian Towns.

X. LANCASTER SOLDIERS, 1812-14. PAGES 271-2.

XI. LANCASTER SOLDIERS IN CIVIL WAR.

XII. PERSONS, MISCELLANEOUS.